THE CHALLENGE OF
WORLD POVERTY

A World Anti-Poverty Program in Outline

Also by Gunnar Myrdal

Objectivity in Social Research

Asian Drama: An Inquiry into the Poverty of Nations

Challenge to Affluence

Beyond the Welfare State

Value in Social Theory

Economic Theory and Under-Developed Regions (American edition: Rich Lands and Poor)

An International Economy, Problems and Prospects

The Political Element in the Development of Economic Theory

An American Dilemma: The Negro Problem and Modern Democracy

THE
CHALLENGE
OF WORLD
POVERTY

A World Anti-Poverty Program in Outline

---

by GUNNAR MYRDAL

with a Foreword by Francis O. Wilcox

THE CHRISTIAN A. HERTER LECTURE SERIES

The Johns Hopkins University School of Advanced International
Studies, Washington, D.C.

 PANTHEON BOOKS
A Division of Random House, New York

Foreword

In the winter of 1964 the faculty of the Johns Hopkins School of Advanced International Studies decided to establish the Christian A. Herter Lecture Series in order to help pay tribute, in some small measure, to the distinguished American who had founded the school some twenty years earlier. It was the hope of the faculty that our lecture platform here in the nation's capital might be used by highly qualified individuals to present different points of view about international relations and to examine in depth some of the basic issues that confront the United States in a rapidly changing world.

For the 1969 series the faculty extended an invitation to the noted Swedish scholar and public servant, Dr. Gunnar Myrdal, who had just published his monumental three-volume work *Asian Drama: An Inquiry into the Poverty of Nations*. Dr. Myrdal readily accepted our invitation with the idea in mind that his lectures might form a logical sequel to *Asian Drama*. Accordingly, in March, 1969, he delivered three lectures at SAIS under the general title "The Rich and Poor Countries: A Strategy for Development in the 1970's."

This book is the direct outgrowth of those lectures. As the titles would suggest, the basic theme remains the same but a number of new topics have been developed and much new material has been added to the original lectures. The result is a book of policy conclusions which should have real relevance for both the developed and the developing countries.

As we move into the 1970's, two great problems stand out above all others: (1) how the world community can avoid the kind of conflicts that might lead to all-out nuclear war; and (2) how we can utilize world resources so that mankind may be able to meet the urgent challenge of poverty and then move on to better things.

The sad truth is that we have not made very much progress on either of these fronts. On the economic side, there has been a great deal of talk but not nearly enough capital for development purposes and not nearly enough effective action. Ten years ago the United Nations declared the 1960's the Decade of Development. In the intervening years the momentum of development in the new countries has slowed up perceptibly and the Western countries have become less and less inclined to support foreign aid.

To combat these two discouraging trends, the United Nations has declared the 1970's the Second Development Decade. Whether the second great crusade will be any more successful than the first, only time can tell. But this much is clear. At this particular juncture in history, when every effort will be made to learn from the mistakes of the past, Gunnar Myrdal's words of wisdom should be most welcome both to academicians and to practitioners working in the development field.

On second thought, his suggestions may not be welcome —although they should be helpful—for he pointedly reminds both the Western donor countries and the new nations that both will have to put forth much more effort if the world's development goals are to be met. He does not minimize the need for foreign aid. But he does stress, over and over again, how very much the developing countries must do for themselves and how urgent it is that they do it rapidly and vigorously. Aid from the developed nations, he writes, "though strategically important, is only a minor part of what should be done in order to make possible, and speed up, development in underdeveloped countries. Much more important than this aid are the needed social and economic reforms within these countries themselves."

Dr. Myrdal has properly earned a world-wide reputation for his vision and his foresight. In 1944, in his book *An American Dilemma: The Negro Problem and Modern Democracy,* he accurately forecast many of the difficulties and problems that beset this nation in the 1960's in the field of race relations. That book was at least fifteen years ahead of its time. This one may be out in front by an equal margin. Personally, I find his diagnosis of the world's ills logical and sound. Some of his prescriptions, however, may not prove acceptable until time has made sufficient inroads into the traditions, the pride, the prejudices, and the practices of both the poor and the rich nations. Even so, the world would do well to ponder his ideas, which are distilled from long years of practical experience and careful study.

Indeed, I can think of no one better equipped to undertake a policy study of this kind than Gunnar Myrdal. When I first met him he was an international civil servant, directing, with as much imagination and enthusiasm as the situation would permit, the activities of the United Nations Economic Commission for Europe. As a young man he studied law and economics at the University of Stockholm, where he was made Professor of Political Economy and Public Finance at the age of thirty-four. Later on he served as Minister of Commerce and as a member of the Swedish Senate. With this background he is admirably equipped to bridge the gap between the academician and the policy maker, to temper theory with practice, and to offer meaningful suggestions about tomorrow's world.

In evaluating the prospects for the future, the author

carefully avoids the dangerous pitfalls of optimism and pessimism. He is neither a Pollyanna nor a Cassandra. As he points out in one of his earlier chapters, "optimism, like pessimism, means nothing but a biased view." What the student should seek, therefore, "is realism, even if he then conflicts with prevailing ideas within his own profession."

This, of course, is sound advice. It is particularly sound in a democracy such as ours where the executive branch tends to "oversell" programs like foreign aid in order to win congressional approval for them. Normally, a candid appraisal of the probability of success is not enough. The virtues of foreign aid are highlighted and the complexities of the problems involved are played down. The net result is that very often achievements fall short of expectations, a credibility gap arises, and some members of Congress become disillusioned with foreign aid. In this situation the dangers that flow from an overly optimistic approach are apparent. Foreign aid and economic development are replete with complexities and problems, and these must be clearly understood if we are ever to reach the promised land.

In any event, we can all agree that the challenge which confronts the world as it moves into the 1970's is a tremendous one. What is needed, of course, is a dual response: (1) a much greater concern for the problems of the new countries and a much greater willingness on the part of the rich nations to make substantial sacrifices for the common cause; and (2) a much greater willingness on the part of the developing countries to put into effect the far-reaching economic and social reforms essential for real progress. It is my hope that this book will help both sides understand more clearly than they now do the nature of their interlocking responsibilities.

Francis O. Wilcox
Dean, The Johns Hopkins University
School of Advanced International Studies

Washington, D.C.
July 4, 1969

PREFACE

When I was originally planning an earlier work of mine, *Asian Drama: An Inquiry into the Poverty of Nations* (New York: Twentieth Century Fund and Pantheon Books, 1968), I felt it should conclude with a section on policy. It is true that as I am always working with explicit value premises, in this case the modernization ideals, I could in the several chapters and sections have drawn policy conclusions from what I thought I had established as facts and factual relationships. But the book does not contain a comprehensive epitome of what main policies the underdeveloped and developed countries should follow in order to facilitate and speed up development in the former countries.

I found, however, that the questions I was asked at press conferences and interviews, and also the questions discussed in many reviews, actually concerned that missing eighth part of the book which should have contained the main policy conclusions I wanted to draw from my study. And as I appreciate such a practical turn of public interest, as I moreover had reached rather definite views on the policy issues, and as I am a squarehead, I willingly answered those other questions. I was sometimes misunderstood.

I am thus fully aware that *Asian Drama* was often mistaken as rendering arguments for not bothering to try to aid the underdeveloped countries in their development efforts, which pleased the conservatives and still more the reactionaries in Western countries. I also found that some of my liberal friends, apparently under the same false impression of where my arguments led, by their own good intentions were made unable to read my book with ordinary care and comprehension. I have the feeling that I was better understood in the underdeveloped countries themselves.

When I was invited by the Johns Hopkins University School of Advanced International Studies to give three lectures, with the understanding that they should be enlarged into a book, I was happy to accept the invitation and to use the occasion to spell out the missing eighth part of the earlier book.

In *Asian Drama* I had been eager to stress the fact that I was concerned only with the nearly one-third of mankind living in South Asia—all the countries south of the Soviet Union and China, from Pakistan in the west to the former French Indochina in the east, and including Indonesia and the Philippines.[1] More particularly the analysis was focused on the two countries that emerged from the partition of British India—India and Pakistan. The reason for this was not only the huge size of the populations living in this subregion, but also the fact that statistical and other materials are far more abundant and better organized there and, even more important, that the discussion of development problems has been pursued far longer there and at a higher level of sophistication. This last point was the more decisive as the study was directed at problems and did not pretend to be in any sense a comprehensive survey of prevailing conditions in the region.

As I now turn to formulating the main policy conclusions from that study, I will continue to think, first, of South Asia and, in particular, of India and Pakistan. But as general as my treatment of the policy problems must be in this brief volume, it will often have relevance for the whole underdeveloped world.

I will restrict my analysis in this book, however, to the non-Communist world. This may be deemed a not entirely well-motivated decision. The underdeveloped Communist countries meet, of course, many of the same problems as other underdeveloped countries. But in several ways they deal with them in a radically different manner. Also, any cooperation between developed Communist and non-Communist countries to aid underdeveloped countries, while rational, is still in a rudimentary stage. The main reason for excluding the Communist world from consideration in this book is, however, the practical one of limiting the study within a manageable scope.

This book being in the nature of a continuation of *Asian Drama,* in a sense also a guide to it, and indeed, a brief summary of it made from the policy point of view, I will feel free to give numerous references to that book for a fuller treatment of the several problems and also for sources in the literature. With the same justification, I will permit myself to refer to earlier works of mine where a fuller exposition is given on one point or another. When citations of other authors are made in the present book without proper bibliographic references, those are given in the sections of *Asian Drama* referred to in the Notes. As the Notes refer almost exclusively to *Asian Drama,* it is hoped that the very frequent note numbers in the text will not disturb the ordinary reader, who is invited to ignore them.

This is a *political* book and should thus, according to my philosophy, be directed not only to experts, officials, and professional politicians but to interested persons among the general public. I have therefore labored to make my message as direct and simple as possible, though without giving up my intention that my policy recommendations should stand out as rational conclusions from facts and explicitly stated value premises. I have taken no political or diplomatic precautions but have tried to speak as plainly and frankly as I can. I could take as a motto a statement of John Kenneth Galbraith made in the summer of 1969 when he retired as national chairman of the Americans for Democratic Action:

> We are determined that there will be a new standard of candor in liberal politics—it will henceforth be a matter not alone of pride but of necessity to say exactly what we mean and think. If necessary, we will oppose men, otherwise qualified, who are given to political rhetoric and where we suspect some gap between promise and performance.

The subtitle of this book may sound pretentious; in any case the indefinite article "a" should be emphasized. I am fully aware of the fact that there is nothing resembling unanimity of opinion on the problems to be discussed in the pages to follow. To keep this in the reader's mind, I have often formulated my opinions about facts and policies in the first person.

That subtitle is apt to bring to mind the anti-poverty program of the United States. Undoubtedly there is a close parallel between the international problems of the poverty in underdeveloped countries and the poverty problems in the United States and also between the ways in which these two complexes of problems have surfaced to popular consciousness and been dealt with policywise. To begin with, they were both raised to public awareness and political importance by what I have called an intellectual and moral catharsis.

In the international field this catharsis occurred soon after the Second World War and the great political changes following in its wake. In the United States the awakening to awareness of the enclaves of people living in economic, social, and cultural misery and of the necessity to do something about it did not occur until the end of the 1950's and the beginning of the 1960's. Intensive statistical studies, carried out by the secretariats of the intergovernmental organizations, served as both cause and effect of the catharsis in the international field. In the United States the catharsis was in the same way prodded along by statistical investigation, books, speeches, and conferences.

With regard to the international issue, the 1960's were on President John F. Kennedy's proposal declared "the Development Decade" by a unanimous decision of the General Assembly of the United Nations. And in the United States, President Lyndon B. Johnson declared in early 1964 the "unconditional war on poverty" and later held up the vision of the "Great Society." Similar pathetic declarations about lifting the underdeveloped countries out of poverty had been commonplace ever since the end of the Second World War.

As will be hinted at in this book, there are also great substantive similarities between the two complexes of problems. In a very real sense the United States has groups of people held apart spatially, socially, and economically from the majority of Americans who live in comfortable circumstances, and therefore has development problems similar in many ways to those in the underdeveloped world. However, there are also significant differences, most of them related to the fact that while in the United States the really poor are a small minority, they are the majority in the underdeveloped countries, and actually in the world.

There are additional similarities. The anti-poverty program in the United States was from the beginning thought of in too diminutive terms, not really corresponding to the scope of the needed reforms and the stirring declarations. It was unplanned. And it became spurious and was not well administered. Nevertheless, it was possible to hope that it represented the beginning of something bigger to come, and that it would then be fortified and better coordinated in the frame of comprehensive and realistic planning. The fact that what we have had of a world anti-poverty program suffered, and suffers, from the same deficiencies, though to a still greater degree, is obvious and will be further brought out in this book.

The intellectual and moral catharsis in regard to poverty in the United States has in recent years lost momentum under the influence of many forces, among them the rapidly escalating participation of the United States in the Vietnam war. This military engagement has engrossed the interest of the people, and particularly of their rulers in Washington. It has also impounded available financial resources, as one of its effects has been inflationary development at home. There are also deeper psychological effects of a war which has been seen by many Americans to be founded on wrong ideas about the United States' relations with the world and, in addition, felt to be illegal, cruel, and immoral. Others, in the face of this growing opposition to the war, have been driven to harden their hearts even in regard to the needy at home.

In regard to the international anti-poverty programs, we have seen in the 1960's a parallel movement that in many rich countries, and particularly in the United States, has caused a decrease in people's willingness to aid the underdeveloped countries. Meanwhile the actual development in those countries has generally tended to slow down. The unfolding of these last two tendencies will, of course, be a main topic of this book.

There are also crucial differences which make analogies less pertinent. In the United States there is a political and administrative machinery which, though cumbersome and fettered by vested interests both at the center and in the localities, could have made possible realistic planning and an attempt to reach a purposive and efficient implementation—if there had been a will to do it. For the world at large there is no government, and thus no unified administration carrying out its decisions. And there will not be one as far ahead as we can now see.

Intergovernmental organizations in our age are merely agreed matrixes for the conduct of national diplomacy in a multilateral setting. They can have importance nevertheless by facilitating intergovernmental agreements. In addition, many of them are in a position where their secretariats, in addition to undertaking studies, can take

initiatives and even become instrumental in the implementation of agreements between national governments.

The intergovernmental organizations themselves can be
blamed only partly for the deficiencies in planning and
coordination of the aid to underdeveloped countries and
still less for the recent tendency of the unilateral aid to
stagnate and to decrease in terms of the relation to the
national incomes of the developed countries. In fact, their
secretariats, within the bounds of what they can dare to do
without being censored by the governments, have not
only been publicizing the widening gap between developed and underdeveloped countries but have also been
propagating increase of aid and furnishing some outlines
for its planning.

In their own aid activities, they have even succeeded in
reaching a respectable degree of coordination. Thus the
practical cooperation between the International Bank for
Reconstruction and Development and the Food and
Agriculture Organization (FAO), for instance, has resulted in the FAO being able to dispose of a much larger
amount of funds than it could ever finance on its own
budget.

But the aid channeled through the intergovernmental
organizations is a very minor part of all aid which continues to be mostly—nearly 90 percent—rendered unilaterally by the national governments in the developed
countries. Moreover, as will be stressed in this book, aid
from the developed countries of both types taken together,
though strategically important, is only a minor part of what
should be done in order to make possible, and speed up,
development in underdeveloped countries. Much more
important than this aid are the needed social and economic
reforms within these countries themselves.

The Stockholm University Institute
for International Economic Studies

October 1, 1969

                                          GUNNAR MYRDAL

CONTENTS

THE APPROACH

Chapter 1

CLEANSING THE APPROACH FROM BIASES

To reach rational conclusions on a policy program for the planning of development of underdeveloped countries [1] we need—aside from relevant and significant value premises that are explicitly accounted for (see below)—a realistic conception of conditions in underdeveloped countries.[2] It is my view that our conceptions of underdevelopment, development, and development planning as presented in most of the scientific and popular economic literature and, still more ominously, in the Plans of the underdeveloped countries, is heavily biased in a direction that is basically opportunistic. Our policy conclusions, therefore, are founded upon ideas about reality that are systematically, though unintentionally, falsified.

This should not be surprising. *There is a tendency for all knowledge, like all ignorance, to deviate from truth in an opportunistic direction.*[3]

The fact that conceptions about reality, and ideologies

and theories, are influenced by the interests as commonly perceived by the dominant groups in the society where they are formed, and that they so come to deviate from truth in a direction opportune to these interests, is easily seen and, in fact, taken for granted when we look back at an earlier period in history. But in our own intellectual endeavors we ordinarily preserve a naïve non-awareness about such influences working on our minds—as, indeed, people have done in every earlier epoch of history.

We believe—as they did and with equal firmness—that we are simply factual, basing ourselves on observation of reality when we think, argue, and conclude. A first pre-condition when trying to unfetter our minds from biases in order to reach a truer perception of reality is to see clearly the opportunistic interests affecting our search for truth and to understand how they operate. In this attempt to overcome naïveté, a backward look becomes helpful.

In colonial times and right up to the Second World War, the popular as well as the more sophisticated explanations of the poverty of the peoples living in what were called "backward regions"—most of them were then not "countries"—were, it is now clear in retrospect, plainly apologetic, aimed at relieving the colonial powers and the rich nations generally from moral and political responsibility for the poverty and lack of development of these peoples.[4]

It was taken as established by experience that the peoples in the backward regions were so constituted that they reacted differently from Europeans: they normally did not respond positively to opportunities for improving their incomes and levels of living. Their tendency toward idleness and inefficiency and their reluctance to seek wage employment were seen as expressions of their wantlessness, very limited economic horizons, survival-mindedness, self-sufficiency, carefree disposition, and preference for a leisurely life.

These attitudes were, in more sophisticated writings, often understood to have their roots in various elements in the entire system of social relations and institutions as fortified by religious prescription and taboos, with which the colonial powers for good reasons were reluctant to interfere. Occasionally, it was noted that undernutrition, and inferior levels of living generally, lowered stamina and so affected to some extent the willingness and ability to work and to work intensively. But as there were so many other causes of such mental traits and of the resulting low productivity and inferior levels of living, it was not assumed that such explanations could lead to a real possibility for development.

Climate was seen as a crucial cause of these peoples' attitudes to sustained work. Dominating this kind of thinking was the racial-inferiority doctrine which, of course, even more definitely closed the door to any policy approach other than the established one of laissez-faire and non-interference in social matters.

Not much serious research on conditions in the backward regions was done at that time except to some extent by Western cultural anthropologists, who usually had to be accepted by the colonial authorities and were sometimes used by them in their efforts to size up the peoples they ruled.

The anthropologists' interest was to find out how these people lived and survived. With few exceptions their approach was static; changes were ordinarily dealt with as "disturbances" of established social relations. Though they were reacting against European ethnocentricism and wanted to give sense and purpose to the social organization of even the most primitive peoples—this was the ethos of anthropological research—the static character of their approach actually gave backing to the colonial theory I hinted at.

The most remarkable thing is, of course, that in the colonial era economists did not bother more about the problems of poverty in the backward regions, in spite of the fact that they obviously fell in their field of study. On the whole, the masses there were then as poor and their lives as miserable as they are now. The economists' flagrant lack of interest was, of course, a reflection of the world political situation. *The colonial regimes were not such as to call forth large-scale research on economic underdevelopment by giving political importance and public interest to such research.*

Now the situation is changed in a radical fashion. Since the end of the Second World War, a swelling flood of research has been devoted to the problems of what were coming to be called the "underdeveloped countries," a term implying the dynamic conception that they should develop. The tide is still rising, the lead having been taken by us economists studying the problems of underdevelopment, development, and development planning in terms of social dynamics.

This abrupt and prodigious change in direction as well as in volume of research efforts has definitely not been an autonomous and spontaneous development of the social sciences. Instead, *it has been a result of vast political reversals* that are causally interrelated: first, the rapid liquidation of the colonial power structure; second, the craving for development in the underdeveloped countries themselves, or, rather, among that educated and articulate elite who think, speak, and act on their behalf; and, third, the international tensions, especially the cold war, that have made the fate of the underdeveloped countries a matter of foreign policy concern in the developed countries.[5]

That the social sciences seldom blaze the way to new perspectives—the continual reorientation of our work regularly coming from the sphere of politics—is a general rule, though seldom or never have we seen it confirmed in such a sudden, radical, and wholesale change. This time it was not merely a move pioneered by some of us, which only gradually won more general adherence when social and political conditions became more ripe for it in one country after another—as, for instance, the Wicksell-Keynesian approach to business fluctuations.[6] That the whole profession in the Western world began to accept new value premises for their work and a new direction toward a field they until then had not been cultivating has apparently concealed from most of the researchers the political conditioning of this vast change.

That research is directed by what in our society is felt to be politically important should not be criticized. It only means that we scientists follow the call from the society we are part of to elucidate the problems that are on people's minds and in relation to which they want to be better informed—though we could wish that more generally we as scientists were better able to see in advance the writing on the wall, so that our societies would not regularly have to be taken by surprise and have to extemporize their policies.

By itself, however, this continuous redirection of our work in response to the unfolding of the political forces cannot be a cause of biases invalidating the results of our research.

But although this shift of *field* represents a rational adjustment of our work to the needs felt by our society, the awareness of it and of how sweepingly radical the change has been should make us suspect that the effects of the same political changes would be a conditioning also of the *approach* used in our research efforts. Such a conditioning, different from the mere redirection of research, is apt to introduce irrational biases.

The current international political situation bristles with violent tensions and emotions; governments and nations feel their vital interests to be at stake. A major source of biases in economic research carried on in the rich countries on the problems of underdeveloped countries will then be the political interests of the former countries in what happens, or ought to happen, in the latter countries, as those interests are officially and popularly felt and expressed.

I have developed this theme in greater detail elsewhere.[7] In the present context I will restrict myself to pointing out that this opportunistic tendency does not usually lead to an "unfriendly" approach to the problems of underdeveloped countries—as long as they have not been hopelessly lost to the other camp in the cold war.

On the contrary, *research tends to become "diplomatic," forbearing, and generally overoptimistic:* bypassing facts that raise awkward problems, concealing them in an unduly technical terminology, or treating them in an excusing and "understanding" way. Indeed, the tendency to think and act in a diplomatic manner when dealing with the problems of the underdeveloped countries has, in the new era of independence, become a new version of the "white man's burden."

If the intellectuals in underdeveloped countries understood how much this approach to their problems is tantamount to condescension, they would feel offended. But for reasons I will touch upon below, they are generally—and even more strongly—inclined to the same type of biased view.

The common agreement to change over to various euphemistic expressions for the term "underdeveloped countries" is an indication of this mental conspiracy. One such is "developing countries." [8] This term is, of course, illogical, since, by means of a loaded terminology, it begs the question of whether a country is developing or not or whether it is foreseeable that it will develop. Moreover, it does not express the thought that is really pressing for expression: that a country is underdeveloped, that it wants to develop, and that perhaps it is planning to develop.

Such a terminological *politesse* may seem to be unimportant *per se*. But it is important to observe because it indicates the deeper biases in the scientific approach to the problems of underdeveloped countries.

The tendency to systematic biases in this particular direction has been strengthened by a more mechanical cause, related to the rapidity with which we economists have undertaken massive research in a previously almost uncultivated field.[9]

Since by logical necessity research must start from a set of analytical preconceptions,[10] it was natural that the theoretical tools that had been forged for the study of the developed countries were used without careful consideration of their adequacy to reality in the underdeveloped countries.

This could be done the more easily as our empirical knowledge about facts and factual relationships in the underdeveloped countries has been so extremely deficient. When data were then assembled and analyzed, these did not disturb the conventional or what, to avoid deprecation by terminology, I will refer to as the "postwar approach"[11] very much, as these data were assembled and analyzed utilizing the conceptual categories implied in that approach. The resulting mountains of figures, for instance about "unemployment" and "underemployment"[12] (see below), have either no meaning for understanding economic reality in an underdeveloped country, or an entirely different meaning from that imparted to them.

In this way empirical economic research became shallow and faulty and, at the same time, less conducive to testing the concepts and theories implied in the approach. Rather, at least for a time, the very fact that the researcher now got figures to play with tended to reinforce him in his original and biased approach.

My main point is that, while in the developed countries an analysis in purely "economic" terms—employment and unemployment, savings, investment, and output, all in aggregate terms; and demand, supply, and prices, all

assuming markets and fairly effective markets at that—
may make sense and lead to valid inferences, this is so
because these concepts and the models and theories in-
corporating them are fairly adequate to reality in developed countries.

But in underdeveloped countries this approach is simply
not applicable, except at the price of making the analysis
irrelevant and grossly faulty. The assumed aggregation of
the "economic" terms mentioned above (and many others)
cannot be carried out when markets are non-existent or
grossly imperfect.

The more fundamental deficiency is, however, that *this
approach abstracts from attitudes and institutions.* In
developed countries these are either rationalized to the
extent that they give passage to development impulses or
are rapidly and smoothly adjusted to allow development.
This assumption is not valid in underdeveloped countries.[13]

There attitudes and institutions are of a character to
make an analysis in terms of markets unrealistic. They are
less permissive of development and they are much more
rigid. For these and other reasons *they should be given an
important and explicit place in the theoretical model applied in analysis.* It is true that all theoretical analysis
must be simplifying; but it is not permissible to simplify
by abstracting from what is crucially important in the
society under study.

In yet another respect does the postwar approach give
an unduly optimistic slant to the economic analysis of
underdeveloped countries. The high levels of income attained in developed countries and their social security
measures make it possible in these countries to consider
nutrition and more generally levels of living only from
the point of view of people's welfare interests and not of
their willingness and ability to work and their efficiency
when working. In our Western growth models they can
therefore generally be left out.

This simplification is, however, not permissible when

analyzing the problems of underdevelopment and development in underdeveloped countries. *Their very low levels of living have consequences for productivity* which cannot be abstracted from in a realistic economic analysis of underdevelopment and development.[14]

I was characterizing what I called the postwar approach of dealing with the problem of underdevelopment and development in "economic" terms as of a more mechanical nature, a function of the speed with which research was begun in a nearly untouched field and our natural inclination to utilize research methods with which we were familiar. But the matter is more complicated.[15] Generally speaking, *this approach abstracts from most of the conditions that are not only peculiar to the underdeveloped countries but are largely responsible for their underdevelopment and for the particular difficulties they meet in developing.*

The unwarranted simplifications implied in the postwar approach are thus leaving out of account much that is awkward, difficult, and undesirable in underdeveloped countries. Constructing development models in "economic" terms therefore serves the earlier mentioned biases toward diplomacy and overoptimism. *The two sources of biases converge and reinforce each other.*

In presenting their concepts, models, and theories, economists are regularly prepared to make the most generous reservations and qualifications—indeed, to emphasize that in the last instance development is a "human problem" and that planning means "changing men." Having thus made their bow to what they have become accustomed to call the "non-economic" factors, they thereafter commonly proceed as if those factors did not exist.[16]

Most economists do this without offering any apology. Some excuse themselves by stressing that they do not feel competent to deal with these non-economic factors. In either case they commonly fail to explain what the neglect of these factors implies for the validity of their research.

The most benignant interpretation of this attitude to economic research—stressing, on the one hand, the importance of the so-called non-economic factors while, on the other hand, neglecting them almost entirely in the models and theories applied in research and planning—would be that the economists assume one or the other of two things: one, that induced "economic" changes (in most planning models still mainly physical investment) are of paramount importance for development, or, two, that it is a methodologically valid procedure in research to establish first an "economic" theory, preserving the possibility of *adding* considerations of the non-economic factors.

It is apparent from most theorizing by contemporary economists that they actually operate on the basis of the first assumption, sometimes in blunt contradiction to their stressing in general terms the importance of the non-economic factors. A theme running through all the chapters in *Asian Drama* is the refutation of that assumption in considerable detail for the several problems. In the present volume this main theme will be resumed in the chapters to follow.

If our conclusions on this point are valid—that the non-economic factors, broadly attitudes, institutions, and the productivity consequences of very low levels of living, are of such paramount importance in underdeveloped countries that they cannot be abstracted from in economic theory and in planning—the second assumption, that it is possible to take account of the non-economic factors by adding considerations regarding them to a simplified and basic economic theory, must be scrutinized as of crucial importance. I mean that this assumption is generally not valid.

For one thing, this amplification of the economic theory has simply not been carried out. As already mentioned, most economists continue to deal with both the theoretical and the practical problems in underdeveloped countries in terms of their simple conception of economic facts and relationships.

Moreover, it cannot be carried out. In spite of the appearance of precision and rigorousness that economists often succeed in creating by this simplification, there is a basic logical confusion in their way of thinking that is hidden by a common lack of clarity in their definitions of concepts and assumptions.[17] In reality there are no "economic" problems; there are simply problems, and they are complex.

The very act of clarifying what should be meant by "economic" problems or "economic" factors must, in fact, imply an analysis that includes all the "non-economic" determinants. *From a scientific point of view, the only permissible demarcation—the only one that is fully tenable logically—is between relevant and less relevant factors.*

And that demarcation will vary with the characteristics of the society under study. It has already been pointed out that the factors commonly excluded in economic theory are of particular importance in underdeveloped countries.

In the present context I will restrict myself to giving only an illustrative example of what has been said: the use of the Western concept "unemployment" and the attempt to approach conditions in underdeveloped countries by also accounting for "disguised unemployment" or "underemployment." While referring to *Asian Drama* for a more thorough criticism,[18] some of the assumptions for use of the concept "unemployment" in developed economics may be pointed out.

Implied are the existence of a fluid labor market, where for particular occupations working hours and working conditions have been standardized by established customs and sometimes by legislation, collective bargaining and collective agreements, and where individual differences in the quality of labor input, which is to say skill, intensity, and efficiency, are also diminished by standardization or can be reduced to a common scale.

Within this fluid and organized labor market the members of the labor force are regularly aware of the employment opportunities or lack of such opportunities. They are equally regularly willing to work; in any case, inability to find work is clearly distinguished from unwillingness to work.

The unemployed can then be defined as workers who have the skills needed, who are aware of employment opportunities when they appear, and who are seeking employment at the market rate of wages without succeeding in becoming employed. A sufficient rise in the general demand for labor will create "full employment."

With many reservations, among them for "structural unemployment"—the existence of which many economists in the United States tried to deny until the moral and intellectual catharsis when the poverty problem rose to public awareness in the early 1960's—these conditions prevail in the developed countries, and they make possible the use of the concept "unemployed" and the statistical measurement of the number of workers who are unemployed. There is a definable "labor reserve."

In the underdeveloped countries the situation is entirely different. Increasing the demand for labor, or creating opportunities for productive work by the self-employed, will by itself not lead to a better labor utilization of the labor force or will do so only to a minor extent.[19]

Such policy measures have to be supplemented by other policy measures directed not only at investment and expansion of labor demand but also at changing attitudes and institutions and often levels of living. The exclusion of non-economic factors from the ordinary theories and models used in economic analysis and planning has in this case led to a serious distortion of our conception of reality.

In *Asian Drama* I was led to discard entirely the concept of "unemployment"—and "underemployment"—as inadequate to reality in South Asia and to base my analysis of labor utilization on the simpler behavioristic concepts that all relate to observable facts: which people work at all; for what periods during the day, week, month, and year they work; and with what intensity and effectiveness. [20]

The general thesis, which by this example I have wanted to illustrate, is that it is not possible to throw the yeast into the oven after the bread has been baked. The non-economic factors cannot simply be added to a supposedly pure economic theory. *The true institutional approach must work with concepts that are adequate to reality from the beginning, i.e., in the very approach to a problem.*[21]

There are strong interests backing the superficial post-war approach, abstracting from the non-economic factors. Quite aside from the cold war and the opportunistic tendencies emerging from it, we in the developed countries are, in the great humanitarian tradition of our civilization, inclined to be hopeful for people in distress—once we have begun to become more aware of their conditions, as we did under the pressure of the momentous changes of the international political situation after the Second World War.

Clearly, the problems we meet when trying to aid their development efforts would also be immensely simplified and brought down to more easily managed proportions if that research approach were realistic. Aid could be cheaper for us. And apart from all selfish interests, it is, as I have said, our earnest hope that these countries will succeed in their development efforts, now that such efforts are being made.

These feelings are, of course, shared by us economists who, in addition, must sense a vested interest in holding onto a scientific approach that has brought us so much success when applied in our own countries. Nor are Western economists uniquely subject to the optimistic biases emanating from our methodological conservatism. Our confreres in underdeveloped countries are afflicted as much, if not more.

Many have been trained at Western universities or by teachers who acquired their training in the West. All have been exposed to the great economic literature in the Western tradition. Familiarity with, and ability to work in accordance with, the theories that have emerged in that tradition are apt to give status in their native countries as well as abroad.

Their motivation for sharing in the Western biases is fairly independent of their political attitudes. The radicals among them must have wanted to believe in the rapid success of planning. In this connection it should be stressed that today the Communist approach in regard to the basic concepts and theoretical development models used is not different from the Western one.

We should also remember Marx's assumption—now so widely adopted also by Western economists, though they usually do not refer to its source and are often unaware of it—that the effects of industrialization and of investment generally (in the final instance Marx's changes in the "modes of production") spread quickly to other sectors of the economy and also determine the whole "superstructure" of culture, including attitudes and institutions.[22]

This assumption of course makes the postwar approach more plausible. But it is unrealistic. In reality the "spread effects" from industrialization are a function of the level of living, particularly the availability of educational facilities and their use, and of existing attitudes and institutions, and are for these reasons generally slow and incomplete in underdeveloped countries.[23]

The conservatives, on their side, and the privileged classes generally in underdeveloped countries are, of course, happy to hear as little as possible about attitudes and institutions which should have to be changed radically in order to promote a speedy development, and about the productivity effects of raising the levels of living of the poor masses.

But there are deeper causes for the support of the biased approach among the economists in the underdeveloped countries and more generally their intellectuals. The equally opportunistic colonial theory which we sketched above, explaining the poverty and backwardness of these peoples and their lack of progress and, indeed, the apparent absence of great possibilities for progress, was naturally felt to be condescending, humiliating, and offensive.

Adopting the post war approach served as expression of a deeply felt protest against the colonial theory.[24] It gave wholesale release at one stroke from all the objectionable elements in a colonial theory which had been developed to prove the hopelessness of their situation and thereby to free the colonial powers from responsibility for it. It was a relief to forget about not only this conclusion but the premises upon which it was founded.

The disappearance of the racial doctrine is, of course, an obvious advance, as it has no scientific validity.

More serious is the almost total disregard of climatic factors, which had played such a prominent role in the colonial theory. In the developed countries, all located in the temperate zones, differences in climate have never had much economic significance and could therefore safely be left outside considerations. This is not true, however, in the tropical and subtropical zones where the underdeveloped countries are situated (see Chap. 2, below).[25]

But in spite of the obvious importance of climatic factors, they are almost never touched upon any more in writings on underdevelopment, development, and plan-making along the lines of the postwar approach. One can read hundreds of books and articles without finding a mention of the word "climate."

Attitudes and institutions were given a prominent role in the colonial theory, though usually only dealt with in a crude and heavily biased way. Now they are almost totally excluded in the postwar approach, particularly in the economic model-building reflected in the Plans.[26]

The rise of corruption in most underdeveloped countries, and the very serious effects it has for national consolidation and all planning and plan fulfillment (cf. Chap. 7, below) is seldom mentioned in the economic literature on underdevelopment, development, and development planning. When very occasionally noted, this is usually done in order to play down its role and importance.

Even when those factors excluded by the postwar approach are sometimes dealt with by writers in the behavioral sciences or by persons working on practical problems such as community development, agricultural extension, or family planning, they live a life apart, in special books and articles and in separate chapters in the Plans. Seldom—and never effectively—is their importance for development discussed in a way that would challenge the economic theories and their implicit assumptions.

Considering the form in which the colonial theory had usually been propounded and the apologetic laissez-faire conclusions it had served to rationalize, the indigenous intellectuals' protest against this way of thinking is understandable as is also the strong emotional momentum it gave to their acceptance of the postwar approach.

In the general diplomatic accommodation to the political independence of the colonies, it was natural for economists in developed countries to sympathize with the feelings of protest among the indigenous intellectuals against the colonial theory.

Reacting in this way was also in line with the general

tendency to avoid awkward problems and see things in the most hopeful light for reasons of diplomacy in research. By ignoring attitudes, institutions, and the productivity consequences of very low levels of living, they could also uncritically apply a theoretical approach with which they were familiar and which they easily mastered.

In this way all the forces of prejudice interacted and reinforced each other in rapidly building and firmly establishing the postwar approach to the study of underdevelopment, development, and planning. The pendulum of bias had swung from one extreme to the other.

It should be clear from this sketch of the field of vested interests backing that approach that a criticism of it will be resisted in almost all quarters. To these vested interests should be added the inertia and conservatism of scientific thinking in economics, whenever the question is one of the structure of theories and not only of specific arrangements within its framework.[27] There is no vested interest so powerful as that of our broadest conceptions and preconceptions.

And so a scientific rebellion against the prevalent biased approach to the economic problems of underdeveloped countries is up against *a veritable "establishment," entrenched by weighty vested interests* held by the great majority of all who are involved in these problems, either as students or politically and practically.

Nevertheless I feel certain that the massive research efforts now devoted to conditions in underdeveloped countries will in ten or fifteen years' time necessitate an entirely new approach in line with what I call an institutional conception of the problems.[28]

This will in time be as radical a change as that from the colonial theory to the postwar approach. We will have to do away with much of what among economists is often miscalled "sophisticated" methods and much rigorousness and unwarranted precision—though not in regard to the

definition of basic assumptions and concepts, I hope,
where there is much carelessness in the conventional postwar approach.[29]

My confidence is built upon the trust that research has
an inbuilt, self-cleansing capacity.[30] Facts kick, and do so
even—though with some delay—when data are first assembled under categories that correspond to the biased
approach applied but are inadequate to reality. This has,
at least, been my own research experience.

The sociologists and other researchers in the behavioral sciences have for a long time been warning us
economists that we should not forget this or that. They
have then proceeded, however, to carve out separate dis-
ciplines for themselves; they quote each other, develop
their own rather unnecessarily eccentric terminology, and
do not, on the whole, disturb us economists much. They
practically never have had the courage really to challenge
our main approach to the development problems in underdeveloped countries and still less to work out an alternative macro-theory to deal with these problems.

In line with traditions that are now more than two centuries old, we economists have this slightly paranoid but
socially useful bent of mind: we naturally accept the responsibility for taking a broad view of an entire country,
and indeed the whole world, and for thinking in dynamic
terms of national and international policies. Place any
economist in the capital city of an underdeveloped country and give him the necessary assistance and he will in
no time make a Plan. In this regard we are unique among
the social scientists. No sociologist, psychologist, or an-
thropologist would ever think of trying to do such a thing.

And for this reason—and welcoming all research contributions from our colleagues in the other social sciences
—my trust is in the profession of economists when they
once have become informed and have seen the necessity
of taking into account attitudes, institutions, and the pro-

ductivity consequences of levels of living where those are very low.[31]

For what a state needs, and what politics is about, is precisely a macro-plan for inducing changes simultaneously in a great number of conditions, not only the economic, and doing it in a way so as to coordinate all these changes in order to reach a maximum development effect of efforts and sacrifices. This may, in popular terms, be a definition of what we should mean by planning.

Quite generally, as pointed out above, economists are also eager to appear open to ideas from outside their own traditional and narrow field and to be broadminded. After having made the most generous reservations and qualifications, they tend, however, to go on as before, reasoning in purely "economic" terms.

Recalling their general reservations and qualifications, their reaction to a criticism of the type rendered in this book—and more fully substantiated in *Asian Drama*—will predominantly be that the author is behind his time and is pushing through open doors. He might even be classified as a "sociologist," a term that to a true economic theoretician is slightly derogatory and, in any case, demarcates a group of outsiders who do not grasp the sophistication of his abstract economic models.

To that pretended sophistication also usually belongs having very scanty knowledge of the history of ideas and of the philosophy and sociology of science. The raising of the problem of the role of biases in research therefore passes by without even being understood.

This lacuna in their understanding of social problems has in recent decades been fortified by the way in which economists are being trained. Up till around the First World War, practically nobody began his scholarly career as an economist. He either, in former times, was a man of practical affairs who at a mature age turned to economics, or he had a previous training as a mathematician, moral philosopher, lawyer, historian, etc.

Economists never started out as economists, which has now for about half a century been the common pattern. The result is that a student has been able to become professor of economics while having only the most fragmentary knowledge about the society he is studying.

Unfortunately, it is not true that the approach to the development problems of underdeveloped countries is already reformed, and that there is no point in this criticism. Continually and regularly, the problems of economic development are conceived of as having their core in physical investment, occasionally with the addition of skills, management, etc. And continually the reasoning is rendered in terms of national aggregate or average income, saving, employment, and output within the setting of markets, prices and technical coefficients, without much concern about what these terms can mean in these countries and by what statistical witchcraft they have been ascertained.

This conservatism in basic approach has in very recent years been highlighted when a group of economists rediscovered the importance for development of education.[32] This is, of course, nothing new to the educationists or economic historians and had also been appreciated by the classical and neo-classical economists from Adam Smith to Alfred Marshall. When it is now a discovery for economists, the explanation is simply that it had been forgotten by members of our profession, particularly since the time after the Second World War when in our development models we thought merely in "economic" terms and, more specifically, in terms of physical investment.

More striking, however, is that this newest school of economists—who feel no restraint in looking at their contribution as an important innovation in economic theory—is not radical enough. They restrict themselves, in fact, merely to widening the concept of investment—ordinarily up till then understood as physical investment—in the capital/output model so as to include also "investment in man." Otherwise this model, so basic to the postwar approach, is left unchanged and as sovereign as before. Particularly in regard to underdeveloped countries, this construct in terms of financial input and output of education is, however, meaningless.

Adam Smith and Alfred Marshall, as institutionalist as they were, would never have thought of it; Marshall even warned against a translation of the factor of education into financial terms of investment and output. It can only block the way to realistic and relevant research of the crucially important problem of the role of education in development (see Chap. 6, below).

This problem has to be attacked primarily in relation to the content of education and its impact on attitudes and institutions, in particular those of economic and social stratification, and the impact of these factors back upon education. *These are the real problems of the role of education in development, which are actually evaded in the investment-in-man formula.*

Meanwhile, Plans for underdeveloped countries are continually presented, discussed, and later evaluated as financial plans, actually as fiscal plans for public investments.[33] As most of the policy measures needed for development, whether of the short-term operational type or implying alterations in attitudinal or institutional structures aimed at being more permanent, have no or only the most incidental relation to costs and returns in financial terms and thus to a fiscal investment budget, *this implies the possibility of having a Plan without real planning.*

A fiscal budget is, of course, needed for orderly conduct and control of public administration and public expenditure, and it is rational indeed to try to make it for several years ahead. But that type of "planning" cannot be laid even as basis for real planning which must encompass induced changes in all sorts of economic and social conditions carried out in a coordinated fashion.

That the coefficients for interrelations between different changes in the circular causation of a cumulative process [34] are not well known is no defense for substituting a model in simply economic terms—mostly reduced to financial and, indeed, fiscal magnitudes. This is so particularly since the attitudes, institutions, and levels of living in underdeveloped countries are of so very much greater importance for development than they are in developed countries.[35]

One general remark should be added in order to characterize the institutional approach attempted in *Asian Drama* and in the present book.[36] The conventional postwar economist is apt to believe that his own approach is "quantitative" while that of the institutionalist is "qualitative." This is, of course, contrary to the truth.

The institutionalist's approach induces him to press harder for research that can give quantitative precision to his theories and bring them to the empirical test. Since he is basically more critical, he regularly finds the conventional economist's claim to quantitative precision unwarranted, usually on logical grounds.

Neither is the institutionalist "adverse to models." [37] Model-building is a universal method of scientific research, in the same way that quantifying knowledge is a self-evident aim of research. But to construct models in the air, out of uncritically conceived concepts that are inadequate to reality and not logically consistent, and so pretend to knowledge when none has been established, does not represent scientific progress; it comes nearer to being an intellectual fraud.

This judgment refers to underdeveloped countries, as do generally *Asian Drama* and the present book. For developed countries econometric models even of the macrotype referring to an entire country are more possible and useful than in the time when Alfred Marshall denounced them as unrealistic. The statistical material is more complete and reliable. And the "non-economic" factors are less important in the economic analysis as they either are adjusted or will rapidly become adjusted to let the economic impulses through. In underdeveloped countries the contrary is true.[38]

On the necessity of working with explicit value premises, tested for their relevance, significance, and feasibility, I will in this context be brief, referring to earlier contributions.[39]

There is in economic theory a tradition, established by John Stuart Mill in his earliest writings, that in order to reach practical and political conclusions there must be added to the knowledge of facts definite value premises. The remarkable thing is that throughout the history of economic theory until now that rule, though often presented in introductory passages, has never been adhered to. Economists have always arrived at policy conclusions without accounting for their value premises, as they do today.

To "objectify" this remarkable ability to free themselves from their own self-imposed methodological rule, they have constructed a supposedly objective value theory and a welfare theory that in their assumptions have implied, and imply today, elements of the outdated hedonistic psychology and the metaphysical moral philosophy of utilitarianism that is merely the elaboration of the still older philosophy of natural law. Otherwise these theories would have no substantial content.

Added to this, however, is the fact that *value premises are needed even in the theoretical stage of establishing knowledge about facts and factual relations.* Answers can only be given when questions have been asked. A view is impossible except from a viewpoint. "Things look different, depending upon where you stand."

A "disinterested" social science has never existed and can never come to exist—for logical reasons. Valuations are always implied in our search for truth as in all other purposive behavior. The valuations can be hidden, however, and the researcher can even keep himself unaware of them. As they can then remain unlucid and undefined, this is what opens the door to biases.

Seen from the opposite point of view, the only means that logic places at our disposal to free ourselves from biases is the requisite of stating our value premises explicitly. The need to do this will be the more clearly felt the less naïve we are about how our approaches otherwise tend to become determined by the tradition in our science, by the influences from the society we are a part of, and, of course, by our own personality as determined by our individual history and experiences, our mental make-up, and our inclinations.

In *Asian Drama* the modernization ideals have been used as instrumental value premises: rationality, development and development planning, rise of productivity, rise of levels of living, social and economic equalization, improved institutions and attitudes, national consolidation, national independence, democracy at the grass roots, and social discipline.[40]

All these value premises and a number of derived value premises are interrelated under the quest for rationality and get, in fact, their more precise definition only in the course of study.[41]

Actual conditions are, of course, always far from the ideals. The meaning of postulating these ideals as value premises for research is that *a change in the direction toward their realization is the desired goal in planning.*

The reason for adopting the modernization ideals as value premises for our study of underdeveloped countries is not merely that very commonly they are pronounced to be the goal determining policy by the governments of practically all those countries and, indeed, generally by the articulate members of their peoples. In many under-developed countries they have acquired the role almost of a state religion.[42]

To this reason is added the important fact that, particularly in view of the present and foreseeable rates of population growth, rapid strides toward the realization of the modernization ideals must be made to avoid not only stagnation but a turn sooner or later to actual impoverishment with increasing misery for the masses.

These countries may not succeed in reaching far toward realizing these ideals. But a return to traditional society is excluded. They have all passed the point of no return.

To postulate the modernization ideals as value premises may seem to imply a study of the problems of under-developed countries in Western terms or, rather, in terms of conditions in developed countries generally. It is true that in developed countries these ideals have been realized to a very much greater extent than is foreseeable in the underdeveloped countries for a long time to come.

The choice of these value premises stands, however, in no contradiction to the main thesis of this chapter: that the underdeveloped countries should be studied in terms that are adequate to the reality there, nor to my criticism of the postwar approach which abstracts from attitudes, institutions, and the productivity consequences of the very low levels of living of the masses of people.[43]

The value premises determine only the point of view from which reality is studied. That point of view does not determine, however, what facts and factual relationships are brought within the scope of observation and analysis. It is my conviction that economic study must be comprehensive enough to be adequate to reality, and that this reality is very different in the underdeveloped countries from what it is in developed countries. No value premises prescribe that a study should not be realistic and relevant to the maximum extent.

One final observation should be added to this introductory chapter. In many quarters it has been held that it is a mistake to apply the modernization ideals in research on, and the plan-making for, underdeveloped countries.

It is emphasized that these valuations [44] are foreign to underdeveloped countries. They originate from the developed Western and Communist countries. *The underdeveloped countries should be permitted to develop according to their own traditional valuations*, it is asserted.

This view is often expressed in a way reminiscent of the old, static anthropological approach that tended to view changes as "disturbances."

I believe that this view is mistaken for a number of reasons. For one thing, the traditional valuations are not directed upon inducing changes. They are static. They are therefore not of a nature that they can be used in determining goals for planning.[45]

From this comes the competitive strength of the modernization ideals, organized under the rationality principle. As soon as development becomes set up as a desideratum, the modernization ideals must be accepted. They are further strengthened when it is realized that with the present and foreseeable population development there must be a rather rapid development toward the modernization ideals in order to prevent economic stagnation and even regression.

Moreover, when the traditional valuations are brought up on a "higher," more articulate level, they are often found not to be in conflict with the modernization ideals.[46] Indeed, for the most part they either support these ideals, or, at least, remain neutral.

There is, thus, for instance, not a development interest in changing modes of dress, and still less people's attachment to their history, philosophy, religion (on the "higher" level; see Chap. 3), literature, art, etc. Many traditional customs represent also a pragmatic accommodation to actual conditions, for instance often in the construction of houses, and are then in accord with rational considerations in planning.

In some cases there are conflicts, however, between the modernization ideals and traditional valuations. The traditionally adverse attitude in India to cow slaughter runs thus contrary to rational animal husbandry. The attachment there and in many other parts of the underdeveloped world to separate languages and, even more, separate scripts runs counter to the most rational use of schooling and often also to national consolidation.[47]

These traditional valuations represent, then, inhibitions and obstacles to planning. If they are so strong that they have to be accepted, they imply opportunity costs that should be accounted for in the calculations carried out for a Plan.

The traditional valuations have to be studied as important facts among all the other conditions in underdeveloped countries that must be taken into account in planning. It is, indeed, part of my accusation of the postwar approach that this has usually not been done. *But the idea of seeking the goals for development in these valuations amounts to abstaining from rational planning.* This the underdeveloped countries could not afford and have not chosen to do.

Chapter 2

DIFFERENCES IN CONDITIONS

The criticism of the postwar approach in the preceding chapter was founded upon the judgment that conditions in underdeveloped countries raise very much stronger inhibitions (among those in power) and obstacles (among the masses of people) [1] to development than in the developed countries where this approach is more applicable. These attitudes are fortified by institutions, acting as both causes and effects of the attitudes. The productivity of the labor force is also held down by the very low levels of living of the masses of people. In regard to attitudes and institutions—though less generally to levels of living—this would hold true even if a comparison were made to the developed countries at that earlier time when they were undergoing their industrial revolutions or even in previous centuries.[2]

In regard to political institutions, one obvious difference is that the now developed countries were independent and had for the most part become fairly consolidated nation-states, able to pursue national policies, well before their industrial revolutions. They formed a small world of broadly similar cultures, within which people and ideas circulated rather freely.

In this small world, long before the industrial revolution, rationalism had been fostered and traditionalism weakened as the Renaissance, the Reformation, and the Enlightenment, successively, revolutionized concepts and valuations. Modern scientific thought developed in these countries and a modernized technology began early to be introduced in their agriculture and their industries, which at that time were all small-scale.

The great discoveries and the colonization of the non-European world had helped to widen horizons. Indeed, they brought about changes of attitudes and institutions in the European countries more than in the colonies themselves, except where the latter were sparsely populated as in the New World, where the natives could be killed off or segregated in various ways to make room for immigrating Europeans and their offspring.

By contrast, most of the underdeveloped countries today have only recently become independent and have yet to become consolidated nation-states capable of pursuing national policies effectively.

The modernization ideals, which very generally have become adopted as a sort of state religion by their ruling educated class, are not indigenous, and attempts to realize these ideals meet strong inhibitions among this class as well as obstacles among the masses. And for many reasons, which will be made apparent as we go along, change there must be rapid rather than slow, as was the case in the presently developed countries.[3]

All this is, on the whole, true of the underdeveloped countries in Asia and Africa. The Latin American countries are different in many respects. The latter countries have a longer history as politically independent countries. Theirs is not in the same sense a traditional society with its roots several hundreds or thousands of years back. They are, rather, like the countries in the New World, European settlements which, however, have gone awry almost from the very beginning.

And so their present situation, not least in regard to the attitudes and institutions which act as inhibitions and obstacles to development, is not too different from that of the rest of the underdeveloped world. Though average levels of income are generally considerably higher in most Latin American countries, their masses of people in the rural and urban slums are often equally destitute and far away from modern life.

There are several other conditions in underdeveloped countries that are less favorable to development than they are, or once were, in the now developed countries. Those other differences should be briefly pointed out before we come to discuss our main policy conclusions. Even though they are not among those that *per se* invalidate the postwar approach—as they can easily be included in an "economic" theory and planning—we find that the deeper biases implied in that approach have led to their being played down in contemporary literature on the development problems of underdeveloped countries and in the plan-making.

For one thing, *the underdeveloped countries are often less well endowed with natural resources than the presently developed countries were when they began modern development.* I disregard, as in this whole book, the spots on the map of the underdeveloped world where there is plenty of oil and other minerals of the types that are in brisk and rising demand in the developed countries. Those spots often, rather, become enclaves integrated more closely with the economy of one or several developed countries.

South Asia, with almost one third of mankind and two thirds of the people living in non-Communist underdeveloped countries, is on the whole a region rather poorly endowed with natural resources.[4] In Africa and Latin

America the stock of natural resources is, on the whole, very much more plentiful. But it should be remembered that their economic exploitation mostly requires heavy investment of capital, which is not easily available. The African countries in particular meet great difficulties on that account.

The resource basis should, however, not be too important for development. Several of the most highly developed industrial economies—as, for instance, Denmark, Switzerland, and Japan—have built up their industries mainly on the basis of imported raw materials. This may be less possible for most underdeveloped countries, at least on a large scale.

In any event, such a pattern of development is more difficult at the very beginning of a developmental process. At a more advanced stage of development, when capital costs have increased and wages, in particular, have reached higher levels, raw-material costs become a much smaller portion of total production costs. Developed countries should for that reason be less dependent on having a natural resource basis.

Climate constitutes another major difference between underdeveloped and developed countries.[5] Almost all underdeveloped countries are situated in the tropical or subtropical zones. It is a fact that all successful industrialization in modern times has taken place in the temperate zones. This cannot be entirely an accident of history but must have to do with some special handicaps, directly or indirectly related to climate.

As already mentioned in the preceding chapter, climate was given an important role in the apologetic colonial theory but has now almost disappeared from the literature and the plan-making. This is, of course, an extreme example of the new opposite biases.

Although research, public discussion, and planning based on the postwar approach tend systematically to bypass the complications arising from attitudes, institutions, and modes and levels of living, the relevance of these factors to problems of development is at least "accounted for" by interspersed reservations and qualifications and by the common declarations that development is a "human problem." Climatic conditions, on the other hand, are either entirely ignored or casually dismissed as being of no importance.

Even if, for this reason, little research has been carried out about the importance of climatic conditions in development planning, it is clear that, generally speaking, the extremes of heat and humidity in most underdeveloped countries contribute to a deterioration of soil and many kinds of material goods; bear a partial responsibility for the low productivity of certain crops, forests, and animals, and not only cause discomfort to workers but also impair their health and decrease the participation in, and duration of, work and its efficiency.

Almost all of these unfavorable effects can largely be avoided or counteracted by planned policies. But overcoming these unfavorable effects—and occasionally turning them into advantages, which in regard to agriculture is in several countries quite possible—requires expenditures, often of the investment type. And since capital and all other real cost elements such as administration are scarce, *climatic conditions often impose serious obstacles to development.*

The present population density and the prospective rapid growth of population constitute another very important difference between underdeveloped and developed countries.[6]

In pre-industrial times the secular trend of population growth in Europe had been comparatively slow, though it speeded up somewhat as the industrialization phase was approached. By contrast, the populations of most underdeveloped countries have been increasing over a long period of time, though not so rapidly as today. As a result some underdeveloped countries—as for instance India and Pakistan, with soon 700 million inhabitants—now start out with a considerably higher man/land ratio than the European countries in earlier times. This puts them at a disadvantage in regard to prospects for development.

Other parts of South Asia, most parts of Latin America, some parts of West Asia and, of course, Africa (except its northern parts), and many individual areas even in the countries with a high average man/land ratio are sparsely populated and often have huge reserves of cultivable though as yet uncultivated land. But as a matter of fact, people mostly live crowded even in those countries and areas that have large land reserves.

Bringing these reserves to effective usage hinges on domestic institutional reforms, especially in land ownership and tenancy, improved education and training, and, prior to these, a political climate hospitable to substantial social and economic reform; it also usually requires large investments and in some cases favorable trade outlets in the developed countries.[7] If these conditions are not created by policies at home and abroad, *a country can remain "overpopulated," even if there are abundant natural resources nearby.*

Much more detrimental to development is, however, the population explosion which in recent years has raised the rate of population increase in all underdeveloped countries to around 3 percent a year or even higher.

The population explosion is the most important social and economic change that has taken place in the underdeveloped world in the postwar era. It has been far more important than any reform or development efforts, and it has done a great deal to thwart these efforts. In Chapter 5 we shall give the reasons why it is not to be expected that the rate of population increase can be brought down substantially within the near future.

Such a high rate of population growth—which implies a doubling of the population within twenty to twenty-five years—raises a formidable obstacle to development.[8] It does so even when the man/land ratio is low.

The developed countries—except for periods in some of those countries in the New World where conditions for development were extraordinarily favorable and where immigration of adults played a large role—have never experienced a population increase of that dimension. It is doubtful whether the industrial revolution could have occurred in these countries, or could have proceeded so fast and with such relatively mild unfavorable repercussions for the poorer strata, had their populations been increasing that rapidly.

International trade was an "engine of growth" in the development of the presently developed countries. Typically, rising demands for their exports played a crucial role. That, together with the relative political stability, made it possible for the newcomer to borrow funds in the international capital market, often for a rate of interest of 3 percent or even less.

Though the initial stimulus had been increasing exports, imports could thus increase even more. This largely explains why during the nineteenth century the volume of trade could for the most part expand even faster than production.

There was in colonial times a similar impetus rendered to many underdeveloped countries which increased their exports.[9] In their case the operating factor was often foreign investments, for the most part in plantations and mines. For many reasons these development spurts have occurred almost regularly in enclaves with weak spread effects to the rest of the economy.[10] In colonial times they practically nowhere resulted in an industrial revolution.

When these countries are now planning for development they meet formidable difficulties. The developed countries, at the time they began to develop rapidly, all had small populations. They stood out as islands in an ocean of backward people.

Now, when the underdeveloped areas are trying to emerge from political and economic dependency, they cannot simply repeat the development process of the developed countries. While being a latecomer in the nineteenth century was not a disadvantage but often quite the opposite, it is in the twentieth century a serious disadvantage.

As a matter of fact, *ever since the First World War most underdeveloped countries have seen their trading position deteriorating.*[11] They have experienced a shrinking demand for their exports relative to the development of world trade. Their terms of trade have not deteriorated equally sharply, but this is because the increase in their production of export products has generally been slow. The outlook for their exports is not bright.

There are many causes behind this unfortunate development. Rapid and all-round technological development in the developed countries has slowed down the rise of demand for primary products by permitting substantial cutbacks in the amount of raw materials used. At the same time technological improvement has increased the developed countries' ability to produce such materials cheaply in rising quantity. Protectionism in the developed countries has magnified these effects. Industrial substitutes have been developed, particularly in the field of rubber and textile raw materials.

Generally speaking, except to some extent for rubber and a few other raw materials, most goods traditionally exported by underdeveloped countries have a low income elasticity, and almost none are products for which there is a rapidly rising demand as a result of economic development in the developed countries.

In the industrial field discriminatory tariffs in the developed countries, rising in line with the stage of processing, hamper the development of export industries in the underdeveloped countries. Even apart from that obstacle, the possibility of building up a manufacturing industry that could successfully compete in the world market is severely limited by the markedly superior conditions under which the entrenched industries in the developed countries operate, among them the advanced skills in producing as well as in selling products, the external economies, the heavy investment in research, and the ever more rapidly accelerating advances in technology.[12]

Meanwhile, the import needs of underdeveloped countries are rising. For one thing, the population explosion has in many of these countries increased their need to import foodstuffs—at the same time as it tended to decrease export possibilities in regard to this type of goods in the food-surplus countries. More important is the rising need to import development goods.

Under these conditions a gap has ordinarily developed between import payments and export returns. This gap has to a very small extent been filled by credits on the private capital market, where investors are reluctant to lend funds both because of the bleak and uncertain economic prospects of these countries and because of their frequent lack of political stability since the colonial power structure has been liquidated. There has been some direct investment, but the volume is small in the larger part of the underdeveloped world.

As the capital inflow from these private sources has only made a dent in the need for it, the gap has to a great extent had to be filled by grants and loans from governments in the developed countries and to some extent also from intergovernmental organizations, mainly the International Bank for Reconstruction and Development (the World Bank).[13]

Grants have been a decreasing part of the public funds placed at the disposal of underdeveloped countries. It is true that some public loans have been given at concessional rates of interest and repayment conditions. Nevertheless, the debt servicing has become an ever more serious burden on their exchange resources. As I shall discuss in Chapter 11, the recent tendency has been for this public capital flow to stagnate and for its quality in various respects to deteriorate.

Even the financing of those regular development loans channeled through the World Bank needs the guaranty of the governments in the developed countries. In spite of this the effective rate of interest is more than double that for which developed countries could once borrow money at the time when they were beginning to develop rapidly.

Under these circumstances the underdeveloped countries are trying to develop through import substitution.[14] One dilemma inherent in this policy is that starting new industries ordinarily requires large imports of capital goods, and often continuing imports of spare parts, semimanufactured goods, and raw materials. The building up of auxiliary industries to substitute for these imports will again raise the need of importing capital goods in particular.

The more serious difficulty with the import-substitution policy is, however, that *the choice of line for substitution is usually not open for rational planning*. Ordinarily the first thing that happens is that an underdeveloped country gets into exchange difficulties; it then is often forced to introduce import controls of one type or another. For natural, and, indeed, rational reasons it tries to curtail imports of the least necessary goods, which thus automatically get the highest protection.

From a development point of view, this is *unplanned protection*. That the result, in spite of all sorts of discretionary controls, generally tends to be a non-competitive, high-cost industry is also natural.

The differences in initial conditions accounted for so far all make economic development of underdeveloped countries more difficult today than it once was for the now developed countries. One advantage they should have is the much more highly developed technology, which they can simply take over without having the burden of creating it.[15]

There are some reasons for discounting that advantage. One is related to the fact that this technology to be maximally useful should be adapted to the different factor proportions in underdeveloped countries. Other initial difficulties are the lack of a supporting industrial structure, which takes time to build up, and the shortage of skills on different levels.

Nevertheless, on balance the tremendous advance of technology since the industrial revolution in the now developed countries should be an advantage. And this is hopefully stated, and often given pathetic expression, by economists and by all the political and intellectual leaders in underdeveloped as well as in developed countries. That this is a static view is regularly not observed.

In the developed countries, with huge resources at their disposal, science and technology are now progressing at an ever faster pace.[16] What is almost inexplicably concealed in economic writings is the obvious fact that *scientific and technological advance in the developed countries has had, and is now having, an impact on the underdeveloped countries which, on balance, is detrimental to their development prospects.* When this has not been seen, it has been due to another outflow of the general biases accounted for in the first chapter.

This stands out the more clearly, since the elements of this dynamic influence are, of course, observed in all specific studies. The fact that technological advance in the developed countries is to a large part responsible for the deteriorating trading position in underdeveloped countries, referred to above, is, for instance, a commonplace, and is intensively studied in relation to the development of their trade.

It is also a well-known fact, and one frequently dis-

cussed in realistic terms, that the continuous technological
advance in the developed countries, and not only their
present high level, is partly responsible for the difficulty
underdeveloped countries have in breaking through by increasing their production and their export of manufactured
products.

It is only the coordination of those thoughts that is regularly missing. As by far the greater part of all research
is carried on in the developed countries and is financed
by their governments, their foundations, universities, and
industries, it would, indeed, be unreasonable not to expect the research and development efforts to be directed
to their own advantage.

In the rich countries we will continue to raise agricultural productivity, make savings in the use of raw materials, and develop substitute products. We may, for
instance, as the report of a committee of the United
States Congress suggests, soon be able to produce syn-
thetically not only coffee but also tea and cocoa.

The Atomic Energy Authority in Britain has reported
that British scientists believe they have discovered a way
to produce, inexpensively, a fiber four times tougher than
steel and much lighter, offering a cheap substitute for
metals in a wide range of uses. It is also worth mentioning
that nickel and aluminum, the two metals for which demand is increasing most rapidly and which would probably have the best chances of competing with the new
fiber, are produced mainly in developed countries.

It would be contrary to the very spirit of our civilization
to stop such advances. The only contribution we in the
developed countries could make to prevent the underdeveloped countries from being hurt would be to direct
a larger part of the development of science and technology toward problems whose solution would be in the
interest of these underdeveloped countries. To an extent
this is already being done, as we shall point out in several
of the chapters to follow.

To raise these efforts to a level where they would really countervail the primary detrimental effects for underdeveloped countries of the exceedingly rapid technological development in the developed countries would imply more aid of this other type by the developed countries, indeed, such aid on a larger scale than anything previously done or now contemplated in the way of technical assistance. To this I shall return in several of the following chapters.

Naturally, there are instances where technological advances in developed countries can be applied immediately in underdeveloped countries, as when growing concern for the water supply has led to heavy investments in research on desalination of sea water. The advance in the techniques of birth control has been of the same nature. But I am talking about the general trend, particularly in the manufacturing industry.

The true significance of this dynamic factor can only be grasped when we realize that *the levels of science and technology are now not only rapidly rising but can be expected to rise at an accelerating speed, following an exponential curve.*[17] A telescoping of change in time has become the only alternative, not only to continued stagnation but to regression.

Contrary to a common misconception, change was not rapid in the now developed countries. They had the advantage of gradualness—and in addition, as we have pointed out, had from the beginning the advantage of attitudes and institutions that more easily permitted or readjusted to change.

The onslaught of modernization from outside, without the gradual transition once experienced by the developed countries and concomitant to the population explosion, leads to a situation where elements of modernism become sprinkled throughout a society in which many conditions have remained almost the same for centuries. As Jawaharlal

Nehru said of India: "We have atomic energy and we also use cow dung."

To take the optimistic view that the spurts of modernism are important "growing points" is to assume a number of things: that the hampering effects of the population explosion at home and of the ever more rapid technological advance in the developed countries can be overcome, and that the spread effects within the underdeveloped countries can be made to operate more effectively than they have done up to the present time.

It is obvious that such a development will not come about by a "natural" evolution, and this constitutes the case for planning, including radical reforms of the type being discussed in the following chapters. The aim of planning is to engender development by coordinated state policies, in spite of the greater difficulties they encounter which we have noted in this chapter. To be at all effective, planning must then be directed also toward many other things than those contained in the biased postwar approach of which I spoke in the first chapter. Above all, policies must be initiated to influence attitudes and institutions directly.[18]

The usual view that differences in levels of development have only a "dimensional," not a "qualitative," character, and more specifically that there is only a "time lag" between developed and underdeveloped countries—which, like much else in the postwar approach, goes back to Marx—is mistaken.[19] As these thoughts have been developed in the so-called theory of the "stages of growth," they are based on metaphysical preconceptions of the teleological variety.[20]

Unwarranted optimism is part of the national disposition of mind in the United States, what George Kennan once called "the great American capacity for enthusiasm and self-hypnosis." It is also a natural urge for the intellectuals in underdeveloped countries. A testimony to that is that the planning there regularly tends to err in the optimistic direction. In the Communist countries optimism is programatic, and mistrust of it is classified as "bourgeois" deviation.[21]

Optimism is often defended as useful for supporting courage in meeting difficulties. But it should be clear that even from that practical point of view the courage founded upon unwarranted optimism is apt to lead to disillusionment. Everyone talks about disillusion—recently not least in regard to the development of underdeveloped countries—without reminding himself that it ordinarily assumes previous illusions.

From the point of view of the student, *optimism, like pessimism, means nothing but a biased view*. What he should seek is realism, even if he then conflicts with prevailing ideas within his own profession. And if he has carried out his work sincerely and effectively, he has the right to protest if his more realistic views are simply labeled pessimistic.

For my own part, when my strivings toward realism lead to a more serious view of the prospects for development than the one that is still current among most of my fellow economists, this does not lead me to defeatism.

My conclusion is, instead, that development requires increased, and in many respects more radical, efforts: speedier and more effective large-scale reforms in the underdeveloped countries and greater concern and more substantial sacrifices in the developed countries.

And my deepest moral criticism of the optimistic bias in current thinking as represented by the postwar approach is that it has encouraged complacency in the underdeveloped countries and lack of solicitude in the developed countries.

The problem of speeding up development in the underdeveloped countries is one of the world problems today —putting a stop to the reckless and still accelerating armament race is another—where cheap optimism can be disastrous. A realistic view today should rationally demand a courage and a determination almost of desperation.

After the introduction in this and the preceding chapter, the main practical policy problems will now be taken up, one after the other. In Part Two, the policies for which there is a rational need in the underdeveloped countries themselves will first be discussed. In Part Three the problem of what the developed countries should do to promote development in the former countries will be raised.

By far most important are the needed reform policies in the underdeveloped countries themselves. But the difficulties they encounter are so great that most of them will have slight chances to succeed without more aid from the developed countries.

The crucial problem of development as depending on politics will be taken up in the fourth and final part: the feasibility of reforms without revolution in the underdeveloped countries depends very much on the policies of the developed countries, dealt with in Part Three.

Part Two

THE NEED FOR RADICAL REFORMS IN UNDERDEVELOPED COUNTRIES

Chapter 3

THE EQUALITY
ISSUE

I *Some General Points*

The social and economic stratification in by far the
greater part of the underdeveloped world is inegalitarian
and rigid—though to different degrees in the several countries. With very few exceptions—in South Asia, Ceylon
may be one [1]—economic inequality seems to have been
increasing in recent times.[2]

The equality issue is central in the development problems of underdeveloped countries. Inequality relates to
all social and economic relationships. The equality issue,
therefore, becomes an element, often a main element, in
all specific policy issues such as community development,
agricultural policy, educational reform, and of course
taxation. We shall thus meet the equality issue in all the
chapters to follow in this Part Two.

The equality issue has, however, not been given that
position in the economic literature on the development

problems of these countries or in planning. Indeed—as will be illustrated in the next chapter in regard to a particularly important development problem, that of agriculture—it has in recent years been evaded ever more completely.

The conclusion I have reached is that *inequality and the trend toward rising inequality stand as a complex of inhibitions and obstacles to development* and that, consequently, there is an urgent need for reversing the trend and creating greater equality as a condition for speeding up development.

Traditionally, Western economists for the most part assume, on the contrary, a conflict between economic growth and egalitarian reforms. They take it for granted that *a price has to be paid for reforms* and that often this price is prohibitive for poor countries.

This attitude goes back to the compromise thinking of the classical economists when they had to protect themselves against the radical policy premises, placed at the very basis of their theory, which they had taken over from the moral philosophies of natural law and utilitarianism out of which economic theory once branched off.[3]

Modern economists, who usually are less sophisticated in regard to the philosophical foundation of economic theory than their spiritual ancestors, mostly assume simply, without many scruples, that there is such a conflict. Very little empirical research has ever been devoted to proving this assumption.

Even in the West today we lack detailed knowledge of how factors such as the savings ratio, labor input, and labor efficiency react to different degrees of equality in the distribution of income and wealth. Discussion of these matters remains mostly abstract and speculative.

Meanwhile, large-scale egalitarian reform policies have been set on foot in all the developed countries, and this reform activity has been escalating ever since the First

World War.[4] These countries are now all "welfare states."
The important thing to note is, however, that not only the
economists but even the propagators of these reforms generally did accept the traditional common assumption that
a price had to be paid for the egalitarian reforms.

*The reforms were argued in terms of reaching greater
social justice,* the importance of which was gradually becoming recognized so widely in the developed countries
that the political conditions were created for their passing
through the parliaments. The reforms were coming to be
considered worth their price.

Only in the most advanced welfare states and only in
very recent years has the thought emerged that the welfare reforms, instead of being costly for a society, actually
laid a basis for more steady and rapid economic growth.
To attempt empirical study of the effects on economic
growth of these reforms has mostly been an interest appealing to sociologists, social workers, and statisticians,
while economists have mostly stuck to their guns—only
in recent years becoming less eager to predict ruinous effects of new reform proposals, as so many such warnings
had quite flagrantly been proved wrong by experience.

I have wanted to give this bare sketch of the ideological developments on the home ground of Western
economists in order to make their position on the equality
issue in underdeveloped countries more understandable.

When after the end of the Second World War they
hastily (see Chap. 1, above) came to direct their research
interests to the development problems of these countries,
a preconception, almost self-evident to them, was that
these extremely poor countries could not afford to think
in terms of social justice and to pay the price for egalitarian reforms. Social justice would have to be sacrificed
in order to accomplish economic growth. This attitude is
exemplified in the following quotation from a recently
published book on the development of Pakistan:

A conflict exists ... between the aims of growth and equality ... the inequalities in income contribute to the growth
of the economy, which makes possible a real improvement
for the lower-income groups.[4a]

This thought is often rationalized by a saying, which
throughout the development of economic thinking has
also been popular in developed countries, viz., that "production goes before distribution." Professor D. R. Gadgil,
the present chief of the Planning Commission in India, has
been among those who consistently have pointed to the
logical confusion implied in this type of reasoning: "Production before Distribution is ... no more than a plausible
cliché used as a cloak for a policy which its protagonists
find it difficult to avow openly." Production and distribution are interdependent within the same macro-system.

The idea of a conflict between greater equality and economic growth—where priority in these poor countries has
to be given to growth—is commonly supported by an
analogy from the history of the now developed countries.
The Western countries and even Japan experienced rising
inequalities in the early stages of their industrialization.
The crude exploitation of the poor is then assumed to have
been the condition that made possible the rise in savings
and the aggressive entrepreneurship that gave momentum
to the industrial revolution.

These historical comparisons should not necessarily be
regarded as conclusive.[5] For one thing, the underdeveloped countries today have mostly declared equalization
as a practical policy goal, which rarely happened in the
now developed countries at that earlier time.[6] Many of
the former countries today are committed to direct and
spur development by means of national planning, which is
another difference.[7] And equalization is regularly declared to be an important goal for their planning, and
indeed, for all state policies (see below).[8]

What would have happened in the now developed countries under such different conditions is open to speculation.

In any case, a straight conclusion built upon this analogy is not permissible.

As Jawaharlal Nehru explained in his *Discovery of India*:

The idea of planning and a planned society is accepted now in varying degrees by almost everyone. But planning by itself has little meaning and need not necessarily lead to good results. Everything depends on the objectives of the plan and on the controlling authority, as well as, of course, the government behind it. Does the plan aim definitely at the well-being and advancement of the people as a whole, at the opening out of opportunity to all and the growth of freedom and methods of co-operative organization and action? Increase of production is essential, but obviously by itself it does not take us far and may even add to the complexity of our problems. An attempt to preserve old-established privileges and vested interests cuts at the very root of planning. Real planning must recognize that no such interests can be allowed to come in the way of any scheme designed to further the well-being of the community as a whole.[9]

But even Nehru could not escape ambiguity on this point: "To some extent that [increasing economic inequality] is inevitable in a growing economy."[10] But again Nehru explained: "But in order to prevent it one has to take measures. Namely, if you leave things to themselves, wealth grows into more wealth."[11]

Next we should note that there are prejudicial elements in the economic models generally resorted to in plan-making according to the postwar approach. Development is simply defined as an increase in national output; it is ordinarily made a function of physical investment. The Plan is then constructed in financial terms (see Chap. 1, above).

This implies that the costs of egalitarian reforms are accounted for in the fiscal budget, which is the core in financial planning, while no benefits in terms of higher productivity are calculated. Moreover, all those reforms that have no reflections or only incidental ones in expenditures on the budget—merely implying induced changes of attitudes and institutions—tend to fall entirely outside the type of Plan prepared in line with the biased postwar approach.[12]

Even when, as mostly is the case (see below), greater equality is pronounced to be one of the important goals of planning, the interest is then mainly focused only on economic equality. This is, of course, by itself, a biased view in line with the postwar approach, discussed in Chapter 1.

In my opinion, there are a number of general reasons why, contrary to the ordinary conception of a conflict between the two goals of economic growth and greater economic equality, those are often in harmony, and why *greater equality in underdeveloped countries is almost a condition for more rapid growth*.[13]

First, the usual argument that inequality of income is a condition for saving has much less bearing on conditions in underdeveloped countries, where landlords and other rich people are known to squander their incomes for conspicuous consumption and conspicuous investment, and sometimes, particularly (but not only) in Latin America, in capital flight.

Second, since large masses of people in underdeveloped countries suffer from undernutrition, malnutrition, and other serious defects in their levels of living, in particular lack of elementary health and educational facilities, extremely bad housing conditions and sanitation, and since this impairs their willingness and ability to work and to work intensively, this holds down production.[14] This implies that measures to raise income levels for the masses of people would raise productivity.

Third, social inequality is tied to economic inequality in a mutual relationship, each being both cause and effect of the other. Greater economic equality would undoubtedly tend to lead to greater social equality. As social inequality is quite generally detrimental to development, the conclusion must be that through this mechanism also greater equality would lead to higher productivity.

Fourth, we cannot exclude from consideration that behind the quest for greater equality is the recognition of the fact that it has an independent value in terms of social justice, and that it would have wholesome effects for national integration.

When we recall the miserably low levels of living of the poorer strata in the underdeveloped countries, and if we take these general reasons for beneficial productivity effects into consideration, there should be less reason to trust the largely speculative thesis that reforms in the interest of greater equality would be detrimental to economic growth.

I mentioned above that the studies which very recently have been made in those highly developed countries which are most advanced as welfare states, with their much higher levels of living for the lower income strata, tend to prove that continued egalitarian reforms even there have been productive. This should *a fortiori* imply that reforms in the same direction would be productive in the underdeveloped countries.

We might end this section by quoting a summary judgment of the Secretariat for the Economic Commission for Asia and the Far East, who are nearer the life of underdeveloped countries than speculative economists, particularly in the West:

> To judge from actual experience, large and growing income disparities have not proved conducive to brisk economic performance and a strong thrust of development. It seems more likely, in fact, that heavy income concentration has often impeded healthy economic expansion by acting as a powerful disincentive (both material and psychological) to public participation in development. It cannot be overlooked that the prevailing *laissez-faire* attitude towards distributional aspects of development policy lends convenient support to maintenance of the political and social *status quo* in Asian countries.[15]

So far, I have been discussing the equality issue in underdeveloped countries in highly abstract and general terms. *The equality issue has, however, to be brought down to earth and to be discussed in relation to concrete policy issues.* In the next chapter I shall attempt to do this for the overwhelmingly important problem of agricultural policy.

But before that I want to look a little closer into the broad facts of inequality in underdeveloped countries and, more particularly, ask the question why the social and economic chasms have been retained and even seem to be widening.

II Inequality and Power

Inequality in underdeveloped countries can take very different forms. It can be equally harsh in a society where no one is really well off economically—for instance, in an Indian village in, say, West Bengal, in which the land is owned in small parcels by high-caste persons who do not work, while half the labor force or more are working the land for the owners, themselves being landless [16]—as where there is a small rich class of a few landlords, often absent from the village, and their managers at the top with many more landless or almost landless workers at the bottom of the social structure—for instance, in parts of Sind and Pakistan, and in many Latin American countries.

It is possible to distinguish between social inequality and economic inequality. Social inequality is clearly related to status and can perhaps best be defined as an extreme lack of social mobility and a severely hampered possibility of competing freely, this taken in a much broader sense than when the term "free competition" is used in economics. Economic inequality is the simpler concept and is related to differences in wealth and income.

But there is a close relation between the two, since

social inequality stands as a main cause of economic inequality, while, at the same time, economic inequality supports social inequality. In most situations social and economic inequality are a joint affair, which can be split into its two components only by means of an analysis, which must be institutional in character.

There are several relationships between poverty and inequality. One forms the general theme of this chapter: that, as we argue, social and economic inequality stand as a main cause of the poverty of a nation. From a planning point of view this means that *greater equality is a precondition for lifting a society out of poverty.*

Another relationship is that *the poorer a nation is in aggregate or average terms, the more severe hardship will economic inequality wreak on those who are the poorest.*[17] Even if the degree of overall inequality were comparable to that in the developed countries in terms of a "Lorenz curve," showing the share of total income received by any given percentage of the population—which is generally not the case, though the crudity of available data does not preclude the possibility in some of these countries—it would have very much more adverse effects for people in the lower income strata in underdeveloped countries.

A third relationship is that *economic and social inequality may itself be not only a cause of the prevailing poverty and of the difficulty for a country in rising out of poverty, but also, at the same time, its consequence.* Observing the broad correlation between degrees of inequality and poverty in South Asia, it is legitimate to ask whether or not poverty breeds inequality.[18]

The causal mechanism would be that at very low economic levels there will be little room left for human generosity, while a stronger need will be felt for maintaining social distinctions of all sorts. "When the trough is empty, the horses will bite each other," as a Swedish saying puts it. If this is true and important, it should not be considered a historical accident that the typical villages in India and

Pakistan, with their extremely low average economic levels, ordinarily display particularly harsh cleavages.

A village in Thailand or Burma may not be very much richer, but few villagers are so short of food as in India and Pakistan. The greater human equality in the former two countries could well be related to their higher economic levels. We may also note that historically, in the developed Western countries, greater equality of opportunity has generally come about *pari passu* with rising economic levels.

But the causation of inequality in underdeveloped countries is, of course, a much more complicated matter and poverty cannot be its only cause, sometimes not even the main one.

The greater equality in countries like Thailand and Burma has often been related, instead, to the Buddhist religion in these two countries. That explanation should not fully satisfy us. Islam in its manifestations on the learned and higher level is no less egalitarian than Buddhism.

Moreover, there are reasons to be generally skeptical when Western, as well as South Asian, writers so often think they are saying something important about the peoples in the region when they refer loosely to the impact of Hinduism, Buddhism, Islam, or Christianity—which they then think of as general conceptions and doctrines, mostly in the intellectualized and abstruse form in which they exist in sacred literature and learned religious teaching.[19]

A study of the influence of religion should have reference to religion as it actually exists on the popular level: a ritualized and stratified complex of highly emotional beliefs and valuations that regularly give the sanction of sacredness, taboo, and immutability to inherited institutional arrangements, modes of living, and attitudes. Quite commonly, without much difference among them, the several religions as they exist among the masses of people in

underdeveloped countries are heavily overlaid by super-
stitions and all sorts of irrational taboos and prescriptions
that have little in common with the rarefied doctrines on
the "higher" level.

A common characteristic of popular religion is that *it
acts as a tremendous force for social inertia,* supporting
any degree of social and economic inequality that is inherited. If ever Marx's dictum that religion is the opiate of
the people is justified, it is among the poorer masses in
underdeveloped countries.

The existing social and economic stratification that is
the product of history is supported by custom. In turn,
this custom gets from religion a support that often means
that the underprivileged themselves do not question, or
protest against, their plight but instead look upon their
fate as ordained by the gods and the whole paraphernalia
of supernatural forces.

The progressive leaders in the underdeveloped countries now usually avoid challenging popular religion. They
are likely to set more trust in a general move toward
greater rationality following education and more effective
communication. In South Asia even the Communists are
careful not to oppose religion.

Having made these general points, we should next
note a strange paradox.

*The policy declarations of all underdeveloped countries
favor greater equality.* For their planning they have quite
generally and prominently set as a practical goal raising the
level of living for the masses. None of the governments
in these countries, as far as I know, has announced as a
goal the creation of greater inequality by enriching the
privileged few.[20]

As the Secretariat of the Economic Commission for Asia
and the Far East recently summed up:

> Most of the plans clearly state or imply that their govern-
> ing purpose is to secure substantial and continuing im-
> provements in living conditions for the population at large

and that the promotion of rapid economic growth is to be regarded as a major means to this end, though not as an end in itself. The fundamentally "social" orientation of development planning is frequently re-emphasized in the statements of political leaders in the region and in some countries is further reinforced by constitutional commitments.[21]

In India, with more than a third of all the people in the non-Communist underdeveloped world, the most extravagant language is used to express the official egalitarian ideals. Thus it is common to use the terms "welfare state," "classless society," and "cooperative commonwealth" not just to indicate the type of society India aspires to become but to describe in what direction it is actually moving and, occasionally, its present character.

It is also quite common to talk about an "economic and social revolution" to describe what has been going on in the country. "Socialism," or various expressions containing the word "socialist," as a practical policy goal is still often propounded by big businessmen as well as by politicians.[22]

While India is extreme in the common use of a radical vocabulary, the adherence to an egalitarian ideal and the pretense that this ideal is actually informing practical policy are, with great differences in emphasis, quite common in practically all underdeveloped countries. Indeed, of all the modernization ideals that are everywhere adopted as goals for planning policies, none is pronounced with greater apparent conviction.

The paradox arises because in almost all underdeveloped countries *economic inequality seems instead to be increasing.*[23] And social inequality, it is fair to state as a general impression, has usually not been decreasing.[24]

The difficulty in demonstrating these trends more accurately is due not merely to the general inadequacy of data in underdeveloped countries, but to a natural tendency by those in control to avoid facing this paradox by not inquiring too deeply into what is happening to inequality.[25] This, as well as the general tendency to give radical motivations to what, in fact, are conservative policies tending to increase inequalities,[26] produces other examples of the all-pervading tendency to opportunistic biases that was commented upon in Chapter 1.

An explanation of this paradox—the contradiction between the emphatic declarations in favor of greater equality and the apparent trend toward greater inequality— *must relate to the distribution of power in underdeveloped countries.*[27]

Fairly independent of the form of government, political power in underdeveloped countries is held nearly everywhere by privileged groups, the first rank including big landowners, industrialists, bankers, merchants, and higher military and civilian officials. Under these upper-upper-class groups, definitely high above the masses of very poor people, are those other groups who in these countries ordinarily are called the "middle class," which usually includes all the "educated."

In this "middle class" is mostly also reckoned what in India is often called the "rural elite." This comprises peasant landlords and privileged cash tenants, who live in the villages, as well as managers, traders, moneylenders, officials, and others who on the local level together with them are in usually rather unchallenged social, economic, and political control.

This nomenclature is, of course, grossly incorrect from a scientific point of view. The persons in the groups called the "middle class" are middle class only in terms of Western societies—in the former colonies, more specifically, the societies in the Western countries that ruled them. The term "educated" gets its real political, social, and economic import from the fact that so very few are educated.

In underdeveloped countries all these groups must be understood as belonging to the upper class. Even with the addition of all the "educated" and generally the "middle class," the upper class remains a rather tiny top layer in their societies.

But we should at this point observe that in underdeveloped countries many of the tax and other reforms that are propagated as aiming at greater economic equality are there said to be in the interest of the middle class, at the expense of what in reality is an upper-upper class. In a realistic view, these reforms—which usually, where instituted, are not very effective even for that limited purpose—can at most be seen as a redistribution of income within the upper class in the broader sense of the term.[28] *Real progress toward greater equality should concern the masses of poor people.*

These masses are mostly passive, apathetic, and inarticulate. They seldom become organized for promoting and defending their interests. As Jawaharlal Nehru once said: "The really poor never strike. They haven't the means or the power to demonstrate." Long before Marx had complained about the contentedness and lack of demands of the poor.

They can be brought to riots and concerted mob violence by religious fanaticism, by ethnic prejudices, envies and dislikes, and by the opportunity to relax the inhibitions on stealing land and household property from each other, and on looting the shops.

This type of breakdown of the social order was experienced on a vast scale on the Indian subcontinent in the wake of the partition between India and Pakistan and later by many similar events on a smaller scale in both countries.[29] In Nigeria religious and ethnic hatreds led to civil war, and the same type of struggle has broken out, or is brooding, in many other parts of the now independent Africa. Occasionally such uprisings can take on a semblance of a class struggle as when, as part of the general turmoil following partition, many Hindu landowners were driven out of East Pakistan, or in the recent tumults in

Malaya, which resulted in the substitution of an emergency government, tantamount to an authoritarian regime, for its constitutional parliamentary democracy.

There have been sporadic peasant revolts against the landowners from time to time in many parts of the underdeveloped world.[30] But rather regularly they have been as inconsequential as the many slave revolts in the United States in the centuries before the Civil War. They have lacked organization and a clear plan, and have been easily suppressed.

When it comes to public policy, *the masses of people in the underdeveloped world are the object of politics but hardly anywhere its subject.* They are ruled by compromises, accommodation, and sometimes infighting among the various groups that together constitute the upper class, as defined above.

When references are made to "public opinion" in various underdeveloped countries, what it really means is mostly the opinion among the articulate, which usually means the members of the upper class. This is usually not made clear by those who speak or write, whether they belong to these countries themselves or are Westerners.

This misnomer is frequent even in scientific writings on the political development in underdeveloped countries. It affords another example of the type of opportunistic bias, assuming conditions that are similar to those in Western developed countries, which we commented upon in Chapter 1.

India, as opposed to most other countries in South Asia, was able speedily to establish, and thereafter to preserve, a parliamentary system based on universal adult suffrage. It has been functioning with a higher rate of participation in elections than in the United States and with possibly no more illegal or legalized infractions. Civil liberties and, in particular, freedom of expression have been rather jealously guarded.

Nevertheless, *the Indian government has remained a*

government of social and economic stagnation.[31] Democracy has not enabled the majority of poor people to grasp, and organize themselves for utilizing, political power to advance their own interests. The power struggle has mainly remained one between individuals and groups in the upper class in the broader meaning.

The fact that political power belongs to persons and groups in the upper class, while the masses remain passive, is a common pattern in South Asia which is not broken by the fact that public discussion among the articulate in the upper class is left more open and free in some countries, those which have succeeded in achieving and preserving the forms of parliamentary democracy and extensive civil rights.

The coups in some of the other countries in South Asia which have led to more authoritarian forms of government have not, from this fundamental point of view, made much difference. *Changes of political regime have never occurred in response to pressure from the poor masses' having become politically aware of their interests and organized for collective action.*[32]

Instead, they have regularly implied a reshuffling of the power position among the various upper-class groups, usually maneuvered by higher military officers grasping and thereafter holding on to a measure of monopoly of power. Power is, however, always shared to different degrees with other upper-class groups.

Reasons for throwing out an earlier government have ordinarily been provided by mismanagement and corruption under that government (see Chap. 7, below). *The masses of people were without political influence before as well as after such a coup, and the coup itself evolved above their heads.*

The most recent tumultuous political upheavals in Pakistan, which still have not reached an end while this is being written, do not imply an exception to this general rule. The front against the authoritarian government in power since 1958, headed by former President Ayub Khan, was formed among various upper-class groups, not least those belonging to that somewhat broader layer of the class calling itself the "middle class," including the students.

The "democratic" regime prior to the putsch in 1958 had been a total failure in practically all respects, and had led to wholesale corruption and economic, social, and political stagnation.[33] Ayub Khan and his government made a good start, punishing a few of the worst offenders, establishing a measure of social discipline, and coming out in favor of the whole gamut of the modernization ideals as goals for planning—except that the quest for greater equality for the masses was played down or given only lip service.

The new regime was, in fact, mainly a defensive regrouping of the old ruling class, and the danger could be foreseen that it would in time again deteriorate politically, ideologically, and morally.[34] But until the recent outbreak of violent rebellion, the regime had to its credit accomplishments in economic growth made possible by two factors: it had emerged out of almost total stagnation during the previous "democratic" era, which had its obvious advantages for the new regime, and it had received over two times as much per head as India of various sorts of "aid," mainly from the United States. The accomplishments of the authoritarian regime were highly appreciated in the United States and were advertised particularly by the Harvard group of economists who participated in planning but who are now, according to reports in the press, being driven out. [35]

But the new incomes and the resulting wealth showed a tendency to go to members of the upper-upper class, and to some extent to the "middle class" in agriculture, while wages to the salaried classes in the cities were held down. Corruption again became fantastic and tarnished higher military and civilian officials, ministers, and even Ayub

himself, and/or their relatives. As an industrialist is reported to have explained: ". . . corruption in this country
is now worse than ever before. When the men at the top
are getting rich, everyone does it. All of us—businessmen,
bureaucrats, Cabinet ministers—have formed an association to exploit the people." [36]

*This other side of the Pakistan success story was not
reported to the American people* and apparently not to
their government—until the bubble burst and the professional reporters were brought to take a closer look.
It is not unusual that the journalists have to find and
make known the truth to the people—while the diplomatic
and intelligence sources are not likely to find it out, and
the professors keep silent about what is awkward.

There was thus much to protest against for the "middle
class" and for those in the upper-upper class who had remained immaculate or had simply been kept away from
the fleshpots, particularly some of the politicians from
the earlier regime. Against the Ayub regime were also the
reactionary mullahs—another "middle-class" group—who
had always been suspicious of the modernization drive.

When in February, 1969, Ayub was brought down to
become a lame-duck president, negotiating with his political opponents, an important operative cause was also
that he could no longer rely upon solid support from a
united military establishment. The dissatisfaction in the
officer corps had been brewing since the military debacle
in the war against India in 1965. It had produced a bitter
nationalistic resentment that was shared rather widely
within the whole "middle class."

As could have been foreseen,[37] the rebellion of the
"middle-class" groups, represented by a number of loosely
organized political parties, had very little of a common
program, except the restoration of parliamentary democracy and uninfringed civil rights, including the lifting of
the curbs on the freedom of the press. As it did not calm
down, agitation spread to some lower strata of the popula-

tion, first to that small class of factory workers in large-scale industry—who in a country like Pakistan are nearer "middle-class" status—but also to all sorts of people in East Pakistan, where nationalistic resentment is ripe and widespread against West Pakistani "colonialism."[38] At that stage, slogans of egalitarian reform were beginning to be heard more often and more loudly.

But mainly, particularly in East Pakistan, the movement, when it showed signs of becoming a mass movement, took on the familiar character of aimless rioting, roaming, killing, burning, looting, and generally unorganized mob violence. The military establishment had then to pull itself together again under the leadership of another general, withdrawing Ayub Khan's concessions to the uproarious "middle-class" groups who had started the rebellion, imposing martial law again, abrogating the constitution and various other laws, dissolving the legislatures, and banning all organized political activity.

It seems probable that peace will now again be restored for some time. Pakistan will then return to a tighter rule by the military and those upper-upper-class groups who do not have to be sacrificed to regain some of the prestige of the government. The now widely spread dissatisfaction in East Pakistan may still remain explosive, however. It will probably be some time before new experiments with democracy and greater civil liberties will be ventured upon. Ayub Khan's experiences in recent years will probably stand as a warning.

To what extent the new authoritarian government will vigorously stamp out the rampant corruption, which in Ayub Khan's later years had flourished and provided nourishment for the protest among the "middle-class" groups, remains to be seen.[39] It is equally uncertain whether the new regime will be able to restore much of the *élan* from the early years of the previous government when Ayub Khan had the courage to take various steps in line with the modernization ideals. It is also uncertain whether, and for how long, the military establishment will now stand united.

Under no circumstances will real power come to be exerted by the masses of people in Pakistan—so far as can now be foreseen.

The only clear exception in South Asia to the general rule of the political passivity of the broad masses is the gradual awakening to social and political consciousness of the people in Vietnam.[40] A main explanation of the different development there is clearly the character of France's colonial rule before the Second World War; during that war, when the colony was under the control of Vichy France collaborating with the Japanese; and after it. From the point of view of the Vietnamese, the colonial war has now lasted more than a quarter of a century. To an increasing number of the Vietnamese people this war has become a fight against military intrusion by a foreign, white, and rich nation—first France, aided by the United States, and after 1954, the United States alone.

The imposition and intransigency of these white foreigners, and their cooperation with privileged groups in the country, have resulted in the mass diffusion of a type of Vietnamese nationalism that now has become permeated by a radical social and political purpose.

The speedy, unreserved, and even generous retreat by the British from its Indian empire,[41] on the contrary, left independent India as a country where not even the most complete version of political democracy could raise the masses to active political participation. The economic and social revolution promised in the liberation movement soon lost its momentum.[42]

Like the French in Indochina, the Dutch after the Second World War made protracted military attempts to keep their East Indies under continued colonial rule. This, and Holland's holding onto West New Guinea—and the not totally unwarranted suspicion that the United States through its Central Intelligence Agency (CIA) and otherwise had supported insurrectory movements—gave Sukarno the basis for carrying on a wildly nationalistic propaganda with a strong anti-Western bias.[43] He could build upon anti-white and revolutionary sentiments, intentionally encouraged by the Japanese before they had to leave, and also upon the tension between the indigenous Indonesian majority and the Chinese minority that naturally developed because of the economic role of the latter but had also been deliberately incited by the Japanese. All this probably served as an influence in Indonesia, though much weaker than in Vietnam, to awaken the masses to organized political activity.

As in Vietnam, the new social revolutionary movement reaching down among the masses took the form of a sort of nationalistic Communism. The present type of military government supported by the landowning upper strata in the Moslem parties—and aided by the United States and other Western countries—that resulted from the ghastly events in the fall of 1965 may not be too stable.[44]

Western interference, particularly when it takes the form of military involvement, may thus become a force which otherwise would be missing to bring the masses in an underdeveloped country to a higher degree of political awareness and activity. *It is an ironic thought that this new mass activity, engendered by Western interference, then becomes directed against the West and—particularly in the world-setting of the cold war—becomes easily allied to Communism.*

I have had in mind Vietnam and perhaps, to an extent that will be revealed only in the future, Indonesia. But there are some parallels in other parts of the underdeveloped world. In Latin America an egregious presence of United States economic and, occasionally, military power, and the common awareness of American subterfuge activities by the CIA and other agencies, undoubtedly tends to make even parts of the broad masses more alert and politically conscious. Such a movement then becomes anti-American and tends to take on a radical taint.

As an American economist, Martin Bronfenbrenner, pointed out long ago in a brilliant article,[45] the political effects of large-scale foreign investments can change character in a revolutionary situation. Instead of remaining a powerful support for the social and political *status quo,* they can become a temptation to confiscatory measures. When the investments are large enough, such measures can be calculated to be to the economic advantage of a revolutionary government.

It is undoubtedly true that compared with all the modernization ideals *nationalism is the easiest to spread among the masses in underdeveloped countries,*[46] and that this is particularly true of a resentful nationalism directed against foreigners from the rich, white Western world.

It should therefore not be surprising if in South Africa, South-West Africa, and Rhodesia there is a brooding popular resentment spreading among the Negro majority, and a will to overthrow the white minority governments which hold them down. Neither should it be surprising that this nationalistic resentment then may turn against all white people and, in particular, against the great Western powers.

It is so clearly visible that these powers not only have been unwilling to use effective sanctions against the governments there in order to uphold the decisions of the United Nations, but also that they actually permit their business interests to keep up, by investments and in other ways, the boom in South Africa. That in Britain political support for these business interests is generously provided by the workers, afraid of losing employment and incomes, does not make these attitudes among the Negro population less nationalistic and strong.

There is also evidence that the Negro rebellion in Portugal's colonies in Africa is beginning to stir up the masses there to political awareness and activity. The fact that almost the whole white Western world is actually backing the Portuguese colonizers by trade, investment, and even delivery of weapons—through Portugal's membership in the European Free Trade Association (EFTA) and its active participation in the whole commercial and military organization of the Western world—tends to give this new nationalism a broader anti-Western and anti-white character.

In a very interesting interview published in *Newsweek*,[47] one of the wisest African leaders, President Kenneth D. Kaunda of Zambia, had among other things this to say:

> But the only countries that seem to be prepared to help the freedom fighters [in Rhodesia, South-West Africa, and Portuguese Guinea, Angola, and Mozambique] are the Eastern-bloc countries. The Western nations will not help them with weapons at all. The truth is that there is heavy Western investment in racialist-controlled countries of southern Africa. Moral values, spiritual values have taken second place to material benefits which, I must point out, are of short-term value to the West. In the long run, the West must accept the fact that these guerrilla fighters are going to be the leaders of their countries one day....
> I hate to say it, but I can see not only a racial conflagration but also an ideological one. And I fear that in the end it's likely to be a fight in which, like the Vietnam war, the Western Powers will fight alongside the racialists in South Africa against the black people on the pretext that Communism is coming in.

President Kaunda means that through diplomatic pressure the Western powers could solve the problems in all of South Africa "to the satisfaction of a majority of the people. If they did that, it would be more important than supplying arms." But "the lives of my own countrymen in Zambia are being destroyed and property is being destroyed by Portuguese troops using weapons that have been supplied to them by NATO powers. We all know that without these weapons the Portuguese would be completely helpless.... As I look at this situation here ... it's like being in a canoe on the Zambesi River heading for Victoria Falls."

More generally, these and the other rebellions of non-white people tend to spread resentful nationalism among the articulate layers throughout the rest of the underde-veloped world, which is mostly colored. And as already mentioned, resentful nationalism seems to be rather easily spread even among the masses, and it may become an ever more important vehicle for arousing these masses from their stupor.

If thus under certain conditions the policies of the developed Western countries can spur the activation of the masses in underdeveloped countries and give it an anti-Western, anti-white, and radical slant, the more prominent influence from the policies of the former coun-tries, at least in the present stage of world history, is to support the privileged groups in their hold over their countries' policies.

In the worldwide colonial power system as it functioned until the Second World War, *there was a built-in mecha-nism that almost automatically led the colonial power to ally itself with the privileged groups.* Those groups could be relied upon to share its interest in "law and order," which mostly implied economic and social *status quo.*

To support its reign, the colonial power would thus generally feel an interest in upholding or even strengthen-ing the inegalitarian social and economic structure in a colony. This was a major element in the laissez-faire tendency of colonial rule, to which reference was made in Chapter 1. Often it even happened that new privileges and new privileged groups were created by the colonial power in order to stabilize its rule over a colony.

There is no doubt that a similar mechanism has been operating after the liquidation of colonialism and that, now as before, it also has its counterpart in relation to those underdeveloped countries that were politically independent, primarily in Latin America. *This is the main justification for the use of the term "neo-colonialism."*

When the political stability provided by colonialism had disappeared, it was only natural that the rich Western countries should feel a special sympathy for such a newly independent country where the rule was tightly kept by a conservative regime that preserved the social, economic, and political power situation inherited from colonial times.

That business interests in the West would be more willing to invest in such a country was equally natural. It was also natural that they preferred to deal with the rich and mighty there. That this, in turn, strengthened those groups at home is equally self-evident.[48]

The mechanism—i.e., the natural and almost automatic unfolding of the tendencies referred to—is stressed in order to emphasize that events would tend to take this course rather independently of any policy decisions in the developed Western countries. Business interests in, say, Sweden—where no state policy upholding inequality in underdeveloped countries would be possible but where strong pressures from all popular organizations are exerted for the opposite policy—would tend to react in precisely the same manner as in the United States, and with the same effect in those countries.

The operation of this mechanism became, however, strengthened by the cold war that had its beginning and further development *pari passu* with the process of decolonization. The United States, which felt its responsibility to be the leader of the "free world," placed state policy as a powerful engine to support that mechanism, especially in the Dulles-McCarthy era when anti-Communism was a determining motive in its foreign policy.

In this era, financial and military aid was with great determination awarded to utterly reactionary regimes, which then could often exploit their advantage by threatening to collapse if not helped by the United States. A glance at the present distribution of financial, commercial, and military aid does not show a great change, except that the total amounts allocated for aid, as well as its quality in various respects, have been decreased (see Chap. 11, below).

But enlightened intellectual and political leaders in the United States have with increasing resoluteness in recent years noted the dangers implied in letting this mechanism, inherited from colonial times, function undisturbed. They have seen the risk of the effect, in a second stage, becoming exactly the opposite, as I described above—awakening the masses in the underdeveloped countries to participation and activity, but then steering this new activity into an anti-American and often generally anti-Western direction, and even driving them to some form or another of nationalistic Communism. The grandiose failure of the United States policy in Vietnam is bound to strengthen the impact on the whole American nation of their criticism.

It is understandable that this reaction will sometimes be turned against the United States' giving much aid to underdeveloped countries, or any aid at all on the theory that it may engage the United States in commitments that in the end might result in military intervention. My conclusion is, however, that we need instead to increase our aid to underdeveloped countries very substantially, as well as change the whole theory of aid and its practical application (see Chaps. 9–11, below).

Even more fundamentally, we should change our view of the underdeveloped countries, particularly in regard to their social and economic stratification, and their attitudes toward, and accomplishments in, reform of that stratification.

As much as fifteen years ago Justice William O. Douglas expressed his opinion that it would be in line with America's unique history and deepest ambitions to be in the lead of the world revolution instead of, as up till now, being lined up with political reaction all over the globe. And he was then not thinking in terms of blood and killing, but meant instead radical reforms that could prevent and substitute for the violence of political revolutions.

We will have to return to the problems raised here in Parts Three and Four.

Even if the influences from abroad have to be accounted for, the main problem in regard to equality in underdeveloped countries is nevertheless what forces are operating at home more or less independently. The ordinary distribution of political power in the larger part of the underdeveloped world, with masses that are passive while upper-class persons and groups rule, has been stressed in order to explain the paradox of egalitarian pretenses while inequality is actually preserved and even increased in most underdeveloped countries.

It was persons in the upper class, particularly among the intellectual elite, who had adopted the Western egalitarian ideals and given them currency among all the "educated," including practically the whole upper class. The fact that in this regard the influences from the Communist countries have not been different has increased their impact.[49] These ideals ordinarily played their role in the liberation movements that preceded independence.

Continuously, some leaders in these countries are harping at the paradox [50] and urging greater efforts toward the realization of the generally accepted egalitarian ideals. As one official report in India explains: "The rich, the high-caste, and the powerful must show a greater sensitivity towards the condition of their unfortunate brethren and be prepared to make the necessary sacrifices."

It is the present author's opinion that *ideals are important facts when they are rooted in institutions and in people's hearts*. When some of my colleagues believe that they are particularly hard-boiled and scientific in excluding from their analysis the fact that people plead to their consciences, I believe that they are simply unrealistic. Particularly in the longer run, the spread of egalitarian ideals in practically all the underdeveloped countries may be of decisive importance—ideals that had come to flourish in the Enlightenment and thereafter have never been absent from our thinking either in the liberal West or in the Communist East.[51]

But in the day-to-day view, the ideals are too often and too effectively kept down by the valuations on a lower level that are determining our behavior.[52] *To become important, the egalitarian ideals need pressure from below.* And that is exactly what is missing in most underdeveloped countries.

It has never occurred in recorded history that a privileged group, on its own initiative and simply in order to give reality to its ideals, has climbed down from its privileges and opened its monopolies to the unprivileged. The unprivileged have to become conscious of their demands for greater equality and fight for their realization. At that point, the general acceptance of ideals can become operative and important. And this is the reason why in my opinion it is not insignificant that the egalitarian ideals are commonly accepted on the level of principles in the ruling upper class.

But when that pressure from below is almost totally absent, as in most underdeveloped countries, we should not be surprised that the inegalitarian social and economic stratification from colonial times is preserved and that development moves in the direction of greater inequality.

It then happens that even policies which are motivated to assist the poor masses are either not enforced or are directed to favor instead the not-so-poor. We shall have occasion to give examples of the working of this mechanism in the following chapters.[53]

It should, finally, be stressed that the explanation of the gulf between ideals and reality is far more complex than mere hypocrisy. People are usually not simply hypocritical, still less cynical, when in their daily strivings they compromise their ideals. The intellectual elite in an underdeveloped country usually do believe they should identify themselves with the nation. The most ardent try.

The upper class is privileged; but historically it has been, and is today, the bearer of egalitarian tidings. Its moral situation can be said to be weak if ever it is challenged by events.[54]

In Part Four, "The Politics of Development," this discussion about the power situation in underdeveloped countries will be continued. We shall then discuss developments in these countries which might make the masses more alert, and also developments which might strengthen or weaken the resistance against egalitarian reforms in the ruling upper strata.

Chapter 4

AGRICULTURE

I *The Crucial Facts*

Perhaps in no other field of economic activity are there greater differences among the main underdeveloped regions in South Asia, Northeast Asia, West Asia, Africa, and Latin America, as well as among individual countries in these regions, and even between districts in the several countries,[1] than in the field of agriculture.

This should be remembered as a general reservation throughout this chapter on agricultural policy. For every single statement made in the following text, it is easy to point to exceptions where what is said is not true. Nevertheless, there are some general conditions in agriculture in all, or most, underdeveloped countries which need to be stressed.

Broadly speaking, farming as practiced today in developed countries is of two distinct types.[2] The first type, extensive land use over large areas, is practiced in sparsely populated areas in North America, Australia, and Russia. In these areas there is sometimes a low output per unit of land. The second type, intensive land utilization with high yields per unit of land, is practiced in regions with a higher man/land ratio, as is found in varying degrees in Europe and Japan.

Agriculture in most parts of the underdeveloped countries fits into neither of these main groups. It forms a third and very unfortunate group, namely, that characterized by extensive land use combined with a high man/land ratio. Naturally, this correlation results in disastrously low real incomes. For not only is agricultural yield per acre low, but a very large portion of the total labor force is tied up in producing that low agricultural output.

Thus in South Asia only about one out of every four workers is available for activities other than producing the meager crops, while in the United States more than nine out of ten and in Europe more than two out of every three workers are employed outside agriculture. Overall comparisons such as these indicate the dimensions of the basic economic problems of the South Asian region. They are fairly indicative of the situation in other underdeveloped regions, too.

Let us first face the fact that *in most underdeveloped countries the yields per acre are low*,[3] leaving for later consideration the other fact that labor utilization is also low. There are three main exceptions to the rule of very low yields per acre.

One is the countries where plantation crops play a major role, such as several countries in Latin America, and Ceylon and Malaya in South Asia, particularly where the plantations are owned and managed by West Europeans. This type of highly commercialized use of the land resources—always for export—should more correctly be considered industry.[4]

The plantations are, like enterprises in manufacturing industry, highly specialized productive units employing wage labor on a regular basis, where capital investment is relatively high and important, and technology advanced. In many countries capital intensity is quite low, however, and technology backward. But this is often true even in traditional manufacturing industries in underdeveloped countries.

The plantation industry, not considered further in this chapter, is ordinarily not a rapidly expanding industry today, except in some countries of western Africa.

The second exception is sometimes, but not always, that part of agriculture producing non-food cash crops which are usually exported. In perhaps most underdeveloped countries that sector of agriculture is more profitable than food-producing agriculture.

Thus there is little rationality in attempting to increase food production by decreasing the areas devoted to cash crops, and for this reason little hope of success also for such a policy.[5] The attempts that have occasionally been made in countries such as India and Pakistan to increase food production through "grow-more-food" campaigns have regularly not been very consequential.

As with the plantation industry, there is usually not much scope for expansion of this agricultural sector devoted to non-food cash crops, at least not if we disregard the competitive situation existing between the several individual countries and think in terms of the underdeveloped world as a whole. The products do not belong to those for which the demand in the developed countries is rapidly rising.

The third exception to the rule of low yields per acre is a very few areas in the underdeveloped world, such as Egypt, with perennial irrigation and a very high man/land ratio.

The overwhelmingly largest part of most agriculture in underdeveloped countries is devoted to producing food, and it is this sector to which the observations in this chapter shall be mainly devoted. This can be done with the fewer reservations as the productivity development in the sector devoted to non-food cash crops has usually been nearly parallel to that of food production and subject to the same causal factors of change and inertia.[6]

Not only are the yields in agriculture exceedingly low in the greater part of the underdeveloped world, but *yields have remained low for generations, probably always.* In such a huge area as British India, yields seem even to have fallen for a long period before independence.[7]

In all the underdeveloped regions taken together there has been an increase of production in the postwar period, but it has barely kept abreast of the population increase.[8] Owing mainly to unfavorable weather conditions, there was an actual decline in 1965, and the rise in 1966 was only 1 percent with the result that food production per head fell by 4 percent during these two years. But the following two years have taken the development back to about the established trend line.

This slow increase of production in underdeveloped countries has until recently been due mainly, though decreasingly, to an increase in the cultivated area.[9] There is general agreement that, in the future, increased production in these countries must primarily be sought by achieving higher yields, as suitable cultivable land is becoming more scarce and as its cultivation requires rising capital investment.

To an American expert, Lester R. Brown, the central question of agricultural policy in the underdeveloped world is: "How quickly can the less-developed countries make the transition from the area-expanding method of increasing food output to the yield-raising method of increasing food output." This is particularly true if the policy goal is defined as increasing food production as much and as fast as is urgently needed to overcome both undernutrition and malnutrition in a rapidly rising population.

To this should be added that yields per acre tend to be lowest in some very populous, poor countries, such as Pakistan and India, and in districts in other countries that are poorer than the average.

Yields in agriculture represent one of the most important differences between underdeveloped countries and those developed countries which are not profitably applying an extensive agriculture in very sparsely populated areas. In the latter countries, yields are not only much higher but also have been rapidly increasing for a long time, particularly since the Second World War, thus creating a widening gap. *This widening gap in agricultural yields represents an important part of the widening income gap.*[10]

To the low yields correspond serious nutritional deficiencies in underdeveloped countries.[11]

People in most underdeveloped countries are estimated to have an average calorie intake below what is required for full health and working capacity. Because of the great inequality of income in these countries, a very substantial portion of the population receives even less food. As we have pointed out in the previous chapter, economic inequality seems to be increasing in most underdeveloped countries.

Even more common than a deficient calorie intake is an inadequate provision of proteins, vitamins, and certain important minerals, such as iron, calcium, and phosphorus.

The situation is often aggravated by irrational food habits which generally discriminate against the protective nutrients mentioned, though the Chinese, for example, exhibit great sophistication in their choice of food. While mostly irrational food habits are widespread among all income classes except the very highest, lack of protective nutrients, usually present only in the more expensive foods, must be particularly serious among the poorer classes.

To this should be added that the spread of infectious and parasitical diseases—caused by a tropical or subtropical climate, low living levels and, in particular, bad housing, deficient food intake, the low level of public and private sanitation and hygiene [12]—also reduces the capacity of the body to utilize the food consumed.

An increasing number of studies lead more and more definitely to the conclusion that the "hidden hunger" due to a low calorie intake and particularly to the lack of protective nutrients gives rise to serious health risks and, more generally, to lethargy and lack of initiative and drive.

Some of the characteristics commonly ascribed to South Asians—their bent to contemplation, their otherworldliness, their passivity, and their appreciation of leisure, etc., sometimes on a more intellectualized level reflected in religious doctrine, philosophy, or the belief in specific "values" of a country or of all Asia—may, in fact, be due to deficiencies in nutrition and health.[13]

A recent report of the secretariat of the Economic Commission for Asia and the Far East (ECAFE) thus refers to "ethnical characteristics [such as] laziness ... or an enviable philosophical attitude toward life" and notes that "they might be due to important environmental factors like ... undernutrition or malnutrition." Similar ideas in regard to common ethnic and cultural characteristics ascribed to people in other poor countries may also have this explanation.

Protein deficiencies are particularly harmful to small children and to pregnant and nursing women. In recent years attention has been drawn to the consequences for small children of protein deficiencies, which decrease the number of brain cells and thwart mental development.

As the Food and Agriculture Organization (FAO) has pointed out, *the majority of people in underdeveloped countries must thus to some degree or another be assumed to suffer from undernutrition and/or malnutrition.* It gives a special accent to their state of poverty to note that this goes together with a very high percentage of their income being spent on foodstuffs, in South Asia about two-thirds or much more.

The nutritional situation in the underdeveloped countries has generally not improved since before the Second World War. In many countries it might even have deteriorated, particularly for the huge agricultural proletariat.

The existing food deficiencies among the masses of people, the population explosion, and the slow increase in food production in the underdeveloped countries raises the specter of a world hunger crisis. As Professor Earl L. Butz expressed it a few years ago:

> The world is on a collision course. . . . When the massive force of an exploding world population meets the much more stable trend line of world food production, something must give in. Unless we give increased attention now to the softening of the impending collision, many parts of the world within a decade will be skirting a disaster of such a proportion as to threaten the peace and stability of the Western world.[14]

In several very large countries, such as India and Pakistan, and in many smaller countries in all regions of the underdeveloped world, *the hunger crisis would have already broken out a decade ago*—and in many countries, among them those mentioned, would have become very seriously aggravated in 1965 and 1966 had it not been for the historical accident of the United States having acquired, against the intention of its agricultural policy, huge surpluses which could be made available to these countries under Public Law 480.

This redistribution of food in the world on the basis mainly of huge surpluses produced in, and made available on concessional terms by, the United States cannot be relied upon to be more than temporary, at least on that scale. Also, it mainly entails meeting acute caloric deficiencies only.

The real amplitude of inequality between the rich developed countries and the poor underdeveloped countries —which is revealed, or rather concealed, in the abstract income gap that is constantly widening—becomes first visible when we consider who gets the proteins and other protective nutrients.

Professor Georg Borgström has done public enlightenment a service by reiterating unceasingly the fact that a number of underdeveloped countries are continually exporting large quantities of high-quality, protein-rich food products to preserve and increase overeating in the affluent, developed countries: for instance, fish meal from African and Latin American areas, more critically short of protein than even South Asia, to feed the broilers and livestock of the United States and Europe; soya beans, oilseed cakes, tuna fish and other food fish, and even meat from various countries in the underdeveloped world are going the same way.

The result is that the inhabitants of the rich countries take an altogether disproportionate share of the protective food available in the world and use it in a less economical way than would be necessary in the underdeveloped countries, at the same time that they use up an equally disproportionate share of grains for feeding purposes.

The low yields per acre in underdeveloped countries become particularly shocking when we consider that the labor force for these scanty crops is very large, usually well above 50 percent of the total labor force. In India the agricultural population is 70 percent of the total population but it has not for a long time produced the country's food needs even at the very depressed nutritional levels in that country.

This means that not only productivity of the land but also *productivity of the labor force is exceedingly low in most underdeveloped countries.*[15] Again, *there is a gap in labor productivity between developed and underdeveloped countries that is larger and has been widening even more quickly than that for yields, and widening for a longer time.*

The exceedingly low labor productivity in the agriculture of underdeveloped countries has an implication that is seldom realized. Particularly in those underdeveloped countries which have a high ratio between the labor force in agriculture and the tilled area, the general notion is that theirs is a labor-intensive cultivation of the land. This may be true, to an extent, of a country like Egypt —which also has high yields per acre (see above), even if not high enough to feed the growing population—but it is not true of the larger part of the underdeveloped world where yields are very low. Contrary to the common conception, *work practices in agriculture are not labor intensive but, instead, labor extensive.*[16]

The labor input per worker is generally low in terms of man hours and is of low efficiency. *The low yields per acre are therefore largely a consequence of an underutilization of the labor force.* The other side of this is that an increase of the labor input—achieved by improving participation ratios, and the duration and efficiency of work [17]—would raise yields, even without any technological innovations or additional investment, except work.

Though this conclusion is seldom drawn, the truth of it is obvious from the existence of differences in agricultural yields between countries, districts, and individual cultivators, as demonstrated in detail in all farm-management studies. They show that the yields differ greatly even when there are no differences in the quality of soil and other physical conditions for cultivation, nor in the agricultural techniques generally known and applied by some farm enterprises in the surrounding area. Technical innovations can increase yields still more. But this should not be permitted to conceal this more fundamental fact of the prevalent underutilization of labor even at the now available level of technology.

In many underdeveloped countries a part of the labor force does not engage in any form of work at all, though the frequency of this varies between the countries. Much more general and important is the fact that most of those workers who do work, work only short periods—per day, week, month, and year—and not very intensively or efficiently. This is what in a false analogy to conditions in the West and in the European Communist countries, and in line with the biased postwar approach, is described in terms of "unemployment" and "underemployment."[18]

These behavior patterns in underdeveloped countries are deeply rooted in attitudes hardened into mores by a long historical process. They have been given a foundation by institutions, particularly those of economic and social stratification, in the first hand related to landownership and tenure, that have been consequential in determining the use of land.[19]

They are supported by the low nutritional levels, which themselves are caused by poverty and, more particularly, the low yields. In turn, they impair the willingness and the ability to work and to work hard, keeping down the yields. And this process of circular causation [20] is the main reason why, if well planned and under otherwise favorable conditions, aid for development in the form of grants of food can be made to have the effect of raising yields in agriculture.

How this complex of attitudes, institutions, and levels of living in underdeveloped countries can act as inhibitions and obstacles to work and also to the effectiveness of policy attempts to raise labor utilization and yields in agriculture will be discussed in more concrete terms later in this chapter. But looking at this situation *in abstracto,* it should have its silver lining. *The very backwardness of agriculture in underdeveloped countries should be a favorable factor.*[21]

As M. L. Dantwala, a leading economist in India— where the average grain yields are less than one fourth of those in Japan or Britain—emphasizes: "There is so much scope for the wider application of known techniques, involving hardly any additional capital investment, that in the initial period, at any rate, progress can be very rapid."

One of his equally distinguished Indian colleagues, S. R. Sen, elaborates this point:

> ... differences [of yields] are noticeable not merely as between different areas but also between different groups of

farmers. In the same area, the best farmers are known to have produced yields per acre several times higher than those produced by average farmers. . . . In fact . . . the difference between the best and the average is much wider in India than in the technically advanced countries. This is both an index of the backward character of Indian agriculture and a measure of its potentiality for development.

And he goes on to characterize the development of agriculture as a "bargain sector" for planning.

This should be equally true for most, if not all, underdeveloped countries. The explanation for the failure to capitalize on the existing potentialities for higher yields must be, first of all, the prevailing work practices that keep down labor utilization.

We should, in passing, make the observation that the big differences in yields between countries, areas, and individual farms, which so clearly are related to a different input of work hours and differences in labor efficiency, prove that the stereotyped assumption in economic discussion, based on the biased postwar approach, that the marginal productivity of labor is zero is factually incorrect as well as theoretically invalid.[22]

The major scope for improvement of agricultural yields is thus simply inducing a change in those work practices that result in the underutilization of the labor force and that imply that cultivation is mostly extensive even when the man/land ratio is high. To this we shall return.

With favorable results for the yields, the input and intensity of labor can be raised in the year-round work on cultivating the land and raising and harvesting the crops. Added to this is the fact that *there is everywhere in the underdeveloped countries a need for the type of additional labor input that can be considered investment* because it promises to raise future yields.[23]

Such work as, for instance, building roads, bridges, irrigation canals, soil conservation terraces, warehouses for storing crops and farm supplies, draining ditches, wells, and tanks, and laboring on afforestation and pasture improvement is all highly labor intensive and requires few resources to complement labor beyond those locally available.

Other uses of the villagers' spare time relate more directly to consumption: construction of school buildings, dispensaries, village privies, and gutters; clean wells for drinking water and other household uses; paving of village streets to do away with dust and mud; improving the houses; manufacturing simple furniture; killing rats; or merely washing the children, and keeping flies away from the eyes. It is generally recognized that these undertakings in the service of consumption are also highly productive.

These various possibilities to use surplus labor represent what the late Professor Ragnar Nurkse characterized as a "disguised saving potential." On no other point has there been a greater unanimity among all experts, in the Western and Communist developed countries as well as in the non-Communist underdeveloped countries themselves. In many of the latter countries the Plans have often contained daring proposals to utilize this saving potential, but usually little has come out of these proposals.

The difficulties are several. For one thing these undertakings presuppose collective action, and hence organization, as the scale of effort required mostly surpasses the immediate interests and resources of individual households. The understanding of the common advantage of such collective action and organization assumes a degree of rationality and social cohesion that is often absent in a faction-ridden village.

Such action, moreover, immediately raises questions of the distribution of benefits and costs and thus the equality issue discussed in the previous chapter. Should the landless workers be paid, and if so how much, when the benefits accrue mainly to the landowners and others in the higher strata, who often are not willing either to work or to pay others for working?

Even more generally, efforts to organize the labor force for such collective undertakings meet, of course, strong resistance from the established work practices, founded on the system of landownership and tenancy, which itself holds down the quantity and quality of individual inputs of labor (see below).

From one point of view, the underutilization of the labor force in underdeveloped countries can be seen as the result of using a primitive technology. For it is an empirically testable general rule that, *with very few exceptions, technological advance would not be labor-saving but, on the contrary, would require a higher and more efficient input of labor.*[24]

This important relationship between labor utilization and technology is often bypassed in the discussion of agricultural policy. Too often it is tacitly concluded from a high man/land ratio that agriculture in underdeveloped countries is labor intensive—even to the degree that the marginal productivity of labor is commonly assumed to be zero.

It then becomes natural to conclude that the problem of the application of a more advanced technology need only be concerned with the productivity-per-acre of the land—as labor is abundant and will continue to have a zero marginal productivity. This whole way of thinking is built on invalid assumptions and, as we have already noted, is apt to be grossly misleading.

Technological reforms generally do not decrease the demand for labor but, almost without exception, increase it. This is true when it is a question merely of reaching a wider use of techniques that are generally known and applied by some cultivators in the local surrounding. It is equally true when the problem is one of technological innovation, that is, the introduction of entirely new techniques or the improvement of old ones.

All types of technological improvement should lead to more abundant crops requiring more work at harvesting. Most improvements also raise the demand for more work in the period of preparing the soil, sowing, weeding, and caring for the growing crop. Some improvements consist in, or depend upon, considerable labor investments in advance, for instance, in constructing irrigation works and keeping them in good repair.

Mechanization forms a special case. It *can* be used for a substitution of capital for labor, particularly when the units of land cultivation are large. Consequently there have been examples, particularly in some parts of Latin America, where mechanization has been depriving workers of employment opportunities, thus increasing underutilization of the available labor force.[25]

But in the more normal case, the type of mechanization that is at all consistent with conditions as they prevail in most underdeveloped countries will conform to the general rule, namely, raising the demand for labor.[26] In countries that normally are in exchange difficulties and where also normally the growth of home industry has to be promoted and regulated, it should be a natural policy to restrict the availability of such agricultural machinery that simply substitutes for labor without increasing the demand for it.

In this context I have to restrict myself to these general assertions, referring the reader to *Asian Drama* where I have gone into considerable detail in analyzing the several lines of technological improvements in regard to what they would imply for labor utilization.[27]

Overcoming the prevalence of a primitive technology in agriculture—which from one point of view is what is needed in order to increase labor utilization and to raise yields even more—meets many and various difficulties.

One general difficulty is the foreseeable rapid increase of the size of the labor force in agriculture that is already underutilized.

It is natural that the underdeveloped countries have seen in industrialization their main avenue to escape from poverty.[28] The principal difference between the underdeveloped and the developed countries appears to them to be that a much larger part of their labor force is in agriculture. One of the euphemistic synonyms for the term "underdeveloped" has also been "underindustrialized." [29]

In the long run, the interest of the underdeveloped countries in industrialization is entirely rational. With the foreseeable population development (see Chap. 5, below) it is indeed difficult to believe that a densely populated country such as India, with now 70 percent of its huge labor force in agriculture, could even preserve the present miserable levels of living of the masses up till the end of this century if a much larger part of its labor force were not then employed outside agriculture. And this conclusion would stand even if ever so big improvements in technology and labor utilization in agriculture were realized.[30]

To a varying degree, the same is true of most other underdeveloped countries. Almost all of them have good reasons to press on as fast as they can with industrialization, which should not, however, imply that they should reduce their efforts to raise the productivity of land and labor in agriculture.

Another supporting force behind their concentration on industrialization has been that, as opposed to a policy aimed at raising yields in agriculture, industrialization did not have to cope with strong vested interests. Even state undertakings in the industrial field were ordinarily planned so as to be in the interest of private industry.[31]

It is natural that the underdeveloped countries have seen a main motive for industrialization in *the need to "skim off" the underutilized labor force in agriculture.* The whole theory of "underemployment" is founded upon the idea of the possibility of the "removal" of a large part of the agricultural labor force.[32] And such a development is very often understood actually to be taking place on a large scale.[33]

But the fact is that in the shorter view—say, for a couple of decades ahead—*even a much more rapid industrialization than is actually achieved, or planned without being achieved, cannot be expected to raise the demand for labor very much.*[34] The main reason for this is the low level of industrialization from which they start out, and the character of modern industrial technology (see below).

The effect of industrialization on aggregate labor demand may be, for a considerable time, to decrease it. This "backwash effect" is due to modern industry competing with existing labor-intensive traditional industry and crafts. When this has not been clearly perceived in the Plans, the result has quite commonly been an unexpected increase in what is accounted for as "unemployment."[35]

There may be, and in most underdeveloped countries actually has been and is, a greater flight from agriculture than corresponds to new demands for labor caused by industrialization.[36] These "refugees" from the poverty-stricken villages to the cities tend in their new environment to swell the various "open occupations" where labor productivity is very low.[37] This cityward migration, which simply swells the labor force in tertiary occupations where labor is underutilized, is in the literature often uncritically, and in a false analogy with developed countries, conceived of as progress in development.[38]

This type of migration, usually implying the increase of squalor, sanitation deficiencies, overcrowding, and inadequate housing in the city slums, cannot be desirable from a national planning point of view. It cannot be seen as a means to solve the problems of underutilization of the labor force in agriculture, as these laborers are also under-utilized in the cities.

Moreover, as initially such a large proportion of the total labor force is in agriculture, this cityward migration will often make little dent in the rate of increase of that labor force. Even in Latin America, where in many countries this migration to the cities has reached very large proportions, the agricultural labor force has nevertheless continued to swell very rapidly, around 1.5 percent per year on the average.[39] None of these countries has actually had a shrinking agricultural population.

According to the Indian censuses, the proportion of the total population engaged in agriculture in the two census years of 1951 and 1961 had remained virtually unchanged, while during this decade India was industrializing faster than most other underdeveloped countries. Referring to all the underdeveloped countries in Asia, a recent report from ECAFE concludes: "The proportion of population dependent on agriculture . . . has declined marginally only or remained much the same in most of the developing countries."

This implies that for the next few decades—the time perspective for any realistic planning—agriculture in most underdeveloped countries must absorb by far the larger part of the expected rapid natural increase, in the first place the increase in the agricultural labor force, but also that in the national labor force.

The development goal in planning must be, therefore, to increase the utilization in agriculture of the now greatly underutilized labor force—in terms of participation and, in particular, of duration and efficiency of work. The fact that this labor force will be continuously and rapidly increasing makes efforts to reach this goal still more difficult.

The failure of the industrialization drive to "create employment" has undoubtedly played an important role in recent efforts of some countries to stress agriculture over industrialization in development Plans.

But there are a number of other reasons for this redirection of policy planning: the accelerating population increase, the magnitude of which was not realized by the planners until after the censuses around 1960; in most countries the slower than expected increase in agricultural production, and in several of them disastrous crop failures in the middle of the sixties; and, last but not least, the increasing pressure from countries giving food aid, particularly the United States.

This change of policy goals has ordinarily been discussed in terms of priorities, and mostly has been translated into transference of "development expenditures" on the budget from industry to agriculture. This is for many reasons a superficial way of thinking. It is a reflection of the faulty method of planning in financial terms (see Chap. 1, above).[40]

It is assuming a competition for funds which often is not real. Generally speaking, there is a positive correlation between a country's industrial development and its productivity in agriculture. From a policy point of view, a greater stress on the need for agricultural improvements might rationally be a reason for a redirection of industry —toward producing fertilizers, pesticides, and all sorts of agricultural implements, machinery, and tools—more than for a slowing down of the industrialization drive.

Also, some of the most important agricultural improvements—as for instance land reform (see above) or organized efforts toward collective investment of labor (see below)—do not compete much for capital and even less for foreign exchange.

It has been pointed out above that, in view of the long-run effects of industrialization and the need for a changed distribution between occupations of the increasing labor force, underdeveloped countries and particularly the more populous ones cannot afford to lessen their industrialization drive. What they need is, rather, a "bigger Plan," [41] containing all that they can do to speed up industrialization and *at the same time* valiant efforts to raise labor utilization in agriculture.

At this point a reminder: the tremendous rise in labor productivity in the agriculture of the developed countries —one that has been going on for generations—could develop almost from the very beginning while the labor force in agriculture was decreasing, first as a proportion of the total labor force but very early also in absolute terms.

This represents *a fundamental difference in initial conditions between the now highly developed countries generations ago and the underdeveloped countries today.* In order to explain this difference we have to realize that the former countries often started on a higher level of industrialization and, moreover, that the early technology in industry had been more labor intensive than today. A third difference is that their total labor force increased much less rapidly.

When now trying to industrialize, the underdeveloped countries have certain limited opportunities to use a somewhat more labor-intensive technology.[42] In industry they have, however, mainly to take over the most modern and advanced technology, the availability of which is rightly considered their great chance. And the possibility of protecting traditional crafts, which are more labor intensive, can only be temporary and limited. Even such protection, to be successful, requires efforts to modernize technology utilized in the crafts, although this new technology is labor saving.[43]

The consequence of all this is, however, that while in the developed countries improving the agricultural techniques could proceed almost from the beginning while their labor force in agriculture was diminishing and rapidly being absorbed in industry, this is not so in the underdeveloped countries today. *Their new agricultural technology must therefore become utterly labor intensive,* as prescribed by the fact that the labor force, confined in agriculture, is now underutilized and that in most underdeveloped countries it will be rapidly increasing for decades ahead.

This prospect should not be too bleak, since their agriculture is now not labor intensive, and almost all technological improvements are apt to increase the demand for labor. Also, with the tremendous quantitative and qualitative food deficiencies, agriculture should not face any market limitation for a long time, if they succeed in translating nutritional needs into effective demands. This they must attempt to do, as it is an important element of development. There is a huge backlag of undernutrition and malnutrition.

And, unlike traditional crafts, the agricultural sector is not vulnerable to backwash effects from industrialization, at least not in the near future.[44]

II Policies

The fact that agricultural technology in underdeveloped countries has to become highly labor intensive while it has now in the developed countries become extremely labor saving, implies that *in agriculture modern technology cannot be taken over as directly as in industry.* Adjusting agricultural technology to the different factor proportions in underdeveloped countries becomes very much more important.[45]

Some specific techniques, such as artificial insemination of cows, new methods of preventing plant disease, and killing of rodents, are applicable, but even these often have to be radically adjusted. More generally, new research is urgently needed, even though it can often build on fundamental research done in the developed countries.

Moreover, modern agricultural technology in developed countries has been the result of intensive and localized research on climate, soils, seeds, etc. It has mostly been limited to countries in the temperate zones. One of the most urgent tasks is, therefore, to carry out on a large scale that same type of research for the tropical and subtropical regions where most of the underdeveloped countries are located.[46]

These various research tasks, which must be carried out in order to make our scientific knowledge better applicable to countries with such different factor proportions, climate and everything else, raise demands on financial and personnel resources which cannot be met by the underdeveloped countries themselves on a scale even nearly equal to the needs. This represents, therefore, *one of the strategically most important requirements for foreign aid from the developed countries.*

But assuming that these difficulties will be gradually overcome so that the most rational and relevant agricultural technology is made available, this represents only the beginning of agricultural reform. *Millions of tillers of the land must be induced to use the new technology.* Pilot projects on a small scale can even in the best case only be a beginning.

These countries, and particularly their agriculture, have been stagnant for a long period. The people, bound up in agriculture, must acquire an ambition that today is often missing [47] if they are to raise their incomes and levels of living. Inducing them to do that, and getting them to raise their technology from a primitive level, requires an educational effort of staggering dimensions.

One particular additional difficulty is that *it is almost never a question of learning to do one specific thing in a new way, but of accepting and giving effect to a package of induced changes.* What is needed is an overall improvement in farming methods, accepting a great number of induced changes to be applied simultaneously. Otherwise, neither good results nor profit is forthcoming.[48]

More water supplied by irrigation becomes really profit-able only in a system of double or triple cropping. In the same way, fertilizers are largely ineffective without water, while in turn irrigation does not pay except in conjunction with fertilizers. Likewise, improved seeds require both water and fertilizers to raise yields substantially.

The same rule of complementary changes is valid in regard to all other improvements of agricultural tech-nology: deeper plowing, soil conservation and improve-ment of soil structure, green manuring and the use of natural fertilizers, better weed control, plant protection, improved crop rotation, etc.

The development of fast-maturing varieties of seeds may, by speeding up the pace of agricultural operations, help to overcome one of the deterrents to double cropping, but this requires, in the first place, irrigation. And the availability of cheap fertilizers may encourage the culti-vation of waste land or land now used as pasture, but only when other adjuncts to improving farming are applied.

To teach millions of very poor, mostly illiterate, and often diseased cultivators in a backward and stagnating agriculture one particular new technological method and to get them to apply it faithfully and effectively may be difficult enough. To get them to accept a whole package of new methods to be applied simultaneously must often border on the impossible. But the agricultural situation in most underdeveloped countries is so desperate that it must be attempted.

As has already been pointed out, almost every element in that package of technological changes, which applied together are rational and profitable, requires not only a greater labor input but more intensive and effective work. The new technology implies in this way generally over-coming the underutilization of labor. And this must be accomplished while the labor force is steadily and rapidly increasing.

In this connection it should be noted that, by itself, the

increase in the labor force tends all the time to push a larger part of it down into the poorer strata and to make the social and economic structure more inegalitarian and rigid.[49]

And there we touch what is, nevertheless, the major difficulty overshadowing all the other difficulties mentioned, viz., the inegalitarian social and economic stratification in most underdeveloped countries. *What is broadly referred to as the problem of "land reform" or "agrarian reform," tenancy reform included, has to be attacked in order to create a situation where the labor force has the opportunities, and feels the incentives, to exert itself very much more.* And so we face an immensely important, practical, and concrete aspect of the equality issue.

Among the grossly underutilized laborers in agriculture are the totally landless workers who seldom form less than a quarter of the whole labor force and often more. As a result not only of the population explosion but also of other factors that tend to depress agricultural workers to lower status in the village hierarchy, the landless workers are generally an increasing portion of the labor force in agriculture. Farmers who own land but very little of it are broadly in the same situation, and are particularly vulnerable to the factors that tend to rob them of the little land they have. These groups are foredoomed to be passive and not in a position to experience incentives to increase their labor input and labor intensity.

The widespread system of sharecropping is conducive neither to technological change nor to investments in labor and money, nor, generally, to the increases in the quantity and quality of labor input that would be implied.[50] The sharecropper, often paying the landowner more than half of the gross yield of the land he tills, is held down in poverty and apathy.

The rent-payment system leaves him only a part, and most often a smaller part, of any increase in yield. To this is added his insecurity of tenancy, which implies that he has no legally guarded rights to land improvement, even if he by his own labor produces it.

At the same time, it is a common experience that under a sharecropping system, with few exceptions, the landowner, whether he is a big or small absentee landlord or a peasant landlord or privileged tenant living in the village, is no more interested in working, investing, and improving than is his tenant or subtenant. Land has a high, usually stable, or even a steadily increasing value, and the landowner gets a high and secure rent in kind even without taking upon himself any new risks or any additional trouble or worry.

I draw the conclusion, and find it confirmed by a great number of intensive studies which have been made, that in South Asia the sharecropping system stands as the cause of a complex of inhibitions and obstacles which work effectively against any attempts to improve technology and increase labor utilization and yields: such a system "constitutes [an] all-but-insuperable disincentive to vigorous participation in development by the rural masses and not only an affront to social justice." [51]

I have a less thorough personal experience of the Latin American latifundia and the minifundia existing under their shadow. But according to what I have read and the few observations I have been in a position to make, that system—which also often contains elements of the sharecropping system—is equally inimical to technological advance which would raise labor utilization and yields.

This impression is supported by the fact that average yields are low, and not rising very much, in countries and districts where this other system is reigning. The remarkably honest and pertinent study of agriculture in Latin America that has recently been prepared by the Secretariat of the Economic Commission for Latin America (ECLA) [52] spells out in considerable detail how the system of landownership, landlessness, and tenancy in various countries of Latin America prevents progress in agriculture:

> The bulk of the rural population has no surplus income and not even enough land to permit an increase in investment, while those who own most of the land and income are seldom interested in developing their property, stepping up production and raising productivity, or have the capacity to do so. The profits made on large estates are hardly ever ploughed back into the land; instead they are spent on urban investment and luxury consumption, or sent out of the country. Under the existing tax systems, the State is unable to collect a large enough proportion of these profits to increase its investment in agriculture.[53]

There are, of course, a great number of landowning and tenancy systems in different countries and even districts of a single country in the vast underdeveloped world. But very generally an agrarian reform of one type or another (see below) should almost everywhere be an absolutely necessary condition for implementing policy efforts aimed at introducing improved technologies.

Another generalization that seems to be well founded is that with few exceptions—mostly where there has been a revolutionary situation or where outside domination and pressure has played a role, as for instance in the case of Formosa—*not much has come out of all the talk about land and tenancy reforms in underdeveloped countries since the Second World War*. Even when legislated, they have mostly been mini-reforms or an outright sham. And in regard to the landless workers, the reforms were regularly not even meant to give them land of their own. For the huge region of South Asia this has been discussed in some detail in *Asian Drama*.[54]

It has also been shown there that the main explanation for the failure of agrarian reform in this region has been the resistance of the powerful landowning interests. Even small landowners joined the bigger landlords in what they felt to be an interest solidarity.

The fact that investment in land is considered a safe and convenient way of preserving personal wealth has had the result that big and small capitalists in the cities have been eager to acquire land. In a country like India probably almost the whole upper class, as defined in the previous chapter, own some land, though there is no statistic that can prove it.

This wide diffusion of landownership even among the urban upper class and non-cultivators in the rural areas, both groups including many government servants in the lower as well as in the higher ranks, creates a formidable anti-land-reform bloc. This bloc is powerful not only because of its voting strength in countries where elections are held, but because it embraces almost the whole literate and articulate population in the urban as well as in the rural areas.

Even aside from the fact that they often own some land themselves, it was only natural that the officials who were supposed to administer the reforms mostly entered into collusion with the upper strata in the villages to make the reforms non-operative.

The poorer strata in the villages, in whose interest the reforms were propagated and sometimes legislated, were mostly apathetic. They were not organized to perceive their common interests and still less to fight for them. In the existing social situation they were powerless, illustrating the general thesis developed in the previous chapter, that ordinarily all the power is held by different constellations within the upper class, while the masses remain inarticulate, unorganized to defend their interests, and passive.

In Latin America, though the landowning and tenure system there is in many ways different, the development in regard to agrarian reform has been similar to that in South Asia. There, too, agrarian reform became a generally proclaimed policy goal, and this was solemnly agreed to in the Charter of Punta del Este in 1961. In the already cited study of agriculture in Latin America by the ECLA Secretariat, published in 1968, a whole chapter was devoted to "The System of Land Tenure and Other Institutional Obstacles to Agricultural Development." [55]

The authors had to conclude that very little had come out of these policy efforts and that this "largely reflects the influence which the big landowners have exerted and continue to exert on the formulation of agricultural policy in the different countries." [56] Comparing "actual results with agreed and realistic targets," the authors find:

> ... the Latin American countries have achieved very little in absolute terms and practically nothing in relation to the needs or targets. ... Although the enactment of land reform legislation and the establishment of land reform institutes were expected to signal the beginning of a new era of profound changes in the structure of land tenure, in fact most of the reform programmes have constantly been watered down and many of them are now almost at a standstill. ... The number of families settled thus far is only a fraction of the annual natural increase in farm families. ... In other words, thus far land reform activities have made only a very small dent in the land tenure system, and none of the programmes have reached the proportions of a real land reform. [57]

In West Asia, and in an African country like Ethiopia, the problems of landownership and tenure are, though varying a great deal, not too different from those in South Asia. In most of independent Africa south of the Sahara, the situation is—from a historical development point of view—less "mature." In many parts of that region, the problem is, rather, one of deciding upon whether to reorganize a tribal system of collective ownership or to establish anew a system of individual ownership. The fact that in many of the newly independent countries Europeans had acquired land, and mostly the best land, raises problems of a particular kind, both when the Europeans stay on and when they prefer to leave.

It is commonly noted that in order to have the most

beneficial effects from a productivity point of view, *agrarian reform should be supplemented by a large number of other and complementary institutional reforms*, including agricultural extension; provision on favorable terms of credits and of supplies of fertilizers, seeds, and other farm implements; improved market outlets for the produce, etc.

A usual policy line in the whole underdeveloped world has been that these reforms should be accomplished through cooperation. In many countries—among them all those in South Asia—these reforms have been motivated and seemingly directed so as to aid in particular the poorer strata in the villages and thus work toward greater economic and social equality.

In *Asian Drama* there is a rather full discussion of these policy measures as applied in South Asia,[58] including credit and other cooperatives, community development and agricultural extension, local self-government, and cooperative farming. The whole ideology behind these strivings is strongly egalitarian. *They were often presented as revolutionary in their effect of fostering greater equality in the villages.*

But by the logic of the existing inegalitarian social, economic, and political stratification in these countries and not least in their villages, they have almost regularly had the opposite effect. Ordinarily only the higher strata could avail themselves of the advantages offered by the co-operative institutions, and profit from the subsidies given for their development. *The net effect has been to create more, not less, inequality.*

While land reform and tenancy legislation, if implemented, are devices for producing fundamental alterations in property rights and economic obligations, these other institutional measures fail to incorporate a frontal attack on the existing inegalitarian power structure. Indeed, their aim is to improve conditions without disturbing that structure, and this represents, in fact, an evasion of the equality issue.

This is also true of the all-embracing rural uplift program, generally known as community development, to which so much hope has been attached both in the underdeveloped world and in the Western developed countries. "In this early period, a good deal of the discussion about community development was held in an atmosphere of euphoria since it was widely believed that the movement held the key to revolutionizing economic and social life in Asia's countless villages." [59]

The one most important explanation for the failure of this program is that as it has been operated *it has essentially been an attempt to bypass the equality issue, while all the time it was argued in terms of aiding the poor.*[60]

India, which has been ahead of all other underdeveloped countries in pressing for these other complementary institutional reforms, is also the country where realistic evaluations have continually been made and where there has been the most enlightened discussion. The point made here is honestly recognized in these evaluation studies. As one official report in India stresses: "As long as the present pattern of society and habits of thoughts remain, the fruits of development are bound to be most unevenly distributed, the weaker sections receiving the smallest portions." The report goes on to document the failure of all the supposedly ameliorative policies, among them community development, to reach the poorer people in the villages.[61] It then concludes: "The crazy-quilt pattern of cultivation makes it well-nigh impossible to improve and rationalize agriculture to any appreciable degree. Whatever little improvement is possible, does in the very nature of things benefit the biggest landowners far more than the petty-holders."

Implied in this statement is the conclusion that in India these complementary institutional reforms, contrary to the egalitarian motivation commonly given them, will actually result in greater inequality, as long as the basic inegalitarian system of ownership and tenure is not radically changed. Wherever such reforms have been attempted elsewhere in the underdeveloped world, they have in the same way tended to be a boon for the better-off strata in the rural areas and to aid the poor masses very little or not at all.

This very serious development has in the last few pages been discussed from the point of view of the egalitarian ideal, which was the aim of land, tenancy, and other complementary institutional reforms. What we face is a clear failure.

The reforms have either not been realized or have actually led to greater inequality. And this has been happening *pari passu* with a very rapid population increase which, as already mentioned, by itself tends to push more people downwards in the social and economic system and to render this system more rigid and unyielding.

But this development can also be viewed from a productivity point of view. Undoubtedly some of the members of the upper class in the villages—mainly those in the group of peasant landlords and privileged tenants, who cultivate the land themselves with their families and with hired farmhands—learned that money can be earned by the modernization of cultivation, and that liberal aid can be obtained from the government for this purpose.

Though no reliable statistics are available, and even though conditions vary in different districts and countries, this group is usually quite small, while, taken together, the sharecroppers, the more traditional farmers employing workers, the landless laborers working for them, and the very small peasant landowners are the great majority.[62] The land tilled by this great majority of the rural population will in South Asia also normally be a considerably larger part of all land.

Even from a productivity point of view this development, therefore, cannot yield very important results. But undoubtedly progressive farmers of that type, few as they are, have been largely responsible for much of what increase of yields there has been in underdeveloped countries. The former Director-General of FAO, Dr. B. R. Sen, whom we have already quoted, notes about India that evaluation reports suggest that it is "the substantial farmers and better-off villagers" who have benefited from community development, and he means that this "should be welcomed."

He then continues: "Thus community development can play a dynamic role in modernizing Indian agriculture." Sen probably does not make this judgment and give this recommendation in comparison with the very much more widespread effects which would incur if these other institutional reforms aimed at assisting cultivators in various ways had been combined with effective reforms of the landowning and tenure structure. The absence of the latter reforms prevented the other institutional reforms from reaching and benefiting the great masses of tillers.

Nevertheless, if one should accept as a factual situation that in an underdeveloped country in broadly the same political situation as India there is no hope of honest, effective land and tenancy reforms of the type planned and largely legislated, then the whole problem of agrarian reform and rural uplift should be reconsidered. It is then also taken for granted that a political revolution, implying an uprising of the poor masses against the present holders of power, is not within sight (Chap. 3, above, and Chap. 12 below). In *Asian Drama* such a reconsideration has been attempted.[63]

Under the two assumptions mentioned it was deemed worthwhile to try *an entirely fresh approach in regard to the agrarian structure.* To begin with, the government should lay down a definite policy which under the existing social and political conditions could really be carried out.

The policy would be to *abandon land and tenancy reform along the lines that have so far been unsuccessfully attempted,* as the political will does not exist, nor is the effective administration for its implementation available.

Although it has failed to produce radical action, the climate of radical declarations and legislation has had the unfortunate effect of creating uncertainties among those individuals in the agricultural structure who should possess the opportunity and the capacity to respond to economic stimuli.

The result has been that agricultural policy has courted the worst of two worlds: equality has not, in fact, been promoted, while potential efficiency in the rural upper class has been held back by these uncertainties.

It would under these conditions seem to be preferable to make *a deliberate policy choice in favor of capitalist farming by allowing and encouraging the progressive entrepreneurs among the group of peasant landlords and privileged tenants to reap the full rewards of their strivings.* This might encourage more such farmers to act in the same way and, in particular, to give up relying on sharecropping.

The fundamental issue of equality would then have to be approached from a different angle and by different policy means. What is detrimental both from an equality and from a productivity point of view is the form of quasi-capitalism now prevalent, combining the least favorable features of unrestricted capitalism with powerful remnants of feudal patterns of economic organization.[64]

For one thing, a genuinely capitalist path of development cannot tolerate passive and parasitic landownership on the part of persons who sap the surplus of the agricultural sector but do not contribute to its productive performance. *Sharecropping as a system of tenancy, absentee landownership, and the prevalence of "cultivators" who in fact are not doing any cultivation should be eliminated.*

Much could be accomplished by a tax system that placed severe penalties on the income of non-participating landowners. More could be accomplished through laws prohibiting the future transfer of titles to non-farming persons and, in particular, non-residents. Laws of the latter type are in existence in many democratic countries, of which Sweden is one, even though the evil of absenteeism there is infinitely smaller.

It is an indication of the power situation in India that while there have been, and continue to be, plenty of radical pronouncements even in official documents along the conventional line of a "social and economic revolution" and "the land to the tiller," such a straightforward, practical line of reform has never been suggested.

If more landowners were to become progressive farmers, prepared to introduce technological improvements, this would generally raise the demand for labor. If in a particular case some type of mechanization would, instead, have labor-displacing effects, its use could easily be checked in a country forced to control enterprise and investment and regularly struggling with exchange difficulties and bottlenecks in the provision of industrial goods.[65]

The rising demand for labor and the gradual abolition of sharecropping would be in the long-term interest of the agricultural labor force that is rapidly increasing. It should be stressed that genuine rural uplift of the masses of poor people in the villages cannot be accomplished unless the traditional distaste for diligent manual work and, in particular, for work as wage employees is weeded out from the social system and from the minds of the people.

But it is important to devise additional measures to protect agricultural workers. Such measures are equally important as those aimed at creating incentives for genuine entrepreneurship on the part of the landowners. The attempts in India to legislate minimum wages are, at least for the near future and with anything like the present underutilization of the labor force, even more inoperative than the land-reform and tenancy legislation.

But a high priority should be accorded to a program

to give a small plot of land—and with it dignity and a fresh outlook on life, as well as a minor independent source of income—to members of the now landless underclass in the villages. Even in densely populated areas it would be possible to give at least small plots on acreages that are now uncultivated waste. The existing pattern of cultivated holdings need not be seriously disturbed—in some localities it would not need to be disturbed at all.

It would be essential in such a scheme of very limited land redistribution, however, that *unrestricted right to own and use the land pass into the hands of the landless as individuals.* The Indian system, applied in the very small-scale attempts to give waste land to the landless, viz., to press them into cooperatives under the control of the village panchayats (mostly dominated by the higher landowning castes) must be suspected to have been devised in order to prevent low-caste persons from acquiring the dignity of landowners, however small the plot.[66] In any case it has had that result.

These policy measures taken together would, in fact, if carried out, add up to *a very radical land reform, though of a different type than that prominently discussed and attempted by legislation.* It would be far more effective for the purpose of raising productivity in agriculture. At the same time it would more effectively change the rural community toward greater equality and a greater mobility within the economic and social structure.

There are people who would assert that the development in India is actually moving in the direction of those proposals. Except for the lessening interest in trying to implement the conventional type of land redistribution and tenancy legislation, this is, however, not correct.

For one thing, the radical goal of redistributing the land to the tillers has until recently been continually pronounced in all sorts of official reports, keeping alive the uncertainty about landownership.

Even more important is the fact that there is apparently

no thought given to taking measures against the share-cropping systems and against absenteeism and passive and parasitic landownership generally.

Neither is there much interest shown in taking practical steps toward strengthening the bargaining power of the landless by giving them small plots of land.

Politically, prospects for steering agricultural policy in India along the new lines I have suggested above are far from bright. Urban absentee landowners and non-cultivating "cultivators" enjoy positions of power. And share-cropping, though wasteful, is so profitable that those who pluck its fruits will not be inclined to support change.

The rural underclass, on their side, are passive and not organized to defend their interests. And it cannot be hoped that they should be sophisticated enough to see their paramount interest in the spread among the land-owners of progressive entrepreneurship, least of all as it would imply that sharecroppers should become employed workers, which many of them would see as a social degradation.

It should be easier for them to understand the type of land redistribution of small plots to the landless. But the resistance to giving the landless—most of whom are low caste—even a minor stake in individual landownership is strong, particularly in India.

The attachment to a radically egalitarian ideology—though of a vague, non-committal type—continues to pre-dominate, creating an anti-incentive reaction among the landowners but otherwise without practical consequences.

Meanwhile, the population explosion tends to increase the underutilization of the labor force and to press down an ever larger part of it into the submerged underclass.

But *this is exactly the type of situation crying for in-tellectual and political leadership.* It is in order to stress this that I have written the foregoing pages.

Another reason has been that considering this alterna-tive line of land reform affords a particularly forceful demonstration of how the demand for greater equality can be made compatible with the need for higher productivity. The two are complementary in the accentuated meaning that they stand as prerequisites for each other.

Because of its tremendous size, India is particularly important. More than any other underdeveloped country it had also established a pattern of planning, even if it broke down under the trials of 1965 and 1966. And it has had a freer and more penetrating public discussion of all social issues than almost all other underdeveloped countries.

There are other countries in the underdeveloped world where a land reform of this non-conventional type could also be the most advantageous one. But it should be stressed that conditions in regard to landownership and tenure differ immensely among the underdeveloped countries.

The problem, therefore, should not be discussed as if there were only one solution to it all over the world, ordinarily assumed to be a more or less equal redistribution of the land to the tillers, but sometimes thought of instead in terms of a radical consolidation of land in some form of collective farming.[67]

The land-reform problem should, instead, be treated separately for each country and sometimes for each district in a country. The discussion should be based on the traditions and the actual conditions as they differ among countries and even among smaller regions.

There are countries where the conventional scheme of a redistribution into individual farms of about the same size would be the appropriate land reform. This could apply not only to countries where the land is already nearly equally divided among a class of peasant proprietors, but sometimes also when most of the land is owned by big absentee landlords, as is the usual case in Latin America.

If in the former case there is a very large class of landless workers—as in Thailand where they make up perhaps 40 percent of the rural labor force—there is the additional problem of giving these workers some land of their own, even though it would not be practical or feasible to distribute the land equally among all the families in a rural area.

There are other countries where a cooperative form of ownership and management would be the most advantageous one. But it should then be a genuine cooperation and not the fake it has been for the most part in India, which is the one country that has tried cooperative farming.[68] There are countries or at least districts where large-scale municipal or state farming could have much to recommend it, particularly when new areas are opened up for cultivation.

The one requirement any type of land reform should meet is that it should create a relationship between man and land that does not thwart his incentives to work and to invest—if nothing else, to invest his own labor. This will regularly require greater equality if the incentives are not to be operative only among a very small upper-class group.

Attempts to improve technology in agriculture and to raise yields will never have great results if that relationship between man and land is not established. And leaving landownership and tenancy as it has been, and is, in most underdeveloped countries will not only imply a very great limitation for the application of an improved technology but, at the same time, will tend to increase inequality in a country.

III *Peculiarities*

There have been some rather extraordinary peculiarities in the discussion of how to direct agricultural policy in underdeveloped countries, particularly in recent years. They need to be pointed out, as they are apt to mislead people into making irrational choices of policy.[69]

For one thing, *the tremendous underutilization of the labor force in agriculture is played down.* Even less attention has been given to its present tendency to increase, as the labor force will be rising in many countries by approximately 2 percent or more yearly, almost until the end of this century. When the underutilization of the labor force has been mentioned, it has been more in passing, usually without stressing the dynamic character of this factor and without attempting a coordination of this insight with the choice of policy.

It has been given importance only in the discussion of "unemployment" and "underemployment" along the line of the biased postwar approach.[70] "Underemployment" has been isolated by dealing with it as a static factor, unrelated to policy—otherwise the term could not be defined in the way it has been defined [71]—and by defining both "unemployment" and "underemployment" in the totally unrealistic and unpractical way as a surplus that could be "removed." [72]

In India, Mohandas K. Gandhi faced the issue, but then he dealt with it in moralistic terms. He spoke about the "traditional laziness" of the Indian people and stressed that idleness had no justification.[73]

> If you spend your next vacation in some far off village in the interior, you will see the truth of my research. You will find the people cheerless and fear-stricken. You will find houses in ruins. You will look in vain for any sanitary or hygienic conditions. You will find the cattle in a miserable way, and yet you will see idleness stalking there.

Nehru occasionally, particularly in earlier years, also used to protest against idleness when there was so much work just crying out to be done.

But gradually these types of complaints have died out

in India as elsewhere. Since decolonization, foreigners have been careful not to utter any complaints of that sort, acquiescing to the indigenous protest against the colonial theory of which we spoke in Chapter 1.

The present author is the last one to denounce a treatment of social and economic issues in moral terms. But the issue needs to be stated realistically. The widespread idleness has reasons and causes over which the individual himself is not master. First there are the inferior health conditions which depend upon many things, above all the poverty of the broad masses.

Then, and even more fundamental, there is the landowning and tenancy system which does away with the possibility of the tillers raising the yield by a more labor-intensive cultivation, and which deprives them of the incentive to invest any funds they could acquire or even their own labor in order to improve the land.

This causes that extreme degree of poverty that robs the mind and body of the strength to do even the things around the individual family dwelling that would be in the obvious interest of health and comfort.

Against this background, the ones to blame are not the masses of poor tillers but the much smaller upper class who under the present system have the political power and who prevent an agrarian reform that would make a higher labor utilization possible and worthwhile.

In different degrees, these remarks are valid in regard to most countries in the underdeveloped world.

The main remedy for the vast underutilization of the labor force in agriculture would be, as I tried to show in Section II of this chapter, a general spread of the application of a modern technology which almost without exception is more labor intensive. A prerequisite for this is a land and tenancy reform which creates such a relationship between the tillers and the land as to make that possible, and which gives them incentives for investing such funds as they can dispose of or acquire, and above all their own labor, in order to increase the productivity of the land.

A second peculiarity, not unrelated to the first one, is that except for almost ritualistic reiterations in some underdeveloped countries of the need for this type of reform—often expressed in uncompromisingly radical terms—*land and tenancy reform is generally given less and less attention when practical questions of raising productivity levels in agriculture are discussed in underdeveloped countries.*

To a certain degree, this might be a natural reaction to the failures in deciding upon and implementing such reforms upon which we have also commented in Section II. The political situation in this regard may have seemed hopeless.

Also, as these reforms can only give results in a raised labor input and higher yields in the somewhat longer run, and would, moreover, assume large-scale complementary public investment in agricultural extension, credit and marketing facilities, etc.,[74] the very aggravation of the agricultural crises in recent years may stand as a reason to turn down the request for them.

In the short-term view, landlords and moneylenders may then even seem to perform a useful function by squeezing out by a non-market process food for the urban market from a half-starved agricultural proletariat. As an Indian author, writing in the Congress Party's official journal, expresses the thought in the protective guise of technical language:

> By redistribution [of land] we will be transferring land to that section of the population whose income elasticity of demand for food grains is nearly unity. . . . This will be disastrous as any shrinkage in the market surplus will be a check to rapid industrialization.[75]

Although such clear confessions are rare, this cruel thought may not be exceptional in policy-forming circles in underdeveloped countries. It can also be used to condone the redirection of the other complementary institutional reforms to serve the upper strata, and thereby foredoom them to failure insofar as uplift of the poorer strata in rural areas is concerned, as we have noted above. And as the poor are so many, it sacrifices progress *in the somewhat longer run.*

In any case, land and tenancy reforms have, on the whole, in recent years lost out in the public discussion of the agricultural problems in most underdeveloped countries. A prominent Indian economist, K. N. Raj, views this development with anxiety:

> It... worries me that generally in India today we find among planners and policy makers in government a movement toward what I would describe as a technocratic approach to all the problems. . . . But the institutional framework of a very traditional society like that in India cannot be left as it is if we really want a significant increase in production. I have in mind measures like land reforms on which, until now, the position has been that at least we said that we wanted to carry out far-reaching changes. . . . now, even the talk of land reform has disappeared.

On the part of the government representatives of the developed Western countries in the various assemblies of the United Nations, there had earlier been some willingness to vote, together with the representatives of the underdeveloped countries, for resolutions which in general and often sweeping terms urged the underdeveloped countries to undertake land reform.

And President John F. Kennedy had placed land reform and taxation reforms as major goals for the Alliance for Progress. As already mentioned, this was solemnly agreed upon by the representatives of the Latin American governments in the Charter of Punta del Este in 1961.

In the face of the non-fulfillment of these appeals and undertakings, all such recommendations from Western developed countries are now dying down.[76] The discussions by their experts and officials are increasingly centered only upon technological improvements.

Whether the present system of landownership and tenancy is a hindrance to the spread of technological advance is no longer asked. Still less is it discussed whether a limited application of the technological improvements may instead accentuate the inequality gap in underdeveloped countries, and how this could be prevented. The reminder by one American expert with practical experience as well as technical knowledge, W. A. Ladejinsky, that "unless those who work the land own it, or at least are secure on the land as tenants, all the rest is likely to be writ in 'water,'" was not only received very critically in India, where he first met difficulties even in having his study published, but was almost entirely ignored in the United States and other Western developed countries.

Meanwhile, the United States, as chief provider of food aid, has pressured aid-receiving countries to increase their efforts to raise the yields. But this advice now regularly does not include recommending land reform.

Many of the American experts, while highly trained in technical matters, are rather ignorant about the institutional conditions in underdeveloped countries. They are also moved by considerations of the ruling circles in the underdeveloped countries who, as we said, have been moving away from any practical thoughts on implementing land reforms.

But it should be noted that their attitudes also fall in line with old colonial policies and thus can be viewed as, in fact, an outflow of neo-colonialism.[77] As was mentioned in Chapter 3 above, the colonial governments regularly sought support from the privileged strata. They were also reluctant to interfere with the life and customs of indigenous populations.

A frontal attack on those deterrents to labor input and efficiency that were built into the traditional agrarian structure was precluded by considerations of law, order, and expediency, and by the general colonial policy of laissez-faire and indirect rule.

The bias in favor of relying on merely technological improvement was strengthened after decolonization by the postwar approach to economic planning, with its evasion of the problems of attitudes, institutions, and the productivity consequences of very low levels of living, and its diplomatic tendency to avoid awkward problems and remain overoptimistic (see Chap. 1, above).

One flagrant illustration of the tendency to deal with the agricultural problems in underdeveloped countries as if they were not dissimilar from those in the developed countries—which is the essence of the biased postwar approach—is provided by the treatment of prices on food products and of price policies.

Practically the whole discussion at the present time in developed countries, and increasingly also in the underdeveloped countries themselves, stresses *the importance of keeping prices high for increasing the supply of food.* As a matter of fact, prices had been rising, not least in countries where and during years when there was acute shortage of food. *This was, however, less an effect of intentional price policy than of the shortage itself.*

But this does not mean, of course, that higher prices could not be brought about by policy measures. We know from many studies that a change in *relative* prices for different food products often has caused rapid and substantial changes in production and supply of these products. The effect of a *general* rise of prices for all or most food products is a more complicated matter.

It is not impossible that in some underdeveloped countries such a general rise of food prices would have the effect of higher production or, at least, a greater output in the food market—though sometimes at the expense of grave consequences for masses of poor people, which should then not be passed over in silence as is usually done. But in perhaps most underdeveloped countries, including such a vast part of the underdeveloped world as India and Pakistan, the situation is not so simple, as has also until recently been stressed by competent researchers.[78]

To mention some of the complications: Only a few of the farmers, in India perhaps only one out of four, ordinarily have any food to sell. This implies obstacles to the signals from the price system reaching the producer. A considerable part of what comes to the market, particularly but not exclusively that produced by sharecroppers, is extracted from cultivators by landowners and moneylenders. *This extraction process is governed not by ordinary market forces but by custom and by economic and social power in the village.*

In spite of this, as a rule a very large part of the total farm output never reaches the market but is consumed within the agricultural sector. In India this accounts for about two thirds or three fourths of the crop and in Pakistan for even more. Therefore, an increase in farm consumption has a totally disproportionate effect on the market supply. This may imply that contrary to the assumed Western model *a higher price may even cause a fall of supply in the market, instead of a rise.*

The masses of the agricultural population are so poorly nourished that if food prices rise because of a bad crop, those cultivators who are in a position to do so may actually reduce their sales and consume more themselves, a development that tends to drive prices still higher. If prices fall, they might instead be compelled to sell more in order to meet their commitments, with the result that prices sink further.

To this must be added the fact that fluctuations in crop size are often greater and more frequent in most underdeveloped countries because of climatic conditions and inferior farming practices. As a consequence of the facts mentioned in the previous paragraph, the volume of marketed supplies will tend to be even more volatile and unstable than total production.

For all these and other reasons *the market becomes more speculative* than in Western developed countries, where it is also largely "nationalized" and in the hands of governmental and cooperative organizations. The fact that poor cultivators are forced to sell some of their crop as soon as it is harvested—often so much that they later have to buy food themselves—results in *very large seasonal fluctuations*.

Deficiencies in transportation and storage facilities, and sometimes—as in India—rivalries between different provincial political authorities, tend to nullify governmental attempts to establish nationwide markets and increase their stability over the crop year.

The relative smallness of the non-agricultural sector, and the very high percentage of income that goes to food, make it *impossible to subsidize agriculture* as is commonly done in developed countries. To raise prices on food products means, for this reason—and for some of the other reasons accounted for above—incurring inflation as was experienced during 1965 and 1966 in India.

When considering these and other complications present to a varying degree in most underdeveloped countries, many of them fundamentally depending on institutional factors, it is rather astonishing to meet increasingly in the discussion of agricultural policy in these countries the unqualified and usually blank assertion that prices should be high in order to call forth an increase in production and supply in the market.

If it were possible to reason in this simple way, agricultural policy would, indeed, be a much easier problem. This is, however, a carelessly overoptimistic view. For the most part, also, the recommendation would work in the interests of the rich but against those of the poor.

This way of reasoning is, of course, in line with the biased postwar approach, generally patterned on the market economy of the rich Western countries and evading attitudes, institutions, and the productivity consequences of the very low levels of living in underdeveloped countries. *It caters to the vested interest of the land-*

lords, the moneylenders, and generally the upper strata in the villages.

In recent years there has been a very important technological advance, which, however, has spurred the biases toward optimism and, in particular, toward forgetting the need for agrarian reform: *the availability of high-yield varieties of cereals*, in particular wheat and hybrid maize developed in Mexico and rice provided by the International Rice Research Institute in the Philippines.

The work on maize and wheat was begun in the early 1940's by that remarkable, forward-looking agency for human welfare, the Rockefeller Foundation. One recalls its important pioneering anti-malaria campaign begun almost immediately after the Second World War in Ceylon; that campaign later spread, effectively improving health and decreasing the death rate in the entire underdeveloped world. Later the Ford Foundation joined in partially financing the work on rice. Development work is continuing and also embracing other cereals.[79]

Only in the last couple of years have the new varieties begun to be introduced on a fairly large scale, particularly in Pakistan, India, and the Philippines—too late to have been commented upon in *Asian Drama*.

There is no denying that this is a most promising technological advance. This I want to stress, even if I will have to be severely critical of the almost euphoric policy conclusions drawn. It has commonly been announced as offering "an unprecedented opportunity for a breakthrough in agricultural production in developing countries," to quote the most recent publication from FAO available at this time.[80]

There are, however, a number of other conditions, also enumerated in that publication, that must be fulfilled for such a breakthrough to become realized. The most important ones are that the new seeds should be used in conjunction with adequate inputs of both fertilizers and water, careful attention to protection from pests and diseases—as the new seeds planted on large areas may be more susceptible to disease and infestation [81]—weeding, and generally high standards of farming.[81a]

When the new seed grains begin to be used, it is in areas and by progressive cultivators meeting these requirements. Any further spread must be deemed more problematic and it will meet greater difficulties.

But without being able as yet to scrutinize scientifically the extent to which the still limited use of the new seed grain has contributed to the rise in agricultural yields, which in the countries mentioned has taken place in the last few years after the famine years 1965 and 1966, it has commonly been loosely suggested that their share in causing this rise has already been of very substantial importance.

The future wider spread of the use of the "wonder grains" is, moreover, often simply assumed to take place, without much consideration and with still less scientific analysis of what that would presuppose in regard to increased availability of water and fertilizers or whether increases on that scale are feasible. Neither have there been any calculations of the needed qualitative and quantitative rise of agricultural extension far beyond what seems at present to be possible, except by extraordinary policy measures, which should then be specified.

My criticism is, however, not primarily directed against the lack until now of careful study of what inputs of these various complementary factors are needed to make possible one degree or another of the spread of the new seed grains, and with one speed or another. There has been too short a time to carry them out.

But the really serious, opportunistically biased mistake in this outburst of technocratic optimism is that the availability of the new seed grains has been used to undergird the flight from the need of large-scale reforms of one type or another of landownership and tenure, which I commented upon above.

Better seed grains can certainly not be a substitute for agrarian reform. Their wider spread, and their becoming important for raising yields substantially, rather presupposes such a reform being carried out. An author in a recent number of the ECAFE *Economic Bulletin for Asia and the Far East,* who first stresses that "The application of modern technology, of new seeds and the farm regime they require, should permit a number of Asian countries to advance appreciably the date of self-sufficiency in food," then adds: "Whether these hopes are realized will depend on the efficiency of social organization which motivates farmers to respond to economic opportunities." [82]

The spread of the use of the new seed grains, as of other improved techniques, will not reach far without an agrarian reform. Indeed, without such reform, the availability of the new seed grains will join the other forces of reaction that are now tending to increase inequality among the rural populations in underdeveloped countries (see Chap. 13, below).

These accusations of a reactionary bias call for some substantiating illustrations. I will choose papers from two prominent experts and officials in the United States government, Lester R. Brown and Lyle Schertz. [83] They were both, in turn, acting as Administrators of the International Agricultural Development Service of the Department of Agriculture during the transition period between President Johnson's and President Nixon's administrations.

Both authors express themselves in exuberant language. According to Brown, we stand "on the threshold of an agricultural revolution in many of the hungry, densely populated countries of the less developed world, particularly in Asia."

Both dutifully interject warnings that much remains to be accomplished. Schertz is most expressive: "The agricultural revolution, like so many other dramatic improvements, has not occurred everywhere. Nor is its permanence automatic." And Brown stresses that the new developments do not decrease the need for a vigorous population policy: they may only "give food supplies a few years' lead in the race with human numbers." But these warnings do not seriously inhibit their exuberance.

Both rely simply on technological advances and on governmental efforts to give them spread. In regard to the political and institutional problems they are rather silent. What they do say falls in line with a reactionary attitude.

Brown observes, quite correctly, that "the new varieties are often quickly adopted by a relatively small group of farmers—the larger, more commercial farmers who have adequate irrigation and credit." In an earlier paper he had observed that "the socio-economic gap between the landowners and the landless may widen" and that even among the former group "the income gap between those owning fertile, well-watered land and those with marginal land is also likely to widen." [84]

But he does not raise the question whether or not poverty and passivity among the masses, absentee land-ownership, and the sharecropping system build barriers of inhibitions and obstacles against the further spread of this new agricultural technology. Neither is he interested in the question whether the profitable adoption by that small group of well-to-do and progressive cultivators makes the resistance against agrarian reform stronger.[85]

Schertz is more outspoken. Besides the availability of the new seed grains he recognizes as driving forces in the agricultural revolution the "efforts . . . of the developing countries themselves in improving their agricultural in-stitutions." He attributes these efforts to "inspired leader-ship in the developing countries." Though the text is not very clear, he then seems to think primarily of "price policies"—which he apparently believes have been the cause of rising food prices (see above).

There is a bare mention of the fact that "many farmers have been bypassed," while those who have "thus far benefited the most are those with enough capital and water." He also notes that "increased incomes have not generally been passed on to labor," and that "income distribution problems among regions, and among groups within regions, are bound to become increasingly sensitive." He gives an example from an area of marked progress in rice production where "a serious class conflict has recently broken out between landlord and tenant groups."

But from these assertions he draws no policy conclusions whatsoever. Instead, he points to "grass roots politics" as having had favorable effects: ". . . farmers have started lobbying for more government assistance. They have realized they need fertilizer, irrigation, credit and better marketing systems. They have found, as U.S. farmers have known for a long time, that political action can influence these conditions."

He does not say so but he should be aware that this type of "politics" implies the increase of all sorts of policies to aid and subsidize agriculture which, in the absence of land and tenancy reform, have been redirected from the often lofty declarations about assisting the poor masses to serve instead the higher strata in the rural hierarchy.

Land reform is mentioned only once, and then with the quite correct [86] observation that the higher land values which follow agricultural progress for some may cause the landowners to "exert pressure on the governments to give land reform lower priority." Schertz leaves the reader with the impression that he considers this a "hopeful, political effect of the high yielding variety programs," though again he is not too clear.

In any case, there is not even a hint that something ought to be done to prevent agrarian reform from being pushed aside or that embarking upon such a reform might have better rights to be classified as "institutional improvements," stimulated by "inspired leadership," than merely letting food prices go up and assisting the already privileged rural upper class.

As this has become the dominant official policy of the

United States, one could expect that criticism would have been raised by the large number of agricultural experts at the universities and in research institutions. But the opposite is mostly the case. There are a few lonely individual students and institutions still interested in the forgotten subject of land reform, but they are kept outside the limelight. Ordinarily the scholarly world lines up with official policy.

At a recent conference on agricultural development at the Asian Studies Center of Michigan State University,[87] the issue of agrarian reform was almost entirely bypassed by the participating experts as being of minor importance in the "agricultural revolution" that will follow technological change.

Not a word was said about non-cultivating and often absent "cultivators," or sharecropping. In line with the official experts, the academic ones now talk about "farmers" as if the tillers in these countries were like the ordinary Danish or the better-placed American farmers, that is, those outside the rural slums. The sharecroppers and other impoverished and dependent peasant groups are euphemistically referred to as "small farmers" or "little farmers."

Only Kusum Nair, who was present—and who should know the Indian villages—raised the problems created by the fact that only a very minor part of the "farmers" could be expected to use the new varieties of seeds, so that perhaps not more than 10 percent of the land would be so used. She considered the fate of the great majority of tillers an urgent problem.

> To transform these, what are generally described as subsistence farmers into commercial farmers is going to be a very different proposition than making the few commercial farmers still more commercial and more responsive. *This* is the nature and, in fact, the main crux of the problem of change in South Asian agriculture. The *majority* of the farmers here are not presently involved in the market and

its opportunities and cannot, therefore, be expected to respond to its signals, rationally or otherwise.[88]

But in the American surroundings even she did not touch the problems of landownership and tenure and of changing the relationship between man and land so as to give man the opportunity and the incentive to strive for higher yields. She kept safely out of that *political* problem by talking only about "values, beliefs and attitudes," without pointing out that those could hardly be changed except by changing the property institutions.

In 1965 a number of liberal American Congressmen succeeded in getting inscribed in the United States Foreign Assistance Act the so-called Title IX, which instructs the Agency for International Development to use its influence to assure "maximum participation in the task of economic development on the part of the people of developing countries, through the encouragement of democratic private and local governmental institutions" in the interest of "sustained economic and social progress." [89]

Going through the recurring debates in Congress on Title IX and other similar declarations, and the considerable literature referring to Title IX, it is striking that one searches almost in vain to find a very few oblique references to land and tenancy reform. So far as agriculture is concerned, the interest is instead focused on credit cooperatives, community development, and other similar institutional reforms, which in the absence of an agrarian reform have mostly aided the better-offs, even if the motivation has been uplift of the masses.

In the summer of 1968 there was a conference devoted to the problem of the implementation of Title IX, which remained in continuous session for five weeks and was attended by forty experts plus a large staff.[90] Again, not a word was said about land and tenancy reform, in spite of the fact that the goal of Title IX was defined as:

"Popular participation . . . should be set alongside economic development to form the twin pillars of the foreign assistance program." [91]

There is in my mind not the slightest doubt that the liberal sponsors in the United States Congress of Title IX would be strongly against the gross and increasing inequality prevalent in agriculture of most underdeveloped countries and would be in favor of agrarian reform, if the present political climate had not caused everybody to turn away so completely from that topic.

I have already touched upon some explanatory factors: the need felt to cooperate with those in power in the underdeveloped countries, who have been responsible for the failure of almost all attempts toward agrarian reform—and, of course, the general influence of the biased postwar approach to their development problems, turning interest away from institutional problems.

The present technocratic euphoria in Washington and many other centers of research has certainly also something to do with what could perhaps be called a compensatory psychological reaction. The American experts are, of course, as depressed as the present author by the strongly downward trend of their nation's aid to underdeveloped countries (see Chap. 11, below). In order to preserve the customary American alacrity to grapple with difficult problems, it must then be a temptation to counterweight that distress by an overdose of optimism in another direction. In Chapter 1 it was pointed out that that type of systematic bias is not a strange or an unusual reaction in America.

It must also be recalled that more reactionary views of the underdeveloped countries' problems of agrarian reform may be more natural for American agricultural experts who work within a national agricultural support system that has left masses of the cultivators impoverished in slum conditions, while a minority could use technological advance and capital investment to raise the productivity of land and labor immensely and so become the main producers. American farm policy has not had that strong streak of social responsibility, demonstrated in Europe and particularly in Scandinavia, preventing the rural masses from becoming, or remaining, impoverished.

So the United States acquired its problem of the rural slums. It is serious in itself, and also partly responsible for the even more serious problem of the urban slums. But in the United States—with for a long time far less than 10 percent of the total population in agriculture, a portion that has been steadily declining—the problem is nevertheless child's play compared with, for instance, India's problem, where the agricultural population is 70 percent, without hope that it will rapidly decrease, or, indeed, decrease at all within the next decades.

To have let the development take its course, and have had an "agricultural revolution" caused in the main by technological advance, without protecting and involving the poor, has turned out to create grave problems not yet solved in the United States. *In India and many other underdeveloped countries it threatens the majority of a relatively very much larger agricultural population, which is fettered to agriculture for a long time ahead and will be continuously growing, with misery and everything that can result from that.* I shall come back to this problem in Chapter 13.

A further explanatory factor is the strange tendency in recent years toward conformism in policy questions where experts in the American universities and other research centers so often tend to take their tone from Washington. I reflected on that at the time when the policy of the United States was to bring Britain into the Common Market. The professors tend to "sing in chorus" with an official policy line, which they so often even feel they have contributed to shaping. The result is a conformism in policy questions which has deadened public discussion.[92]

There are many forces which work in this direction: the

legacy of the cold war and the pressure for national discipline felt under the John Foster Dulles–Joseph McCarthy era; the pattern of increasingly bringing experts from the universities to Washington for consultation; and the huge amounts of government money dealt out for research on specific topics by agencies in Washington, not least those responsible for foreign policy in the wider sense. It is more and more possible to speak about a "government-academic complex" and not only the "industrial-military complex" about which the late President Eisenhower warned the nation.

When an issue becomes very important to the nation and when it is really causing a definite split, as is the Vietnam war, the conformism disintegrates, but even then rather late and less completely. In recent years there are indications that such a healthy process has been on the way in many other issues of national and foreign policy, making more real and possible the following out of the American ideal of "government through discussion." But the problem of agrarian reform in underdeveloped countries does not reach up to even that level of national concern.

When all this is said, trying to explain the ideological trend in the United States away from interest in an agrarian reform in underdeveloped countries, it must be added that a similar trend is also visible not only among people in and around governments in the underdeveloped countries themselves, but in the other Western developed countries as well. On this issue the United States has really exerted leadership in "the free world."

As all the interested governments are on the same line —the Communist countries have felt less and less inclined to discuss the agrarian problem for non-Communist underdeveloped countries—the issue of land reform also tends to disappear from the agenda and the publications of the intergovernmental organizations.

In the last issue of FAO's *The State of Food and Agriculture 1968*, it is barely mentioned. The small section in the FAO Secretariat for land reform has persistently and courageously been carrying on its studies and has continuously stressed the paramount importance of land reform for agricultural development and its great urgency.[93] Even if that section's activity will now not be scaled down, it will probably not be allowed to influence the main policy line of FAO very much.

As this is being written, FAO has just published its voluminous *Provisional Indicative World Plan for Agricultural Development*.[94] It is prefaced by many reservations, but without any doubt this work of both fact-gathering and analysis will be a basic source for the discussion of agricultural problems in the years to come. The authors attach particular importance to the term "indicative" in the title, yet this first global attempt to present orders of magnitude and to show how the different targets are related in quantitative terms constitutes an important step in the right direction.

The study gives due weight to the problem of labor utilization. It contains a chapter on "Land Reform as an Instrument of Progress" and rightly places it in the part dealing with "Mobilization of the Human Resources." It notes that conditions differ in different countries and even in districts within one country, and stresses that the land reform problem has to be approached "pragmatically."

Nevertheless, it is feared that attention will be focused only on the abstract relations and the excessive precision conveyed by expressing population growth and technological prospects of increasing yields in percentages with several digits. It will then support the technocratic euphoria of which I have spoken.

In the United Nations *1965 Report on the World Social Situation*,[95] written before the influence on opinions and policy of the new seeds, there was one short section on the "incentive value of agrarian reform." [96] Its main point was a flat assertion that "experience shows that land redistribution has not always proved successful."

The authors then continue with the cryptic observation that "Political and socio-economic conditions may militate against the redistribution of land, and a system of tenancy may therefore have to be retained." On this point they more clearly indicate that the main obstacle to improving the tenants' position is the political and social power of the landlords. A reform is necessary, according to the authors, but the reader is left in the dark about exactly what they mean should be done.

The Report for 1967,[97] which is generally a more distinguished work, devotes considerable interest to the land reform issue in both Asia and Latin America. It states the present situation and its origin clearly, but leaves the reader generally uninformed about its relation to productivity and about what should be done.

Most outspoken in regard both to stating the facts and to raising the policy issue have been the Secretariats for the regional Economic Commissions for Latin America, Asia, and Africa. As a former official of the Economic Commission for Europe and as a close collaborator of the Secretariats of the other Economic Commissions, I have felt pride and happiness in citing a few of their recent general conclusions about agrarian reform and the equality issue.

There is one development which would seem to give governments, officials, and experts in developed countries rational reason not to bother about agrarian reform in underdeveloped countries any longer, viz., the palpable failure in most of these countries to carry out such a reform. Given the present political power situation in underdeveloped countries, they may see agrarian reform as a dead horse.

For such a judgment there are, as I have shown, some solid reasons in the distribution of political power in most underdeveloped countries. But it is not honest to rationalize such a defeatist conclusion into technocratic optimism, concealing the serious limitation it must present to a wider spread of the technological advances, and concealing also the equally serious effects of the limited spread in causing a widening of the inequality chasms in the vast agricultural populations in underdeveloped countries.

In the somewhat longer view the further question should be asked: *What are the effects of this type of "agricultural revolution" on political stability in these countries?* (a problem to which we shall return in Chap. 13).

Moreover, it should be questioned whether the reasons for such a defeatism really are conclusive. It is a fact that the governments in developed countries, and in particular the government of the United States, are exerting pressure upon the governments in underdeveloped countries in regard to their agricultural policies. Is it really necessary that this pressure should completely bypass the equality issue which is so important also for productivity?

One effect of this is that all liberals—not to speak of the radicals—in underdeveloped countries find more nourishment for their conviction that *developed countries, and particularly the United States, stand for political reaction in their home countries.*

In any case, the independent students have no right to conform to the diplomacy of the governments. It is their plain duty to do their work without blinkers, to seek unbiased realism, and to criticize their own and other governments when they are shortsightedly opportunistic and are strengthening the reactionary forces in underdeveloped countries. Political defeatism, whether in the guise of "optimism" or "pessimism," cannot be accepted in objective research (see Chaps. 1 and 2, above).

IV   Concluding Remarks

It is hoped that this chapter has established a number of things: (1) the crucial role in development of agrarian reform of one sort or another, adjusted to the conditions and opportunities in the several underdeveloped countries, but aimed at creating such a relationship between man and land that the tiller has opportunities, and feels incentives, to exert himself; (2) the need for such a redirection of all other institutional reforms—providing and subsidizing agricultural extension, market outlets, and availability of fertilizers, water, seeds, machinery, and other agricultural implements—that they will serve the masses and not, as now, cause a widening of the gap between the rich and the poor; and (3) the importance of agrarian reform for making that redirection of other reforms effective.

All these reforms in the interest of greater equality are needed also for spreading technological advances and raising labor utilization and yields.

The one important point to be added is that *all these huge reforms in the interest of greater equality and a more rapid rise of production must be carried out by the underdeveloped countries themselves.* They must legislate the reforms, improve administration, and secure implementation.

The main responsibility of the developed countries in regard to these institutional reforms is *not to strengthen the powerful vested interests that have been delaying, distracting, or stopping those reforms in underdeveloped countries.* By setting up a virtual taboo on even discussing the institutional issues, we have lately been doing exactly that.

This taboo is now increasingly becoming accepted and observed by the students in the developed as well as the underdeveloped countries themselves. Together they are carrying the biased postwar approach to a point where it has become increasingly dangerous for the progress of underdeveloped countries, because they then support the reactionary forces in those countries. As has also been pointed out above, this is in a sense an expression of neo-colonialism.

What the developed countries can do, and have come to do on a scale that should now be very much enlarged, is, first of all, to *focus their efforts on research*. Intensive and localized research on physical and biological conditions for agricultural production in tropical and subtropical areas should be speeded up to an extent that the underdeveloped countries have neither the financial nor the personnel resources to do. The recent advances in procuring high-yielding and highly responsive varieties of grains are other and rather glorious examples of what research aid by the developed countries can accomplish.

But such accomplishments should not be taken as an excuse for running away from the needed institutional reforms. In fact, they make these reforms even more urgently needed.

The developed countries must continue to carry responsibility for *emergency aid to prevent hunger in the underdeveloped world*. Food aid should be a responsibility shared by all developed countries and managed in the multilateral setting of the World Food Program under the United Nations. It should not be operated under the hazard of the United States having a food surplus that it wants to get rid of and then finds suitable to integrate into its foreign policy as "Food for Peace," later renamed "Food for Freedom."

As has been shown in a number of FAO studies and to an extent tested out in practice, food aid can be turned into a positive means of causing a rise in labor utilization and production. Capital aid can increase the availability of water, fertilizers, and agricultural implements of all sorts.

But there is no exaggeration in insisting that *by far the most important changes must be induced by the under-*

developed countries themselves and that the crucial changes concern the institutional structure of these countries: realizing greater equality and at the same time higher productivity of land and labor.

Chapter 5

POPULATION[1]

I The Facts

While most economic terms, like "national income" or "output,"[2] are so inadequate to reality in underdeveloped countries that they can be used only with the greatest caution in scientific analysis of the economic problems, or, like "the savings ratio,"[3] "unemployment," or "underemployment,"[4] cannot be used at all, the concepts available for an analysis of the quantitative population problems do not suffer from such logical defects. Births, deaths, population size, age and sex distribution, and even migration in space are plain facts of human biological existence.[5]

Furthermore, the quantities of these population factors are interrelated in such a simple and clear logical mechanism that data can be cross-checked and corrected for mistakes and the consequent inconsistencies. The age structure, for instance, can be checked against births and deaths in earlier periods, and all three can then be adjusted so as to make better sense.

What nevertheless obscures our knowledge of the population development is the paucity and unreliability of the original observations and the calculations based on them. Few underdeveloped countries have reliable statistics even on population size. And in general the data become still more deficient as the degree of differentiation progresses from a single count of total population in a country to a count of the populations in the different districts and the number of males and females in particular age groups in the country and in these districts.

The superiority of the conceptual apparatus for analyzing population problems refers, however, only to formal demography. As soon as we proceed to studying the causes and effects of the development of one or the other of the population factors, we immediately run into complex social and economic conditions of a non-biological nature. And then we must again resist the temptation of the postwar approach to simplify the analysis by applying concepts and models borrowed from our analysis of conditions and developments in the developed countries.

Awareness of what is now commonly perceived as the population explosion is of rather recent origin.[6] As recently as fifteen or twenty years ago, in most underdeveloped countries the question whether, and in what sense, they were faced with a problem of excessive population growth was still a subject of controversy.

Only in the censuses around 1960 was the fact firmly established that the populations of practically all underdeveloped countries were growing at a yearly rate very much higher than recently assumed. Now that rate is approaching 3 percent in most countries, and in some an even higher percentage.

For example, India's First Five Year Plan (1951–56) assumed a rate of population growth of 12.5 percent per decade, that is, less than 1.25 percent a year. This assumption was retained in the Second Five Year Plan (1956–61). The 1961 census showed a rate of 21.5 percent for the decade 1951–61, or some 70 percent higher than the estimate relied upon only five years earlier.

The Draft Third Five Year Plan (1961–66) assumed then a population growth of 2.2 percent per year, but by

1961 the Planning Commission was forecasting a growth rate by 1976 of no less than 2.4 percent compounded annually. Later forecasts—if not counting on rapid results of the policy efforts to spread birth control among the masses of people—give still higher future growth rates.[7]

The experiences in most other underdeveloped countries have been broadly similar, though somewhat differently placed on the time axis.

The demographic mechanism of this dramatic change of the population trend is simple. Mortality rates have declined so rapidly as to have no historical precedent, while fertility rates have remained, on the whole, at the very high levels that seem to have prevailed as far back as any reliable estimates exist. The rates of natural population increase have therefore gone up suddenly and rapidly, reflecting to the full the decline in mortality.

The explanation cannot be sought in any improvement in the levels of living of the masses, as these levels have not changed appreciably. Nor have there been advances in education or attitudes toward hygiene great enough to have had much influence on morbidity and mortality.

It is commonly accepted that *the cause of the decline in mortality has instead been the great advances in medical technology,* based on recent scientific discoveries. This new "non-conventional" medical technology has made available effective and very inexpensive means of curing and preventing a number of fatal diseases which have been rapidly applied in all the underdeveloped countries.[8] It was particularly efficient in preventing and sometimes curing a number of infectious diseases which, while they took a heavy toll of life in underdeveloped countries, had already been almost exterminated in the developed countries by the earlier "conventional" medicine.

Further advance is to be expected. The true levels of mortality in underdeveloped countries, as reflected, for instance, in life expectancy at birth, are still considerably higher than in developed countries, even though the crude birth rates often have come down to comparable levels because of the higher concentration of the populations in younger age cohorts.[9]

But after the successful elimination of malaria and with other similar public-health campaigns, advance will be slower. To control other diseases, more active participation of the populations will be needed. The great scarcity of medical personnel, equipment, clinics, and hospitals must be overcome, which is expensive and takes time. And in order to provide a safe water supply, sewerage, and drainage, heavy investments have to be made.

These efforts, and a higher level of personal hygiene, are particularly important for bringing down infant mortality rates. It should perhaps be noted that, contrary to what is often assumed from a false analogy with the more recent development in the developed countries, the decline in mortality has usually not been particularly pronounced for infants.[10]

A study of the various factors that determine fertility—including the improved health conditions of women of childbearing age—would, rather, point toward a rise in fertility, if contraceptive practices were not to spread further.[11] And a study of fertility differences within and between countries in South Asia as well as other indicators lead to the conclusion that there is little likelihood of a considerable decline in fertility due to a spontaneous spread of birth control.[12]

These conclusions from a study of one of the regions can probably be generalized to have validity for most countries in the underdeveloped world.

It is important to stress that *the fall in mortality is largely "autonomous,"* in the specific sense that it is not connected with any preceding or concomitant rise in incomes and levels of living or any other conditions of life, except the new medical technology and its application.

The *high rate of fertility is also "autonomous"* in the same sense. In the absence of determined policy measures to spread birth control among the masses, fertility will remain at its high level.

At this point we meet the dictum of the demographers that, in the long run, deaths and births must again approach balance. If fertility cannot be adjusted downward to the new, lower levels of mortality, mortality must rise again at some future time. This thesis is sometimes presented as a simple inference from demographic logic.

But it assumes what we will presently come to discuss, viz. that the present population trend, if not reversed, is bound to thwart development efforts and lead, in the end, to a progressive deterioration of incomes and levels of living. At a certain point, mortality will no longer be "autonomous" in relation to levels of living.

The Malthusian checks—and particularly, intensified hunger and diseases—will at that point again come progressively into operation. What the application of modern medical technology has accomplished, in other words, is merely to have lowered in a radical fashion the level of living where the Malthusian checks begin to raise their heads—that is, to have made these checks inoperative except at levels of income and living which are much lower even than those now prevailing.[13]

In a society constantly undergoing short-term alterations of all economic conditions it is not likely that stagnation and an ensuing retardation will be apparent as a sudden turn which can be identified with a definite point of time. Only in retrospect will it be possible even to specify a period during which—with some intermittent ups and downs—economic development efforts were entirely frustrated. It is, indeed, not impossible that future historians looking back on what is now happening in a country like India will identify these recent years, or some years not far in the future, as that period—if fertility does not decrease substantially and very soon.[14]

One corollary of the present autonomous character of mortality is that mortality statistics become a deficient measure of morbidity and the general health situation in a country, though they are commonly used for this purpose. Even aside from all the non-fatal diseases and debilities, it is conceivable that a large part of a population may be diseased, or at least lacking in normal vigor, all or most of the time, even though rates of mortality are still decreasing and life expectancy is increasing. It is even conceivable that people live longer only to suffer debilitating conditions of ill health to a greater extent than before.[15]

Before we go further it is necessary to spell out one rigid value premise for our study: *any attempt to depress population growth is restricted to work on the fertility factor.* Complacency about or even tolerance of a high level of mortality because it slows down population growth is simply not permissible.[16]

This value premise is presented here for what it is: a moral imperative for population policy. It also has a utilitarian foundation. Besides all the human unhappiness caused by ill health and premature death, they are costly. Ill health is also among the important causes of low labor utilization, since it prevents people in the underdeveloped countries from working as much, as hard, and as well as they would be able and willing to do if they were healthy.

Part of the effect of a decline in mortality is, however, to increase population growth. But a high child mortality rate is generally assumed to be one of the factors upholding fertility. If more children were to survive, parents would be less eager to give birth to additional children.

Like all categorical norms of public ethics, this moral imperative may tend to become a more relativist precept when it must compete for scarce resources for its realization. But even that admitted, preventing and curing diseases will in the somewhat longer run become an ever more important policy goal in underdeveloped countries. And the international community, in this case represented by the World Health Organization, will continue to press forward in this direction.

In any case, the ethical norm to preserve life is strong enough that it would be out of the question for population policy to be formulated in terms of increasing death rates. When we now turn to discussing the economic effects of population development, it is these effects as they differ when fertility differs that become the problem, holding mortality constant or, rather, outside our analysis.

To begin with, we need to clear the decks by deprecating some of the approaches commonly applied when dealing with this problem of the economic effects of population development.

One model, widely used in both the scientific [17] and the popular literature, is a straight application of the postwar approach, reasoning in terms of investment, output, and the capital/output ratio, investment regularly being assumed to be physical investment. The model pretends to demonstrate in a simple way the adverse effect of population increase and even to measure it in terms of what is sometimes called the purely "demographic investment" needed to prevent a decrease of average incomes.

With some variation in the numerical values chosen, it is expressed in this standard form:

If population increases by 2 percent annually, and if the marginal capital/output ratio is 3 to 1, 6 percent of the national income must be saved and invested per year in order to maintain the present level of income per head. If it is then desired to increase income per head by 2 percent per year, another 6 percent of the national income must be saved and invested.

This kind of mechanistic and schematic analysis gives the appearance of knowledge where none exists, and gives an illusion of precision to that pretended knowledge. As this type of reasoning is typical of so many other applications of the postwar approach, I would like specifically to refer to *Asian Drama*, Appendix 7, Section 2 (p. 2066), where the logical and factual mistakes implied are pointed out.

Another type of theoretical approach, which is now and then encountered in the discussion of the population problem in underdeveloped countries, centers around concepts like "population optimum," "optimum population growth," "overpopulation," and "underpopulation" (when these last two terms are defined in relation to "population optimum," which is necessary to give them a definite content). This approach is also logically inconsistent, in addition to being inadequate to reality in underdeveloped countries.[18]

All concepts and theories stated in terms of "population," pure and simple, are misleading also because they do not take into account the changes in age distribution which inevitably accompany a primary change in fertility rates.

Basic to our analysis of the economic consequences of population trends is the fact, demonstrated in a classic work by Ansley J. Coale and Edgar M. Hoover,[19] that a decline in the fertility rates would have no substantial influence on the size of the labor force in underdeveloped countries for almost a generation. Its impact on the number of consumers, however, would be immediate.[20]

There would be fewer children to support. If the lower fertility were maintained, this decrease in the dependency burden would continue until the children began to reach working age. The decrease in the population of children would be progressive if the decline in fertility rate were gradually intensified.

A couple of decades hence, when the depleted age cohorts would have reached adulthood, there would also be a decline in the relative number of people in the reproductive age groups. Still further ahead, if fertility were stabilized at a lower level than the present one, the age distribution would also tend to become stable—at a lower dependency ratio than the present very high one.

This *change in the age structure of the population is the major reason why a decrease in fertility would make a people less poor.*[21] The income per head would increase.

A secondary effect of the ensuing higher consumption levels would be to raise labor productivity by increasing both labor input and labor efficiency. This effect would be most pronounced in the poorest countries and in the poorest sections of all underdeveloped countries, where particularly low levels of nutrition and of health and educational facilities depress participation, duration, and efficiency of work more than elsewhere.

Moreover, at progressively higher levels of income per head, more could be saved and devoted to direct investment, and the government could squeeze out more in "forced savings" through taxation or other means. Both forms of saving would, after some initial delay, tend to increase income per head still further with cumulative effects similar to those of the initial rise in income per head due to lower fertility.

We should, in addition, reckon with more subtle effects of the rising levels of living. The great poverty among the masses in underdeveloped countries must account, at least in part, for their fatalism, their apathy, and their unresponsiveness to efforts to change attitudes and institutions, to spread modern technology, to improve hygiene, and so on.

These effects of a decline in fertility to raise economic levels, operating through the changed age structure, are very considerable and they are cumulative, gaining momentum over the years. One important thing to stress is that *they are independent of the man/land ratio.* The same causal mechanism must operate in sparsely as well as in densely populated countries.[22] "It is a false claim," the new President of the International Bank for Reconstruction and Development, Robert S. McNamara, stressed in his first address to the Boards of Governors, "that some countries need more population to fill their land or accelerate their economic growth."[23]

The other line of causation proceeds through changes in the size of the labor force. One brute fact already alluded to has to be faced: those who will be of working age fifteen or twenty years hence are already born or will soon be born. And, as realistic calculations demonstrate, even thereafter a decline of fertility from now on will not make much of a difference in the size of the labor force for a considerable time. *Till the end of this century, the labor force in the underdeveloped countries will continue to increase by about 2 or 3 percent annually,* reflecting present and earlier high levels of fertility.[24]

The consequences, for policy and planning, of this continued rise in the labor force which cannot be prevented have been discussed in Chapter 4 above. In most underdeveloped countries industry cannot realistically be counted on to absorb much more than its present share of the labor force during the next decades, the time perspective of realistic planning.

As further increasing the underutilized crowds in the tertiary urban occupations cannot be desirable, and anyhow has its limits, there can be no question of an actual decrease in the size of the agricultural labor force, or of its stabilization at a higher level.

The aim of the agricultural policy must under these circumstances be to raise labor utilization, and to do so while the labor force is increasing rapidly. The main obstacle to such a development is the institutional conditions, particularly in regard to landownership and tenure, fortified by the political power situation in underdeveloped countries. It has also been pointed out that the growth of the labor force by itself tends to join all the other changes that are now worsening the inequalities in the social and economic stratification and to make them more rigid.

In countries where a larger part of the labor force is already employed in modern industry, as in some Latin American countries, further industrialization can imply a bigger rise in industrial employment. The rise in the agricultural labor force would then be smaller.

And it should be easier to raise labor utilization in agriculture, when much new land can be brought under cultivation, as again in most countries in Latin America and also in Southeast Asia, some countries in West Asia, and Africa. The cultivation of new land, however, usually requires organized migration, clearing and settlement, often large public investment in irrigation or drainage, and, prior to all this, a determined and foresighted government and an efficient administration.[25]

The depressing effects of the rise in the labor force are inevitable for about a generation ahead—though they can be counteracted, or more than counteracted, by a radical and effective agricultural policy. We should at this point recall that the effect of a decline in fertility would immediately be to raise average incomes and levels of living; it would also in many ways help to raise labor utilization and productivity.

It would thus counteract—and if speeded up perhaps more than counteract—the tendency of the continued rise in the size of the labor force to have adverse effects on labor utilization and productivity.[26] For this reason it is urgent to take measures to spread birth control as soon and as effectively as possible. Other reasons are the interest in bringing down during the next generation both the reproduction potentialities and the prevailing rate of the increase in the labor force. This can happen only by bringing down fertility now.

By referring to *Asian Drama*, where these things are discussed in greater depth, I have here presented only a summary discussion of the economic effects of a decline in fertility. One note should be added. The attempts to put the problem in the form of a neat quantitative model, by expanding the simplified model built on the capital/output formula referred to above, do not stand up to criticism.[27]

Any such model would have to be very much more complex in order to be logically consistent and adequate to reality in underdeveloped countries. With the present dearth of empirical data, indulging in this type of model-building does not seem to be a rewarding endeavor.

But even a treatment in terms which for the time being cannot be very precise leads, I believe, to the conclusion that *a consideration of the economic effects of different population trends should give the governments of under-developed countries strong reasons for instituting, as soon and as vigorously as possible, policy measures aimed at getting birth control practiced among the masses of the people.*

II Policy

The experience of the developed countries cannot be very relevant in judging what can happen in regard to fertility or what policies ought to be applied in the under-developed world today.

In the developed countries birth-control practices spread spontaneously even to the masses of people. But that did not happen until levels of living, education, and rationality of attitudes had risen much higher than they have in underdeveloped countries today and much higher than those levels can be expected to rise within a foreseeable future. Indeed, without a spread of birth-control practices, the rise of levels of living and the spread of all the other modernization elements will be severely retarded.

In recorded history we have never seen birth control being spread widely in largely rural, tradition-bound, illiterate, and very poor populations. *What underdeveloped countries are in dire need of accomplishing is something as unprecedented in the world as the rapid fall in mortality and the ensuing population explosion have been.*

The reason why such a task should not, offhand, be deemed impossible springs from two very important advantages in the initial situation of underdeveloped countries when facing the birth-control issue, as compared with the situation of the developed countries when starting a similar movement.[28]

For one thing, *underdeveloped countries today can make the spread of birth control public policy.*

In developed countries birth-control practices had to spread by "private enterprise" in the individual families, not to say "subversive activity," as these changes in behavior of the population met with concerted resistance from public policy and from all the forces of organized society working through the church, the administration, the school, the press, the medical profession, and legislation.[29]

Strong forces of determined public resistance against the spread of birth control, and also its succumbing to private decisions within the families to act against public policy, have been the common pattern in Western countries and in all the developed Communist countries. The differences as to when on the time axis this happened—that the masses of individuals began to revolt against public policy—seem to have had little to do with ideological and even religious dissimilarities among countries and social groups within a country, and to have been mainly related to levels of education, rationalization of attitudes, and structural changes of society, all correlated with economic levels.

In diametrical contradiction to what once happened in the now developed countries, the underdeveloped countries will have to take a political decision actively to effect the spread of birth control among the masses of people. Otherwise birth control will not spread.

The second advantage of the underdeveloped countries today is that *they can from the beginning distribute technical contraceptives.*[30]

When birth control spread spontaneously in the West, conception was prevented mainly by *coitus interruptus*— and this was, in all likelihood, the case in the European Communist countries as well. In all Western countries there was, indeed, legislation to counteract the availability and sale of technical contraceptives. In some of these countries those laws are still on the statute books.[31]

Due to intensive research—most of which was carried out in the United States by research institutions, in the first hand those under the Population Council, that began their work years before the United States government dared to condone aiding underdeveloped countries to spread birth control—*birth-control technology has had, and is having, a virtual breakthrough* that has already made available more acceptable and effective contraceptives. This research is rapidly proceeding further and is now officially supported.

The intra-uterine contraceptive device (IUD), the pills, and the inoculations, preventing conception for a certain period of time, are already available. Pills and inoculations that will be effective for a longer period are on the verge of being invented. The discovery of how to make sterilization reversible, which increases its applicability and acceptance, is also well on the way.

This new contraceptive technology is undoubtedly of greatest importance for the carrying out of a public policy to spread birth control among the masses. One reminder should be made. Particularly now, when the Western developed countries have entered the scene as ardent supporters of such a policy in underdeveloped countries, *it will never be possible to recommend and use a contra-*

*ceptive technique there which is not accepted and used in
the developed countries.*

There will always be nationalistic intellectuals in an
underdeveloped country who then would protest against
their people being used as guinea pigs. All dreams about,
for instance, radically lowering fertility through the spread
of chemicals in the drinking water have to be given up
as entirely illusory, besides being inhumane and incon-
siderate.

The population explosion has been by far the most
important social and economic change in the underdeveloped countries in recent decades, far more important than
any policies or planning up till now. In the decades ahead
the spread through public policy of birth control using
the new technology may be an equally important change.

But the difficulties should not be underestimated.
Among the governments and, more broadly, all the articulate in the upper class who influence public policy *there
are in underdeveloped countries inhibitions against adopting a public policy to spread birth control and, in particular, against their pursuing this policy with vigor.*

Some of these inhibitions are of a religious nature.[32]
Even if, as is commonly observed, there are no explicit or
clearcut strictures against birth control in the scriptures
of the major Asian religions, Hinduism, Buddhism, and
Islam, the priests and religious leaders—especially, but
not exclusively, on the popular level—are apt to feel mis-
givings about a practice that seeks to free people by
artificial means from their prescribed destiny. They may
even see this practice as sinful.

Officially, the Catholic Church, of course, still persists
in its prohibition of birth control by technical means—
which until a few decades ago was even more firmly upheld by the Protestant churches. The Church's opinion has
importance for the governments in Latin America and the
Philippines. The Communists have taken the same line,

though stressing more than the Catholics that birth control is not necessary if a determined development policy is carried out.[33]

A main cause of the rapid decline in recent years of resistance on the part of the Catholics and the Communists against birth control is undoubtedly the fact that, in spite of the official censorship by the authorities, it had been spreading rapidly among their own adherents in the developed countries. But the recently revealed population explosion in underdeveloped countries, and the clear necessity for lowering birth rates in these countries in order to make sustained economic development possible, have at the same time made the continuation of an adverse position toward birth control more and more impossible for both Communists and Catholics, as for all other religious groups.

But there are many other inhibitions making governments hesitate to come out forcefully for a public policy to spread birth control.[34]

Some of these inhibitions are in the nature of false or exaggerated beliefs about facts. In countries with a low man/land ratio, such as Indonesia and most African and Latin American countries, it is continually argued that they have no population problem or sometimes even that they need a high birth rate in order to develop.

They then often forget what it costs to settle people and to give them employment and how long it usually takes. And they forget the effect of a lowered fertility in raising all economic levels, beginning immediately, which we characterized as the main effect of the spreading of birth control.

One belief—which, however, is not entirely groundless —is that it is very difficult or even impossible to influence people's behavior in so private a sphere as their sexual behavior, particularly when they are poor, illiterate, and tradition bound. The failure of India's family-planning policy during the first three five-year plans to have any appreciable effect on fertility easily leads to that conclusion.[35]

In order not to fall prey to sheer defeatism, this belief is often combined with the illusory idea that birth control will spread spontaneously as the levels of living begin to rise.

When the upper classes in Latin American countries, and consequently their governments, have been reluctant to lay down a public policy to spread birth control among the masses, it is probably more because of false beliefs of the types exemplified than because of the position taken by the Catholic Church.

But the Church can undoubtedly, and perhaps more effectively, produce obstacles among the masses against their accepting birth control and thus decrease the effectiveness of a policy directed toward getting them to do it. If the upper-class groups who determine government policy believe that, this will support their inhibitions.

As usual, beliefs are opportunistic. They are ordinarily rationalizations in the interest of prejudices and expediency. But beliefs can be purged, even though bringing facts into the open and analyzing them in rational terms meets resistance. The strongest force for getting the policymakers' beliefs corrected is, of course, the population explosion itself and its easily observable effects.

But it should be realized that the flight into opportunistic and false beliefs must be very tempting, particularly in underdeveloped countries. Their governments are burdened with all sorts of pressing political worries. They operate in a perpetual crisis, as do in fact all governments, though those of underdeveloped countries much more.

To look very far ahead and shoulder a huge policy task, in addition to coping with all the immediate problems, must be uninviting, particularly as the population issue is

almost everywhere controversial.[36] To avoid controversy
whenever possible is the natural desire of every government.

Even assuming that the government of an underdeveloped country overcomes the inhibitions to decide upon
a vigorous policy for spreading birth control among the
masses, *this policy meets very great obstacles among those
masses.* The government will have to attempt to make
millions of individual couples change their most intimate
sexual behavior. Their motivation in regard to breeding
children must be induced to become rationally intentional
and to change in a radical fashion. And the new motivations must effectively control their behavior, not on a single occasion only but according to a sustained pattern.

And this must occur in populations that are very poor,
illiterate or semi-illiterate, often with impaired health and
vigor, and mostly living in static, traditional, and stagnant
communities with an inegalitarian and rigid social and
economic structure, all of which breeds fatalism and
apathy. The birth-control policy must reach the masses
of people to have the desired effect.

During the period of hesitation and experimentation
in regard to population policy a large number of studies
of the receptiveness of people to the message of birth
control have been carried out in many parts of the underdeveloped world, and particularly in South Asia, often by
agencies from the West or with their participation, though
they are not conclusive.[37]

The general impression from these studies is, however,
that there is very commonly an initial sympathetic attitude
toward accepting birth control, reflecting a vague desire
to limit the number of births. But a positive and decisive
will strong enough to motivate the requisite effort to avoid
incurring a new pregnancy and to persist in that behavior
does not usually follow.

In this ambivalence lies the essential difference between

the situation in underdeveloped countries today and in developed countries at the time when birth control was spreading there. It is this ambivalence that policy must overcome. This is, of course, being made easier by the IUD and will be more so by the pills and inoculations when they become effective for a longer period, making one decision enough to prevent conception for that period.

The government of an underdeveloped country must accomplish tremendous things in order to carry out an effective policy of spreading birth control.

First, it must realize the overwhelming importance for its development planning of bringing down fertility, it must overcome the inhibitions referred to above, and it must make *a firm decision to take action by instituting a vigorous public policy to spread birth control.*

About the countries in South Asia it can be said that they now either have taken that decision or are on the way to doing so. But in West Asia, Latin America, and Africa only a very few countries are in the position where their governments have definitely made up their minds and taken a firm decision, though in most of them private organizations are active, sometimes with a measure of government recognition and support.[38]

To effectuate a decision when taken, the government must, secondly, *build up an administrative apparatus for the purpose.* The distance is long between the bureaucracy in the capital and the individual families in the villages or the urban slums. This is particularly true in large countries like India and Pakistan,[39] which just because of their population size weigh so heavily.

Administration, particularly on the lower level, is not the strong side in underdeveloped countries, which are all "soft states" (see below, Chap. 7). When, as in India and Pakistan, goals of bringing down fertility have not been reached, this is often due to the fact that the administrative apparatus has been faltering.[40]

Implied in this second requirement of a sufficient and effective administrative apparatus is, thirdly, *the need to deploy a large staff of medical and paramedical personnel.* For many reasons this staff must often be female. Regularly they must speak the language of the people, which, in a country like India with many languages, narrows the range of those who can be used.

To meet this third requirement must be particularly difficult as such personnel are exceedingly scarce in underdeveloped countries and are also badly needed for their regular curative and public-health duties. Many, particularly among the doctors, cluster in the cities, serving largely the needs of the urban upper class. And they and all the others are difficult to get out into the villages.[41] The scarcity of medical personnel is a particular hindrance if reliance is placed on sterilization and, perhaps even more, on the insertion of IUDs.

There are recent reports from many underdeveloped countries that the retention rate of the latter devices has been lower than expected. The cause of this is that not enough attention has been given to their application and even less to the possible adverse effects in perhaps a quarter of the cases (bleeding, cramps, or backaches).

Every such case increases the rumors that the IUD is dangerous. This will cause more women to take it out, even if it has not been disturbing to them. It then becomes more difficult to gain the popular support necessary for more widespread use of these devices.

Among countries that have encountered these difficulties on a large scale and are far from reaching their targets is India.[42]

The important thing to stress at this point is that all these things must be accomplished by the governments in the underdeveloped countries themselves. There is indeed very little the developed countries can do by means of aid and technical assistance.

The common clamor—in very recent years—in the press and popular discussion in developed countries, repeated very often by their officials and politicians, that when giving aid they should give highest priority to spreading birth control in underdeveloped countries, often reveals a lack of understanding of the true dimensions of the task and of where the responsibility must rest.

To begin with, the government itself of an underdeveloped country has to reach a firm decision to undertake to spread birth control as public policy. But certainly it should mean something that the United States and other developed countries, as well as the World Bank and the other intergovernmental organizations, now take an increasingly positive position on such a policy.

And while in regard to agricultural policy their position has for diplomatic and other reasons more and more become a support for a reactionary policy in underdeveloped countries (see Chap. 4, Sec. III, above), in regard to population policy they have in recent years come out in favor of radical reform.

This is the reason why in this case even a certain pressure on underdeveloped countries in the population issue can be condoned. When the World Bank in its outlook on the underdeveloped world gives high priority to population policy, it implies not only a preparedness to give aid in order to facilitate such a policy which necessarily cannot amount to much (see below), but also that the Bank in all its dealings with underdeveloped countries, and through its missions, will continuously stress the urgency of their embarking upon a radical population policy.

It is, however, useful for retaining a perspective on this problem to recall *how late in the day most developed countries came to their present insight into the problem of population policy.*[43]

In the various organizations of the United Nations an unholy alliance between Communist and Catholic countries—including the Latin American countries—thwarted any practical and effective approach to the population problem in underdeveloped countries for a long time. These organizations are still prevented from engaging in "operational activity," that is, anything other than research and planning.

Even predominantly Protestant countries like Britain and the United States time and again yielded to the pressure of their Catholic minorities. It was for a long time left almost entirely to the Lutheran and more secularized Scandinavian countries to stand for birth control in underdeveloped countries—as well as at home—and also to give some assistance unilaterally.

In the United States, President Dwight D. Eisenhower's administration had as late as 1959 to back away from a committee report that in cautious terms suggested that some aid under the military assistance program could, upon request, be used for family planning.

Not until 1963, under the personal leadership of President John F. Kennedy, was a policy set forth that enabled the government to assist underdeveloped countries in planning and research on population policy. Only in the Johnson era was United States policy entirely freed from all inhibitions.

As I have already mentioned, not only the Communists but also the Catholics are now changing their stand. The recent Papal Encyclical against birth control is probably causing only some delay in the reorientation of the Catholic countries. And as the Communists are changing just as quickly,[44] the intergovernmental organizations should also be set free to sponsor birth control in underdeveloped countries.

But it should also be understood that this new enthusiasm in all the developed countries for spreading birth control in the underdeveloped world, coming as late as it does, must often cause ironical thoughts, particularly in

India, that so early had embarked upon a population policy.[45] Nehru was often very blunt in giving vent to such ironical thoughts.

Sometimes the reaction will be more critical than ironical. The intellectuals in underdeveloped countries, as everywhere else, have difficulty in distinguishing between "large" and "great" and are often under the "number illusion." [46]

Undoubtedly the now flourishing interest in the rich countries in reducing the population increase in the poor countries sometimes produces a backlash effect by supporting the inhibitions in the latter countries against undertaking a firm policy at home for that purpose.

This reaction can sound almost bitter if it is observed that the rich countries at the same time decrease their aid for health work. In United States' aid activity, health programs have for several years been quietly downgraded or phased out in most densely populated underdeveloped countries, while the family-planning programs have been pushed up. When the total aid budget has been decreased continuously (Chap. 11, below) while more and more funds are now spent for family-planning purposes, this development may be looked upon as natural.

Medical experts, however, are increasingly raising their voices against this development.[47] And they can point to the fact that improving health has important effects for raising labor utilization and for making poor people more responsive to development efforts generally, and also that, in particular, a decline in infant mortality is almost a condition for spreading birth control (see above).

Besides keeping up and increasing the aid for health work in underdeveloped countries, such backlash effects in these countries should certainly not be counteracted by an adjustment to a more diplomatic manner of arguing and writing, least of all in texts with scholarly pretensions. But I believe it is very important that both students and officials understand and give expression to the tremendous difficulties underdeveloped countries meet when embarking on a policy to spread birth control.

It should be clearly understood by all concerned that the contributions which the developed countries can make to the implementation of birth-control programs in underdeveloped countries, either unilaterally or through the intergovernmental organizations, are relatively limited.

The most important item has been and will remain research, in particular research aimed at perfecting the available techniques for birth control. Demographic and economic research is important also, mainly for public enlightenment and for overcoming the inhibitions of governments in underdeveloped countries against feeling the urgency of inaugurating a firm population policy. Financially, research of both types is rather inexpensive.

The difficult task of building up the administrative apparatus needed to give effect to a decision to embark upon spreading birth control among the masses must necessarily be the responsibility of these countries themselves. There are some countries which can make use of some expert advice on this matter.

But having seen many useless or even unfortunate results of that type of advice-giving to underdeveloped countries, often rendered without a thorough knowledge of the specific and very different conditions in these countries, I would urge governments to be wary in giving advice. Financially it does not amount to much aid anyhow.

Some aid can be given in the training of medical and paramedical personnel, but this again cannot be on a large scale, particularly as all developed countries have a shortage of such personnel themselves. And for reasons of language they can seldom substitute for the indigenous personnel in the field.

Developed countries can give, as grants, the contraceptives—and this is at present happening on a fairly large scale. But those are very cheap and many countries can produce them at home. If we then add jeeps, medical instruments, etc., as an item of aid, we have completed the list.

The really big contribution from developed countries is the research on the new birth-control technology which has been going on and is continuing. In the United States, as we have seen, it was begun through the support of private foundations, long before the government made up its mind on the matter.

In pointing out how relatively little the developed countries can do—except in the field of research, by educating the public, and by exerting pressure on the governments of the underdeveloped countries—it is of course not my intention to warn against their doing as much as they can. I want, rather, to stress *how very much the underdeveloped countries must do themselves and how urgent it is that they do it rapidly and vigorously.*

This is the rationale for presenting the subject in this part of the book where I discuss the need for radical reforms in the underdeveloped countries.

Chapter 6

EDUCATION

I Introductory Observations

The conceptual framework for a study of education in the underdeveloped countries should be almost as free from *logical* difficulties as that for the analysis of demographic facts.

How many people are literate and how many children attend school, and for how many years, are straight and seemingly unambiguous questions. Neither does the quantity or even the quality of available educational facilities —school buildings, teaching materials and implements, teachers, etc.—raise that type of logical objection which we have encountered when criticizing the postwar discussion of "economic" problems.

When nevertheless *the educational statistics are probably even less satisfactory than statistics in almost every other field pertinent to underdevelopment and development,* the explanation is, in part, an astonishing carelessness in stating and applying clear definitions, though they should not be too difficult to conceive. In part, also, it is simply the great scarcity and often the absence of comprehensive observations and calculations.

In both respects there are opportunistic interests best

served by having the actual situation unrevealed or at least presented in a way that does not raise thoughts about the need for a radical change of educational policy.

In the literature on the educational situation and development in underdeveloped countries two concepts are given a primary role: literacy and enrollment.

To define literacy and to standardize the definition for international comparisons should not seem to be difficult *per se*. To have the definition applied by the census-takers and understood by the persons questioned are admittedly difficult practical tasks. But more meaningful and correct statistics could be produced on literacy.[1]

To give one example of how completely unreliable statistics on literacy can be, I may refer to the seemingly impressive rise in literacy in all age groups of males above thirty years of age in India between the two census years 1951 and 1961.[2] The recorded rise of each age group was uniform. That type of rise in literacy is inconceivable, however.

Even if there had been an extensive and efficient adult education effort—which there had not been—it too, like more schooling, must have had its effects concentrated in certain age groups. This is obvious and should have given rise to a critical appraisal, if not in India itself at least by UNESCO, which disseminates and comments upon these statistics. It should be added that the Indian statistics on literacy cannot be suspected of being less accurate than those in most other underdeveloped countries.

Figures for literacy are, however, widely quoted without questioning, particularly by economists now venturing into the field of education. For many reasons it must be assumed that *literacy figures for underdeveloped countries generally overestimate the actual spread of literacy*. But a UNESCO writer believes the opposite.[3] Nowhere are any serious attempts made by international or national authorities or by individual students to check the published figures even for a restricted area, though such a test should be easy to perform.

The second main concept employed in the discussion of education in underdeveloped countries is enrollment of children in school.[4] It is commonly, innocently, and uncritically assumed in the literature that the published figures for enrollment are fairly accurate and that these figures— sometimes given as a percentage of total population even disregarding the skewed age distribution in underdeveloped countries—measure the extent to which children attend school. Often very optimistic judgments about the educational situation in an underdeveloped country and the recent improvement of it are based on the enrollment statistics.

How unreliable enrollment figures can be may again be illustrated by an example: according to the 1961 census of Pakistan less than 15 percent of the children aged five to nine attended school, while according to the enrollment statistics about 30 percent were enrolled in the slightly different age group six to ten. And then it must be remembered that in Pakistan pupils in primary classes attached to secondary schools, perhaps more than 20 percent of all pupils, are not in the enrollment statistics for primary schools.[5]

That type of statistical discrepancy is probably particularly prevalent in Pakistan, which in the South Asian region is in the bottom rank in regard to both educational achievements and economic levels.[6] But a scrutiny reveals that very generally *the enrollment figures give an inflated account of school performance,* if by that is meant the extent to which children actually attend school, which is, of course, the important question.

The bias works most strongly for primary schools and more strongly for girls than for boys. As this bias toward inflation of the statistics on enrollment is most accentuated in the very poor countries with the least satisfactory educational situation, such as Pakistan and India, the published statistics tend to underestimate the existing difference between very poor and less poor countries in the region. The same is true of differentials within the individual countries.

In other words, the rate of school attendance for girls, children in rural areas, and generally children in poorer districts and countries becomes more inflated when measured by the enrollment statistics. If we had information on class differentials, we would undoubtedly find not only that the enrollment figures are lower for the children of poor families but also that their lower figures are more inflated.

In *Asian Drama* I made my own estimates on the crucial magnitudes: actual school attendance and retention rates at the end of a stage of schooling. Besides using enrollment figures, I based my estimates on all scattered information I could find in official and unofficial discussion in these countries. These estimates are, of course, extremely uncertain. But they are probably better than the figures based on the enrollment statistics. They also call attention to the really relevant problems and thus constitute a challenge to improve the official statistics.

In my opinion *a major prerequisite for rational planning of the radical reform of the educational system in underdeveloped countries that is urgently needed is very much improved statistics, focused on the crucial questions.* It should have higher priority than, for instance, even demographical studies. This is why I have begun this chapter with a few remarks on the educational statistics.

That education is a very important factor in the development process has always been understood by educationists and historians. It was also seen by economists from the time of the classical authors on.[7] But in line with the biased postwar approach it was largely forgotten by the economists when they began to study the development problems of underdeveloped countries. This was a general consequence of their non-concern about attitudes, institutions, and the productivity consequences of very low levels of living, to which educational facilities belong.

A group of economists have in recent years rediscovered the importance of education to the development process. This by itself was a laudable venture.

But as I pointed out in Chapter 1, they then merely widened the concept of capital investment in their superficial development models to include, besides physical investment, also "investment in man," which was identified with education. A consequence was, however, that it was then treated in the form of financial expenditures having a financial return.[8]

The situation is somewhat paradoxical. While most of the actual planning in underdeveloped countries, and most of the economic literature, continues to be based on the notion that physical investment is the engine of development, there are today an increasing number of economists who denounce that view and regard development in underdeveloped countries as primarily an educational process. But they then immediately fall back into line with the biased postwar approach by confining that process in the shackles of financial and fiscal planning, the inadequacy of which was pointed out in Chapter 1.

Applications—questionable as even they are [9]—of this approach to measuring the financial return of expenditures on education have been made for some highly developed countries. In no underdeveloped country does the available statistical material permit so much as an attempt at that type of application.

The "theory" has simply been transferred by analogy from these studies in highly developed countries to the underdeveloped countries with their very different conditions in all respects. Usually the general assertion that the thought contained in this approach is even more important in those countries is added to the analogy. Without any possibility of quantification, this newest variation of the postwar approach has thus remained merely a general and indefinite dictum on the great importance of education for development. For valid reasons it has hardly ever been utilized in any real research.

Even though this recent approach has thus remained in the sphere of vague generalities, it does imply certain assumptions which are unwarranted and of a nature to operate as opportunistic blinkers in research. Education is thus assumed to be a homogeneous magnitude, measurable on the cost side in terms of financial expenditures. But as shown in considerable detail in *Asian Drama* and also stressed below, *the main reforms needed in education in all underdeveloped countries are of a qualitative nature.*

They concern, first, not the quantity of education, least of all as simply measured by the financial expenditures. The emphasis should be on the distributional spread of the educational inputs among districts, social classes, and the two sexes. Reforms should also concern what is taught, with what intention, in what spirit, and with what effect, for instance in regard to willingness to perform manual work. Unfortunately much education in these countries is now even plain miseducation and apt to raise impediments for development.

More generally speaking, the investment-in-man model implies, like the simpler capital/output formula, that prevailing attitudes and institutions and various items in the levels of living other than educational facilities are of no consequence for the problem, and that the effect of all other policy measures applied at the same time can be disregarded in the study of education.[10]

As these assumptions are logically inconsistent and inadequate to reality, *this extended capital/output model blocks the way to realistic and relevant research.* Though the formula has been left entirely without content of empirical knowledge, particularly on the output side, it operates in conformity with the entire postwar approach as a complex of opportunistic biases of the type characterized in Chapter 1. This is, of course, why it has become so popular in both underdeveloped and developed countries.

II The Heritage

My intensive study of educational problems has concerned that huge part of the underdeveloped world that I have called South Asia; the results have in considerable detail been published in Chapters 29 and 31–33 of *Asian Drama*.[11] The condensed treatment of these problems in the following pages will also be focused on the countries in that region, with only brief comments at the end of this chapter on underdeveloped countries in other regions.

The colonial era ended by leaving the masses of people mostly untouched by any formal education.[12] This holds true particularly for the largest countries in the region, India, Pakistan, and Indonesia. They entered their time of independence with a very low rate of literacy, probably far below one fifth of the adult population.

In the Philippines the Spanish priests and monks of various Catholic orders, closely collaborating with the civil authorities, had for centuries been an important element in spreading elementary education while also sponsoring higher educational activities.[13] The colonial authorities of the United States in its short time as a colonial power in these islands, differing from the English, the Dutch, and the French in other parts of South Asia, likewise placed major emphasis on education of the people.

That Ceylon and parts of Southern India also entered the independence era with a comparatively high literacy rate was again partly due to the activity of Christian missionaries, here using the vernacular language, although in Ceylon the Buddhist tradition of the monastery schools also played a major role. In Burma and Thailand it was almost entirely the latter educational factor that explained the higher literacy levels in those countries.

With all the diversity hinted at above, *the most severe handicap of the new nations as they emerged from colonial rule was the ignorance of the masses of their populations.* To a varying degree all colonial powers had made some significant contributions to education in their dependencies. But their main interest—with the exception of the Americans in the Philippines—had not been to educate the people and prepare them for development. Their objective was to train clerks, minor officials of all sorts, and, particularly in the British colonies, higher administrative functionaries and, to some extent, professionals.[14]

For this purpose secondary schools (usually with preparatory elementary schools attached) and tertiary schools were promoted. It is important to stress that this bent of interest was thoroughly shared by the upper strata in the colonies, who were eager to avail themselves of the opportunities to profit by serving their masters.

These elite schools were regularly of a "literary" or "academic" type—what is now in the region called "general" —even more than in the metropolitan countries themselves at that late time.[15] Little attention was given to science and still less to technical subjects. When schools of medicine and engineering and other training institutes were later established, they departed only slightly from this "academic" pattern.

Students commonly expected—and were expected—to become "deskmen," not soiling their hands. This and the policy of giving a pronounced literary and academic character to all schools were also in line with the colonial powers' disinterest in encouraging indigenous manufacturing industry in their territories.[16]

Again it should be pointed out that this direction of secondary and tertiary education perfectly agreed with the cultural pretensions inherited from precolonial times and the deep prejudice against any type of manual work of the indigenous upper strata in the colonies, then as well as now. The methods of teaching, having students listen, read, and memorize without encouraging them toward critical thought or toward taking an interest in self-education outside or beyond the school, were, indeed, even more an inheritance from precolonial times which colonial influence merely continued to uphold.

More generally, by building up an educated elite while neglecting popular education, *the colonial governments helped to preserve and make more insuperable the barrier between an entrenched upper class and the masses of people.* And it was the hereditary aristocracy and the upperclass strata generally who sent their children to the secondary schools and the colleges.

The fact that the language used by the elite class in their work and often in their social life was foreign tended to raise the class barrier still higher, particularly as only in the Philippines did the colonial authorities—first the Spanish and later the Americans—ever envisage making the foreign language the *lingua franca* of the whole people.

In Chapter 3, I talked about the mechanism that almost automatically led a colonial power to seek its support from the privileged strata and even to create new privileges in order to secure support. Indeed, from the point of view of the colonial powers, the educational system was "functional," It was "functional" also from the point of view of the upper class in the colonies that could exploit the advantages offered.

One further observation should be added. *The entire school system was in colonial times dominated by the colleges,* giving a general, non-professional tertiary education required for entering public service.[17] This was one aspect of the disinterest in popular education.

Importance was placed on passing examinations and acquiring status, while practical training for life and work was ignored. This spirit dominated, above all, the teaching and learning in tertiary institutions. But it was transmitted to the secondary schools where the main objective was to make certain that the students would be equipped to pass their entrance examinations for college. The primary schools, in turn, were imbued with the necessity of preparing pupils for entrance to the secondary schools. This is part of the explanation why education on all levels became "general," "literary," and "academic" in character. This development came particularly to stamp the school system in the British colonies, but was hardly less prevalent in the Dutch and French possessions or in Thailand.

The resulting character of education on all levels has not changed much in the independence era, least of all in India, Pakistan, or even Ceylon. As the Indian Secondary Education Committee explained:

> The dominating influence of University requirements on the one hand, and the . . . present methods of recruitment [for public service] on the other, have had an adverse effect not only on healthy development of secondary education but on the whole field of education in the country.

The Committee noted that India's educational system is "examination-ridden" and that "the dead weight of the examination [at the top level as throughout the school system] tended to curb the teachers' initiative, to stereotype the curriculum, to promote mechanical and lifeless methods of teaching, to discourage all spirit of experimentation and to place the stress on wrong or unimportant things in education." The ten years that have passed since the Committee presented its report have not seen any great change.

In various ways the low standards in education are thus related to the examination system. But that, in turn, is related to the inherited class character of education. Students and parents, as well as administrators and teachers, have resisted proposed changes in the curriculum at all levels and especially proposals that would give greater emphasis to technical and job-directed training at the secondary and tertiary levels.

The effective demand for education comes from the "educated" and articulate upper class, and they have retained most of the political power in the local, provincial, and national governments. The "examination craze" reflects not only the undue influence of the tertiary institutions on the lower schools but, primarily, the concern over status in an inegalitarian and still largely stagnant society.

Wherever there was much of a liberation movement in South Asia, educational reform stood high on the agenda.[18] In India efforts toward such a reform were even begun in the latter decades of the colonial era when Britain permitted a considerable amount of provincial self-government, specifically in the educational field.

When independence was won, Nehru and leaders in several other countries insisted that *the entire system of education must be "revolutionized."* [19] But this is exactly what did not happen in India or in the other South Asian countries, except perhaps to an extent in Ceylon. The principal reforms of the system as it was inherited from colonial times remain largely unaccomplished even today.

One of India's most distinguished educationists, J. P. Naik, later Member-Secretary of the Education Commission, expressed this in 1965 in the following words:

> What has happened [in India] in the last sixteen years is merely an expansion of the earlier system with a few marginal changes in content and technique.

The explanation is, of course, that *the winning of independence has not worked great changes in the people or in their society.* The educational establishment is part of the larger institutional system which includes the social and economic stratification, the distribution of property, and the power structure. A revolution of the educational system would assume that which is often mistakenly said to be what these countries have been going through: a social and economic revolution (Chap. 3, above).

Indeed, *even the outer structure of the school system has been preserved.* The continual domination of education at all levels through the examination system of the colleges, preparing students for entrance into public service, has already been noted.

As a part of the legacy from colonial times many of the schools on all levels, including colleges, are private, though mostly aided from the public purse.[20] This raises grave problems of direction, inspection, and control, and generally impedes reforms of the school system.

These problems have not been solved in any of the South Asian countries with one exception, Ceylon, which some ten years ago decided upon a coordination of all but a very few private schools which preferred to renounce any aid from the state. The purpose was to guarantee "a more equitable distribution of the available facilities and contribute toward providing equal educational opportunities for children from all parts of the island."

When in Kerala, India, the first Communist provincial government enacted legislation in order to take a step in the same direction, it was met by violent demonstrations and later thrown out of power by the central government in New Delhi, inaugurating presidential rule. The Kerala government's action had followed a general recommendation of the Planning Commission in its Second Five Year Plan, but that did not help. Neither does it help that such an assertion of state authority over the school system is taken for granted in all developed countries, in many of them for a century or more.

Another legacy from colonial times is the tuition fees ordinarily levied in both public and private schools.[21] Here again Ceylon is different. It has adopted the principle of free education in all schools, including those on the tertiary level, except for the very few private schools that have chosen to remain unaided. More generally, education in all other South Asian countries is also gradually becoming free in the primary schools which are public.

These observations, and in general the faithful conservation of the school system as inherited from the colonial era, testify to its great inertia as an institutional structure. The system embodies strong vested interests on the part of the administrators, the teachers, the students, and, above all, the families in the powerful upper class who do not want to undermine the bolstering of their positions provided by the inherited school system.

There has been, however, one reform idea continually expressed with seemingly great determination and practically never contradicted: the *extension of popular education and the liquidation of illiteracy.*

According to the statistics from the early 1960's—the last available—the literacy rate in South Asia [22] varies in rather close correlation with the economic levels of the several countries.[23] Pakistan, the poorest country in the region, claimed less than one third of the males over fifteen years of age as literate and only 6 percent of the females. For India the corresponding figures were around 40 and 13, and for Indonesia around 60 and 30. The figures for Burma, which may be the least accurate of all, are around 80 and 40.

In the upper range of economic levels, Ceylon had reached above 80 and 60, respectively, and Malaya [24] should not be far behind, though the statistics available are from the late 1950's. In the middle range Thailand also gave figures around 80 and 60 and the Philippines about 70 for both sexes. The poorer countries but not always the poorest ones (and Burma) showed substantially lower figures for the rural populations as compared with the urban.

I have quoted these figures for literacy, mostly compiled from census reports, as they may give a very broad idea about the rank order of the countries in South Asia, though Burma and probably Thailand are placed too high. More generally speaking, as I have pointed out, there are reasons for the greatest suspicion not only of the accuracy but also of the meaning of these statistics. In most cases they exaggerate the level of literacy, and very much so if to this term is attached any notion of "functional literacy" in the meaning of the literates being able to make their literacy useful to any degree in their life and work. All literacy definitions are given in terms of ability to read and write. It is clear, however, that ability to reckon should be equally or more greatly needed in most life situations.

To liquidate illiteracy was in India a main point in the liberation movement.[25] Since independence it has been consistently retained. All the other South Asian countries have at several regional conferences joined in expressing the same goal.[26]

The elevation to highest significance of the goal of reaching general literacy of the whole population as soon as possible represents the main—and almost the only— break with the elite ideology from the colonial era. It is in agreement with the modernization ideals, adopted as value premises for our study for reasons explained in Chapter 1.[27]

Literacy is needed for acquiring higher skills in all occupations, including agriculture, and for developing more efficiency in all the various types of local and functional cooperation which governments are trying to foster. It is, indeed, essential for acquiring more rational attitudes in all human relations.

It is true that merely "mechanical literacy" is of little significance for a country, as was stressed by UNESCO during the long period when that organization played down literacy and propagated "fundamental education" or "social education." [28] But literacy cannot be put on a par with all the other good purposes of popular education, as it is primarily an instrument whereby the other skills can be acquired.

It is sometimes held, however, that what underdeveloped countries need in the first place for economic development is an increase in secondary education, even if this means a slowing down in the expansion of primary and adult education. In spite of its emphasis on development, this view, which has a certain following among Western experts, conforms rather closely to the old colonial pattern of providing the highly educated elite with an attached lower rank of technical personnel functioning as subalterns, even at the cost of leaving the population at large in a state of ignorance.

Against this way of reasoning it can be pointed out that experience shows it will tend to lead not to a development of the whole national economy but merely to enclaves within an economy that for the rest may remain stagnant. *Any attempt to create an integrated nation with wide participation of the people assumes a more widespread literacy.* That an approach to effective political democracy would have the same prerequisite is clear.

If general literacy were thus accepted as the goal to be reached as soon as possible, we must inquire how the policies actually adopted square with that goal.

For a long time UNESCO and most underdeveloped countries, among them those in South Asia, continually defined the goal as "universal literacy through free and compulsory education." They have, in other words, seen the means of reaching the goal to be increasing the number of children who go to primary schools over a long enough period of time to assure literacy.[29]

This formula implied, however, that *the South Asian countries downgraded adult education,* particularly literacy classes.[30] This is in my opinion a grave mistake.

UNESCO itself has indicated that only if each year a

considerable number of the illiterate adults are given an opportunity to take a literacy course are there good prospects for the eradication of illiteracy within a reasonably short time. *Adult education not only should be more important in underdeveloped than in developed countries, where almost all are literate, but poses quite different problems.*

For another thing, *adult education, with emphasis on literacy, should help to make the school education of children more effective.* All the information we have suggests that children of illiterate parents tend to fall behind in scholastic achievement and that they more easily lapse into illiteracy.

The detrimental effects of an illiterate home and village setting begin in the preschool years, and these are singularly formative years when attitudes are shaped that will tend to persist. Also, illiterate parents are usually less inclined to enroll their children in schools and to keep them there, a fact that helps explain the many dropouts and repeaters in primary schools, particularly in the poorer countries, districts, and classes where the literacy rate is low,[31] a problem to which we shall return.

In most of the South Asian countries there are organizations working to stimulate adult education, and the matter is not entirely bypassed in most of the Plans. But not much has come out of it. In India, J. P. Naik in 1965 characterized the situation as follows:

> The liquidation of adult illiteracy is the most important programme of national development and on it depend several other programmes such as agricultural production, family planning, etc. *This sector has been criminally neglected* and it is extremely desirable to undertake a large-scale programme in this sector and to liquidate mass illiteracy in a few years—five or ten at the most. [Italics added.]

Later, the Education Commission (1964–66) endorsed these views of its Member-Secretary and made far-reaching practical policy proposals. And in the preparation of the Fourth Five Year Plan—which in the temporary eclipse of planning in India was never brought further than to the draft stage—adult education was calculated to be allotted twelve times as much; its share in the total outlay on education to be raised from 1.4 percent to 5.6 percent. These radical proposals have since then been quietly buried.

To an extent Indonesia is an exception. Indonesia has also shown a rather remarkable speed in increasing literacy from one of the lowest levels in the region. Even in the Philippines there has been, almost from the time when it was an American colony, a somewhat greater interest in adult education.

On the whole, this criticism is valid for practically all underdeveloped countries in "the free world." Though in this book I do not usually make comparisons with the Communist orbit, it should be noted that the countries there follow a very different pattern. *When a country becomes Communist, a vigorous campaign is usually waged to make the whole people literate within a few years.*

There should be nothing sinisterly Communistic about this particular policy. It has its historical origin in the practice of rebellious students in Russia during the latter decades of the Czarist regime who went out into the villages to teach the peasants to read, write, and reckon. When they grasped power the Communists took over this practice and made it official policy. They finished off the literacy campaign that in Russia was then already approaching universal literacy, at least in the younger generation.

W. S. Woytinsky, in his book on India, recalls experiences in Russia during his youth and reflects:

> We noticed nothing similar to that crusade in India. We heard complaints about mass unemployment among young graduates of the universities, but we could get no answer to the question: "Why cannot a million of them be mobi-

lized for rural teaching?" Such a mobilization would be possible if Indian intellectuals felt the urgency of primary
education for the villages as keenly as did the Russian
intellectuals in the days of my youth.[32]

The answer to Woytinsky's question is that the young
intellectuals in India and in most of the rest of the non-
Communist underdeveloped world have been so conditioned by the rigid elite and class structure in which they
have been brought up that they do not feel that deep
identification with the poor in their nation which the Russian intellectuals felt. They do not feel it even when in
some countries they are radically indoctrinated. This is
merely one example of the destructive influences of the
fortified class society inherited from the colonial era.

Without entering upon the problems of the "peace
corps" organized not only in the United States but also
in some other Western developed countries, it should be
pointed out how fantastic the very idea must be in the
host countries. Young educated people in the Western
developed countries are being organized in teams and sent
to the underdeveloped countries many thousands of miles
away, very often to go out into the villages to assist and
teach the poor masses. Meanwhile, graduates from schools
in these latter countries themselves would not think of
doing the same, but rather prefer to crowd together in the
cities as "educated unemployed" [33] or press their governments to swell their administrations in order to create
"suitable" jobs.

One thing is certain: *without a fundamental change of
attitudes on the part of the "educated," a large-scale adult
education campaign in the underdeveloped countries is
not possible.* The universities themselves should be engaged in the effort. This, incidentally, would benefit both
the teachers and the students by bringing them nearer to
the acute problems of their countries and so giving to
both their studies and their lives more of a purpose and
meaning.

Assuming that such a fundamental change could be brought about, one could dream about the way in which a large-scale adult education program in an underdeveloped country with much illiteracy should be organized. *It would be unwise simply to take over methods and practices from the Western countries,* where adult education has an altogether different function and a different type of student.[34]

There may be need for entirely fresh approaches. The whole pattern, transmitted from the urbanized countries in the West, of segregating children in schools and then perhaps having "classes" for adults should be questioned. It is quite possible that a program of teaching families or whole communities together would be more effective.

But the basic question remains: How is it possible to do anything substantial in the field of adult education before the increasingly inegalitarian social and economic structure in most of the underdeveloped countries is broken down by radical reform or revolution? This is a problem parallel and similar to the one we raised in Chapter 4 about how the lack of an agrarian reform creates inhibitions and obstacles for agricultural advance.

III   The School System

As, on the whole, efforts for teaching adults were pushed aside—which also, of course, was well in line with the vested interests of the school bureaucracy—the literacy goal was then translated into *a program for rapidly enlarging the intake of children into the primary schools.*[35]

The Indian constitution of 1950 bravely stipulated that within ten years' time compulsory, free education should be the rule for children up to fourteen years of age. In 1951 the Indonesian government set as its goal universal elementary schooling by 1961.

The other countries in South Asia were somewhat more

cautious, in spite of their already having higher literacy levels for the most part and more primary schools. But in the so-called Karachi Plan of 1959, the ministers of education of the Asian member states of UNESCO agreed to the provision of not less than seven years of compulsory, universal, and free primary schooling as a target for 1980.

There is no point in criticizing most of these countries for falling far behind these unreal schedules. Their difficulties in enlarging the intake of the primary schools are simply tremendous, particularly in the poorer countries. Generally, to provide elementary schooling for all children is in South Asia a much more burdensome project than in the developed countries. For one thing, children of school age form a much larger percentage of the populations.

For another, the South Asian countries, and particularly the poorest among them, do not have much of a foundation on which to build. They start out with a considerably smaller proportion of their children in school. And there is at the start less of everything needed to run schools: school buildings, teachers, textbooks, writing paper, etc.

But there is another and more valid criticism to make. Although the declared purpose was to give priority to the increase of elementary schooling in order to raise the rate of literacy in the population, what has actually happened is that *secondary schooling has been rising much faster and tertiary schooling has increased still more rapidly.*[36]

There is a fairly general tendency for planned targets for increased primary schooling not to be reached, whereas they are overreached, sometimes substantially, as regards increases in secondary and, particularly, tertiary schooling. This has all happened in spite of the fact that secondary schooling seems to be three to five times more expensive than primary schooling, and schooling at the tertiary level five to seven times more expensive than at the secondary level.[37]

Even more remarkable is the fact that these tendencies

are rather more accentuated in the poorest countries, Pakistan, India, Burma, and Indonesia, which start out with many fewer children in primary schools and which should have the strongest reasons to follow out the program of giving primary schooling the highest priority. It is the poorer countries that are spending least, even relatively, on primary education.[38]

These considerations have been based mainly on the enrollment statistics, but also on fiscal data that are, unfortunately, utterly uncertain. But, as has already been pointed out, enrollment figures tend to overestimate school attendance very much for primary schools, although less for schools on the secondary levels. These figures are also more inflated for the poorest countries where enrollment is lowest.[39] For both these reasons *the true lag of increase in primary schooling, compared with targets and, still more, compared with the general program announced, is in the poorer countries even bigger than appears in the enrollment statistics.*

When this happens, it implies that the school system has been allowed to follow a conservative laissez-faire line, letting a swelling stream of pupils through the established channels without interfering other than by trying to enlarge those channels where the pressure in society is greatest.[40] Those who can exert pressure are students and parents in the upper class. The higher types of schools cater more to the upper class, and this is particularly true in the poorest countries. Here we see again how the school system is determined by the inegalitarian economic and social stratification and the unequal distribution of power.

A comparative study of educational advance in the several South Asian countries leads to the conclusion that *the differences in attainment of goals are rather closely correlated with economic levels.*

The two small, relatively least poor countries in the region, Ceylon and Malaya, have now reached a situation

where by far the larger number of children not only enroll in the first grade of primary school but attend school
and do so to the end of that stage. They are indeed rapidly
approaching a level of primary education for children comparable with that in the developed Western countries a
few generations ago.[41]

In Pakistan and India, on the other hand, and generally
in the poorer countries, somewhat fewer children enroll
in the first grade of primary school. Much more important,
however, is the very high rate of what in the region is referred to as "wastage" and "stagnation." Children who have
enrolled drop out early or do not attend school regularly.
If they do not drop out they then become repeaters, which
is often a prelude to dropping out.[42] Ordinarily less than
half of those children who originally enroll complete primary school in the regular way. The primary school is also
of shorter duration in most of the poorer countries.

*Those children who do not complete primary school, as
well as many who do, have not attained much functional
literacy.* In an environment where most adults are illiterate, they are also in danger of losing what literacy they
have acquired.[43] The Indian Education Commission in its
report of 1966 concluded that

> ... the system of primary education [in India] continues to
> be largely ineffective and wasteful and many children who
> pass through it either do not attain functional literacy or
> lapse into illiteracy soon afterwards. If we are to continue
> our dependence on this programme alone for the liquida-
> tion of illiteracy, we may not reach our goal even by 2000
> A.D.

In Pakistan the situation is considerably worse. While in
India probably not many more than one child in three ever
enrolls in and completes a course of primary education, in
Pakistan only one in six does. Burma falls somewhere between. In the Philippines and Thailand, where relatively
more children enroll in the first grade, the wastage per-

centage continues to be very high. Indonesia stands somewhat better, though not much.

Irregular attendance, repeating, and dropping out represent a huge waste of resources. If the total expenditure for primary schools were expressed in terms of cost per child who successfully completes primary school, the cost per pupil would be much greater than is commonly accounted for. Unfortunately, the cost per pupil so calculated would be particularly high in the poorer countries and the rural districts. *The wastage is greatest where it can be least afforded.*

Far too little attention is given to this problem. The legislation dealing with compulsory education in most of the South Asian countries is almost nowhere enforced.[44] Particularly in the poorer countries and the poorer districts a general lack of efficiency and discipline permeates the whole school system.

There are practically no statistical or other comprehensive studies to measure the availability of the various facilities which have a bearing on the quality of education in the primary schools in South Asia.[45] The impression from casual observations and from scattered information in official reports and in the rather extensive literature, however, is that *the availability of school buildings, textbooks, writing paper, and all kinds of teaching aids is limited everywhere in South Asia. But the situation is much worse in the poorest countries and in all countries worst in the rural districts where the greatest number of children in the region grow up.*

The availability of adequately trained and motivated teachers is an even more crucial precondition for effective teaching in the primary schools.[46] *All the countries in South Asia operate with a large number of teachers classified as "untrained."* Taking into account the presently available facilities for training teachers, only the Philippines and perhaps Ceylon and Malaya may be able, within the next decade or so, to substitute trained for all untrained teachers—if the capacity of teacher-training schools is not more rapidly increased than now planned.

The classification of teachers as "trained," moreover, has to be viewed with the greatest suspicion. Most of them, particularly in the poorer countries, are not well trained in any sense of the word. The trained teachers also tend to be concentrated in the cities and, more generally, in areas with high literacy.

In India and still more in Pakistan, differing in varying degrees from Ceylon, the Philippines, Thailand, and even Indonesia, *the salaries of teachers in primary schools are exceedingly low and their social status depressed.* In turn this has negative effects on professional recruitment and on their acceptance and performance, particularly in rural areas. Again we see a broad correlation between relative economic levels in the several countries and districts and the functioning of the inherited school system.

In the poorer countries in particular *there is an urgent need for improvement of the teacher-training schools* and, at the same time, for a rise in economic and social status of teachers in primary schools which would encourage talented young people to enter the profession and increase the possibility of the teachers influencing the children and the community.

Improved teacher training would assume a number of things difficult to accomplish rapidly in a poor country: better school preparation before entering the training schools, often a longer period of training, and above all a radical reform of their curricula and, indeed, the whole spirit in which they operate. Raising the salaries meets particular difficulties in the poorer countries, as the teachers' salaries, though so extremely low, represent a very large percentage of total school costs—mainly because so little is spent for equipment and other teaching facilities.

Even at the primary level, *the complex linguistic situation in South Asian countries has serious implications for teaching.*[47] It so happens that the two very large countries which are also the poorest, India and Pakistan, meet the greatest difficulties because of the need to teach several languages—and scripts—in the primary schools, often by teachers who are not very proficient in any one of them.

However good the political reasons might be for this multi- or bi-lingualism of the schools in these very large countries, where national consolidation and popular participation in government assume it,[48] it has rightly been called a "roadblock to educational progress." "The curriculum of any child is bound to be congested on the linguistic side before anything else is learned." The schools are for this reason—and in line with an evil tradition from precolonial and colonial times and under many other severely limiting conditions—becoming much too "bookish," even though very few books and little writing paper are available to the pupils.

In India, Gandhi's intention to make the curriculum more oriented to the life in the community and to incorporate elements of manual work has not been successful. And the basic schools that in diluted form have been started are mostly shunned by the upper-class families.[49]

In the poorer countries and the poorer districts, where by far the greatest number of children in South Asia grow up, the situation in the primary schools must be described as almost desperate.

Instruction in secondary schools [50] begins with the serious handicap that the pupils have generally not been given a satisfactory preparation. This handicap is greater in the countries where the extent of primary schooling is five years or less, that is, in Pakistan, most of India, and Burma.

The barrier to effective teaching created by the linguistic complexities becomes even more serious in secondary schools. Proficiency in languages becomes the yardstick of educational achievement; this is one reason why it has proved so difficult to transform the inherited "general" schools into schools of a more practical type.

No statistics are available on the physical equipment of secondary schools—buildings, libraries, science laboratories, and teaching aids, especially textbooks and writing paper. Judging from general impressions and scattered information in the literature, such equipment is, if not sufficient, at least superior in both quantity and quality to that of primary schools. Secondary schools are more often to be found in urban areas and their pupils come mostly from the upper class—in the wider sense of that term as defined in Chapter 3 above.

Still another impression is that the standards for physical equipment, as well as for qualifications of teachers, though generally low, are considerably higher in the countries that are on a higher economic level—especially Malaya and Ceylon—and, even in the poorer countries, in those private schools that cater mainly to the upper-upper class—in a queer English tradition often called "public schools."

Considering the damaging traditions inherited from colonial times, the poorly prepared pupils entering secondary schools, the largely unqualified and frustrated teaching staffs, and often the extraordinary burden of teaching several languages and scripts, it is not surprising that *the teaching in most secondary schools in South Asia does not measure up to high standards and that this holds true particularly in the poorer and larger countries.*

One dynamic factor holding back efforts to improve teaching in the secondary schools is the unprecedented and unplanned rapid increase of students in secondary schools already referred to. *Particularly in the poorer countries and the poorer districts this expansion has implied the lowering of already low standards in teaching.*

In spite of all efforts in the postwar period to orient teaching to practical life, to impart useful skills, and in particular to give more emphasis to vocational and technical education, *the great majority of all secondary schools in South Asia have retained the "general," preacademic, and literary character* established in the elite types of upper-class education in colonial times.[51]

In no country of the region are there signs that a radical change is under way. The increase in vocational and technical school enrollment—though mostly somewhat larger in percentage terms—has been small in terms of absolute numbers. And almost nowhere has the curriculum of the general secondary schools, where the larger part of the expansion has taken place, been modernized in any appreciable manner.

This may seem astonishing as there has been unanimous agreement among political leaders and experts that in this respect a radical change was needed—in British India even in colonial times such a demand had been raised in official reports for almost a century.[52] The explanation of this conservatism has a number of elements.

We have already noted the influence in this direction of the colleges and the examination system. To this is added the fact that there is actually a need for further preparatory general education of the pupils entering secondary schools, particularly in the poorer countries, with the shorter duration and lower effectiveness of their primary schools. As in primary schools, language study tends to crowd other subjects out of the curriculum, again particularly in the poorest countries.

An additional difficulty is the scarcity of persons who can teach technical subjects, particularly as they are also needed in government and industry where they can expect higher salaries and social status than in the schools. Moreover, instruction in science and technical and vocational subjects requires costly laboratories and other technical aids.

Added to all this is the heavy weight of tradition from colonial and precolonial times. The force of tradition is strengthened by the vested interest of all those employed in the school system, most of whom have good reason to resist change in the light of which their training and methods would seem less desirable.

More fundamentally, the dominating upper class, who are "educated" and articulate, feel a vested interest in maintaining the cleft between the "educated" and the masses. The fact that a more practical and vocational orientation of the secondary schools would often require participation in manual work, which is despised, and that they presumably prepare students for jobs where manual work is part of the regular routine, helps make such schools less popular than the traditional general ones.

The result is a persistent lack of trained personnel at the middle level of industrial management. Those graduates from the general secondary schools who do not continue to study at the tertiary level but who, in the colonial tradition, seek work as "clerks" are usually not even trained to meet modern requirements for that type of desk work, as they have no knowledge of shorthand, typing, filing, etc.

The situation is mostly not improving. As a recent Indian report notes:

> The maladjustment between the education system and the socio-economic needs of our developing economy has further increased. A result of this has been the increase in the number of educated unemployed side by side with the shortage of trained personnel.[53]

The expansion of tertiary education has generally been even more accentuated, not least in the poorer countries.[54] Again, tertiary education is suffering from insufficient preparation in the secondary schools, particularly in the poorer countries where the secondary schools are handicapped by the shorter duration of the primary schools and generally lower levels of efficiency of both primary and secondary schools. The linguistic difficulties are compounded on the tertiary level where functional ability to read and speak a foreign language—now usually English—is needed, though this need is seldom met in a satisfactory way.

In spite of huge investments in buildings, libraries, laboratories, equipment, and teaching aids, the rapid increase of students in these countries perpetuates low standards and, indeed, often reduces them further.[55] The quality of academic teachers is low and has often tended to deteriorate.[56] More than the secondary schools, the tertiary schools have a very high wastage percentage of students who never graduate.[57]

At the tertiary level even more than at the secondary, the schools should, of course, be job oriented and directed toward preparing the students for particular professions. Practically all experts, South Asian and foreign alike, complain, however, that *the tertiary schools continue to produce an oversupply of "generalists,"* who have been trained in the humanities, law, social sciences, and "academic" science, and who swell the ranks of underqualified administrators, clerks, and the "educated unemployed." [58] At the same time, more engineers, agricultural technicians, doctors, dentists, pharmacologists, and, not least, teachers on all levels are needed. With few exceptions, this holds true in all South Asian countries.

The situation has not improved substantially in the postwar period. All institutions of higher education have been free to expand their enrollment very rapidly; technical and professional education has been able to hold its own and, at best, to increase a little more rapidly.[59] By far the most important industry in the region, agriculture, is particularly disfavored.

The difficulties in changing the structure of higher education to meet development needs more adequately are similar to those already mentioned that hinder the efforts to make secondary schools vocational or at least more practical and less "academic": the higher costs of technical education in terms of buildings and equipment

and the difficulty of recruiting the teachers in competition with government and industry. The tertiary schools,
which usually charge rather high fees, have additionally
a financial interest in increasing their enrollments in the
arts and law, where the marginal costs per student are
low. Underlying all these difficulties, and inherited from
colonial times, are the traditional ideas of what upper-
class elite education should amount to.

IV   A Reform Program

One theme that has been running through the preceding account of the educational situation in South Asia is
the rather close correlation between the economic level
of a country and its achievements in the educational
field.

The two less poor countries, Ceylon and Malaya, are
well on their way to giving the whole child population a
primary education of six years. Ceylon in particular is
increasing the number of pupils who also receive a secondary education. Starting out with relatively higher
literacy rates, they are now approaching general literacy
in the younger generations. This should make it more
possible to eradicate that serious obstacle to equality and
development which has as its basis the disdain for manual
work on the part of the "educated." When being educated
is no longer a monopoly of a small upper class it should
be easier gradually to dissolve that class barrier based on
who performs manual work and who does not soil his
hands.

After the war Ceylon and Malaya started out with a
quantitatively less developed system of tertiary education
and a smaller percentage of high school graduates continuing in tertiary schools, which were generally on a
higher level. They relied relatively more on sending
students abroad for tertiary education. Both these coun-

tries are now rapidly building up their tertiary schools and keeping them at a rather high standard. As relatively more children are receiving secondary education, they are thus on the way to breaking through the wall of the upper-class monopoly of higher education. Ceylon in particular has taken a very important step toward democratizing education by making it free on all levels.

On the whole, however, they have as yet not been much more successful than the poorer countries in changing the tertiary education, and still less the secondary education, from the general to the practical and job-oriented type.[60] Even primary education has a curriculum that is unduly "academic." Undoubtedly a change away from the traditional general orientation of instruction in schools on all three levels, if it were courageously followed out, would speed up the eradication of the prejudice against manual work.

Except for children in these two small and less poor countries, the vast majority of children in South Asia either receive no schooling at all or terminate their schooling before they have established a lasting functional literacy. The Philippines and Thailand should, however, be able to emulate Ceylon and Malaya, if they succeed in decreasing the rapid and continuous wastage of dropouts. Indonesia, though relatively poorer, is somewhat better placed in regard to primary education, being the one country where, in spite of exceedingly inferior levels of planning and policy generally,[61] there has been relatively more popular enthusiasm for educational improvement.

The Philippines in particular excels in being able to give a very large part of its youth secondary and tertiary education. Though not always of high quality, this greater supply in the labor market of the relatively higher "educated" should in time counteract their unwillingness to do manual work. Dating back to the colonial era under the United States, the Philippines has also striven to give teachers and schools a higher and more central position in the life of the communities, has shown more interest in attempts to improve and modernize teaching, particularly on the primary level, and has even made a little more advance in adult education than all other countries in the region except Indonesia.[62]

Though all these countries mentioned have policy problems in education not yet solved, the problems are compounded and magnified in the poorest countries of the region, Pakistan, India, and Burma. Together they contain by far the larger part of the population in the region. In considering the policy conclusions I will have this larger and poorer part of the region in mind primarily, but in various particular questions many of the conclusions will have bearing on the other countries mentioned.

Part of the explanation of the less fortunate educational situation of the poorer countries is simply and directly their poverty. There are fewer resources to place at the disposal of educational policy. But the problem is more complicated. These countries are also more inegalitarian, with wider chasms between an educated upper class and the masses.

In Chapter 3, I referred to a causal interrelation between poverty and inequality. *Monopoly of education is —together with monopoly of ownership of land—the most fundamental basis of inequality, and it retains its hold more strongly in the poorer countries.* It does so even when attempts are made to widen the availability of popular education.[63] The mechanism is the class bias in the operation of the wastage, which in the poorer countries also is greater: dropouts, repetition, and failures in examinations.

Among the fewer children in the less poor countries that are enrolled in the first grade of primary school, girls, children from rural areas, and generally children from the most disadvantaged families are less well represented. Irregular attendance, repeating, and dropping out then occur most frequently in these categories. Only a small percentage of all children complete primary school, which is ordinarily of shorter duration and lower quality in the poorer countries and particularly in the poorer districts.

Thus, even at this early stage of education, a severe process of selection is at work which, on the whole, tends to exclude the less privileged groups. This helps to explain why such a high proportion of those who finish primary school can go on to secondary school. The dropouts in secondary schools and later the failures in matriculation examinations imply a further selection along the same lines. Of the still smaller proportion of an age cohort who matriculate, again the majority enter tertiary schools. Once more the pattern is repeated: the relatively fewer pupils from families in the lower social and economic strata are more often the dropouts or fail more often in the examinations for graduation from the tertiary schools.[64]

In this mechanism of selection there are several economic and social operative factors at work, including home environment.[65] The difference in the home environment of the few well-to-do and "educated" families and that of the much greater number of lower-class families is enormous; it is far greater than in the advanced countries. Even if the schools were excellent there would be serious problems attendant upon the children of the poorer families entering schools, remaining in them, and succeeding.

The result is an inbuilt bias strongly favoring the upper class and fortifying its monopoly of education. P. C. Mahalanobis, thinking particularly of higher education in India but aware of the fact that the bias starts at the primary level, observes:

> By and large, it is the rich people who have the opportunity of giving their children the type of education required for posts of influence and responsibility in the country.

He continues:

> ... the power and privileges of a small group of people at
> the top tend to be not only preserved but strengthened. ...
> This has created an influential group of people who natu-
> rally desire to maintain their privileged position and power.

J. P. Naik, giving reference to a particular study, concludes:

> ... the largest beneficiaries of our system of ... education
> are boys, the people in urban areas, and the middle and
> upper classes.

And in another context:

> Educational development ... is benefitting the "haves"
> more than the "have nots." This is a negation of social jus-
> tice and "planning" proper.

And the *Report of the Education Commission 1966*
stressed:

> The social distance between the rich and the poor, the edu-
> cated and the uneducated, is large and is tending to
> widen. ... education itself is tending to increase social seg-
> regation and widen class distinctions. ... What is worse,
> this segregation is ... tending to widen the gulf between
> the classes and the masses.

The situation is not different, but worse, in Pakistan,
though there is less sophisticated discussion of it. Both
these countries have a small, highly educated upper-class
elite; at the same time the masses in these countries have
had little or no education. The ignorance of the masses
stands as a complex of serious inhibitions and obstacles
for economic development holding these countries down
in poverty. At the same time, the harsh inequality in
these countries—stratified and continually strengthened
through the virtual monopoly of the upper class on education—tends to emasculate reforms meant to democratize
education.

We have in the preceding pages seen this mechanism
of upper-class power in operation: when, in contradiction

to the announced aims, adult education has been played down; when the more expensive secondary and, in particular, tertiary education has been permitted to expand much more rapidly than primary education; when the reform efforts to make schools on all levels less "general" and, on the two higher levels, more practical, technical, and job-oriented have been frustrated, and so on. Before going on to enumerate the main policy conclusions which have already been anticipated in the statements on deficiencies, I felt the need to stress the operation of this *mechanism of upper-class power in an inegalitarian society where the masses are very poor.*

Educational reforms are most needed there, but also meet there the greatest resistance. So little power belongs to the poverty-stricken masses. These masses remain inarticulate and passive. Neither individually or collectively are they alert to the need for educational reforms. Like the idea of "the revolution of rising expectations," their "hunger for education" is largely a myth, a reflection of how well-to-do Westerners and South Asians feel they themselves would react if they had to live in such miserable conditions.[66]

I began this chapter by stressing the need for more reliable statistics, focused on the crucial questions. But enough is known—partly summarized above and presented in greater detail in *Asian Drama*—to make it possible to state the main policy conclusions in their broadest outlines.[67]

In support of my conclusions, I would like to refer especially to the Indian *Report of the Education Commission, 1966,* one of the most distinguished examples of the continuation in independence time of the glorious tradition of honest, comprehensive, and penetrating public investigations in British India. The Report was available so late that in *Asian Drama* I could only utilize it for footnote references. But it strengthened very much my reliance on the conclusions I had reached by independent research.

One major conclusion is the need for radical change in the entire educational system.[68] As the Indian Report stresses:

> Indian education needs a drastic reconstruction, almost a revolution. . . . This calls for a determined and large-scale action. Tinkering with the existing situation, and moving forward with faltering steps and lack of faith can make things worse than before.

This holds true for Pakistan and Burma as well as India, and also, though less emphatically, for the middle group, Thailand, Indonesia, and the Philippines.

Much of the current effort to integrate educational policy in the Plans has been rather pointless.[69] It has even tended to draw attention away from the major development interest in raising the literacy levels of the whole population. What is most urgently needed is *planning of education itself as an integrated whole.*[70]

The first requirement is *to maintain and raise the quality of education and, in any case, not to permit an expansion that is not real or that is detrimental to quality standards,* as has been the rule during the whole independence era.[71] As the *Draft Outline of the Fourth Five Year Plan* (1966) points out:

> The expansion of numbers has . . . been accompanied by a certain deterioration in quality. . . . It is obvious that in the immediate future larger and more effective attention has to be paid to factors like consolidation, quality, diversification, terminalisation, and work orientation than has been the case so far.

The second requirement, which largely concurs with the first, is the need to keep a balance between the three stages of education and, in particular, to give reality to the priority that primary education has been awarded in the programatic pronouncements. This requirement should imply *calling to a halt the more rapid increase in enrollment in secondary and tertiary schools or even decreasing it.*[72]

Inasmuch as the South Asian secondary and tertiary schools produce an oversupply of "generalists" there is no reason why technical, vocational, and professional training should not be increased substantially within the present or even a somewhat smaller secondary and tertiary education system—providing more teachers, agricultural extension workers, and medical personnel, to point out only a few of the fields where more trained young people are urgently needed.

Fewer admissions to the secondary and tertiary schools should also make it possible to maintain higher levels of preparation and ability in the students admitted to secondary and tertiary schools and thereby decrease the great wastage of repetition, dropouts, and failures. It should generally permit the attainment of higher quality standards by these schools.

More resources should then become available for primary education. But even so, and considering in particular the present scarcity of well-trained teachers, it should be seriously considered to *reduce for a time, the pressure to increase the number of children who enroll in the first grade.*[73]

Two interrelated purposes should then be easier to attain: one, the raising of the miserably low quality of all physical school facilities in primary schools, and, two, intensive exertions to decrease the tremendous wastage of dropouts and repetitions. As the Indian *Report of the Education Commission 1966* stresses:

> ... the most important programme to be implemented at the primary stage during the next years is to improve the quality of education and to reduce stagnation and wastage to a minimum.

This reduction of the increase of enrollment in primary schools should, however, only be temporary and turn into a new expansion, as soon as the contraction and changed

direction of secondary and tertiary education has resulted
in increased resources for primary education, not least in
an increased number of better qualified teachers, and as
soon as a real advance has been made in reducing that
enormous leakage in the primary school system that is
caused by dropouts and repeaters. If it were prolonged,
it would postpone the length of time many poorer districts have to wait for opportunities to send their children
to primary school.

Throughout South Asia, and not only in the larger
part of the region which is very poor and is least advanced
in primary education, *there is a need for vigorous efforts
in adult education*,[74] both in order to speed the rise in
literacy and to support the exertions to keep children in
primary school and prevent their relapse into illiteracy.
These efforts should be closely related to and, indeed, be
an extension of the activity in the schools.

A crucial task in the reform of the school system must
be to *increase the number and qualifications of trained
teachers*.[75] The Education Commission continually stresses
that *a supreme aim of education should be to change the
attitudes of the children and, ultimately, of the whole
people*—"the values of the people as a whole." The Commission recognizes the need for a "social and cultural
revolution," oriented toward the ideals of modernization.
This would be a hopeless task without teachers who are
not only satisfied with their economic and social conditions and are accepted as intellectual and moral leaders
in their community, but who are also dedicated, enthusiastic, and imbued with the zeal to disseminate useful
and practical knowledge and with the will to advance.

From this point of view *the institutions for teacher
training are strategically important in educational reform.*
They should be the "power plants" that generate moral
and intellectual energy among their students to prepare
the people for development.

Planning and carrying out reforms along these lines imply *a firmer governmental control of educational institutions and an improved administration.*[76] In the region, only Ceylon is on the way to solving this problem.

Educational reforms along these lines require financing.[77] It is true that an essential element of the reform program should be to avoid the tremendous wastage of resources that now takes place. The curtailment of the quantitative expansion would in itself save resources, and to that extent raising quality standards and inducing more students to remain in the schools and succeed in graduating would be "self-financed." But to be really effective many of the reforms will undoubtedly require that a larger part of the national resources be allocated to education.

Even if there are reasons for believing that an improved educational situation is important for assuring and speeding up development, the effects can be expected to be important only after a lapse of considerable time. And to calculate these delayed effects in terms of a financial "return" is not really possible. The demand for more funds for educational purposes will therefore have to compete for priority with other demands, and in particular with those for physical investments where returns can be calculated and seen within a shorter time.

In the very poor and educationally backward countries we have in mind, the dominating upper class are already "educated" and get their children "educated." They feel no urgent need for the reforms.

And even though it would be possible to reach agreement in general terms on every point in the reform program sketched above, there is in the power structure of these countries a built-in resistance to the reforms. The preceding pages of this chapter, where the educational situations and trends were reviewed, should serve as an antidote to an assumption that the needed reforms can be easily decided on and carried out.

The Indian Education Commission asks for "a revolution in education" and believes, I think quite correctly, that this revolution, if it is really carried out, "in turn will set in motion the much desired social, economic and cultural revolution." [78] But the initial lack of the "social, economic and cultural revolution" itself represents a tremendous inhibition for giving an impetus to the "revolution in education." This dilemma is also inherent in the problems to which we shall have to return in Part Four on the politics of development.

The Indian *Report of the Education Commission* expressed its request for radical reform in the following way:

> We need to bring about major improvement in the effectiveness of primary education; to introduce work-experience as an integral element of general education; to vocationalize secondary education; to improve the quality of teachers at all levels and to provide teachers in sufficient strength; to liquidate illiteracy; to strengthen centres of advanced study and strive to attain, in some of our universities at least, higher international standards; to lay special emphasis on the combination of teaching and research in agriculture and allied sciences. *All this calls for determined and large-scale action.* [Italics added.]

At the end of the document in which the Commission had spelled out in considerable detail what this should imply, it reiterated that its report "is not a substitute for action."

As to a timetable, it concluded: "... *the future of the country depends largely upon what is done about education during the next ten years or so*" (italics added). In the four years that have already elapsed since the Report was published, the trend in Indian planning and politics has not gone in this direction. Nothing very different has happened in the other extremely poor countries in South Asia.

For other parts of the underdeveloped world I am not at present in the position to be as specific as in regard to

South Asia. A cursory study of the literature, however, confirms the impression that *almost everywhere there are broadly similar problems*—though with great differences of the type we have also noted within South Asia, particularly as between less poor and very poor countries.

Everywhere there is general consensus on the high national priority to be given to reaching universal literacy as soon as possible. Adult education is played down everywhere in the non-Communist world, however. Primary education has been expanding, but often at the price of low-quality standards. Wastage in the form of dropping out and repetition is common, particularly in the poorer countries and poorer districts, and is tending to increase.

Secondary education, and tertiary education in particular, have been permitted to expand more rapidly, often concomitantly with the sacrifice of quality standards and increase in the numbers of students who fail. Almost everywhere the efforts to change the curricula so as to make the schools less "general" and to direct secondary and tertiary education toward becoming more vocational and professional have been less than fully successful.

The distortion of educational efforts from commonly expressed general goals has its basis almost everywhere in a social, economic, and political stratification, giving a small upper class a dominant position. Status and degrees are given undue importance, reflecting the system of valuations in an elite society.

The historical background and many other conditioning factors are very different in Latin America, in West Asia, and in North Africa, and the considerable similarities in educational situation are for this reason surprising. The one unifying common trait is the political domination by a small upper class. The independent African countries south of the Sahara are still in a "becoming-born" situation, but there are more than exceptional signs of the establishment of an elite class structure in many of these countries.

The educational reforms needed in the underdeveloped world must all be fought for, planned, and acted upon in the underdeveloped countries themselves.

In regard to population policy, as in regard to health policy, I noted in Chapter 5 that the developed countries and in particular the United States have been in the position to aid the underdeveloped world very substantially by spurring a virtual breakthrough in the technology of birth control. In the field of education there is little scope for similar assistance.[79]

Health, sex, and birth control relate to simple biological phenomena. There exists a body of exact science about such phenomena, continually strengthened by new research which, in turn, forms the basis for an ever more effective medical technology that is applicable everywhere. In contrast, the educational problems concern people's minds and not only their bodies.

And their minds are conditioned by a very different culture which cannot, and should not, be obliterated. The problem of conditioning the traditional culture so as to make a place within it for modernization is a complicated one, raising the necessity for sophisticated new teaching methods and not for simply taking over those applied in the Western world.

In the educational field there is, therefore, no real counterpart to the technology of birth control which researchers in the developed countries could experiment with and then offer to the underdeveloped countries for immediate application. Conditions, and therefore people, are so different in these countries that Western educational experts have very few contributions to make in regard to educational methods.

There is, for instance, not only a greater need for adult education in underdeveloped countries, but adult education of a different type. Generally, the methods of educating young and old people have to be different and often have to be thought out anew. Educational experts from the West are, more often than in other fields, misfits in these countries—although usually not so bluntly as in John Kenneth Galbraith's novel *The Triumph,* which is now a best-seller in Latin America, drawing much laughter.

There are important exceptions to this, particularly when technology can be combined with financial assistance. The use of audio-visual aids, for example, can contribute to teacher efficiency, whatever the person has to teach and however he should do it. There are many other types of physical equipment for teaching, including books and paper, which could greatly aid the underdeveloped countries if placed at their disposal free of cost or at concessional prices. Sometimes aid to finance their production in these countries themselves would, however, be more in line with development.

One could even think of financial aid aimed at making it possible for the poorest countries to begin raising the salaries of teachers, which is such an important precondition for educational advance. As in these countries their salaries are largely consumed in the form of food, it would even be possible to give food aid in this direction.

Even financial aid to improve educational facilities more broadly could be important. Such improvements— like higher salaries for teachers—do not ordinarily raise much new demand for foreign exchange. It can therefore be said that they do not require special foreign assistance, though, as with many other reform policies, perhaps more unallocated foreign funds.

But undoubtedly, foreign assistance specifically aimed at educational reforms would make it possible for the aid-giving organizations or countries to exert pressure on underdeveloped countries to proceed more courageously along certain strategic lines in the educational field— provided aid-givers were enlightened enough to want to use such pressure in the right direction.

The developed countries have shown great generosity

in making it possible for students in underdeveloped countries to study at their universities. Behind this type of foreign aid there are undoubtedly many excellent motives of good will for less fortunate young people. Often there is also the hope of bringing them over to political opinions favored in the aid-giving countries— a hope which is not always realized. In any case, a seasoned professor in the great liberal tradition could never want to close universities anywhere to students from any part of the world.

But the question is whether directing substantial aid to this purpose is really practical and productive. In many fields—particularly the social sciences but also, for instance, agriculture—the result is giving students from underdeveloped countries training that does not correspond to the needs in their home countries. This very often implies plain miseducation. If, as is usually the case, they belong to the upper strata and have good "connections," they might get positions at home for which they have not been trained in the best way. Or they will join the "brain drain," and remain abroad. Technical assistance by foreign experts should also, in the best case, be counted as aid for education.

The main point to stress, however, is that *in the educational field foreign aid can be of only marginal importance. Of overwhelming importance is what the underdeveloped countries themselves decide to do, and succeed in accomplishing, in regard to educational reforms.* What they need to do is not simply to add more education to what they are now offering their people but to *change in a fundamental way the whole structure, direction, and content of their educational system.*

Chapter 7

THE "SOFT STATE"

I A Pervasive Feature

The underdeveloped countries are all, though in varying degrees, "soft states." This stands out as a significant feature among other conditions that together make a country underdeveloped. Without more social discipline, development will meet great difficulties and, in any case, be delayed.[1]

The term "soft state" is understood to comprise all the various types of social indiscipline which manifest themselves by: deficiencies in legislation and in particular law observance and enforcement, a widespread disobedience by public officials on various levels to rules and directives handed down to them, and often their collusion with powerful persons and groups of persons whose conduct they should regulate. Within the concept of the soft state belongs also corruption, which will be given special attention in the second section of this chapter. These several patterns of behavior are interrelated in the sense that they permit or even provoke each other in circular causation having cumulative effects.[2]

The laxity and arbitrariness in a national community that can be characterized as a soft state can be, and are, *exploited for personal gain by people who have economic, social, and political power.* While the opportunities for large-scale exploitation opened up by the soft state are, of course, only at the disposal of the upper class, even persons quite low on the social ladder often find such opportunities for petty gains. But even aside from those personal interests, *there will in a soft state be a much wider spread, in all strata, of a general inclination of people to resist public controls and their implementation.*

The broad conspectus of this immensely complex phenomenon attempted in this chapter will again be focused on South Asian countries, whose conditions I have studied more intensively. The soft state is an aspect of *all* problems of underdevelopment, and it will in this chapter be particularly difficult to give sufficient supporting cross references to *Asian Drama*. Only a few brief comments will be added concerning other parts of the underdeveloped world.

This characteristic feature of an underdeveloped country has apparently little to do with its form of government. A country under authoritarian rule such as Thailand or Indonesia, both before and after the violent events in the fall of 1966, can be as soft, according to the definition given, as India or Ceylon with parliamentary governments dependent on regular elections—or even softer.

It is true that, for example, the putsch in Pakistan in 1958 was preceded by a general demoralization in public affairs during the preceding "democratic" regime and that it was defended as necessary to restore order and confidence.[3] And more generally, a military regime can often show some immediate accomplishments in that direction, as Ayub Khan's government in Pakistan demonstrated and also the first military government in Burma in 1958.[4]

But as was also revealed in these countries, these accomplishments may not be lasting. This is not unrelated to the fact, upon which I commented in Chapter 3, that changes of government, or even of form of government, occur high above the heads of the masses of people and mainly imply merely a shift of the groups of persons in the upper strata who monopolize power.[5]

Before proceeding further I find it even more important than in earlier chapters to stress the fact that the following attempt at *an analysis of the soft state should not be understood in moralistic terms.* In regard to social indiscipline, as in other respects, the underdeveloped countries are as they are not because of any inherent evil character traits of their peoples but as the result of a long history, very different from that of developed Western or Communist countries, during which a particular economic, social, and political power structure had developed.[6]

The role of social research is to lay bare the interplay of causes and effects as seen from the viewpoint of the value premises, in this case the modernization ideals—not to accuse or excuse. To be effective, research should be uncompromisingly realistic and not diplomatic. When in writings on development the topic has been commonly shunned as awkward, this is merely another, and major, example of the biases in postwar economic research that were characterized in Chapter 1 and that have made its results grossly faulty and superficial.

In precolonial times there was undoubtedly "integration" of a sort in the rural areas of South Asia, as there was in premedieval and medieval Europe. There was a considerable degree of local "self-government," again of a particular type not much like what the term implies in modern times. Whatever the basis and distribution of power and the relationships to a more central authority, the system functioned to preserve the social and economic balance in a stagnant and largely self-sufficient community.[7]

Its essence was a network of obligations, regulating in the first place the right to cultivate land but also ensuring the upkeep of roads, canals, water tanks, and other facilities whose use was shared. Particularly in the countries with a more egalitarian structure—such as Burma and Siam—there were rules of custom for mutual help with labor, a sort of "cooperation," though again very different from what in modern times is attempted in South Asia as part of the effort to engender development. The obligations were mostly between individuals, families, or groups with different status rather than in terms of a common community interest.

There was a machinery for upholding these traditional rights and obligations and for correcting and punishing transgressions. In South Asia, as in Europe, obligations usually fell most heavily on the poorer strata of the population—although with great differences among countries and over time. There was probably, however, a considerable laxity in the observance of the obligations and, particularly in those countries where the social and economic inequalities were greatest—as in the subcontinent that now is made up of Pakistan and India—much arbitrariness. Cruelty toward the lower strata was accompanied by petty obstructionism and lack of discipline on their part, and indulgence on the part of the privileged groups toward their low levels of performance, efficiency, and punctuality.

The present difference between Europe and South Asia came about gradually. In Western Europe, despite periods of decay, the long-run trend has been toward perfection of the inherited systems of rights and obligations and the transformation of the obligations from a network of individual, family, or group relationships into obligations to the community. This was one aspect of the socio-cultural evolution by way of mercantilism and liberalism, industrialization and urbanization, which macrosociologists have variously referred to as the shift from "status" to "contract," from "mechanical" to "organized" solidarity, from *"Gemeinschaft"* to *"Gesellschaft,"* etc.

From the beginning, even frontier settlements in the New World rapidly equipped themselves with a modern community organization. The more recent Western development toward the welfare state based on political democracy has meant, not least in regard to these earlier systems of rights and obligations within the community, radical steps toward their more precise definition, a sharp reduction in laxity and arbitrariness, and a more egalitarian distribution of the burdens. Today no one, whatever his position in society, escapes these systems of strengthened community controls.

South Asia did not experience a similar evolution from the primitive and static village organization. Instead, colonialism ordinarily led to a decay of the ancient village organization without the creation of a viable substitute. Indirect rule generally preserved the inherited patterns more than direct rule—Indonesia and Burma, respectively, to give extreme examples of the different effects of the two types of colonial policy.

Generally speaking, the pressure to introduce a Western form of ownership of land, the partial monetization of certain economic relations, the spur by these two changes to moneylending, the internal migrations, the influx of "oriental aliens" in some countries, and the superimposition of a colonial administration that aimed mainly at collecting taxes and maintaining peace and order resulted in a weakening and in some areas the virtual breakdown of the indigenous system of rights and obligations, laws, and procedures. The frequent attempts, particularly in the latter decades of the colonial era, to introduce local self-government after a Western pattern were almost everywhere a failure.

The authoritarian tradition of precolonial times— stronger or weaker, depending mainly upon the degree of inequality in the social stratification but always important—was, rather, strengthened by colonial rule and transferred into paternalism. Within such a system people became accustomed to being ordered about, but also to getting away with as much as they could. The colonial government's interference in the life and work of the people was limited also by the laissez-faire attitude that they should not attempt to meddle too much in social and religious matters—religion on the popular level being mainly a force for preserving the *status quo* in social relations.

Within this limitation and the limitations of available personnel and funds, *interfering in an indivualized way and assuming, to an extent, paternalistic responsibility for people's welfare was a natural role of colonial officials.* Administrative discretionary controls were exercised directly by these officials, assisted by a hierarchy, broadening toward its base, of indigenous officials or trusted feudal chiefs. Except in Indonesia, corruption was rampant, particularly on the lower level. This also contributed to arbitrariness in this system of government.

During the last decades of colonial rule, the liberation movements in those countries where they played a role, as in Imperial India (including present-day Pakistan), Indonesia, and for an even longer time French Indochina, had been rebellions against the foreign rule. Disobedience to authority was their natural weapon.

In India, Mohandas Gandhi built up a philosophy and a theory of political tactics on non-cooperation. In those South Asian countries that lacked a Gandhi or even much of a liberation movement, disobedience and non-cooperation were nevertheless a natural protest and defense against the enforced colonial power structure. They could spread among the broad strata the more effectively as they were in line with the general indifference and heedlessness inherent in the traditional authoritarianism. It left *a legacy of more anarchic attitudes which the new indigenous governments now find turned against themselves.*[8]

These governments want, however, to attain development and they prepare Plans for engendering it. Independent of whether they seek their power basis in free elections, as in India and Ceylon, or are dictatorships of one type or another, as in Pakistan and Burma, they try to have what is variously called "democratic planning," "decentralization," or "basic democracy." [9] They have good reasons for wanting the backing and support of the broad masses because those masses can block any attempts at development by passive resistance, for which they have been well trained. With the legacy I have tried to characterize and with their weak administrations shot through by much corruption, it is understandable that they shun efforts to strengthen and build up a system of community obligations which, from a modernization point of view, would seem to be the obvious need in all these countries.

Even in a country like India, where until recently planning has been a going concern and where successive Plans have taken account of such a wide variety of issues, one has, for instance, to scrutinize the Plans very closely indeed to find a few references to the need for regulations that place obligations on villagers. The first two Plans did touch on the desirability that the states, which are responsible for agricultural policies, should have land-management legislation preventing dilapidation of land. But this recommendation, presented without conviction, has not been acted upon, except tentatively in a few states, and there the laws have not been enforced.

On the whole, the need for greater discipline is systematically avoided in public discussion—in India much more, in fact, now than in Gandhi's time. Instead, *resort is taken to inducements of various sorts: exhortation, education, training, and subsidies.* With the absence or great imperfection of markets for labor, capital, and products, *the subsidies in particular can seldom be given by means of general, non-discretionary interventions through the price mechanism.*[10]

Mixed with the other types of individualized inducements, the subsidies have instead to be distributed by what I call discretionary controls within the programs of community development, cooperation, and new organs for local self-government. Through these means, literally hundreds of thousands of subsidies are distributed in India. These policies are overtaxing the weak administration and are opening up a vast new field for corruption.

They have been aimed at aiding the poorer strata, but with the inegalitarian social stratification and the power structure in these countries, not least on the local levels, they have mostly benefited the better-offs,[11] as was illustrated in Chapter 4. Partly for this reason the educational inducements also included in the programs for rural uplift have been disappointing.[12] A general reason for their ineffectiveness has also been that they have not been complemented by any attempt to build up a system of community obligations. In principle the policies have not been different in the other South Asian countries.

This policy choice to rely almost exclusively on the carrot rather than the stick is thus explainable by the legacy from the colonial era and from the circumstances under which these countries gained their independence. It is also understandable, perhaps, that they made a virtue of what to some extent was felt to be a necessity. Their bias of policy is generally explained with pride as testifying to the new government's *abhorrence of using compulsion and their determination to work only through the positive means of persuasion and incentives.*[13]

In the climate of the cold war it was then opportune to represent this as constituting a stand against Communism and, especially, against terror and regimentation. Everyone who wants to prevent the use of state power to induce egalitarian reforms, and all those who become defeatist by being aware of the political and institutional obstacles to such reforms acquire an interest in this rationalizing interpretation.

In the Western countries, with their preoccupation

with saving the underdeveloped world from Communism, the stand against using compulsion has mostly been innocently accepted at its face value. And the Communists themselves can have little interest in advising the use of more compulsion. They probably also believe that this cannot be done until after a revolution which they are careful not to propagate at this stage. And so the whole discussion remains in unresolved confusion.

The real and very serious dilemma, covered by this verbal fussiness about the ideal of voluntariness, is *that there is little hope in South Asia for rapid development without greater social discipline, which will not appear without legislation and regulations enforced by compulsion.* All these countries, independent of their type of government, have in general placed many fewer obligations much less effectively upon their peoples than have Western countries. The dictum of the highly respected, conservative American jurist Learned Hand that "law is violence" would not appeal to, or be understood by, the greater part of the South Asian intellectual elite.[14]

In principle, *social discipline can be effected within the framework of whatever degree of political democracy a country can achieve;* in the end nothing is more dangerous for democracy than lack of social discipline. But the political and social conditions in these countries block the enactment of regulations that impose greater obligations. Even when laws are enacted, they are not observed and cannot easily be enforced. This is ultimately what I mean by the term "the soft state."

This feature of the South Asian countries is traditional and conditioned by their history during precolonial and colonial times. But behind the resistance to overcome social indiscipline are also *strong vested interests, mainly among the upper strata but spread down into the masses.*

In strange contrast to the reluctance in South Asia to place their peoples under specific and firm obligations sanctioned by state power, their declared abhorrence of compulsion, and their reliance on inducement lies the fact that in all South Asian countries, though to a varying extent, there has been *an ambition to prepare and enact sweeping legislation of a general character* aimed at modernizing their societies and, in particular, countervailing the legacy of authoritarianism, paternalism, particularism, and anarchy which I have hinted at above.

All of these countries enacted, or prepared to enact, constitutions with general adult suffrage and guaranteed civil liberties. A more or less complete, modern family legislation was prepared and enacted in many of the South Asian countries, in most cases particularly directed toward giving women equal status with men. In India caste was abolished in the constitution, and special legislation was decreed to stamp out the practices associated with the caste system. All countries declared themselves in favor of land reform, and legislation for carrying it out was gradually placed on the statute books.

Generally speaking, these pieces of broad reform legislation were framed to defend the interests of the underprivileged in the masses. They have resulted in *infinitely less social change than was said to be their aim* or has commonly been pretended to have been accomplished.

As mentioned in Chapter 3, people in the upper strata were the transmitters of the modernization ideals and in particular the egalitarian ideal. These new legal rights were in early independence time handed down by the political elite in power. They were less eager, however, to give reality to these rights. To avoid doing so was the easier as there was no pressure from below.

In most West European countries general adult suffrage came after decades of organized efforts on behalf of the disfranchised, usually not on a full scale until after the First World War. Greater equality for women in civil law matters was likewise gradually attained after a struggle stretching over an even longer period. This implied that

when the rights were finally granted there were eager
and organized groups of citizens prepared to make use of
them.

This was not the case in the countries of South Asia.
In many of them various forms of a more authoritarian
regime were substituted for the democracy, with general
suffrage sought by the elite but never asked for, or even
thought of, among the broad masses of people.

Quite generally it can be asserted that whatever
changes there have been in political regimes have as a
rule resulted from infighting among the upper strata at
the top of society, as was pointed out in Chapter 3. In
no case have they been the result of an uprising against
oppression among the poor masses—except now in Vietnam after twenty-five years of armed revolt, first against
the French and then against the Americans, both seeking
their allies among the privileged groups. In India, where
a parliamentary system based on general adult suffrage
has up to now been preserved, the broad strata of the
electorate have not been organized to press for their interests. Parliamentary democracy as functioning in India
has been a force for social and economic *status quo.*

Similarly, the legislation against caste in India was
never pressed for by a broadly based and organized
movement among the masses of untouchables. Most of
them probably continue to this day to believe that their
lowly status is ordained by the gods and their karma.
Sullen, aimless dissatisfaction does not represent an effective social and political force. As caste has been excluded from the census, a main result of the legislation
has been that Indian intellectuals, particularly when
abroad, can maintain that caste has disappeared. In reality the caste institution may be on the whole more effective than ever, particularly in the rural areas.[15] Voting in
elections and many other changes have given caste new
fields for operation.

Likewise the legislation for equal rights for women has meant little change among the masses in the villages or in the cities. Few women in the lower strata have any inkling that these rights exist, or what they are all about.

In one sense the land and tenancy legislations have had the same nature. Hardly anywhere in the region can they be said to have been pressed for by an effective movement of the landless.[16] They have been propagated by the more radical in the intellectual and political elite. At an early time the idea got such prestige as an obviously sensible and just demand that it was generally accepted though realization was in the future. In India, for instance, the principle that the land should belong to the tiller was on the program of the National Congress long before independence and has never been abandoned.

There is this difference, however, that *if such reforms were really carried out, they would materially change the social and economic stratification in a radical fashion.* They could not, like the legislation against caste or about women's rights, be kept as an adornment without much practical importance.

This explains the different fate of these proposals.[17] Legislation about land reform was delayed, as for instance in Indonesia, or restricted by a very high ceiling, as in West Pakistan. Or, as almost everywhere, escape clauses of various types were included. Or, again as almost everywhere, the legislation was simply not enforced, mostly because of collusion between the officials and the landlords. As stressed in Chapter 4, in most underdeveloped countries land and tenancy reforms have been a sham, except when carried out in a revolutionary situation of some sort. To an extent this was the case in East Pakistan where so many of the landlords were Hindus and were driven out in the course of partition.

The taxation laws on income and wealth have this in common with land and tenancy reforms: *if they were*

*strictly formulated and effectively implemented, they
would have effects on the social and economic stratification.* But exactly for this reason tremendous vested interests are mobilized to emasculate them.[18]

It starts with the formulation of the laws. They quite
generally contain escape clauses and exceptions taking
the teeth out of any proposed law. Often they are deliberately written in such unclear terms that the scope for
tax avoidance is increased. Then comes tax evasion and
non-payment of assessed taxes. These ways of escaping
taxes are facilitated by astonishingly lenient penalties and
by keeping the administration for tax assessment and tax
collection too small and not competent enough. The low
salaries of the officials increase the possibilities of bribery.

There are, of course, tax avoidance and tax evasion
even in the developed countries. But these practices have
taken on colossal proportions in the countries of the South
Asian region and in underdeveloped countries generally.
Even though national accounting is extremely weak, this
can, within wide margins of uncertainty, be demonstrated
statistically. And it is common knowledge among educated and articulate people living in these countries. The
press, when it is free as in India and the Philippines, continually hammers at it as a national scandal—usually
without anything being done in a systematic way to purge
the situation.

*When policy measures have been instituted specifically
aimed at ameliorating conditions for the lower strata, they
have either not been implemented and enforced or have
been distorted so as to favor the not-so-poor and to discriminate against the masses.*[19] In Chapter 4 we commented upon this for the vast agricultural sector. The
same is broadly true of various assistance schemes outside
agriculture.

The foreseen difficulty or impossibility of enforcing a
law aimed at aiding the poor rather than the better-offs
may indeed make it easier to get such a law passed in a

legislature, as the representatives of those who should make a sacrifice can feel sure that nothing much will be changed. An Indian state assembly can thus show its generosity to the landless and poorer peasants by passing laws on minimum agricultural wages or by putting a maximum on the landlords' share of the crop or the money-lenders' interest charges without a risk that such laws will be enforced. In regard to its practical effects, *the whole political, legal, and administrative system is thus systematically and heavily weighted against the poor masses of people.* This comes about through lack of enforcement of laws and the distortion of policy measures.

The laws and policy measures are motivated as measures to realize the egalitarian ideal and, more generally, the modernization ideals which have commonly become accepted by the educated upper class whose intellectual and political elite had been the harbingers of these ideals. When it comes to actually formulating the laws and the policy prescriptions and, still more, taking measures to implement them, however, they commonly follow narrower selfish interests.

The masses may harbor a sullen dissatisfaction.[20] But they are too inarticulate, passive, and unorganized to press their interests effectively. The absence of pressure from below thus creates this strange contrast between the egalitarian pretenses, on the one hand, and the crass and increasing inequalities, on the other hand, upon which we commented in Chapter 3.

When dealing with the lower strata, including the very poorest, the state also avoids laying down definite obligations, sanctioned by state power, and relies upon inducements and voluntary adjustments. This gives a sort of conscience-consolation for not giving effect to the laws and policies instituted in their interest. The fact that reforms in the interest of the unprivileged strata are largely thwarted on the levels of both legislation and implementation must make precisely those members of the governments and the intellectual elite who are most devoted to the egalitarian ideal wary of measures that would demand performance from the masses of poor people.

Though for these and other reasons the matter is complicated, *fundamentally the main explanation of the soft state is that all the power is in the hands of the upper class who can afford egalitarian laws and policy measures but are in an unchallenged position to prevent their implementation.* And the systematic shirking from observing and analyzing this political mechanism, its causes, and its effects on development constitutes a major outflow of the biases in the opportunistic postwar approach to the study of the development problem in underdeveloped countries to which I referred in Chapter 1.

Urban communities contain establishments in industry commonly referred to as the "organized," the "modern," or the "modernized" sector of the economy.[21] Even when we include in that sector not only modern private and government enterprises in large-scale manufacturing, mining, construction, transport, commerce, and finance, but also the plantations,[22] together they form only a very small fraction of the total economy, particularly in terms of the labor force they employ.

Even though the traditional sectors—also in manufacturing [23]—are far larger in all the South Asian countries, the organized sector is particularly important from a planning point of view, as enlarging it and, eventually, causing the traditional sectors to adopt its more rational patterns of economic behavior is a main objective for planning. What little discussion has occurred about operational controls [24] over the private economy in the Plans concerns almost entirely the organized sector, though usually that is not clearly stated.[25]

The words "organized" or "modernized" are, however, likely to give exaggerated notions of the similarity of enterprises in that sector to Western enterprises. Ownership, in regard to private enterprises, and management, in regard to both private and public enterprises, show pre-capitalistic traits of paternalism and nepotism. Loyalties to caste, family, and ethnic group play a considerable role; "connections" are also extremely important. Even the foreign-owned plantations, mines, and other industrial or commercial enterprises show quasi-feudal peculiarities.

Only with reservations, therefore, can it be asserted that enterprises in the organized sector are directed according to a rational consideration of price stimuli as they affect costs and returns. They are, moreover, only imperfectly insulated from the much larger "unorganized" economy in which they exist as enclaves. Their demand for labor, as also for managers and technicians, does not operate in markets that show a close resemblance to those in Western developed countries, and the same often holds true of the demand for supplies. The markets for the output of products are also often imperfect in various ways and to varying degrees.

With these reservations it is nevertheless in regard to the organized sector that price policies [26] and other non-discretionary general controls could be expected to be most effective. What we find, however, is that the *governments are all attempting to control—encourage, steer, and restrain—these enterprises with redundance of administrative discretionary controls* (what are mostly called "direct" or "physical" controls), with the result that no major and, indeed, few minor business decisions can be taken except with the prior permission of the administrative authorities or at the risk of subsequent disapproval. Also for this reason, even in the modernized sector, business in South Asia is something entirely different from what it normally is in the Western countries.

The mechanism explaining this peculiar situation is, in broadest terms, the following.[27] To stimulate enterprise and investment, a number of positive inducements are applied: cheap rates of foreign exchange and protection from foreign competition by import restrictions, low rates of interest, low prices for services and goods from the public sector, tax holidays, and generally low effective taxation of profits.

These inducements are provided so generously, however, that they cannot be given according to general rules. Administrative discretion must be exercised to determine who shall be allotted foreign exchange, who shall receive loans, often at concessional rates of interest, and who shall be serviced by the public sector at cheap costs. As this is often not enough, a whole paraphernalia of negative controls have to be applied determining who shall be permitted to invest and produce, and what and where, and from what country he shall import capital goods and production necessities, etc.

An odd situation is thus created. While everyone talks about the necessity of encouraging enterprise, and while a great number of inducements are instituted with this end in view, most officials have to devote much of their time and energy to limiting or stopping enterprise. This is like driving a car with the accelerator pushed to the floor but with the brakes on.

The important point to stress is that *encouraging enterprise beyond practical limits makes necessary a gargantuan bureaucratic system of administrative discretionary controls to harness it.* The abolition or relaxation of some of the inducements would make it possible to reduce the curtailments correspondingly and also to manage both the inducements and the curtailments by price policies and other non-discretionary controls.

The widespread existence of conflicting controls has thus the implication that there is need of *more* controls and that *a larger part* of them must be of a discretionary type than would otherwise be necessary. This is particularly unfortunate from a development point of view, as one of the most serious bottlenecks in the South Asian countries is the great scarcity of administrators of competence and integrity.

One important reservation to what has been said should be stated. Undoubtedly the South Asian countries more often than developed countries are in need of discretionary controls and occasionally of controls that counteract each other—as the developed countries have been under the impact of the war on their economy.[28] The basic reasons are their poverty and underdevelopment, which are reflected in imperfect markets, where bottlenecks and surpluses are more normal than a balance between demand and supply.[29]

But it is equally certain that this reliance on discretionary controls would not be necessary to the extent that it is commonly practiced. Although the operational controls are generally bypassed in the Plans [30]—which is a main reason why the Plans cannot be classified as operational—it is clear that the overgrowth of administrative discretionary controls is in the region generally considered to be the essence of planning. In India and other countries committed to a "socialist pattern of society," the willingness of a government to employ discretionary controls is looked upon as a particularly "socialist" trait, a misconception frequently shared by Western writers who often even succeed in convincing themselves that it has a "Marxist" origin.

The scarcity of foreign exchange acts generally as the master bottleneck. We should therefore not be surprised that the bureaucratization with conflicting controls mostly of a discretionary character has gone furthest in India, Pakistan, Burma, and Indonesia. Malaya, the Philippines, and Thailand have fewer curtailments of a discretionary type though their inducements, for instance their tax exemptions for new undertakings, are to an unusual extent a matter for political and administrative discretion.

This general preference for individualized, administrative, discretionary controls of private business is, of course, in line with the legacy of authoritarianism and paternalism from precolonial and colonial times. But the absence of any strong will to use instead as far as possible general non-discretionary controls needs more of an explanation than this simple reference to history.

This sketch of an analysis of the government controls of the modernized sector in private business would be grossly imperfect if we avoided raising the crucial questions: *Cui bono? Who is profiting from this type of arrangement of public controls over private business?* [31]

We should then note that although businessmen in the South Asian countries, as everywhere else, are apt to complain about government interference and bureaucratic controls, the complaints are muted and weak to an extent that should arouse the suspicion that they are not so seriously meant.

The "too high" inducements, which often have to be complemented by curtailments, create "too high" profits —"too high" according to what would be necessary from a planning point of view to call forth an undertaking.[32] These "too high" profits are, moreover, not very effectively soaked up by taxation, because convenient loopholes are provided in the tax laws and because large-scale tax evasions are the rule. For several reasons *established businesses and, in particular, large-scale enterprises are in a strategic position to be chosen as recipients of both the inducements and the permissions.* This tends to restrict competition, to favor monopoly or oligopoly, and to pamper vested interests. These enterprises also control "business opinion" and even "public opinion." [33]

Indeed, whenever they succeed in getting a permit, a license, a loan, or an allocation of foreign exchange, they get a gift. As the system operates they are the ones who have the best chances of getting the paper slips that are worth money. And that makes it very worth their while to break their way through the jungle of administrative discretionary controls, planted to encourage enterprise but to keep investment down to the level where demands can be satisfied by supplies.

That, also, the *officials and politicians who operate the administrative discretionary controls have a vested interest in their preservation and further proliferation* is obvious. It gives them a wealth of power, and power is always sweet. The power is the greater because the controls are not integrated into the Plans and the directives for their use tend to be vague: application becomes, then, more a matter of administrative judgment.

Particularly in a setting where caste, family, economic and social status, and, more generally, "connections" mean so much, collusion between business and officialdom becomes a natural tendency. The result is often corruption. The corrupt then get a vested interest in the system.

Even if the large gains can be reaped only by higher officials and politicians, corruption among them tends to spread downward, indeed into the villages. At least it acts as a powerful inhibition to any attempt to stamp out petty corruption in the lower strata of public servants.

II Corruption [34]

One of the most flagrant examples of bias in the postwar approach is the virtual taboo against including the important facts of corruption in the analysis of the development problems of underdeveloped countries. As mentioned in Chapter 1, it is possible to read hundreds of books and articles on underdevelopment and development without even encountering the word "corruption."

The two main sources of bias in the postwar approach—diplomacy in research and the utilization of Western models that are not adequate to reality by abstracting from, in particular, attitudes and institutions—have here joined in leading to a situation that is preposterous from the point of view of the ethos of truth-seeking in scientific work and of rendering it relevant for the formation of rational policies.

When occasionally the problem of corruption is touched upon among Western economists and social scientists generally—which happens much more often in conversation than in writing—the excuses put forward for not treating it as a serious matter are irrelevant, apparently thin, or bluntly false.[35] A very few economists—usually Americans, because other Westerners remain more completely silent on this issue in their writings—even put their erroneous thoughts into print, for instance that "bribery ... is a necessary and not harmful lubricant for a cumbersome administration," while the truth is that corruption is one of the causes of administration becoming cumbersome.[36]

Indigenous students usually observe the taboo in writing equally politely—or apologetically. I recall how I once tried to interest a group of young sociologists in India in carrying out empirical research in order to pinpoint and analyze the type of difficulties a poor landless worker or sharecropper would encounter if he ventured to insist upon getting his due from the landlord or moneylender. My suggestion met with complete disinterest. "We know all about it without study," one of them remarked, which is certainly a strange attitude for a scientist.

Singapore is one of the few spots in the underdeveloped world where a clean government has with apparent success fought corruption which otherwise, there as elsewhere, would tend to be common and on the increase. At a meeting with leaders for the trade unions of public servants in Asia, the minister for foreign affairs and labor, S. Rajaratnam, courageously gave as the title of his address: "Bureaucracy *versus* Kleptocracy."[37] He criticized the taboo upheld by most economists against discussing corruption:

> It is amazing how otherwise excellent studies on development problems in Asia and Africa avoid any serious reference to the fact of corruption. It is not that the writers do not know of its existence but its relevance to the question of political stability and rapid economic development appears not to have been fully appreciated. It may also be that a serious probing of the subject has been avoided lest it should offend the sensibilities of Asians.

Rajaratnam then went on to quote a few of the exceptional authors who have touched on the topic and who have implied that it is unscientific "moralism" to believe that corruption is damaging.

> Bribing bureaucracies, they argue, can in developing countries promote bureaucratic efficiency, innovation and rapid economic development.... [To which Rajaratnam said,] I have yet to see convincing evidence that corruption assisted economic development or strengthened political stability.

He quoted another author:

> ... corruption is not a mass of incoherent phenomena, but a political system, capable of being steered with tolerable precision by those in power.

To this Rajaratnam answered:

> But his contention that it can be "steered with tolerable precision" is at odds with facts as we know them in Asia. A kleptocracy will steer itself, whether those in power want it or not, into more and more corruption and finally into economic and political chaos. This has been the life cycle of societies in Asia during the past two decades.

The disinterest among the great majority of economists in the facts of corruption stands in strange contrast to *the very lively interest shown in South Asian countries among the average literate people.*[38] Few issues penetrate the minds of people so deeply among all "educated," even among those otherwise only slightly alert, as this one. Few are debated with so much excitement. Where there is freedom of public expression, as in India and the Philippines, the newspapers devote much of their space to alleged cases of corruption. There are popular periodicals almost specializing in this matter. I have sometimes felt that corruption takes the same place there as sex and race in contemporary American civilization.

Political assemblies, where they function, devote much time and interest to the matter. Periodically, anti-corruption campaigns are waged: laws are passed, vigilance agencies set up, special police establishments assigned to investigate reports of misconduct; sometimes officials, mostly in the lower brackets, are prosecuted and punished, and occasionally a minister has to resign. And committees are appointed to set forth a general strategy for counteracting corruption.

Yet the articulate in all these countries believe that corruption is rampant and that it is growing particularly among higher officials and politicians, including legislators and ministers. The ostentatious efforts to prevent corruption and the assertions that the corrupt are being dealt with as they deserve only seem to spread cynicism, especially as to how far all this touches those higher up. I have already noted that the little island-state Singapore represents an exception, the only one in the region. That this has strengthened the government there is apparent.

People's beliefs about corruption and the emotions attached to those beliefs are themselves important social facts. They have their causes and also their effects, and there is no excuse for not making them the object of intensive research. The same holds true in regard to *public policy measures: political, legislative, administrative, and judicial actions.* Both types of social facts should be fairly easy to ascertain and analyze, as they are on the surface of social reality.

This should be the first research task. With public debate quite open in many South Asian countries, and gossip flourishing in all of them, it should not be too difficult to proceed from there to ascertaining the facts in individual cases of wrongdoing. The wider research task is, however, to establish *the general nature and extent of corruption in a country, its incursion upon various levels and branches of economic life, and any trends that are discernible.*

The empirical research which should form the basis for answering these questions has almost entirely yet to be done, thus reflecting the taboo upheld by the students. What is said about the facts of corruption in *Asian Drama*,[39] to which I have to refer in this brief condensation, is based on extensive reading of parliamentary records, committee reports, newspapers, and, even more, on conversation with knowledgeable persons in the South Asian region, including Western businessmen, as well as to a minor extent on direct personal observations.

The relative level of corruption in the several South Asian countries is at present not possible to assess with any certainty. It is, however, very high in all countries and unquestionably much higher than in the Western developed countries—not excepting the United States—and in the Communist countries. It has been rising in the independence era, particularly in regard to higher officials and politicians. Continually the trends seem to be upward.

As for the different branches of administration in the South Asian governments, it is generally accepted that the public works departments and government purchasing agencies in all South Asian countries are particularly corrupt, as are also the agencies running the railways, the offices issuing import licenses and other permissions, and those responsible for the assessment and collection of taxes and customs duties. Corruption has spread to the courts of justice and to the universities.

Both as cause and as effect, corruption has its counterpart in undesirable practices among the general public. The business world has been particularly active in promoting corrupt practices among politicians and higher officials. One important question on which the official reports and the public debate are silent is the *role played by Western business interests competing for markets in the South Asian countries or embarking on direct investments in industrial enterprises there, either independently or in joint ventures with indigenous firms or with governments.*

Western business representatives never touch on this matter publicly. But as I can personally testify, in private conversations they frankly admit that it is often necessary to bribe high officials and politicians in order to get a business deal through and to bribe both high and low officials in order to run their enterprises without too many obstacles.

They are quite explicit about their own experiences and those of other firms. These bribes, they say, constitute a not inconsiderable part of their total cost of doing business in South Asian countries. Although hardly any foreign company can make it an absolute rule to abstain from giving bribes, it is apparent that there is a vast difference in regard to the willingness to bribe, not only between companies, but also between nationalities.

Among the Western nations, French, American, and especially West German companies are usually said to have the least inhibitions about bribing their way through. Japanese firms are said to be even more willing to pay up. On the other hand, I have never heard it alleged that individual bribes are offered or paid by the commercial agencies of Communist countries. These widely held opinions are part of the social setting in South Asia, as are all the other elements that make up the folklore of corruption. To what extent they accurately mirror actual business practices should be established by research.

That *grants offered by Western governments and in*

particular the United States have often been dissipated in large-scale corruption, particularly in countries like Laos, South Vietnam, Thailand, and even the Philippines, is common knowledge and, in the frank American tradition, has been reported not only in the press but in Congressional inquiries.

Apparently *the International Bank for Reconstruction and Development and the International Monetary Fund and other agencies within the United Nations family have on the whole been able to avoid playing into the hands of the corrupt*—except to an extent when aid is rendered in the form of commodities which sometimes have appeared on a black market instead of reaching their intended destination. The World Bank, in particular, has increasingly exerted its influence to see to it that its loans are used in a way to preserve fair competition among suppliers.

The folklore of corruption, the political, administrative, and judicial reverberations of popular beliefs and emotions, the actual prevalence of corruption in the several countries, and the present trends—*all these social facts must be explained in causal terms by relating them to other conditions in South Asia.*[40]

Corruption is fundamentally nothing but one specific manifestation of the soft state, as defined above and having the general historical background I have sketched. It is the general setting of the soft state that makes corruption possible, while, in circular causation with cumulative effects, the prevalence of corruption is a mighty influence to keep these countries soft as states.

In this brief condensation only one point shall be stressed. Corruption as a pattern of life in these countries implies *a difference in mores as to where, when, and how to make a personal gain.* While, on the one hand, it has proved difficult in underdeveloped countries to introduce rational profit motives and market behavior into the sec-

tor of life where they operate in developed countries—
that is, the sphere of business—it has, on the other hand,
proved equally difficult to eliminate motives of private
gain in the sector where they have been largely suppressed in the developed countries—the sphere of public
responsibility and power.

The two differences are complementary and, to an extent, support each other. Indeed, they are both remnants
of the precapitalist, traditional society. Where there are
no markets or where those that exist are exceedingly imperfect, "connections" in the wide sense of the word have
to be substituted. In "plural societies" this implies a
fragmentation of loyalties and, in particular, little loyalty
to the community as a whole, whether on the local or the
national level.

The power position that is exploited to make a gain for
self, family, or "community" (in the South Asian meaning of the term) may be the high one of a minister, a
member of the legislature, or a superior official, whose
consent or cooperation is needed to obtain a license or
settle a business deal. Or it may be the lowly one of a
petty clerk who can delay or prevent the passing of an
application, the use of a railroad car, or the prompt opening of the gates over the tracks.

When explaining the presence of corruption in South
Asia, the legacy from traditional society must be taken
into account. But as a theory it then remains in the realm
of social statics. The rising level of corruption which is
commonly reported—and which has changed a country
like Indonesia from being largely free of corruption, as
it was in colonial times,[41] to becoming thoroughly cor-
rupted, as it has been in recent years—must be explained
in dynamic terms. *Practically everything that has happened in the independence era has afforded greater incentives to, as well as greater opportunities for, corruption,*
particularly large-scale graft by politicians and higher
officials but spreading downward to petty bribery.

The winning of independence and the transition from colonial status to self-government were preceded and accompanied by profound disturbances in most of the South Asian countries. At the same time, politicians for the first time became important as now holding power. The repatriation of a large number of officials from the metropolitan countries left these countries few competent administrators at the top level with the stricter Western mores. This scarcity was much greater and more damaging in Indonesia, Burma, and even Pakistan, than in the Philippines, India, and Ceylon. The general trend toward decreasing salaries to officials when measured in terms of real income, not least to those at the lower and middle levels, has been another fateful change.

At the same time the wholesale resort to discretionary administrative controls, upon which we commented above, increased the demands on administration. Such controls themselves breed corruption. The spread of corruption, in turn, gives corrupt politicians and dishonest officials as well as their customers, particularly businessmen, a vested interest in retaining and increasing controls of this type.

To all this is added the influx of private funds and business activity from the West, now no longer controlled by administrators from the old metropolitan countries, who at least in the British and Dutch dependencies were largely incorrupt themselves and laid a certain restraint on the Western businessmen. The controls are now in the hands of indigenous politicians and officials who have not demonstrated an equal degree of integrity.

There is also quite generally a circular causation with cumulative effects working within the system of corruption. Among the sophisticated the situation may become rationalized in the idea that corruption is unavoidable in a "developing country." The effect of this is to spread cynicism and to lower resistance to giving and taking bribes.

One effect, though not the only one, of the widely spread awareness of corruption and the feeling to which I referred above that effective measures are not taken to punish the culprits, particularly those who are highly placed, may be to underpin cynicism.[42] In turn, this may discourage even a national leader, who himself is not corrupt and who knows about the spread of corruption, to resist demands for bolder and more systematic efforts to cleanse government and administration of corruption. This seems to have been Jawaharlal Nehru's inclination:

> Merely shouting from the house-tops that everybody is corrupt creates an atmosphere of corruption. People feel they live in a climate of corruption and they get corrupted themselves. The man in the street says to himself: "well, if everybody seems corrupt, why shouldn't I be corrupt." That is the climate sought to be created which must be discouraged.

This analysis of the immediate effects of the folklore of corruption is probably correct. But Nehru's practical conclusion, that he should not use his tremendous personal authority and the angry popular outcry for taking radical measures against the spread of corruption in high places, probably belongs to one of his serious mistakes, as many of his friends told him.

As mentioned above, one of the opportunistic rationalizations of the neglect of research on the problem of corruption is its alleged unimportance, or even its alleged usefulness for development under the conditions prevailing in South Asia. I believe that this idea—for the support of which no respectable analysis in terms of causes and effects has ever been presented—is thoroughly wrong, and that *corrupt practices are highly detrimental for development.*[43]

Corruption is part and parcel of the general condition in underdeveloped countries of their being soft states. It is a major inhibition and raises serious obstacles against all efforts to increase social discipline. Not only are politicians and administrators affected by the prevalence of corruption, but also businessmen and, in fact, the whole population.

Corruption introduces an element of irrationality in all planning and plan fulfillment by influencing the actual course of development in a way that deviates from the Plan. If such influence is foreseen, it limits the horizon of planning.

A common method of exploiting a position of public responsibility for private gain is the threat of obstruction and delay; hence, *corruption impedes the processes of decision-making and execution on all levels.* It increases the need for controls to check the dishonest official at the same time as it makes the honest official reluctant to take decisions on his own. In both ways it tends to make administration cumbersome and slow.

The influence of corruption in slowing down the wheels of administration and in prohibiting rational delegation of authority is particularly damaging in South Asia, where, on the one hand, there is a scarcity of competent administrators coupled with, on the other hand, a tendency to introduce on a vast scale methods of public controls that increase the need for administrative discretionary decisions.

When the "excessive bureaucracy" in these countries is commonly said to be a legacy from colonial times, this is only part of the truth. The trend to increasing corruption carries much of the blame. When even highly competent Western administrative experts fail to mention this connection,[44] this is part of the unscientific diplomacy I have criticized throughout this book.

Even more important is, however, the effect of corruption in *endangering the stability of government.* The new governments inherited a traditional society where loyalties were fragmented. Their development efforts must attempt to modernize people's attitudes by overcoming this fragmentation. Yet corruption, and the widespread knowledge of corruption, counteract the strivings for national consolidation and, in particular, decrease respect for and allegiance to the government.

No South Asian government can remain firmly in control unless it can convince its articulate groups that effective measures are being taken to purge corruption from public life. It is a fact that wherever a political regime has crumbled in Asia—in Pakistan and Burma, for instance, and, outside South Asia, in China—a major and often decisive cause has been the prevalance of official misconduct among the politicians and administrators, and the concomitant spread of unlawful practices among businessmen and the general public.[45] To every South Asian government today, wherever its locus is on the democracy-dictatorship axis, taking effective measures against corruption is literally a question of self-preservation.

The foregoing remarks are founded upon my observations of that huge part of the underdeveloped world that is located in South Asia. The legacy of old times is shaped very differently in the countries of Latin America.

Nevertheless, and although no comprehensive survey is available, what I have seen and read about these countries gives me the impression that, with individual deviations in one direction or the other, *the end result has been very much the same in Latin America as in South Asia:* rampant and, on the whole, increasing corruption. The historical background has been, and remains, a soft state. Foreign involvement has for a long time been even more important in Latin America than in South Asia and never hampered to a noticeable degree by the civil service of any metropolitan country.

The folklore of popular beliefs about corruption is equally potent. And it is even more charged with emotions, as to a higher degree it relates corruption to influences from abroad, in the first place the United States. In regard to the effects of corruption the similarities are greater than in regard to causes.

Again, with many individual gradations and differences the same seems to be generally true about underdeveloped countries everywhere in the world. Most of *the newly independent countries in Africa are reported to have lapsed rapidly into a spreading pattern of corruption* with the tiny new upper-class groups of "educated" not able to withstand the temptation to exploit their power in the new era of independence.

My demand for the taboo to be broken and for comprehensive and intensive research to be directed at the reality of the soft state and corruption also in these other parts of the underdeveloped world stands equally motivated. We economists will have little possibility of really understanding what is happening there and of framing rational development policies if we remain in a strange state of innocence about these facts of life and continue to deal with their development problems by the biased postwar approach, criticized in terms of principle in Chapter 1.

What has been attempted by the remarks so far in this chapter, and in the whole book, and which in *Asian Drama* has been substantiated and developed in greater detail, has been to establish facts and factual relationships when *taking a view from the viewpoint of the modernization ideals.* For the purpose of their employment as value premises they have been explicitly stated and motivated. The knowledge about social reality reached in this way should then make possible *rational policy conclusions,* where again the value premises are brought into play together with that knowledge of the facts.

The one who sees reality differently has to account for his different viewpoint and his value premises, and to explain his motivation for choosing them. A "disinterested" or "neutral" view is not possible—for logical reasons.[46]

It is a fact that the modernization ideals are relatively much more fully realized in the Western developed countries than in the underdeveloped countries. The economic, social, and political life develops within a "harder" and "stronger" state, where also corruption has been brought down to much less significance. This is particularly true of the small Protestant countries in Scandinavia but also of Britain and Holland.

In a sense the assertion that the viewpoint chosen for our analysis is a Western one is true. This is sometimes formulated as a criticism, which is, however, neither a relevant nor a correct one. The modernization ideals which have been chosen as value premises are in a more fundamental sense simply rational, if the goal is development. That they are more fully realized in the Western countries corresponds to the fact that those countries are also more developed. When the underdeveloped countries have actually chosen these ideals as development goals for themselves, they have done it *because they are seen to be rational for development, not because they are Western.*

Because of its size and its great practical importance for all relations between the developed Western world and the underdeveloped world, it should be noted that *the United States shows traits in the system of law, law observance, and law enforcement that in some respects place it nearer the situation in underdeveloped countries than that of the countries mentioned in northwestern Europe*—though, in the United States, still very far from the situation in the underdeveloped countries and with a very different economic, social, political, and ideological background. When working on *An American Dilemma* more than a quarter of a century ago, and outlining in the first chapter of that book the American ideals, I devoted several sections to discussing in general terms the peculiar legal tradition in the United States.[47] To this earlier book of mine I want to make specific reference, as I cannot develop the theme in the present book.

Americans, like people in the underdeveloped countries but unlike those in the countries of northwestern Europe, not infrequently inscribe their ideals in laws which are then inadequately observed and enforced. Administration has never been very effective in the United States. The nation's rapid economic growth has occurred *in spite of* this. This was possible because of a number of conditions very different from those in the poverty-stricken underdeveloped countries today.[48] And the United States is still not as free from corruption, particularly on the state and city levels, as the European countries mentioned.

This last cultural lag is due to many interrelated facts, among them the spoils system since President Andrew Jackson; the consequent relative lack of a firmly established and politically independent civil service; the clustering in the cities of disadvantaged colored and immigrant groups; the rise of machine politics; and, particularly, the relative lack of integration of the lower classes of its still very heterogeneous population.[49]

A large part of the research on the development problems of South Asia as of other underdeveloped countries is carried out at American universities and by American students. It might perhaps be suggested that the prevalence of the biases in this research and, in particular, the almost total disregard of the problems of the soft state and corruption, could be due to an opportune blindness developed in the peculiar American civilizational setting.

This suspicion is, however, not warranted. To begin with, there has been no greater interest in the institutional aspects of the problem of development of underdeveloped countries in the writings of students from those other countries mentioned. Moreover, American students have not developed a blind spot for these important problems at home, but have instead, from the muckrakers on and even earlier, made them an important object of study. Not entirely unrelated to this, but, of course, also in line with other changes in the American society, the state has in recent decades continually become less soft, while the development in underdeveloped countries has gone in the opposite direction.

Under these conditions, I rather see reasons for hope that American students will begin to make really significant contributions in laying bare the facts of the soft state in underdeveloped countries and will also investigate the practical and political problem of how gradually to improve the possibilities for development by strengthening and hardening the state. From what they know about the society where they have grown up, they should have a greater initial understanding of the problems raised in this chapter.

III   Policy

The underdeveloped countries have to struggle on a broad front to make their states less soft.

This implies making their *legislation more functional,* more appropriate to fulfilling its purposes of determining people's behavior, less full of loopholes, and backed by effective sanctions. In many cases *this would imply a retrenchment.* It is of doubtful value to legislate reforms that have no chance of being realized for the time being.

The vision of reforms that can only be realized in the future has its legitimate place in the political programs of political parties, of organizations of various sorts, and of individual statesmen and scholars. It can even be a source of inspiration in adult education which, as all schooling, should attempt to change people's attitudes.

But to legislate ideals without the possibility or even the intention of realizing them is apt to breed cynicism and also to cause new elements of uncertainty and arbitrariness in the state when they can be implemented in only a few cases but not generally. It also provides those who in their hearts are against social change with a pretense that it has already been achieved. This is exactly the type of new legislation the underdeveloped countries should not embark upon if they want to harden and strengthen the state.

All underdeveloped countries need to improve their administrations. Indeed, *large-scale administrative reform belongs to the most important tasks for making possible and speeding up development.* Administrative reform would in many respects also *imply a retrenchment.*

This is, to begin with, of importance for what is asked of the administration. It has been pointed out above that the underdeveloped countries to a varying degree all show a tendency to manage the direction the state wants to give to private business by administrative discretionary controls—what are called "direct" or "physical" controls —instead of by non-discretionary controls like price policies, custom and excise duties, and other policy measures that have a general effect.

Granted that their situation in various respects necessitates more discretionary controls, they are not needed to the extent actually practiced. This is not a plea for less control over private business but for its being carried out by different means and thereby more effectively. As shown above, the present system with overgrown discretionary controls actually works to give established and big business more oligopolistic power and permit profits that are "too high" from a planning point of view.

Administrators with competence and integrity are scarce in all underdeveloped countries, though more so in some than in others. A changeover as far as possible from individualized discretionary to general non-discretionary controls would decrease the demand for this scarce resource and make it more available for carrying out all the important tasks that are now unmet. Meeting the needs for more efficiency in the administrative system, less

cumbersome bureaucratic procedures, and more delegation of authority downward would then also be more
possible.

Another urgent administrative reform is also in the nature of retrenchment. Certainly in no underdeveloped
country are there too many administrators of competence
and integrity. But the overburdening of administration by
unnecessary discretionary controls, and also the clumsy
procedures and lack of rational delegation which are
partly caused by tradition and partly by the proliferation
of that type of controls, have tended *to dilute the corps
of officials by employing persons of less competence and
less integrity.*

Almost everywhere there has been *a huge increase of
public employees on the lower levels of administration.*
In South Asia it has taken on tremendous proportions.[50]
Even in Latin America and elsewhere in the underdeveloped world the same trend is noticeable. This has happened under political pressure. Public employment as
petty officials has often been a means of bringing down
the number of the "educated unemployed," created by
the asocial school system that was discussed in Chapter 6.

When I discussed this problem with an important Indian minister, he confided to me that his whole staff, under
the highest level, was of virtually no use. With half or
even a third of his total staff his ministry would function
more efficiently. But politically it was not possible to fire
them and shrink his staff to what would be practical and
economical.

This system of keeping too large a cadre of public servants on the lower levels is, of course, not unrelated to
their *very low salaries.* This, in turn, makes them more
amenable to bribe-taking. A retrenchment of their numbers should be accompanied by a substantial increase in
salaries; at the same time, vigorous attempts should be
made to stamp out corruption.

Generally speaking, and not least on the higher level of

officials, *corruption plays a decisive role in keeping down administrative efficiency.* The dishonest official has a vested interest in preserving the administrative discretionary controls over private business. As these controls, on the whole, work to the advantage of established and big business, there is little resistance among leading businessmen against them.

The dishonest official also has a vested interest generally in cumbersome administrative procedures which create more opportunities for delays. Unfortunately, the honest official will often share this interest. If he works in an administration widely suspected of being corrupt, he will tend to play for "safety" and shun taking personal responsibility.[51]

In all attempts to strengthen and improve administration, and in all other efforts to make the state less soft, the suppression of corruption must play a crucial and strategic role.

The state in the northwestern European countries two hundred years ago was generally much less soft than the underdeveloped countries today. But even in the countries in northwestern Europe, where corruption is now quite limited, it was rife at that earlier time. This was the situation even somewhat later, indeed until the liberal interlude between mercantilism, with its many vestiges of feudalism, and the modern welfare state. *During the liberal interlude, the strong and hard state came into being.* One of the characteristics of the liberal state became a system of politics and administration marked by a high degree of personal integrity and efficiency.

While the liberalization of production and trade, and particularly the liquidation of the craft guild system and the arrangements protecting urban industry and commerce, inherited from the previous era, have been closely studied by historians, they have shown much less interest in how the corrupt state was changed into the strong, incorrupt liberal state. It was probably accomplished by a strengthening of morals in the higher strata, backed by legislated sanctions, together with salary reforms in the lower strata, often by transforming customary bribes into legalized fees.

Undoubtedly, the underdeveloped countries should have something to learn from what happened in these Western countries a little more than a hundred years ago. There is, however, a fundamental difference in initial conditions. The relatively high level of integrity in politics and administration was achieved there during a period when state activity was reduced to a minimum. When the state again intervened in the economy on a large scale, it had a political and administrative system whose high quality only needed to be protected and preserved.

The underdeveloped countries today, on the contrary, have to *fight rampant corruption in an era of their history when almost everything that happens tends to feed corruption* and when, in particular, the activities of the state are proliferating—and when, as I pointed out, preference, even beyond what is necessary, is now being given to discretionary controls.

But *the underdeveloped countries have no other choice than to do their utmost, against the odds, to cause the trend to turn and corruption to decrease.* More generally, they must strive to strengthen and harden their state, making their legislation more effective and their administration more efficient and, in particular, less corrupt.

There is an interrelation among these several lines of action making success in one direction a condition for success in the others. But certainly the fight against corruption should be given high priority, as the spread of corruption creates inhibitions all around. In this sense it can be called *crucial and of strategic importance.*

There is no lack of proposals about what needs to be done in order to fight corruption. The remedies are spelled out in considerable detail in many committee reports in several underdeveloped countries, for instance in the excellent Indian *Report of the Committee on Prevention of Corruption, 1964.*[52] They range from simpler and more precise rules for political and administrative decisions, less scope for administrative discretion, speedier prosecution of offenders, more severe punishments, and more publicity around administrative decisions, including tax assessment. Like the individual scandals, the reform proposals tend to create great excitement when they are presented; but it dies down when nothing substantial comes out of them.

On one point there is virtual agreement: *the efforts should first be directed toward punishing corruption of these higher up:* ministers and higher officials. Also, the big bribers in the business class should be brought to court. If the disease is not attacked on that level, corruption all the way down will be protected.

Indeed, in some branches of public administration there is a systematic sharing of bribes among officials at different levels of responsibility. When there is not, and each takes care of his own interest, a tacit collusion develops. The conclusion widely drawn in public discussion is that it is hopeless to fight corruption if politicians and higher officials are not required to observe a higher degree of personal integrity.

But *these persons and the businessmen and others whom they are in collusion with form the power elite.* They can in general protect themselves—and all the small fry of malefactors under them—from prosecution. Now and then a scandal will come to a head where one of them will have to resign. More seriously, widespread corruption may be part of the build-up of a situation where a putsch becomes possible, and a change of regime, mostly in the direction of a dictatorship of one type or the other. But if nothing else has changed, the new regime may in a short time be just as corrupt as the one liquidated.

What we are facing when in general it becomes impossible to attack corruption at the level where it must be attacked if an anti-corruption drive should be effective is again *the inegalitarian power structure in underdeveloped countries.* If a large part of the upper class both among politicians and officials and among businessmen and others are out to make the short-term gains from corruption, nothing substantial can be done to stamp it out, however angry the protests of a somewhat lower level of the educated and articulate. Before the power structure has been changed by evolution or revolution it will be difficult to decrease corruption or even hinder its continual increase.

In this connection a reminder is in order. It is commonly observed that the installation of a Communist regime regularly is followed by a forceful extinction of corruption—though often also of the corrupt.[53] It may sometimes not be long before a new bureaucracy and a new upper class develops, leading again to a measure of nepotism and petty corruption as we have seen in the Soviet Union and the other Communist countries in Eastern Europe. But the initial popular acceptance of a Communist regime, when this can be seen to be the effect of a Communist revolution, is probably partly due to the fact that it offers the people for the first time an incorrupt regime.

As in the case of the adult education drive, which also follows a Communist revolution, this should not *per se* be viewed as a sinister development but, rather, as a reform activity which the non-Communist underdeveloped countries should have excellent reason to emulate, though with different means. For *we should not accept the idea that only Communism can save us from corruption.*

The strengthening of social discipline in an underdeveloped country and the overcoming of the inhibitions and obstacles for development inherent in its being a soft state must be accomplished by that country itself. There is very little space for foreign assistance in this matter.

Expert advice on various problems of legislative and

administrative reform can occasionally play a role. The experts from developed countries must then be chosen with utmost care. They must not only be good lawyers and highly qualified experts on administration but be capable of acquiring a thorough understanding of the very different conditions of a particular underdeveloped country: its peculiar traditions, initially sunk in much corruption; its widespread lack of loyalty to the national community, not least among a large part of its upper class, including higher officials and businessmen; and finally its great poverty and lack of functional literacy among the masses. To make available experts of lower qualifications to an underdeveloped country is not only of little value but can be detrimental to it, as, unfortunately, many examples show.

Financially, such technical assistance can not amount to very much. In the rather exceptional cases where competent experts with these qualifications are available, even the poorest countries could afford to pay them from their own purse.

It would undoubtedly also be important if the developed countries used their influence to *press the underdeveloped countries in the direction of establishing more social discipline* and, in particular, to take effective measures against corruption. The World Bank has from the beginning exerted its influence in that direction, and that pressure could be intensified.

Individual developed Western countries can have little prestige in this important matter, however, as they unfortunately are compromised by their own citizens' activity in underdeveloped countries. As I mentioned, private Western business interests are commonly deeply engaged in corrupting politicians and officials in all underdeveloped countries.

This activity is without any doubt *damaging to the long-term interests of Western business and Western countries.* They are already stigmatized in the eyes of many intellectuals in underdeveloped countries as being associated with exploitation, colonialism, and imperialism.[54] In a large part of the upper class the retention of this view is supported by protectionist feelings that indigenous expertise and business are losing out in competition with foreigners.

To these sources of resentment is added the fact that, in the eyes of these intellectuals, foreign business appears now to be conspiring to undermine the integrity of their politicians and their higher administrators. The damaging effects of this are, of course, strengthened when Western unilateral public aid can be viewed in this light, which, as I mentioned, is sometimes warranted.

To this comes another effect similarly damaging to the West. A Western company that tries to maintain higher business standards finds itself caught in unfair competition with other companies that resort to large-scale bribery. In regard to the national problem, it has gradually become recognized that it is not in the interest of the business community to tolerate unfair competition. Anti-bribery legislation usually has the full support of business organizations in all Western countries.

If anything is certain it is that *collectively Western business has much to gain by stamping out that type of unfair competition.* I have often discussed this problem with enlightened Western businessmen and they have agreed in principle.

This would seem to constitute a problem where remedial action could be expected from their own international organizations, among them the International Chamber of Commerce. Some years ago I got the chairman of the national delegation to that organization from a small country to raise the problem informally at the meeting of the Chamber. In that country businessmen have developed more than usual interest in maintaining high moral codes at home and abroad. Consequently, their business concerns suffer most from unfair competition because of their generally higher standards.

However, he had sadly to report that he had met vigorous opposition even against hearing about the problem and still more against having it publicly discussed at the meeting. The United States delegation had been particularly eager to shove it under the carpet. This is another example of the shortsightedness of businessmen and their organizations in weighing their own interests.

Still another example is their attitude toward South Africa. The commerce with and investments in South Africa are peanuts to American capitalism. But they provide a forceful spur to South Africa's business boom and prevent the American government from taking effective measures to uphold the policy toward South Africa it has announced together with all other governments. And they give the United States and American capitalism—like the British even during a Labor government—a bad name all over the world, which cannot be in the true interest of a country that aspires to world leadership. American business practices and their consequences for government policy in several Latin American countries give plenty of examples of similar shortsighted, irrational, and self-defeating attitudes.

In this situation, *the countries with more enlightened businessmen and firmer government leadership should take the lead by putting corrupt practices by their nationals abroad under the same legal sanctions that are applied at home.* Bribing officials of their own state is ordinarily a serious crime. There is no reason why the bribery of foreign officials should go unpunished. Nowhere in the taxation of corporations are exemptions allowed for bribes given domestically. There is no reason why bribes given to politicians and administrators in underdeveloped countries should be deductible as "business expenses."

It is in the last analysis *a moral question for the citizenry of a country how much it will permit in the way of corrupt practices abroad.* Acquiring a better conscience is in Western civilization also worth some cost. Undoubtedly, corporations in a country which came to apply these stricter rules would lose some business in the beginning. But undoubtedly also they would gain tremendously in good will among persons of integrity in the underdeveloped countries. This could soon counteract or more than counteract the lost opportunities.

It would also place the countries with looser business morals against the wall as culprits. It could not avoid bringing the whole problem of the large-scale bribing of politicians and officials in underdeveloped countries out in the open. The International Chamber of Commerce, for instance, could then not avoid placing it on its agenda.

The problem has here been discussed from the point of view of Western interests. It is self-evident that an *abstention by Western business firms from bribing their way into the economic life of underdeveloped countries would be a very substantial aid to those countries in their attempts to overcome the disabilities of being soft states* —an aid that would not cost the developed countries anything but would actually be in their own long-term interest.

That it would also help overcome the present inhibitions toward scientific scrutiny of the whole problem of the soft state in underdeveloped countries and of corruption is equally self-evident.

Chapter 8

NOT AN ALIBI
BUT A CHALLENGE

The numerous references to *Asian Drama* indicate that practically everything said so far in Part Two on the need for radical reforms in underdeveloped countries—in regard to both the pertinent facts and the policy recommendations when drawing rational inferences from those facts and from the value premises—has been developed more conclusively, that is, in fuller detail and with proper references to sources, in that earlier work. The unwieldy length of the original work called for a condensed last part summarizing the main policy conclusions.

Though published separately, the present volume should fill this void. To an extent it has been selective, however. I have not, for instance, taken up the health problem.[1] And the problems of industrialization and the case for crafts and "small-scale industry"[2] have only been touched upon in Chapter 4 on agriculture.

My attempt to deal realistically with conditions in underdeveloped countries has revealed traits that represent *serious shortcomings—from a development point of view.* They stand as the reason why radical reforms are needed. In my experience these shortcomings and the need for radical reforms, when pointed out, have been used in Western developed countries as a justification for turning interest away from what happens in underdeveloped countries and, in particular, for not wanting to increase but rather to scale down development assistance.

This conclusion, drawn by the reactionaries, has apparently disturbed more liberally inclined persons, a category to which by far the greater number of the professional students of development problems belong. In fact, fear of such a conclusion has systematically influenced their thinking. The optimistic biases in the whole development literature, which I criticize, have undoubtedly gained strength from *the fear that a more realistic analysis of conditions in the underdeveloped countries could discourage people in the developed countries from caring to help them.*

Both these views are in my opinion irrational. Recognition of the fact that the situation in underdeveloped countries is much more serious than is commonly perceived by students of their problems should instead give increased emphasis to their need for assistance from the developed countries. It should also motivate more careful planning of this assistance in order to make it to the highest degree a spur to development. *A realistic view certainly does not provide an alibi for the developed countries but raises, instead, a challenge.*

It is true, as I have stressed throughout the preceding part, that the radical reforms which are needed *must be carried out by the underdeveloped countries themselves.* In particular they will have to harness all their policies in the several fields in an effort to counteract the economic and social inequalities that at present are increasing almost everywhere. This is needed not only for reasons of social justice but in order to overcome major inhibitions and obstacles for development (see Chap. 3, above).

They must then see to it that their several attempts to come to the aid of their poor are not distorted to favor instead the better-offs. This type of distortion, which is now almost a rule in underdeveloped countries, is one of the wheels in the mechanism that works for increasing inequality.

In agriculture they must radically change the relationship between man and land so that man is afforded the opportunity and the incentive to exert himself and to invest whatever capital he can dispose of, in the first instance his own labor. Without a reform of landownership and tenancy, technological advance will lead to still greater social and economic chasms in the large, continually and rapidly growing agricultural population (see Chap. 4, above).

They must spread birth control among the masses, which in the larger part of the underdeveloped world is a much more difficult task than is ordinarily understood in developed countries (see Chap. 5, above).

They must acquire the ambition to stamp out illiteracy among the population within a limited number of years by organizing adult education. They must reorient and improve their schools in an equally radical fashion (see Chap. 6, above).

They must improve their ways of legislation and their administrations. They must consolidate and strengthen their state. They must take up a struggle to liquidate corruption, which is now commonly increasing (see Chap. 7, above).

The gravity of their situation—and the justification of so many "musts"—is signified by the fact that the reforms are a condition for national consolidation and sustained development, and the further fact that, as we have seen, the reforms all meet great resistance, mostly because of vested interests within the upper class, which is regularly in control of politics on both national and local levels.

The difficulties are greatest in the poorest countries, which need development most. On the other hand, as development will generally make the reforms more possible, this implies that reforms, if once started, could release a cumulative process with development and reforms in mutual circular causation.

Only in one respect have we found that the developed countries can *directly* help the underdeveloped countries with the reforms: by preventing their own businessmen from corrupting officials and politicians in those countries. This would remove one of the potent causes for the tendency of corruption to increase. This "aid" would not cost the developed countries anything but, in fact, would be strongly in their own interest (see Chap. 7, above).

With the understanding of the importance for development of the internal reforms comes the question: Is there anything the developed countries can do to influence the underdeveloped countries to see the reasons for reforms and to urge them to undertake reforms?

I may be excused for mentioning first a reorientation of our scientific work. As now pursued *it is commonly directed so as to conceal the conditions in underdeveloped countries that are crying out for radical reforms.* By failing to see and analyze uncomfortable facts, it is playing into the hands of the unenlightened upper-class strata in underdeveloped countries who resist reforms and who distort what attempts at reforms are being made so that such attempts fall in line with their shortsighted interests. That reforms would regularly be in their own long-term interest will be pointed out in Chapter 14, below. The challenge to reforms which honest and penetrating research should raise is thus not given voice.

As we have seen, the biased postwar approach dominating economic research has observed a virtual taboo against even touching the crucially important problems of the soft state and corruption (Chap. 7, above).

It has also followed an old bias in economics by simply assuming that egalitarian reforms are inimical to economic development instead of, as I firmly believe, being a spur to it. In the best case, it has simply bypassed the equality issue (see Chap. 3, above).

In regard to agricultural policy, economists have commonly fallen victim to a cheap technocratic optimism. Increasingly in recent years they have moved away from giving any consideration to the crucially important equality issue of landownership and tenancy, and more generally participation and involvement of the rural masses in agricultural advance (see Chap. 4, above). They are thus becoming accomplices in a development that is bound to lead to increasing and harsher economic and social chasms and that in time will endanger not only economic development but social stability—if that development is not soon modified by giving rational attention to the equality issue.

No economist as far as I know has seen the supreme importance for development of rapidly stamping out illiteracy by means of an adult education campaign. In regard to education in schools on the several levels, economists have recently provided the underdeveloped countries with the utterly superficial and false theory of "investment in man." It serves in the underdeveloped countries as an excuse for not attacking the really crucial problems of quality—the direction, content, and spirit of teaching and learning (see Chap. 6, above). At present the educational system is often planned so as to be inimical to development.

That the general direction of research upon fields of study is dominated by the turn of political interests of the society we are living in, and where we earn our incomes and achieve our status, is natural—even if, as I said, a student could wish that in our profession we showed more foresight than the ordinary man and could see the writing on the wall so that our societies should not always be taken by surprise and have to improvise policy.

But when that field of study which is given increased political importance is demarcated, it is our duty as students to penetrate the problems; we must not allow ourselves to work with the blinkers of popular prejudices in our society. By not accepting opportune biases, we can make an important contribution to rendering policy and politics more rational.

The main bias of economic research on underdeveloped countries at present—and I am thinking of my confreres in both developed and underdeveloped countries—is that we abstract from attitudes, institutions, and the productivity effects of levels of living when those are very low (see Chap. 1, above). If we can move toward an unbiased and truly institutional approach, I have no doubt that our research could have a wholesome influence on policies in underdeveloped and developed countries and that this influence could be considerable.

It is true that people are moved by what they conceive to be in their interests. *But people also have ideals and they want to be rational.* In particular, they are able to distinguish between long-term and short-term interests and to see the superior importance of the former—if this is plainly and convincingly explained to them. Among the glorious traditions in economics for centuries has been a recognition by our profession that we should not remain in ivory towers, remote from issues and people, but should feel our responsibility for explaining and convincing as well.

The faith of our profession is, in the final instance, that we believe that truth is wholesome and that opportunistic illusions are always damaging.

A more unbiased and penetrating research effort could have direct influence on policy formation in underdeveloped countries themselves. Generally *it would give more impetus to the progressive forces that raise demands for radical reforms.*

For understandable reasons, vested interests are much less ubiquitous in developed countries than in underdeveloped countries; likewise, the importance of unbiased scientific work should there be greater. The question is: How and to what extent can the developed countries exert a healthy influence on the underdeveloped countries to turn their interest toward internal reforms?

In answering this question we should first make clear to ourselves that a *"neutral" attitude, in developed countries, to the internal problems of underdeveloped countries is not one of the choices.* We are not neutral, nor can we be neutral. Even without an aid policy this would be so. An aid policy becomes, of course, an additional reason to entangle our interests in the internal policies of underdeveloped countries. In all developed countries it is understood that aid policies are part of a country's general foreign policy—though seldom is it expressed with so few inhibitions as in various Congressional actions and publications in the United States.

The next question is, then: How should the influence of the developed countries be exerted on the policies of underdeveloped countries and what direction should it be given?

Let us assume—as I do—that people in the developed countries desire the fastest possible development of underdeveloped countries everywhere in the world and, in addition, a development "balanced" in the sense of not creating economic chasms that in the long run would not only build up obstacles against development but could even endanger national consolidation and internal peace. Given these assumptions, the improved knowledge about conditions in underdeveloped countries should rationally lead the developed countries to do what they can to strengthen the forces in underdeveloped countries that press for reforms.

Aid policies increase the influence that the developed countries can exert on underdeveloped countries *by the choice of countries to be assisted and of purposes for which assistance is given.* If the aid is increased very much, as I will propose in Chapter 11, this influence could be greater.

The World Bank Group is a principal provider of capital for underdeveloped countries and its present policy is rapidly to increase its lending several times within a short period. It is significant that the President of the Bank is now stressing the necessity for population control. Even if, as I have shown in Chapter 5, there is not much scope for financial aid in this field—other than providing the funds needed for the continually important research to create a still more improved birth-control technology— and even if by far the greater part of the responsibility falls on the governments of underdeveloped countries themselves, there is plenty of scope for pressure in the right direction.

When weighing applications for assistance, the Bank can from now on be counted on to take into consideration whether or not a country has a population policy and, if so, to what extent effective measures are being taken to implement it. This is quite rational even from the restricted viewpoint of the Bank as a bank, since the future population development is crucially important for the economic development of a country and its possibility to meet its financial commitments. And all the teams of experts sent out by the Bank to survey the economic development of the several underdeveloped countries will be instructed not to bypass the question of how the population problem is dealt with.

Likewise, it is important that the Bank is now placing educational advance high on the priority list. Provided that it liberates itself from the biased and superficial theory of "investment in man" and appreciates that the pivotal educational reforms concern other things than merely spending funds and increasing the number of schools and pupils who are enrolled, pressure from the Bank can be of crucial importance. Somewhat more than in the field of population policy, an inflow of capital resources can make educational reform easier, though not much more so (see Chap. 6, above).

But again, in the long view educational reform is important for the development prospects of a country and thus for weighing its credit-worthiness; hence it is entirely rational that a country's policy-posture in the educational field should be given importance by the Bank's survey teams.

The high priority given by the Bank to agricultural progress is similarly well motivated. Whatever the Bank can do to advance agricultural technology and to have it applied will be of utmost importance. But it should be aware of the danger of letting technological advance become an excuse for forgetting the urgent need for land reform of one sort or another. This would limit the possibility of reaching the widest application of the new technology. At the same time it would widen the gulf between the upper class and the masses in the rural population, engendering unforeseeable consequences not only for economic development but for social and political stability as well.

Indeed, now that the Bank is increasingly becoming imaginative and willing to exert its influence in the underdeveloped countries for progressive policies, it could go one step further and actually be prepared to use some of its resources for aiding underdeveloped countries to carry out land reform. Particularly, this meets a need when the contemplated land reform should take the form of dividing up the land, or some of the land, among the tillers or of going over to cooperative or public ownership and management.

For when as in most underdeveloped countries an expropriation of land without compensation to the former owners is excluded, those countries face a difficult financial problem that is bound to prevent or slow down a land reform. Given certain changes in their tax legislation (and implementation) as a condition, *a loan from the Bank for making land reform more possible could mean all the difference between no reform, or a sham reform, and an effective reform.*

That the Bank has shown interest, and within its limited sphere of activity been successful, in counteracting corruption and preserving fair competition, has already been pointed out (see Chap. 7, above). A next step would be for the Bank to place importance in its surveys and generally in its contacts with underdeveloped countries on what these countries are doing or not doing to improve legislation and administration and so to harden and strengthen the state and, in particular, to stamp out corruption, nepotism, and all shades of favoritism.

It should be pointed out that an effective implementation of the Bank's announced policy, in these and other fields, could not be restricted to mild educational advice, however important that would be. It would hardly be possible, nor should it be, to avoid letting the Bank's policy be reflected in *the choice of countries to be given loans, for what amounts, and for what purposes.*

I have discussed the problem in relation to the activity of the International Bank for Reconstruction and Development. But exactly the same considerations should, of course, guide the governments of individual developed countries in their unilateral public aid policies. The vision opened up before our eyes would be *close cooperation between the Western developed countries and the progressive forces in underdeveloped countries.* That such cooperation would be in the long-term interest of both types of countries is undeniable.

What we have seen in reality up till now is very far from that vision, however. As repeatedly pointed out, the power in most underdeveloped countries is monopolized by political elite groups within a tiny upper class whose short-term interests are generally not in line with honestly and effectively carrying out the progressive reforms. They are, therefore, not being carried out. When seemingly legislated, the laws have been provided with convenient loopholes or have not been enforced. In their implementation they have often even been distorted so as to have the opposite effects from those announced.

At home the groups in power have often been able to silence, or even to get active support from, the economists and, generally, the thinkers and writers who determine "public opinion," which is largely an upper-class affair in most underdeveloped countries. I have illustrated this in regard to the more recent discussion of agricultural policy, where the question of land reform has often fallen through a trap-door (see Chap. 4, above). As we have seen, the same has for the most part been true of other urgently needed reforms, for instance, in the field of education (see Chap. 6, above). Corruption, which is such a lively issue on a somewhat lower level of public life, is less and less broached in professional development discussion (see Chap. 7, above).

In the developed countries it is apparently felt to be wise policy to take diplomatic considerations to those in power and in any case not try to thrust reforms down their throats. This attitude is in conflict with the history and present ideology of developed countries. It is, indeed, measuring with unequal gauge. In fact, it is discrimination in the most serious sense, implying that strivings which now stand out as having been beneficial to the developed countries themselves, and indeed having reshaped their societies, are not considered advisable for the underdeveloped countries.

In Chapter 3, I pointed out that in an almost mechanical way passivity among the masses and the absence of any strivings for reforms in an underdeveloped country appeal to Western business interests seeking outlets for investment and enterprise in underdeveloped countries. Their natural allies are the ruling oligarchies. *This is a direct*

continuation of colonial policy and, indeed, the justifica-
tion for the label "neo-colonialism" often thrown at West-
ern enterprise.

In the colonies the same mechanism regularly led the colonial powers to seek support from the privileged groups who shared their interest in preserving "law and order," which always was interpreted as preserving the *status quo.* For a laissez-faire policy to turn their interest away from egalitarian reforms they found the further reason that it was not advisable to interfere with customs, which often had religious sanction.

For present-day Western capitalism dealing with the underdeveloped countries which are now politically independent, the logic of this mechanism inherited from colonialism is not so evident. If and when opposition against a reactionary oligarchy starts to grow, be it violent or not, it is not the most comfortable situation for foreign enterprise to be stranded in close alliance with that oligarchy and to have drawn profits from this alliance. It would be understandable if enlightened Western businessmen were not only advancing the wages and the welfare and promoting the organization of the workers they themselves employ—as they often do—but were also trying to lay a certain distance between themselves and those in power.

For the time being this is, however, mostly a pious dream. In order to carry on their business with reasonable efficiency, they frequently feel the need to collaborate closely with the ruling oligarchies. This must often seem to be quite a legitimate policy—even if in the end it may lead to difficulties. It is less legitimate when their collaboration with politicians and officials is being oiled by bribery. In the longer view this last business pattern works to the disadvantage of Western business, as stressed in Chapter 7.

It is, moreover, easily observable that Western businessmen, however liberal they might be on their home ground, when operating in an underdeveloped country tend to become social and political reactionaries. To many of them a dictatorial upper-class regime, suppressing all opposition, is favored, even if it is extremely exploitative. To have to deal with such a regime facilitates business, which is difficult enough in every underdeveloped country. This attitude is understandable even if in the long run it becomes disastrous, not least for their own interests.

Many enterprises also carry a historical load of reckless exploitation, corruption, and even plain fraud from earlier times when the enterprises were first started and property and concessions acquired. This historical load now and then explodes, as presently illustrated, for instance, by the political reaction in Peru to American oil interests there. But there are many more such potential scandals that must be prevented from exploding by keeping close to the oligarchy and often by bribing them. This is often the situation in Latin America, where there was no colonial regime preventing the most outrageous abuses.

It should be pointed out that the present generation of businessmen can feel personally quite innocent. They themselves would perhaps not now be engaging in the business practices once applied when their firms were laying the foundation for the enterprises. But it cannot be an easy decision to take to pay back and retreat from unjustly acquired rights and properties.

Businesses can also regularly rely on the aid of diplomatic pressure from their home governments, which must bolster their consciences. In Latin America the United States government has an old tradition of backing such pressure by the threat of military intervention or the actual use of it, recently often substituted or aided by subversive activity through the CIA and otherwise.

In the United States the cold war and the ensuing preoccupation with saving the world from Communism has been a most important excuse for those types of pressures on underdeveloped countries. It has released an ideological trend that in the United States and in the underdeveloped countries themselves stands as a cause of diverting interest from egalitarian reforms or any reforms at all.

The American government has in the postwar period been prepared to accept as ally any reactionary regime in an underdeveloped country that takes a firm stand against Communism. From such a regime very little was asked in terms of egalitarian reforms or incorruptibility. In this way the United States acquired an image in the eyes of the whole world, and particularly of the underdeveloped world, of a country that stood for global reactionism.

We all hope that the cold war will now abate. In particular, we can hope that the American interpretation, during the McCarthy-Dulles era, of the role of the United States will change. We should then have the right to expect that there will be an opportunity for liberals in the United States to assert themselves in foreign policy and, more specifically, in its policy in regard to foreign investments.

What I indicated to be a vision—that the developed countries use their considerable influence to strengthen the progressive forces in underdeveloped countries—could materialize. In any case *this is what we should work for.*

Such a turn of policy would be in line with cherished ideals and also with what the developed Western countries have accomplished at home. I would not expect enlightened businessmen with their eyes on the future to be necessarily averse to such a change—though it would undoubtedly assume an abnegation of privileges and properties acquired by exploitation and sometimes fraudulent practices, particularly in Latin America.

And it would certainly contribute to liberating the theory of economic development from some of the influences that have supported its biased limitations. *In order to incorporate progressive reforms into this theory, it would simply have to become institutional.*

In the discussion of aid to underdeveloped countries, stress has been laid on providing more resources for their development. With this I have no contention. Rather, like almost every other economist, I want to argue for raising the level of the resources to which they are given access. But before I take up the discussion of aid, trade, and capital movements in the next part of this book, I need to criticize what I consider to be grave deficiencies in the way economic development is defined and measured.

Development is commonly understood in simple terms of economic growth—national aggregated growth of production or income. Before I go further I would like merely to remind the reader that economists always, and from John Stuart Mill on more systematically, at least made a reservation for the importance of distribution of wealth and income. This important reservation has lately tended to disappear from the economists' analysis of economic development in underdeveloped countries.

But there are many other dimensions of development that are abstracted from when we simply equate development with growth of production or income. The social system is complex and consists of a great number of causally interrelated conditions.[3] Subject to the arbitrariness common to all indexes, the movement of the social system of interdependent conditions could, in principle, be represented by an index.

To get the data for changes in all the conditions and to weigh them correctly from the point of view of significant valuations is, of course, far beyond present possibilities. But we should retain the important notion that—as we can easily find out by scrutinizing the inferences we commonly draw—*what in fact we all mean by development is the movement upward of the whole social system.*

In this situation it is defensible, however, to turn to

some indication of development that is easier to ascertain and measure than the ideal index. The rate of growth of the national product or income per head of the population is then a natural choice.[4] But we should remember, however, that we are then using a rough and ready *indicator* of that more complex change in the whole social system that we really should want to record. This reservation is not understood or in any case not accounted for in the commonly used "definitions" of development.

But far more alarming is the use of this definition of development in the Plans and in the whole literature. The discussion is regularly based on *figures for the increase in the national product or income for which there is not a sufficient empirical basis.* These figures for economic growth are often given with a decimal or occasionally two decimals—implying one hundredth of 1 percent!

Comparisons among countries are, moreover, ordinarily made in terms of the official exchange rate to American dollars. With all the various exchange and import controls in most underdeveloped countries and with the differences in all other relevant conditions, this is, of course, not permissible. Even a mention of the importance of this problem is ordinarily missing.

In *Asian Drama* I made a critical examination of the way in which figures for the national product or income are computed in South Asian countries.[5] Because of the lack of clarity of concepts utilized and gross deficiencies in the basic material, I arrived at this conclusion: *"That these figures have any precise meaning at all is doubtful; we see no possibility of estimating even roughly the margins of error."*

The study I undertook of the component parts of the aggregate data—even if disaggregated only for agricultural and non-agricultural pursuits—gave glaring proof of the gross inadequacy of these data.[6] The commonly quoted figures for the savings ratio were deemed entirely useless.[7]

The attempt I made to correct the commonly used comparisons of national product or income among the several underdeveloped countries in South Asia as accounted for in terms of the official exchange rates to United States dollars by deflating the figures by price levels merely illustrated the extreme crudeness of this whole type of statistics.[8]

Throughout the chapters of *Asian Drama* I intentionally renounced the use of most of the multitude of figures on development rates and many other things that are so easily available and commonly used by my colleagues for inferences sometimes in very precise terms. This was certainly not because of aversion to quantification on my part.[9] On the contrary, I view the future development of our discipline as largely dependent on our success in observing and translating into firm figures our now too-vague conceptions of reality.

My accusation against conventional economic research at this point is its *extreme lack of critical scrutiny of the statistical material*. In the field of production and income this uncritical attitude has made it possible to "measure" and compare the rate of development of individual underdeveloped countries from year to year down to fractions of a percent. This is plainly humbug, or, to express it more politely, unwarranted precision. It is not less so when these figures are dressed in impressive-looking econometric models. The models represent *loose thinking presented as particularly rigorous analysis*.

The lack of critical sense is visible in all other fields of the study of underdeveloped countries, for instance in the naïve use often made of statistics on literacy and enrollment (see Chap. 6, above). Indeed, it is difficult to avoid the conclusion that *the last generation of economists, with all talk about rigor and precision, have lowered scientific standards in precisely these respects*.

We economists compare badly with the demographers. In spite of their concepts being simpler and their having

the powerful tool for checking their data for internal
consistency within the population mechanism,[10] to which
we really have nothing corresponding, the demographers
have conservatively retained the scientific discipline of
always wanting to characterize the uncertainty of their
data and their calculations.

There is one book that should be compulsory reading
for all the hundreds or thousands of economists now
venturing into research on underdeveloped countries,
namely, Oskar Morgenstern's classical study *On the Accuracy of Economic Observations.*[11] Even when scrutinizing the comparatively very highly refined statistics of the
United States he finds reason to warn against taking
growth figures for short periods as accurate, except within
large margins of uncertainty and error. Statistics giving
international comparisons

> are among the most uncertain and unreliable statistics with
> which the public is being confronted. . . . This is a field
> where politics reigns supreme and where lack of critical
> appraisal is particularly detrimental.[12]

As Morgenstern—rightly, in my opinion—is not prepared to make "concessions as far as the scientific use of
growth rates is concerned," he concludes:

> As available today, they are worthless in view of the exact-
> ing uses to which they are put. . . . Precise uses of "growth
> rates" are entirely inadmissible, whether for comparing dif-
> ferent countries or short periods of the same country.[13]

But, as Morgenstern stresses, this is exactly the use to
which they are commonly put.

Along the same line as Morgenstern, Donald V.
McGranahan, then at the United Nations Bureau of Social
Affairs and now the Director of the United Nations Research Institute of Social Development in Geneva, com-
plains about the trusting manner in which unreliable
statistics are employed in scholarly publications, and the

"elaborate structures and elegant comparisons sometimes built up on the basis of very fragile data. . . . even in the case of the better statistics, . . . the figures give the illusion of a precision that does not exist." [14]

There are several conclusions to be drawn from what has been said. One is that *we are not permitted to share the certainty of other economists, founded upon uncritical use of the available statistics on the growth of production or income, about whether and at what rate various underdeveloped countries or almost all underdeveloped countries have been developing, are now developing, or will continue to develop.*

Another conclusion is that *far too little attention has been given to improving statistics in underdeveloped countries.* This work should primarily be directed toward clarifying concepts applied and making the "observations" at the basis of the statistics more accurate.

A third reflection that forces itself upon the critical reviewer is that *the loose and to a large extent arbitrary utilization of extremely bad statistics has made it more possible for economists to stick to, and not become corrected from the side of empiricism of, the biased postwar approach to the development problems.*

Part Three

THE RESPONSIBILITY OF THE DEVELOPED COUNTRIES

Chapter 9

TRADE AND CAPITAL MOVEMENTS

I   In Colonial Times and Now

The very idea that the developed countries, in all their dealings with underdeveloped countries, should show special consideration for their welfare and economic development, and should even be prepared to feel a collective responsibility for aiding them, is *an entirely new concept dating from after the Second World War.*

The breaking up of the colonial power system, and the awakening of national ambitions of countries that were formally but not really independent, especially in Latin America, meant that the developed Western world was now suddenly faced with a great number of new independent countries. They were all very poor and obviously had great difficulties in engendering the development that those who spoke and decided for them craved.

The colonial system had served until then as a protective shield for the Western developed world's conscience.

Even though the peoples under colonial rule were just as poor and in need of development then as now, responsibility for what happened out there lay exclusively on a few individual, mostly West European, countries whose subjects they were.

If other countries had wanted to interfere in their rule over their dependencies, they would have resented it— as they actually did when they felt that outsiders wanted to meddle, though such meddling practically never occurred on the part of the governments of other Western developed countries. In some cases and in some respects the metropolitan country did aid a colony in various ways, though the picture is mixed. But this was largely a unilateral—and to an extent a bilateral—relation, even in regard to the motivation.

There was, in fact, no political basis for feeling any degree of collective responsibility on the part of the developed Western nations. When in this chapter and the two following I deal in critical terms with what they are doing or not doing, and what they should do to help the underdeveloped countries, we should remind ourselves how new the very idea of such assistance is. Before the Second World War hardly anyone perceived a common responsibility on the part of all developed countries to aid the underdeveloped countries.

Now such a responsibility is becoming recognized. And this has happened within a time period that is very short, historically speaking. Perhaps for this reason we should not feel disheartened about the future of those international relations.

The reason why underdeveloped countries need international special consideration is because of the very fact that they are underdeveloped, extremely poor, and encounter great difficulties in their attempts to develop. In this chapter I will attempt to analyze why international trade and capital movements have not been more favorable to their development efforts than they have been.

II   A Biased Theoretical Approach

The theory of international trade was not worked out to explain the reality of underdevelopment and the need for development. One might say, rather, that this imposing structure of abstract reasoning implicitly had almost the opposite purpose, that of *explaining away the international equality problem.*[1]

When applying an immanent criticism to the theory of international trade, the biased approach it implies stands out in the unrealistic assumption of stable equilibrium— and a number of other assumptions related to that assumption. Even in later writings, it has been retained more tenaciously than in other parts of economic theory. Another unrealistic assumption is the notion that there are certain elements of social reality which can be characterized as the "economic factors," and that it is defensible to analyze international trade while abstracting from all other factors.

These assumptions opened the way for the ideological predilections that since classical times have been deeply embedded in all economic theory but particularly in the theory of international trade. These predilections—harmony of interests, laissez-faire, and free trade [2]—determine, more than economists usually realize, their approach in present writings.

Biased in this way, the international trade theory developed the thought that trade worked for the equalization of factor prices and incomes, in the first instance wages of labor.[3] Trade would permit industrial activity to adapt itself to the location of natural and population resources in different countries and different regions, and this would have a generally equalizing effect on incomes everywhere.

Two prominent compatriots of mine, the late Professor Eli F. Heckscher and Professor Bertil Ohlin, perfected this classical theory long before the Second World War by carrying out the reasoning in terms of more factors of production than labor. They also drew the major conclusion about trade having equalizing effects more explicitly. After them the econometricians, particularly in the United States, have in recent decades shown a lively interest in elaborating how under very specific, abstract, and usually static conditions this tendency to equalization of factor prices in different countries would be realized.

What we can here observe is indeed a very strange thing. International inequalities of income have been increasing for a long time and are still increasing. After the avalanche of the liquidation of the colonial power structure since the end of the Second World War this development toward increasing inequality has become an ever more pressing concern in international politics. At this very juncture of world history the theory of international trade has increasingly stressed the concept that international trade initiates a tendency toward a gradual equalization of incomes as among different countries— under assumptions that should stand out as obviously unrealistic and against all experience.

The reader of this book will by now not be surprised if I characterize this strange *direction of theoretical interest* —and, in particular, the almost total lack of interest among the economic theoreticians working in the field of international trade to explain the existing and growing inequalities in the world—as *a bias, opportune to people in the developed countries.* In its origin this bias had its moorings much further back in the history of economic thought than most of the other biases operating through what in the first chapter I called the postwar approach.

A third compatriot of mine, the late Folke Hilgert, could almost have made a claim to originality, when he posed the question—without furnishing an answer—How does one explain the obvious deviation in reality from established theory?

But this biased bent of international trade theory—and its implicit predilection for harmony of interests, laissez-faire, and free trade—undoubtedly influenced the way in which the problems of the underdeveloped countries were commonly discussed, and how the peoples and governments of these countries were advised. And this is, of course, why I touch upon the problem in this book.

This was particularly true until the underdeveloped countries joined together in recent years to complain about their trading positions and the trade policies of the developed countries—the outcome of which was the institution of the United Nations Conference on Trade and Development (UNCTAD), established in 1964 despite much resistance from developed Western countries. Much that in earlier years had emanated from the intergovernmental organizations in the trade field—the International Monetary Fund and the General Agreement on Tariffs and Trade (GATT)—can only be explained in terms of this biased view.

The easily observable fact that governments and people in general in the developed countries feel so much less of a bad conscience in the trade field than in regard to aid has undoubtedly much of its explanation in the unrealistic and biased theory of international trade, established as of old.

The fact is that, contrary to that theory, *international trade—and capital movements—will generally tend to breed inequality, and will do so the more strongly when substantial inequalities are already established.*

Unregulated market forces will *not* work toward reaching any equilibrium which could imply a trend toward an equalization of incomes. By circular causation with cumulative effects, a country superior in productivity and incomes will tend to become more superior, while a country on an inferior level will tend to be held down at that level or even to deteriorate further—as long as matters are left to the free unfolding of the market forces.

The former country will continually acquire more external and internal economies. And from every center of growth emanate backwash effects to the other countries on the "periphery," to borrow an expression from Raoul Prebisch. These unfavorable trends are usually stronger, the lower the levels of income—and of education and a number of other "non-economic" factors, as they have been called when economic theory has abstracted from them. The spread effects, on the contrary, are weaker at lower levels of income and everything else that goes along with poverty.

We can see these effects of the working of the market forces also within a country.[4] A "growing point" established by the location of a factory or any other expansional move, will draw to itself other businesses, skilled labor, and capital. It will by the same token have backwash effects that keep down or even impoverish out-regions, if the spread effects are not strong enough. This theory is confirmed by the observable tendency for poorer countries to have greater regional differences in income than richer countries.

The main reasons why these differences are becoming smaller within highly developed countries are, first, that the spread effects become stronger and the backwash effects weaker at higher levels of living.

The second explanation is the state. It can intervene in the play of the market forces, and it does intervene. In the international setting the underdeveloped countries are in a weaker position than the underdeveloped regions in an individual country, simply because a world state does not exist that could legislate, tax, subsidize, protect, and promote underdeveloped regions as the state does in the individual country.

I have developed this theory more fully and with proper qualifications in another context,[5] and will here have to restrict myself to this bare hint of my argument. But I want to point out that folklore in all countries is full of expressions proving the popular understanding of this theory that goes counter to the established theory of international trade. As so often is the case, the Bible gives expression in this ancient folk wisdom: "For unto every one that hath shall be given, and he shall have abundance: but from him that hath not shall be taken away even that which he hath" (Matthew 25:29; cf. 13:12).

It is therefore perhaps not so difficult to understand that when the underdeveloped countries became independent, their political spokesmen showed little respect for the theory of international trade in its established form—even if some of their economists occasionally did so, particularly in more recent decades. In India the early economists around the turn of the century developed a school of thought that could be called "institutional" and that directed its main attack against the type of free trade and laissez-faire the British imposed upon their colony.

In colonial times, the superior, and often cheaper, products from the developed countries outcompeted the products from old crafts and traditional industry in the underdeveloped countries, without opening new markets for any manufactured products from them. Nor could capital movements be relied upon to counteract international inequalities. On the whole, capital shunned the underdeveloped countries.

True, capital was scarce in those countries. But the need for it did not represent much of an effective demand that could compete in the capital market. The bulk of European overseas capital exports went to settlements in the open spaces in the temperate zones which were becoming populated by emigration from Europe.

There was some capital export, however, that went into the construction of railways, ports, and other public utilities—investments made secure by the political controls exerted from outside by the colonial governments or in Latin America by other means. Contrary to Marx's anticipation for India, the construction of railways did not give the start to a steel industry or to an industrial revolution.[6] The materials and capital goods needed for these investments could more economically be imported from the developed countries.

A usually somewhat smaller stream of capital found its way into investment in large-scale enterprises specializing in the production of primary products for export. They were ordinarily so profitable to their owners that they rapidly became self-supporting so far as investment capital was concerned.

These enterprises tended for natural reasons to form enclaves, cut out and isolated from the surrounding economy but closely tied to the economy of the developed country from which the capital and the management came. The economic relations of the foreigners with the indigenous economy were for the larger part restricted to employment of unskilled laborers. They ordinarily imported their capital equipment and the foreign personnel often even spent a large part of their incomes on imported consumer goods or investments at home. This cut down the spread effects in the country where the foreign enterprises were situated.

Racial differences, the immense cultural differences, and the very much lower levels of living generally made segregation a natural consequence. This was clearly the case within the enclaves themselves as between the managers and the workers, but it also worked toward the rest of the population. Segregation hampered the transfer of culture, including technical skills and the spirit of enterprise to the indigenous population. This is part of the explanation why these economic starts in colonial times remained enclaves, and why the spread of expansional momentum was so weak or almost absent.

The main effect of international trade on the underdeveloped countries in colonial times was thus to promote their production of primary products for export, employing unskilled labor. *This still largely determines the struc-*

ture of their economies. Seventy or 80 percent and sometimes more of their export today is composed of primary products.

This highly schematized [7] picture of what happened in underdeveloped countries in colonial times is meant to demonstrate that this development, or this relative lack of development, was not primarily forced upon the underdeveloped countries by devious policy designs by the colonial powers. It was mainly *the natural outcome of the market forces, which do not work for equality but tend to increase inequality.*

When the foreign businessmen and governments took commercial advantage of the working of the market forces, they only "played the game"—as long as it paid. And they established law and order, built up schools of the type we analyzed in Chapter 6, constructed railways and ports, and established banks and other commercial enterprises—primarily in their own interest but also in the interest of the underdeveloped country they ruled.

Where there was a formal colonial rule, however, they also regulated, to an extent, the market forces by putting a damper on too scandalous departures from the rules of business morals. Many Latin American countries still suffer the effects of never having benefited from that type of control of a metropolitan country.

The main interferences in the play of the market forces, however, were made in the interest of the colonial powers and their businessmen. A metropolitan country had, of course, an interest in protecting the dependent country as a market for the products of its own industry, sometimes also in protecting its home market from competition from the colony. Likewise, it had an interest in procuring primary goods and even in investing so as to produce them in quantity and at low cost.

But in all these and many other respects, *colonialism meant primarily only a strengthening of the market forces.*

It built itself into, and gave an extra impetus and a peculiar character to, the circular causation of the cumulative process working all the time toward international inequality.

The market forces did not, as in abstract economic theory, work under free competition. There were many elements of monopoly, almost always working in favor of businesses in the metropolitan country and usually, to an extent, condoned or even promoted by the colonial government. In this chapter I include them in the term "market forces."

This process is continually in operation. Decolonization has not by itself changed much of this situation. And I have inserted this section in the book in order to stress the fact that *the underdeveloped countries have been and are still largely at the mercy of the play of the market forces.* Because of their status of underdevelopment, these forces are adverse to their strivings for development.

To this, two main qualifications should be made. One is that after independence *the underdeveloped countries have gained the opportunity to plan purposive interferences in the play of the market forces in the interest of their own development.* From one point of view the most important negative effect of colonialism had been the deprivation of their right to regulate their own economy in their own interest.

This is important, but what in recent years the underdeveloped countries have learned is that national planning neither rapidly nor effectively lifts them out of economic dependency and poverty. And this would largely be true even if their planning and its implementation were better than they are for the most part and, in particular, even if they were more prepared to carry out the radical reforms discussed in Part Two of this book as needed for development.

The second reservation is even more closely related to their initial state of underdevelopment. They can inter-

fere only with their own underdeveloped and poor economy. That economy is very dependent on the rest of the
world and, in particular, on the market conditions and the
policies of developed countries which dominate world
finance and commerce.

In the absence of a world state that could interfere on
their behalf and to their advantage in the economics and
the policies of the developed countries which make up
this mighty minority, they have to appeal for financial aid
from the developed countries, which shall be discussed
in the following two chapters. They must also press for
acceptance of changes in their commercial policies from
developed countries. This is what that great movement of
the underdeveloped countries that led to UNCTAD is
all about.

III   Trade

With great individual differences, the development
of the trading position of most underdeveloped countries
in the postcolonial era has deteriorated and probably will
continue to deteriorate if nothing is done about changing the trends.[8] This refers in the first place to the far
larger part of the underdeveloped world where there are
no, or less significant, resources of petroleum and some
other minerals that are in brisk and rapidly increasing demand in the developed countries.

This unfortunate trend is largely due to the inherited
structure of the underdeveloped countries' economies and
particularly to the composition and direction of their exports, which it has not been possible to change substantially from what it was in colonial times. The exports from
underdeveloped countries of traditional goods, mostly
primary commodities, have constituted a rather rapidly
decreasing portion of world trade since the end of the
First World War. South Asia, which constitutes such a

very large part of the underdeveloped world, has been particularly hard hit by this trend of change.[9]

Behind this trend have been a number of circumstances. In the present era, primary commodities that are more directly going into consumption, such as various kinds of food and beverages but also textiles and their raw materials, tend, as a general rule, to have a rather low income elasticity and often to lag behind increases in income levels in the developed countries which are the main importers.

For rubber—which otherwise should belong to the commodities that ought to enjoy rapidly increasing demands—as well as textiles and their raw materials, modern technology in the developed countries has created manufactured substitutes. It is possible and, indeed, probable that the same blow will soon hit other traditional export goods like coffee, tea, cocoa, and perhaps some metals (see Chap. 2, above). Even more generally, technology also tends to decrease the quantity of raw materials needed for production of more finished goods.

The forecasts that have been made for traditional exports from underdeveloped countries are ordinarily far from optimistic.[10] The overall outlook seems to be a continuation of the unfavorable trend and in many cases its acceleration.

Meanwhile, the attempts to break into exporting manufactured commodities in competition with the highly developed and industrialized countries meet formidable difficulties. Their established industrial enterprises have a firm hold on the markets. They have built up trade connections, achieved external and internal economies on the basis of a wide and diversified industrial foundation, and built up research departments for continuous rationalization of production and improvement of products. And they have organized marketing facilities through which they are kept aware of their customers' needs and preferences and how these are changing.

Taking foreign markets away from those accustomed to supplying them is difficult for the best-equipped enterprises. For enterprises in underdeveloped countries the difficulties are compounded by a shortage of efficient managerial, technical, and laboring personnel, lack of capital and of business acumen so frequently associated with advanced techniques, and lack of experience in standardized high-quality mass production.

In some lines, cheap labor should give these countries a cost advantage. Unfortunately, however, the inefficiency of both labor and management and the absence of specialized auxiliary facilities often tend to raise the costs of labor per unit of output, and so to negate, in part at least, the low wage scales per unit of time.

Also relevant is a most important inhibition on the part of the industrialists themselves in underdeveloped countries. The import restrictions which most underdeveloped countries have been forced to adopt are made necessary because of their foreign-exchange difficulties. They provide, however, a protection for industries directed upon import substitution. As I pointed out in Chapter 7, this protection is "unplanned": highest for the production of the least necessary products.

After the application of a whole paraphernalia of discretionary controls of enterprise and investment, the protection of those who can slip through the controls is bound to make it possible for high-cost producers to do a profitable business at home. By insulating the internal market from foreign competition, it blunts incentives to produce commodities for export.[11]

Exports of manufactured goods from underdeveloped countries have increased faster than exports of primary goods, though not nearly so fast as from developed countries. But for a number of reasons this increase has not yet had great importance for their development prospects.

For one thing, the basis from which the increase takes place is very narrow. Moreover, most of the manufactured goods exported from underdeveloped countries, such as textiles, foodstuffs, timber products, leather goods, and other products involving simple manufacturing processes, are not far removed from the primary stage and can hardly be expected to give the same impetus to industrial growth as the more processed products making up the bulk of the exports from developed countries.

Finally, most underdeveloped countries are not experiencing much of the increase of even this type of export, which is for the larger part coming from a few countries. Hong Kong is, for instance, responsible for between a quarter and a third of these exports.

While export prospects are not bright, import needs, and actual imports as well, tend to rise for two reasons: population growth and development efforts since the Second World War.

The rapid population growth increases the need for a lot of things, in the first instance food, tending to increase imports in the deficit countries while decreasing exports in the surplus countries. The development efforts raise everywhere the need to import development goods of various sorts.

IV Capital Movements

The result of all this has been, almost everywhere in the underdeveloped world, *a widening gap between the import needs and the actual export returns*. In this situation, and as the export difficulties have been persistent, the import needs have had to be curtailed, reducing development efforts below what would have been desirable, and also the consumption levels, particularly among the masses.

In South Asia and also in many other underdeveloped countries there has remained *a gap even between actual exports and imports.* This "trade gap," as it is usually referred to, has been filled in the exchange balance by inflows of various sorts. From the inflows, however, the outflows have to be subtracted. They are also of different types.

For many countries, particularly in Latin America, the net flow is negative. This means that for these countries movements of funds do not alleviate but, on the contrary, heighten the pressure to increase exports and, to the extent this is not possible, to decrease imports.

Financial aid from the developed countries constitutes one type of inflow. For many years now, such aid has been stagnating and in real terms, decreasing (see Chap. 11, below). As, moreover, aid is increasingly taking the form of loans, it originates later outflows of interest and amortization.

This consequence has been mitigated to an extent by affording a long amortization period, by granting a grace period, and by keeping the rate of interest low. In recent years, however, the average rate of interest has been rising again and the average maturity of new loans and the grace period have been shortened.

The International Bank for Reconstruction and Development has increasingly become an intergovernmental agency for development of underdeveloped countries. It is expanding its loan activity, even if it still accounts for only a small portion of the capital inflow to these countries.

Its regular loans are often said to be given on commercial conditions, which is hardly true, however, as the rate of interest and other credit conditions could not have been kept so favorable without the member government's guaranty of its bonds. In addition, it has by its subsidiary, the International Development Association (IDA), set the pattern for public loan activity containing a very substantial aid element.

For the rest, the capital inflows are composed of private funds (see further in Chap. 10, below). They consist in part of short-term export credits. This latter type of capital inflow has in recent years been rising drastically. They postpone the pressures on the exchange balance but only for a brief breathing space, and these credits are often expensive.

Portfolio investments, which played such a large role in colonial times, have now practically ended.

Much hope is now placed on direct investments. For reasons already given we should subtract what is invested in the petroleum industry and other enterprises for exploitation of certain raw materials for which the demand is rapidly rising; these investments are of less interest for by far the greater part of the underdeveloped world. Though more exact information is not available, this would decrease the aggregate figures usually quoted for private direct investment by perhaps one third or more.

In South Asia private direct investments have not amounted to much.[12] The same is true in West Asia and Africa. They have had larger scope in East Asia and in Latin America. Their importance for the exchange balance depends in the first instance upon whether and to what extent they will decrease the need for imports and/or increase exports.

Then, profits from these investments, when they are taken out of the country and not reinvested, and, of course, the repatriation of investment capital represent an outflow from the point of view of the exchange balance. (For a criticism of the common practice to count the former as capital "inflow" and to disregard the latter, see Chap. 10.)

Another outflow is the capital sent out by the citizens of an underdeveloped country, usually put in banks or in holdings of stocks. This has mostly the character of "flight capital" and offends against the exchange rules. For this reason it also largely escapes statistical observation. It is, however, known that such outflows of capital are often sizable, primarily, but not only, from Latin America.

The development of trade and of capital movements sketched above has resulted in the problem of *the rising debt burdens of underdeveloped countries.*[13] It is calculated that the accumulative debts of these countries have increased from $10 billion in 1950 to $40 billion in 1965, and that they are continuing to increase and will in future years also.

Annual payments of interest and amortization over the same period have increased from $0.8 billion to about $3.6 billion. The ratio of debt service payments to export returns rose from less than 4 percent in the middle 1950's to 9 percent in 1965. It can be foreseen that if present trends continue, all the gross inflows of capital will be swallowed up by the outflows, including the debt service, sometime in the early 1970's.

For almost a decade anxious warnings have been expressed, particularly from the International Bank for Reconstruction and Development, which feels a general responsibility for the development problems of the underdeveloped countries and especially for the capital movements. It is now several years since the then President of the Bank, Eugene Black, saw the danger that "the machinery of economic development could be overloaded with foreign debt until it sputtered to a halt amid half-built projects and mountains of discarded plans." [14] His successor, George D. Woods, talked about the "debt explosion" and repeated the warnings. The remedy could be more public grants and easier credit conditions for public loans. *The trend in regard to such public aid has gone in the opposite direction* (see Chap. 11, below).

Some rescheduling has been undertaken for several underdeveloped countries, which is, however, nothing else than a more considerate way of managing a bankruptcy. It works on the symptoms and does not solve the fundamental problem: how to stop a development that is bound to explode in a payment crisis, if more radical measures are not taken.

V   Trade Policies

The capital movements into and out from underdeveloped countries are either reflexes or represent modifications of what happens to their foreign trade, and especially to their exports. The main problem accentuated by the debt explosion and the rapidly rising debt burden is *how to improve the trading position of the underdeveloped countries.*

As I stressed, the trends in the trading positions of underdeveloped countries in recent decades are in the main the result of the play of the market forces— strengthened by various monopolistic elements that are almost always operating to the disadvantage of the underdeveloped countries. These trends imply, in fact, merely a continuation of what had happened in colonial times. If left unhampered, the market forces in this wider sense work to the disadvantage of the underdeveloped countries.

But, as in colonial times, *the commercial policies of the developed countries have further discriminated against the underdeveloped countries in a number of ways.* In the postcolonial era those policies of the developed countries that are adverse to the development interests of the underdeveloped countries may even have become less considerate. The former metropolitan countries have often felt less responsible for the welfare of a colony once it was on its own.

The commercial policies discriminating against the development interests of underdeveloped countries make up a long and varied list which can here be dealt with only in summary fashion. There are, first, the tropical agricultural products, such as coffee, tea, cocoa, and a number of others. They cannot be produced in the temperate zone where the developed countries are located, and they can thus not serve any protective interest.

Tariffs and taxes on these products were earlier often motivated as a luxury taxation. In affluent societies that motivation has fallen off. They are now purely fiscal duties. From an individual country's point of view they are simply taxation of a particular kind of ordinary consumption. They could most easily be abolished—by being shifted to other taxes, for instance on other consumption or on consumption generally.

Then there is the more regular agricultural protection that often works to the great disadvantage of underdeveloped countries. The generally high protection of the home production of beet sugar is one outstanding example, as is the protection of various vegetable-oil-yielding plants.

Still more obnoxious is the protection in developed countries for manufactured and semi-manufactured goods. With the foreseeable lagging trend in exports of primary goods—even if the type of agricultural protection exemplified above were abolished—the achievement of viable and dynamic economics in the underdeveloped countries rests largely on the chance of these countries to increase exports of manufactured goods.

Expansion of such exports meets formidable difficulties under all conditions. These difficulties have, however, been raised higher by protectionist policies applied in the developed countries.

The more processing involved in the production of a commodity, the higher the tariffs, usually. Even for semi-manufactured goods, which in the beginning should offer relatively easier opportunities for underdeveloped countries to shift away from merely producing primary goods for exports, tariffs raise a protective barrier that is often prohibitive. If the primary material is let in duty-free, the effective tariff on a semi-manufactured commodity is ordinarily much higher than it appears.

This abstract exemplification is enough to show that *the commercial policies of the developed countries are almost systematically rigged against the efforts of underdeveloped countries to rise out of underdevelopment.* These policies become the more damaging as they add their influences to the adverse effects of the play of the forces in the market.

In a rational world, giving due consideration to the egalitarian idea, *it should, instead, be a natural ambition of the world community to make such interference in the unfolding of the market forces that export trends in underdeveloped countries would take another and less disastrous course.*

In fact, no individual developed country—and no underdeveloped country that has embarked upon planning —is prepared internally to let the market forces cause large regions to remain underdeveloped and sometimes even lapse into further impoverishment. Still less could it think of strengthening the adverse effects of the market forces by intentional policies.

The developed countries are now developed and politically consolidated partly because, throughout their recent history, they have interfered in the play of the market forces and framed policies that counteracted and corrected the adverse effects of those forces.

Since the development problems of underdeveloped countries rose to international importance after the Second World War, this line of thought has been stressed by progressive economists and statesmen in all countries. I once formulated the demand for reform in the field of international trade by suggesting that what is needed is a "double standard of morality in commercial policy"— and for once a double standard to the advantage of the weak and not the strong as usually has been the case in a world which is ruled by power and not by moral considerations.[15]

As an Indian official once pointed out: "Equality of treatment is equitable only among equals." The under-developed countries cannot abstain from protecting their economy, particularly their budding industry—though one would wish that they were more free from foreign exchange considerations to plan their protection better and also showed greater ability to do it.

Because they are compelled to use all the foreign ex-change they can acquire—export proceeds, foreign credits, and financial aid—to keep imports up to the highest level, their import restrictions can only shift their import demands from some commodities to others that are considered more important.

Whatever form they are given, these restrictions will not tend to decrease international trade. And so small as their imports are, compared to total production in the developed countries, these shifts can under no circum-stances cause difficulties of any importance in the econo-mies of the latter countries.

The developed countries, on the contrary, should uni-laterally open their boundaries for imports from under-developed countries. In addition, *they should find the means of actually promoting imports from underdevel-oped countries.*

The whole structure of the economies and the interna-tional trade of those countries has become so warped and "unbalanced" as a result of the unhampered play of the market forces during many decades, aided by narrowly selfish policies by developed countries, that nothing less would be really rational.

And I stress again that this is the policy line taken in the internal policies of all developed countries as a matter of course when they face a problem of underdeveloped regions. The developed countries which at home have been most successful in national consolidations and economic progress have been those which have carried out the egalitarian reforms most ardently.

The United States is no exception to the general rule that developed countries have for a long time been interfering in the play of the market process in the interest of less advantaged regions and groups of people within their own boundaries. It is true, however, that as a nation composed of immigrants and their offspring, largely but by no means entirely of European stock, and with the background of Negro slavery, the majority of well-off Americans have become accustomed to tolerate large pockets of very poor people in their midst without taking effective measures to lift them up from poverty and underdevelopment.

As I pointed out in the Preface, the United States in this way has a problem at home that is similar in many respects to the problems of development in underdeveloped countries. As a welfare state, the United States is still relatively backward.

The solution of its urban problem and the parallel problem of the rural slums will take time. It will also involve financial expenditures that few Americans conceive of realistically. The implication is that the well-off citizens of the United States carry a very large "debt to the poor" that has to be paid in order to preserve and improve national consolidation. This, incidentally, makes all its figures for national wealth and income unrealistic and exaggerated.

The long-term direction of change in the United States in regard both to peoples' ideas and to public policies is, however, unmistakable. They are in line with what has happened in other developed countries which are more advanced as welfare states, having had less serious problems to tackle and having gone further in solving them. The United States is, therefore, not an exception to the general rule I have indicated.

These internal policies can now be seen to have been in the long-run interests of not only the backward but also the most advanced regions. There undoubtedly exists to a considerable degree a "harmony of interests." But it has been a "created harmony," reached not by letting the play of the market forces unfold themselves unhampered, but by regulating them and harnessing them to serve the common interests, to which belongs protecting and advancing the lagging regions and groups of people.[16]

It stands out as a paradox that the policies adopted for these purposes in the developed countries often have been framed in such a way that national equalization has been sought and reached at the expense of cutting down the export possibilities of the underdeveloped countries. In any case, the idea that similar policy considerations should be taken to them has hardly occurred in the policy discussion in the developed countries until very recently.

The welfare state is nationalistic,[17] indeed very much more so than a laissez-faire type of state would be. Thus, tremendous forces of vested interests, often spread out among broad layers of the citizens, are so created that they can be mobilized against abstaining from policies that hurt underdeveloped countries. In this case, it is wrong to put the blame on the "capitalists," as is often done by some ignorant radicals. *On this point, the people are the reactionaries.*

In the United States hundreds of opinion polls over the years have established the fact that, even more broadly speaking, it is often the poor who are reactionary. McCarthyism was a popular movement. It was not the upper strata who in the presidential election of 1968 voted for Wallace. In the United States this is the result of the still imperfect integration of the lower classes, lack of a broad-based balanced institutional infra-structure of organizations, and effective popular participation.[18]

Even if this situation has little or no correspondence in

the other developed countries, where nations are more integrated and consolidated internally, in regard to their feelings toward the rest of the world and particularly the underdeveloped countries, they are most often just as shortsightedly selfish in their reactions. The international solidarity basis is lacking or too weak, particularly when it comes to giving up what people look upon as trading advantages, even when they are petty and merely transitional.

Abolishing the policies in developed countries that are adverse to the underdeveloped countries, and, still more, initiating policies that would help them positively, assume that people in the former countries would accept, to one degree or another, the conception of *a welfare world*. Logically, this is implied whenever there is an interest in doing something to help underdeveloped countries in their development efforts.

People in developed countries should draw the inference from their national experience that this can be done with little or no real sacrifice in the long run. They should learn to see the possibility of a "created harmony" even internationally—or, for the foreseeable future, at least be willing to take steps toward such a "created harmony."

This visionary thought, so far removed from the drastically imperfect international reality that exists, needs to be stressed. Without spreading this idea among the people in the developed countries, it will not be possible to counter the broadly based vested interests in preserving the commercial policies that are adverse to the export interests of the underdeveloped countries. Unless this idea spreads it will, of course, be still more difficult to induce people not only to abolish tariffs and other trade obstacles but to take steps in order positively to promote exports from underdeveloped countries.

People in the developed countries must be made to feel something of the *rational generosity* in their relations with underdeveloped countries that has gradually developed in the internal relations.

The United States and other developed countries should not, of course, need to protect by tariffs and other means their textile industry, for instance, against exports from underdeveloped countries. Abstaining from doing so would create transitional problems at home. But these countries are resourceful and wealthy enough to handle such problems without great difficulties.

Similar adjustment problems are constantly created by economic and technological changes and they are handled as a part of normal policy routine. In the efforts to lower tariffs in recent years, culminating in the so-called Kennedy Round, adjustment problems were actually created intentionally in order to win long-term gains. With few exceptions, however, these efforts concerned only the trade between developed countries.

As a general rule, cutting down the restrictions of developed countries against imports from underdeveloped countries should actually be in the long-term interest of the developed countries. The industries where the latter countries could compete—resource-based and labor-intensive—are usually not the industries which it is in the developed countries' interest to promote or even to preserve at home. In the developed countries they are often low-wage industries. Rational planning in developed countries should regularly result in moving their scarce labor resources to high-productivity industries, not in tying them to low-wage industries.

In a country like Sweden, with a tradition of an enlightened trade-union movement which now includes practically the whole labor force, this policy line is accepted even by the union representing the workers in these low-wage industries. The textile industry, for instance, has been forced to rationalize radically and direct its production to higher-grade goods, where the industry can still compete successfully. Meanwhile, the textile workers in the period 1950 to 1968 decreased by around 50 percent.

Worries about their exchange balance are regularly put forward by developed countries as a reason why they are not prepared to scale down tariffs and other import restrictions which now stand as obstacles to the export efforts of underdeveloped countries. The same reason is given for their not being prepared to increase their financial aid, and also for their need to tie the aid they are giving to exports from the donor country (see Chap. 11, below).

It is true that many developed countries are in acute and serious payment difficulties—including the United States—and that almost all other developed countries feel a danger of getting into such difficulties. Without, of course, being able in the present context to develop my thoughts in any detail, I want first to point out that *the payment difficulties of developed countries must be considered self-inflicted.*

They are results of inadequacies in their internal and external policies. Private and public consumption—in the case of the United States also the huge expenditures for armaments and for the Vietnam war, moon flights, etc.— are permitted to rise, without the nation undertaking corresponding increases in taxation. The result is inflation.

As the inflationary rise in prices—or the foreseen rise in prices—is not following a similar pace in the several developed countries, the result is exchange difficulties for some of them, and the risk of such difficulties in the near future for almost all of them. The developed countries, moreover, have not yet perfected their monetary cooperation to the extent of preserving a foreign exchange balance in spite of this.

But leaving aside the cause of the exchange difficulties, or the felt danger for such difficulties in the near future, it is, of course, *a preposterous situation when the rich, developed countries for exchange reasons find themselves unable to take even small steps to liberate imports from underdeveloped countries*—and feel unable to increase even a little their financial aid to underdeveloped countries, and also feel impelled to tie the small aid they are giving to exports from their own countries.

They are not taking like precautions in regard to other policies of far greater consequence for their payment balancing. I pointed to some of these policies when hinting at their proved inability to stop inflation. The armament expenditures, which in the United States have been permitted to increase to amounts that are incomprehensible to a normal person, are only one example.

The fact that developed countries are putting forward exchange difficulties as a reason for not abolishing the obstacles for exports from underdeveloped countries is, therefore, nothing but a demonstration of *how low among their national policy goals they rate the interest to help underdeveloped countries to develop.*

Like all crucial policy choices, this is, at bottom, a moral issue. Governments and officials should not be blamed—except for not taking upon themselves the responsibility to urge more forcefully unpopular policy lines when they are rationally motivated. They respond to their peoples who are prejudiced. As I pointed out, there are vested interests involved. Those interests are rather petty. But they are broad-based among the peoples.

VI The Failure of UNCTAD

The Second UNCTAD Session in New Delhi in the spring of 1968 was almost a complete failure.

In his report on the Conference, the distinguished Secretary-General of UNCTAD, Raoul Prebisch, who has

since resigned, had to acknowledge that what was lacking
was "enough political will":

> [The] great objective was not achieved. The second ses-
> sion of the Conference was able to obtain only very limited
> positive results that are not commensurate with the dimen-
> sions and urgency of the development problem.[19]

Bitterly he adds:

> It seems that prosperity, in people as well as in nations,
> tends to form an attitude of detachment if not indifference
> to the well-being of others. . . . developed countries, with a
> few exceptions, continue to consider the development prob-
> lem as a residual one that can be tackled here and there
> with a few and insufficient measures instead of bold and
> resolute action. [Only] in some sectors of developed coun-
> tries [is there] a far-sighted view of the serious economic
> and political consequences of allowing the Third World to
> continue to drift.

This, he said, was "the real background to the second
session of the Conference."[20]

Small and hesitant steps were taken in the right direction by the developed countries to adjust their positions,
though without committing themselves to do anything in
particular. But even that movement has since then been
proceeding at a snail's pace.[21]

The Conference was not faced with radical demands
from the side of the underdeveloped countries. Largely
this is explained, and perhaps politically justified, by the
knowledge that the developed countries were not prepared to yield much ground, and that they had all the
power. When brought down to concrete issues, the underdeveloped countries also showed interest splits among
themselves, which considerably decreased the force of
their thrust.

For one thing, they wanted to *increase trade among
themselves,* particularly in the several regions. For the
most part, this must be their own responsibility. But it is

important that the developed countries give their support
and, in any case, do not use their power to resist regional
integration among underdeveloped countries.

As late as far into the 1950's, I can testify from my close
observations of what went on in the regional commissions
that the United States and Britain adamantly resisted the
use of these organizations for cooperation in the trade
field, pleading that it would go counter to the principle
of multilateralism in international trade. Other developed
countries remained uninterested and neutral, generally
speaking.

In the last decade or so this has changed. In Latin
America, where the most ambitious efforts in the direction
of regional integration have been launched, the bringing
down of trade obstacles within the region has been seen
as an interest of the foreign, mostly American, enterprises
there to have a larger "home market." This foreign support, incidentally, has in some Latin American countries
dampened the indigenous support for the idea.

Regional integration would in general undoubtedly be
helpful for the development of underdeveloped countries.[22] They certainly would need the protection of a
"common market" more than the continental West European countries. But the difficulties are very great. Aside
from the problems involved in creating a political climate
of solidarity in regions often marked by deeply rooted
national animosities, there are special difficulties of a more
technical nature.

It is thus necessary to prevent the larger and industrially
more advanced countries in a region from overwhelming
the smaller and less developed countries, which otherwise
cannot be expected to join in the efforts. A customs union
or a free trade area is therefore not enough.

What is needed in underdeveloped regions, besides
the lowering of trade barriers among the participant
countries, is *joint planning to decide which countries
should specialize in particular product lines.* National

planning has its serious defects in all underdeveloped countries. As, moreover, planning is not equally advanced in the several countries, this raises a very great obstacle in the way of increasing trade cooperation in a region.

The goal of regional cooperation is no longer a controversial issue and the developed countries could in general terms pledge their support.[23] They undertook no specific obligations, however, except to agree that the problem should be dealt with within the UNCTAD framework, probably by a special committee.

In regard to the *transfer of "financial resources,"* the developed countries agreed to raise the target, earlier fixed at 1 percent of the national income, by some 25 percent by setting it in relation to gross national product.[24] There was no agreement upon a target year for the attainment of this objective. Throughout the Conference, it was referred to as "aid." I will criticize that type of calculation in the next chapter.

In regard to public *aid* proper, general sympathy was expressed for softening its terms by increasing grants-in-aid and by improving interest rates, ammortization and grace periods for loans, and also for decreasing the extent of tying aid to exports of the donor country.[25] No definite promises were given, however, and continually the trend goes in the opposite direction (see Chap. 11, below).

The developed countries were prepared to recognize in general terms the need to provide *supplementary and compensatory financing* in order to protect an underdeveloped country's development plan against the effects of export shortfalls.[26] No definite commitments were made. The request that the developed countries or the intergovernmental organizations should provide financial resources for the *prefinancing of buffer stocks was not accepted.*

The idea often launched that the agreement being reached on the creation of *Special Drawing Rights* within the International Monetary Fund should be used for sending an *extra inflow of funds* to underdeveloped countries was not accepted.[27]

The reform of the monetary system is mainly a concern of the developed countries that dominate international financial relations. The financial problem of underdeveloped countries is a totally different one. These countries are bound to be short of foreign exchange under any system.

I have personally for a long time looked upon the idea, so prominent in many of the monetary reform schemes, of using this opportunity for replenishing the available capital resources of underdeveloped countries as utterly illusory.[28] To smuggle through more financial aid to underdeveloped countries in the guise of the adoption of a monetary reform is a subterfuge which the developed countries will not buy. Financial aid has to be fought for, and agreed to as such. This was now confirmed—though at the same time only the vaguest undertakings of increasing financial aid were accepted.

Perhaps it should be added that it is strongly in the interest of underdeveloped countries for the developed countries to succeed in regulating the monetary system, which is mainly their own affair. Such a reform will remove one reason, prominent in developed countries, for their holding down their aid: the common excuse of their exchange difficulties.

The issue of *commodity agreements* played an important role in the discussion at the Conference. Its history in the postwar era has been discouraging. Few agreements have been reached. They have often broken down.

The difficulties in this field are tremendous. At bottom there is a fundamental difference in approach. What underdeveloped countries really want is "fair prices," that is, "better prices," while what developed countries can accept at most is a stabilization of prices over time.

And they can point to the disorganization of markets with an oversupply of a commodity, which would result from bolstering prices. This is more likely to occur, since agreements on restrictions of production are difficult to reach and to enforce.

There often cannot be a united front among underdeveloped countries, and for many reasons, one being because some are importers and some exporters. For many commodities of importance to many underdeveloped countries, developed countries are also exporters, sometimes the main exporters.

By this I am only hinting at some of the difficulties that meet international efforts to regulate commodity prices. On this issue the result of the Conference could hardly have been different from what it was. It scheduled studies, consultations, and negotiations to be carried out for a number of commodities.[29] Most probably the resolutions passed on commodity agreements will prove to have been written on sand.

In regard to *shipping*, the Conference confirmed a certain advance that had been reached within the UNCTAD framework between the two sessions, giving the underdeveloped countries more of a say, or at least more of a possibility to observe, what is happening in this heavily regulated industry in regard to freight rates and other things.[30]

Shipping is, of course, dominated by the developed countries. But they gave general, non-committing promises of technical assistance and aid to the underdeveloped countries in their own efforts to develop their ports as well as their merchant marine, insurance business, etc.

The really fundamental problem is, of course, *the opening of export markets* for underdeveloped countries in the developed countries. In regard to *agriculture* the underdeveloped countries no longer insisted on a more general scaling down of protectionism but asked that they be allocated a share of any increase in demand.

This was a big retreat. Nevertheless, the only concession they got was a promise from the developed countries to carry out, to the extent practicable, measures providing more favourable conditions of access to their markets for primary products exporting countries, particularly bearing in mind the interests of developing countries, and permitting primary products exporting countries to participate in the growth of the markets of industrial nations.[31]

This is certainly a superb specimen of the type of non-operative and non-committal compromise agreement at which, unfortunately, governments in intergovernmental organizations excel when wanting to conceal that they have got nowhere.

In regard to *manufactured and semi-manufactured products,* Prebisch could report "a limited and incomplete result." [32] The Conference accepted in principle the idea of a system of general non-reciprocal and non-discriminatory preferences.[33] The carrying out of this promise could certainly be, as Prebisch stresses, of "paramount importance."

The United States had for years been stubbornly against giving any favored treatment to underdeveloped countries —while itself continuing in many ways bluntly to discriminate against these exports. Now the United States had felt the necessity to move. But neither the United States nor the majority of other developed countries were prepared to negotiate with the underdeveloped countries even the main elements of a preferential system.

The implementation of the decision was then referred to a Special Committee in UNCTAD with the hope that it should have ready before the end of 1969 a final report setting down a definite proposal for a scheme of preferential treatment of exports from underdeveloped countries. It was not able to have such a report ready by that time.

It is also evident that, if the committee ever reaches that step, the proposal to which the developed countries can agree will not be a far-reaching or generous one. The forces holding them back from rapid and courageous action are organized in the Organization for Economic Co-operation and Development (OECD), which operates as a caucus of the developed countries.

No reference in the resolutions is made to the particularly offensive tariffs and taxes on *oriental products,* in regard to which the developed countries cannot even pretend that they have the valid interest of protecting their own production.

More generally speaking, one can observe a strange thing in relation to this last problem, as to several others. *When a particular problem is taken up for intergovernmental discussion, this is often used as an excuse for individual developed countries not to take rational action on its own part.*

Even a relatively enlightened developed country like Sweden—which in OECD, together with the Netherlands, is pressing for speedy action and substantial concessions in regard to general export preferences, and which has unilaterally abolished half of its already low fiscal burdens on imported coffee—can be caught arguing that a more complete abolishment of its tariffs and taxes on oriental products has to wait for an international agreement.[34]

This is, of course, confusion of thought. Abolishing these taxes on oriental products by all, or most, developed countries would tend to increase prices more than if it is done by one country. Such action would then certainly be of greater importance for underdeveloped countries but the individual country would have to face a bigger rise in these prices.

That a problem has reached the stage of being discussed in an intergovernmental organization cannot be a rational reason for any single country to abstain from doing a sensible thing in line with what it is arguing should be done also by other countries. There is undoubtedly in the activity of our intergovernmental organizations a *built-in tendency for a false and damaging "internationalism." It becomes an excuse for national non-action.*

Coming back to the resolutions of the Second Session of UNCTAD, it should only be added that all expressed sympathy for land-locked countries, for the very poorest of the underdeveloped countries, were against restrictive business practices in the developed countries that hurt underdeveloped countries, and gave advice to underdeveloped countries as to how they should mobilize internal resources, use aid, etc.

But the sad conclusions of Prebisch quoted in the beginning of this short survey of the results of the Conference stand as well founded. And everything that has happened after the Conference makes one fear that *the majority of developed countries, with the United States in the lead, is now intent upon putting UNCTAD on ice.*

And the OECD—which in the international field functions as "the rich men's club"—becomes the instrument for organizing that sabotage.

But the problems will not disappear. They will loom larger and become ever more pressing as the years pass.

Chapter 10

THE OPPORTUNISTIC JUGGLING OF AID STATISTICS: THE "FINANCIAL FLOWS"

I   Insincerity and Hypocrisy

As we have already pointed out in Chapter 9, the commercial and financial policies of the developed countries toward the underdeveloped countries are, like all other crucial political problems, at bottom *a moral issue*. The same point of view will be adhered to in Chapter 11 on aid. The primordial problem is, therefore, *how people in the developed countries think and feel about helping underdeveloped countries in their development efforts.*

In the final instance, the development up till now of

trade and aid policies and the possibilities of altering these policies in the future depend on people's intellectual and emotional reactions in the developed countries to the realities in the underdeveloped countries, and their perception of their responsibility for helping to change these realities.

In the United States, in particular, it has become customary among liberals to put the blame for improper priorities and reactionary policies on Congress. It needs to be pointed out that probably no legislative assembly in the world is more sensitive to public opinion than the American Congress—a fact explainable by the frequency of elections, the Anglo-Saxon tradition of majority elections in small districts, and many other peculiarities in the system of government in the United States.

When there are major faults to be accounted for, the blame has therefore to be laid squarely on the American people. That Congressmen as well as the President and members of the Administration play a role not only in giving expression to but also in forming public opinion does not change this fundamental fact. With variations in modes of political operation, the same is true of other developed Western countries.

Those many persons who, like the present author, want to change a line of policy must try to accomplish, in the end, the changing of public opinion. Influencing experts and politicians, however important, can in a broad and long-term context only be looked upon as an instrumental, intermediary task. Arguing in terms of ideals, and of rational conclusions from those and from knowledge of facts, we cannot accept as unconscionable that broader task of attempting to change, in the end, public opinion.

A general observation should be made within this context: *In the Western developed countries there is an air of insincerity and even hypocrisy in the discussion of their relations with underdeveloped countries.*

On the one hand, exuberant general declarations in terms of international solidarity are continually made, committing the rich developed nations to a policy line of generosity toward the poor underdeveloped countries in order to help them develop.

It started with vague but unreserved declarations in the Charter of the United Nations, prepared even before the end of the Second World War. In its Preamble—and speaking in the name of "We the Peoples of the United Nations"—the Charter bound the governments participating in the organizations "to promote social progress and better standards of life in larger freedom" and "to employ international machinery for the promotion of the economic and social advancement of all peoples." This theme was then further developed in Chapter IX of the Charter on "International Economic Cooperation."

Thereafter followed a sequence of emphatic declarations, ever more explicitly extending promises to the underedeveloped countries. On President John F. Kennedy's proposal in 1961 the 1960's were by a unanimous decision of the United Nations General Assembly designated the "Development Decade," and responsibility for realizing that goal was laid squarely on the shoulders of the developed as well as the underdeveloped countries.

President Lyndon B. Johnson improved upon his predecessor's rhetorical record by explaining that the vision of the Great Society should apply to the whole world and not only to the United States. And in between and beyond these oratorical landmarks there are spread over the years any number of equally extravagant declarations by statesmen representing all developed Western countries.

The secretariats of the intergovernmental organizations in the United Nations family were collecting and disseminating information on the continually widening gap in levels of living between developed and underdeveloped nations and on the misery of the great majority of people in the latter. Through all the mass media, full awareness of these dismal facts has been spread to almost everybody living in the developed countries.

This has generally, however, not released much willingness among their peoples to part with what they have, or to accept even minor adjustment in their trading practices. It is a fact that, as yet, *no Western developed nation has made any real sacrifices in shouldering aid obligations to underdeveloped countries. Neither have they been prepared, on the whole, to abstain from even minor trading advantages that can be shown not to be of real long-term interest to a developed country.* The trend has not gone in the direction of greater willingness to come to the assistance of the underdeveloped countries.

As we shall point out in the next chapter, the aid awarded them not only has tended to stagnate during the Development Decade but has even decreased when measured in real terms and still more when compared with the developed nations' increasing capacity to give aid as their wealth and incomes have been rapidly growing. At the same time, the "quality" of the aid in various respects has radically deteriorated.

Reacting to the weak popular and parliamentary response in most Western countries to demands for sacrifices to be made for aiding the development of underdeveloped countries, government officials, when they plead for acceptance of the small and often concocted aid budgets, rather regularly argue that the aid costs very little and that in reality the money spent is a boon to various business interests at home. This has, in particular, become a line of government pleading in the United States but, as I shall point out, not only there.

In the previous chapter I pointed to the unwillingness of developed nations to do anything substantial to counteract the market forces that in the field of trade and capital movements have continuously been holding the underdeveloped countries down in poverty since colonial times and in their brief independence era, let alone to abolish such commercial policies as are strengthening these forces.

This course of government action in the developed countries and, behind such action, of their people's thoughts and feelings shows *ominous similarities to that in the field of war and peace.*

Every national representative taking the floor in an international assembly—and every journalist writing a leading acticle in a newspaper—is expected to paint in somber colors the pending catastrophe that threatens mankind if the armaments race between the two superpowers is not stopped.

It has not been stopped, however, but goes on at an accelerating pace.[1] The arguments in the field of disarmament reached after protracted negotiations are mostly inconsequential for *that* purpose. They often seem to have been offered as a solace to the alarmed world that something is being done to avert the apocalyptic danger.

Few seem to be really alarmed. And there is astonishingly little popular pressure for disarmament. The peace organizations are extremely weak everywhere and particularly so in the two countries which are running the armaments race. But there are everywhere strongly organized nationalist groups pleading against lowering the guard.

And the military-industrial complex represents a tremendously powerful combine of vested interests, resisting any serious move toward curbing the armaments race— particularly since it has now also involved many universities and actually become a military-industrial-academic complex. In some periods it almost seemed to have taken over the government in the United States.

There is no reason to believe that the situation is fundamentally different in the Soviet Union. It has, indeed, its counterpart in almost every country, big and small, rich and poor. We are all living in strange toleration of an immense danger hovering over our future without joining together to avert it.

In the field of aid to underdeveloped countries as well as commercial and financial policies, the intellectual and emotional confusion in developed countries is equally apparent. It stems from the simultaneous presence in people's minds of two strains of totally incompatible ideas: the realization of the extreme poverty of the masses in underdeveloped countries and their need for help on a large scale, on the one hand, and, on the other hand, a selfish unwillingness to make any substantial sacrifices to aid them.

This must be damaging for people's conception of reality. At this advanced stage of the argument followed in this book, the reader should in this situation expect a tendency to distortion of truth in an opportunistic direction— in other words, a biased view of reality, useful in covering up the incompatibility of these two strains of ideas.

As the poverty in the underdeveloped countries cannot be conjured away, the reader should expect in the field of aid *a twist of the statistics so as to show aid to be larger than it really is.* This is, in fact, what has happened. And again I will have to devote critical attention to figures which are presented and relied upon in both scientific and popular writings.

II *The DAC Statistics*

The Organization for Economic Co-operation and Development (OECD) with headquarters in Paris, includes practically all of the rich and developed non-Communist countries. OECD has a Development Assistance Committee (DAC). The statistics on the disbursement of development assistance assembled from the member countries and, after an "aid review" by officials of the member governments, produced by DAC's secretariat are the main source of information concerning that aid and are practically everywhere taken as authoritative. They are uncritically relied upon by economists and other professional students of development problems, officials, politicians, authors of popular books and articles, journalists, etc., by the secretariats of the other intergovernmental organizations, and by special expert groups set up from time to time.

The first thing to note is that in the table headings the DAC secretariat uses the term "the flows of financial resources." It is legitimate to assume that this term is chosen in order not to have to exclude items that have no aid element, particularly private investments and credits. The fine point that DAC statistics record all sorts of "flows," whether having the character of aid or not, is regularly and systematically forgotten by persons the world over when they make use of the figures.

As noted in the first paragraph of this chapter, the name of the agency that is served by the secretariat producing these tables is the Development Assistance Committee, and its figures for the "flows" become "development assistance" or plainly "development aid." This mutation occurs in scholarly as well as popular and political writings and pronouncements. The DAC secretariat has done little or nothing to prevent this opportunistic misuse of the figures, which is now common throughout the world. In fact, it occasionally supports this misconception itself by some of the titles of tables and comments on the tables.

When the DAC reported (July 10, 1969) [2] that during 1968 the "flows" to underdeveloped countries had increased to almost $13 billion, this implied a decrease in "official flows" but a somewhat bigger increase in "private flows"—which was commonly understood and commented upon the world over as encouraging, showing that "aid" was increasing again.

But the question must be raised: *Is the practice of the*

DAC secretariat of simply adding "private flows" to "official flows" really in the interest of clarity of thought and of honesty? The "private flows" are a very mixed bag of transactions, stretching from direct investment as reported by the Western enterprises to their governments (counted at sometimes padded prices) to export credits.

In fact, the recent increase in the "private flows" was to a large extent due to a rise by $800 million of such export credits. They are often expensive and going to underdeveloped countries that are heavily burdened by debt services for earlier credits. Also, most of these countries are in financial difficulties and need even that type of credits very badly. They can therefore often be exploited by having to pay too high prices for the imports to which the credits are usually tied.

At OECD's Ministerial Council meeting in February, 1969, on "Relations with Developing Countries," the Swedish Minister of Industry, Krister Wickman, pointed out that this composite-flow concept was

> a very bad measuring rod for our financial sacrifices to promote development in the third world. . . . it includes transactions, which, when made between developed countries, never could be called aid. It is important that a distinction be made between development assistance and other flows of capital.[3]

But there are many other and even more serious flaws in the DAC statistics on the "private flows." One is that they are defined as "net values," but the backflows accounted for are only amortization payments on outstanding loans and repatriated capital, again as reported to the governments of developed countries.

Interest payments, payments for licenses, etc., and, in particular, profits taken out from the underdeveloped countries are not included in the backflow, while reinvested profits are reckoned as inflow. Profits of both types can sometimes be fantastically high, particularly on investments made long ago and under the conditions of plain exploitation I touched upon in Chapter 8 and will come back to at the end of this chapter.

Neither is the capital sent out by residents in underdeveloped countries—often flight capital—accounted for. Particularly in Latin America both types of "private outflow," not accounted for in the statistics compiled by the DAC secretariat, amount to huge sums.

With all this in mind, Wickman continued his criticism:

> ... it is very clear, that the net concept used does not come in the neighborhood of the net figures. In 1967 the DAC figure for "net" flows of resources ["official" and "private"] from DAC Members was $11.4 billion. This could be compared with a figure that U.N.'s Secretary General has presented for the total net inflow of resources to the developing countries. This latter figure, which is based on International Monetary Fund statistics, is $3 billion. . . . Due regard being taken to errors and omissions, time lags, and so on, the chief explanation of this [difference] is that the DAC figure represents a very incomplete coverage of the financial transactions with regard to return flows to DAC Members from the less developed countries. Some DAC Members may even find after a close look that their balance of payments with the third world shows a surplus.

But *taking such "a close look" is exactly what people in developed countries do not want to do.* Wickman has his eyes on these opportunistic leanings and their consequences:

> The danger . . . that OECD Members, being preoccupied with their own domestic and external adjustment difficulties, will not pay sufficient attention to the problems of the third world—is . . . very manifest. . . . Overestimation acts as a brake to the expansion of aid programmes. It is thus imperative that the general public and legislators in our countries are correctly informed of the magnitudes of our present efforts to assist the developing countries.

And he expressed the pious hope that OECD and, in particular, the Development Assistance Committee should tackle this problem.[4]

This is not in the cards, however. A "Note by the Secretariat"[5] in answer to Wickman's accusations, makes clear why that secretariat will have to stick to its guns. The arguments boil down to three: that the member governments do not want to change the practice, that the statistical material for other return-flows than those accounted for is weak and difficult to interpret, and that, in particular, the outflow of profits and capital "is essentially a problem for the developing countries themselves."[6]

What has been said implies that *the DAC statistics, quoted everywhere as authoritative, leave entirely open the problem of what the total net private flow of resources from developed to underdeveloped countries amounts to and, indeed, whether there is such a net flow at all to many of the underdeveloped countries or, instead, an outflow.* That it is this other net inflow or outflow which is relevant for the debt explosion and the burden of the debt service in underdeveloped countries, and thereby for their possibilities to engender development, has been shown in Chapter 9.

The DAC secretariat as a professional body cannot be excused for producing its figures for "net flows" without pointing out, *and stressing*, that they do not represent true net values. Salaried professionals acting unethically cannot exculpate themselves by vindicating that they have only acted upon the instructions of their employers, the governments. Neither can the professional world at large be excused for using these figures in the careless and uncritical way they are commonly used—most of the time as meaning "development assistance" or "development aid."

A particular responsibility rests on the secretariats of the other intergovernmental organizations within and outside the United Nations family. They should be credited for having ventured soon after the war into the difficult field of trying to produce worldwide comparative statistics in the several important fields. Quite commonly they have then, however, proceeded with less than the desired degree of professional zeal for clear concepts and for critical awareness of the weaknesses in the primary data they have used as furnished by the national governments.

They have between them their conflicts, particularly in regard to what extent each is responsible for specific fields. But in their accommodations to each other, one polite regard is regularly observed. *They do not question each other's statistics.* That would be bad form.

Thus the statistics on growth of incomes and production, and on rates of growth of underdeveloped countries, that are produced by the statistical office of the United Nations and which I criticized at the end of Chapter 8, are commonly accepted and used by all other secretariats, usually without questioning their meaning, relevance, or reliability.

The UNESCO secretariat produces statistics on literacy and school enrollment which, as I pointed out in Chapter 6, are of very poor quality and grossly misleading. When another secretariat touches on educational problems it would apparently be considered an unfriendly act toward the UNESCO secretariat if its statistics were not taken at face value. Often they are then used with even fewer reservations than the UNESCO secretariat would have dared to do.

This interagency courtesy results in a sort of polite camaraderie that is *unethical from a professional point of view and in its effects decreases the scientific value of the work of the secretariats of the intergovernmental organizations.* As these secretariats have become bureaucratized and, on the whole, are less in a position to attract the most qualified in a certain profession,[7] this has contributed to rendering their output of statistical information stale and less problem oriented.

In the present case this, and the defensive camaraderie I

pointed out, has implied that the DAC statistics have been published year after year without any critical observations from the secretariats of the other organizations. Indeed, these statistics have commonly been quoted and used by them in a totally uncritical way.

The political spokesmen for the underdeveloped countries and their economists have on the whole remained *naïve in regard to this play with statistical figures*. It may seem more excusable, since the experts in developed countries had so unanimously set the tune.

Thus even those spokesmen and experts coming from the underdeveloped countries have almost all uncritically adopted the method of measuring and analyzing development in their countries in terms of the fancy figures for the rate of growth of production and income that I criticized at the end of Chapter 8.

They have also accepted the DAC secretariat's conception of total public and private financial "net flows." This is an even more damaging slip, since this conception is so seriously loaded by a bias that is opportune to the developed countries.

When in 1961, in connection with the emphatic declaration by the General Assembly of the United Nations that the 1960's should be the Development Decade, the developed countries were driven to accept, in principle, a minimum level they should reach for their development aid to underdeveloped countries, this limit was spelled out in terms of these composite "net flows," which should be 1 percent of their national incomes. And when in 1968 at the second meeting of the United Nations Conference on Trade and Development (UNCTAD), this lower level was raised by one quarter by stating it instead as a fraction of the gross national product, it was again these dubious "flows" that should be raised to that next level.

As would-be recipients of the maximum of foreign resources, the representatives of underdeveloped countries have felt, apparently, that they should not be too particular about how these were labeled. But as I have hinted, this is much more than a terminological problem.

The crucial issue of the outflows of profits and capital from underdeveloped countries, which are not accounted for in these statistics, must also to many of the representatives of these countries be a touchy one that had better be left under the rug. They regularly belong to, or are in the service of, a ruling oligarchy, of which many—even if not necessarily they themselves—take personal advantage of the opportunities for private profiteering from their countries' situation of poverty and dependency.

There were, however, in later years enough rumblings from some underdeveloped countries to cause the United Nations General Assembly to express concern over "the increasing rate of outflow of capital from the developing countries which substantially reduces the net volume of external resources available to the developing countries." And the United Nations secretariat has included some estimates of this "net volume" in their publications *The External Financing of Economic Development*.[8]

Though these estimates are too crude to be worth quoting, they give a general impression that *these total outflows, including those of profits and of capital (often capital flight) from the underdeveloped world at large may be of the same dimension as the total private and official "net flows" in the DAC statistics or not much smaller,* particularly as also the figures for "official flows," as we shall point out in the next chapter, are often considerably padded.

For some countries, particularly in Latin America, these outflows are known to be several times larger than total inflows, five times as large it is often contended. A liberal United States Senator, Charles McC. Mathias, Jr., critical of his country's aid policy on grounds which shall be further discussed in the next chapter, recently explained without blinking: "Capital flows *from* Latin America and *into*

the United States are now over four times as great as the
flow south. The countries of Latin America, in a way, are
actually giving foreign aid to the United States, the wealth-
iest country in the world." [9]

Early this year the topic of the "Outflow of Financial
Resources from Developing Countries" was taken up in a
committee of UNCTAD—interestingly enough against
the advice of most member governments of the OECD
group of developed countries. A study made by the
UNCTAD secretariat was requested, "paying particular
attention to the question whether measures could be taken
at the international level to control the outflow of such
resources from developing to developed countries to conform to the development objectives of the developing
countries." [10] It will be interesting to see what comes out
of this study.

The work of the DAC secretariat shows several other
peculiarities. Before their worldwide dissemination, the
figures on "flows" should, of course, have been related to
the inflationary movement of relevant price indices.

The "flows" are presented as "financial," though they
usually do not flow in that form. It should then be of interest for the proper use of the statistics to know more
about the prices put on the various "resources" actually
transferred. And realistic inquiries about profit levels,
taking into account other advantages sought by investors
than dividends, would be highly interesting and relevant.

The DAC figures for "official flows" will be taken up
for critical scrutiny in Section II of the next chapter. That
will *reveal even more deep-seated biases in the DAC statistics, leading to an altogether exaggerated account of
what can be conceived of as genuine public aid.*

But even aside from such touchy problems, studying
the statistics emanating from the DAC secretariat leaves
one with the feeling that the secretariat either lacks normal research interests or is prevented by government pres-

sure from exercising them. Sometimes it even seems to lack an ordinary sense of humor. In the DAC statistics petty fascist Portugal year after year is given the place of honor as having the largest "flows" to underdeveloped countries in comparison with its gross national product.

This does not occasion so much as a footnote explaining that the situation depends on two facts. First, the country has been very poor and largely stagnant for a long time— except for some recent entrepreneurial activity of business interests, mostly from the other European Free Trade Association (EFTA) countries, profiting from the extremely low wage levels. Illiteracy among the masses is high, particularly in the large rural areas. It has a very high child mortality, and extremely low levels of living. Indeed, it is underdeveloped itself as much as three other OECD countries, Spain, Greece, and Turkey, which in the DAC statistics are counted as underdeveloped and therefore not asked to join the club of well-off DAC members. This means that its gross national product, in relation to which the "flows" are posited, is extremely low.

Second, it carries on a protracted colonial war in its "provinces" in Africa to which the "flows" are going—together with some other "flows" reported in the DAC statistics as emanating from other OECD countries.

There are many other problems of great importance which need much more penetrating study than is given them by the secretariats of DAC and OECD or the secretariats of any other intergovernmental organizations, including UNCTAD.

For one thing, we need to know whether the investments represent new ventures or a consolidation of old investments. The latter may have implied concessions to foreign business firms that at present seem unfair and contrary to the development interests of an underdeveloped country.

It would also be of importance to have analyzed in a comprehensive way not only to what countries but also to what branches of the economy of the various underdeveloped countries the "flows" are going. New foreign investments in the petroleum industry and in enterprises to extract other minerals in high demand, located in the few spots on the map of the underdeveloped world where there are such natural resources, may be highly remunerative for the country where they are made, or at least for the rulers of it. But their development efforts may be different, usually less important, than new investments in certain branches of manufacturing industry. The same is usually true of investment in large-scale plantation estates of the type common in Latin America, but not only there.

It is a fair assumption that deeper investigations into such problems, as generally about the "flows" of private capital, would have a greater chance of being carried out in depth and without biases by organizations, which, like the United Nations, are composed of both developed and underdeveloped countries. Even those organizations are, however, not outside the power field, where the minority of developed countries is so strong. There is certainly a need for critical and watchful inquiry from the independent students. Of this we have seen little, however.

III Private Direct Investment

As an escape from the serious problems of the trade gap, the debt explosion, and the rising burden of debt service—and usually without discussing them at all in that context—interest has been focused on *how to encourage private direct investment in the underdeveloped countries.*

In many developed countries but particularly in the United States there has from the beginning been an ideological commitment of faith that the development of underdeveloped countries is best served by private enterprise. As a corollary to this faith the United States policy has been intent upon encouraging private direct investment from abroad in underdeveloped countries.

The International Bank for Reconstruction and Development—explicitly in its general activity of advising these countries as well as in its loan activity—has subscribed to this opinion. In recent years it has modified its stand considerably, however, and might do so still further.

The former President of the Bank, George D. Woods, in his last public appearance in that capacity, stressed the "necessity for new approaches" and confessed that "the World Bank Group is not immune" to the tendency of institutions to stick to "standard formulas." He continued: "In the World Bank Group . . . we have been slow to finance state-owned enterprises because of the problem in many countries of ensuring efficient management of undertakings that, for want of private savings, must operate under government sponsorship." [11]

The underdeveloped countries, in their difficult position, have generally expressed a rather cordial welcome to private investments. Often these enterprises have been awarded favored treatment. Rather generally they have been assured of the freedom to take home their profits and even their capital, if they would choose to do so.

This attitude has been elaborated in several resolutions of the United Nations General Assembly and more recently by a resolution at the Second UNCTAD meeting in New Delhi (1968).[12] In 1969 it was again confirmed in the United Nations Panel on Foreign Investment in Developing Countries, assembled in Amsterdam, composed of business representatives from developed countries and officials from underdeveloped countries.[13]

Usually *the underdeveloped countries want to set conditions,* however. They want a say in deciding in what branch of industry the foreign enterprise is to be undertaken. Often they want it to be a joint enterprise. Often also they set as a condition that a minimum number of their own nationals be trained and employed in higher managerial and technical posts.

For the most part, these conditions are acceded to by the developed countries, at least in their general form. As the U.S. Assistant Secretary for Inter-American Affairs, Charles A. Meyer, recently explained: "... each country must decide for itself how much it [the foreign enterprise] is wanted, and on what terms it is wanted." [14] Behind this consensus there are the obvious advantages to the underdeveloped countries of getting not only a capital inflow but also the technical know-how, management, and particularly familiarity, etc., with markets which ordinarily accompany foreign investments.

Rather generally, however, *the complaint is heard in underdeveloped countries that direct investments are too expensive.* This is primarily a quest for more public aid in the form of grants and loans at concessionary rates. It is supported by nostalgic memories of the portfolio investments which in colonial times could be mobilized from the private-capital market, usually at much lower rates than are now becoming prevalent, and which then played such an important role.

But as public grants and loans are limited, and private portfolio investments are generally not to be expected any more, this complaint does not prohibit most of the underdeveloped countries from being favorable to direct investments.

As a matter of fact, the studies that have been made do not generally show very high profit rates of direct investments. Much reliance cannot be attached to these studies, however. The investment capital is seldom or ever counted at what amounts have historically been invested. The figures are largely arbitrary, and already for this reason there is not much sense in a rate that is put in relation to this capital value.

From the investing concern's point of view, there are quite generally also other substantial dividends flowing from the investments, though they escape ordinary accounting statistics.

For one thing, the investing concern often delivers to its foreign branch machinery, spare parts, and other production materials and makes available patent rights and other licenses. These transactions take place without much outside competition. The commodities and the rights can therefore often be priced at somewhat arbitrary and high levels.

Moreover, once established in a country and "in" with officials and politicians there, the concern will often have opportunities to acquire licenses for imports of commodities that it also produces, and get various advantages that otherwise would not be coming its way.

I have discussed these matters with local officers of several foreign-branch establishments in underdeveloped countries. I have always found them quite open and willing to confirm both the arbitrary manner in which the capital value of their investments is calculated, and the existence of the extra dividends and other advantages, for instance in regard to taxation. In fact, they have often stressed them as a not unimportant reason why the foreign undertaking seemed worthwhile to their concerns.

These experiences convince me that the usually quoted profit rates are unrealistic and too low. They also make me feel that it would be quite possible by openminded and unbiased research to throw more light on how high the true profit rates are.

In the cautious and complicated verbiage commonly used in such international encounters, the Amsterdam agreement contains the following observation:

> The Panel recognized that comparative profitability studies of the same type of investment in different countries, to be meaningful, must take into account all the constituent elements of profits, including possible differentials in prices at which equipment and ingredients are supplied, as well as in royalties and service fees; consideration must also be given to the social, economic and legal situation in both the host and the investing country and the degree of competition. . . . It recommended that further study should be

made of this subject, where necessary on a regional or sectoral basis with the help of appropriate international organizations.[15]

I have already stressed that in most underdeveloped countries private direct investment does not amount to very much—much less than could be assumed from the lively discussion about it.[16] But in some countries, particularly in Latin America, it does, to the extent that it incurs feelings among many of the citizens that *they are losing their independence*, or have already done so.

These fears are naturally particularly strong when the investments are made by concerns from a very big country. That means, in practice, the United States. They are also stronger when the investing concern has interests all over the world. That again means American concerns, for the most part. The fears accumulate when it is seen, or suspected, that the American government will use its power to support American concerns abroad.

The knowledge of these fears should perhaps be *a reason for people in the United States to be somewhat less enthusiastic about direct investment in these countries.* Such a reaction, however, does not appear to be very common. But on the level of the American administration some caution is now and then demonstrated.

The sentence already quoted from Meyer testifies to this. More explicitly, he stated in the same article:

> Most of the resources for Latin America's ultimate development should be generated within Latin America itself. This seems to be inevitable economically; it is probably desired politically.... The United States does not wish to be involved in any case where investment is not wanted, *nor do we want to be involved in any one country so deeply that the sum of our presence becomes uncomfortable.*[17]

From this point of view certain conclusions would seem evident. First, it would be to the common interest of both developed and underdeveloped countries if more of the direct investments came from countries that were not so large and not so near as the United States. For that and other reasons their governments can be expected to be less tempted, and less able, to use political or military strength to defend the interests of their investing concerns. Dispersed in this way, the foreign investments would cause less fear of intrusion upon the independence of an under-developed country, where investments are made.

Parallel or, indeed, identical with that interest would be the interest of having more of the direct investments carried out by concerns that are not so large as most of the American ones now involved in foreign investments.

These conclusions, obvious as they are, have not won much understanding in the United States. Governor Nelson A. Rockefeller, returning from four eventful trips to Latin American countries in the summer of 1969, where he was accompanied by a very large staff of officials and experts in all fields, recently issued a report with the pious title *Quality of Life in the Americas*. He observes there first:

> A great many and probably a majority of the citizens of hemisphere nations regard United States private investment as a form of exploitation or economic colonialism. . . . Fear of domination by United States companies is expressed frequently.[18]

In a most cavalier fashion and without any argument he dismisses this as a "mistaken view" and recommends that "The United States should provide maximum encouragement for private investment throughout the hemisphere."

Professor P. N. Rosenstein-Rodan long ago proposed *a device for transferring technology and management as well as possibly some capital,* which could be helpful in furthering such a development.[19] He called it a "management contract." The idea has been discussed now and then by several authors.[20]

The idea is that a foreign concern should contract with the government of an underdeveloped country to set up and manage a new plant for a limited period, say ten years.

The foreign concern could either make a direct investment for the period agreed upon, or could make it a joint project with the state or an indigenous firm. Or it could even abstain from ownership from the beginning but perhaps provide a fixed-interest-bearing loan for the duration of the management contract.

In any case, the contract should assure the foreign concern a management fee and, in the end, the return at fixed dates of any capital provided, as well as a normal profit on it until then. On its side, it should provide the needed technology and management, but undertake to train and gradually employ personnel from the country itself.

Such a scheme would seem to meet mutual interests. The underdeveloped country would be assured of an industrial start and the needed skills and, perhaps, if so agreed, some capital for a period. Thereafter it would own the plant itself or let it be owned by a selected group of its own nationals.

The foreign firm could in this way profit from selling management and technology without binding capital abroad, or doing so only for a limited period. This should make many smaller industrial concerns more interested and able to go into international industrial ventures.

I have discussed Rosenstein-Rodan's idea with several statesmen in underdeveloped countries but never found much response, which has surprised me. One prime minister explained that he rather preferred to discuss investments with governments and the really big concerns.

He agreed, however, that having fewer big industries among the foreign investors and having them from smaller countries would mean fewer dangers for his country's independence. They would also be more willing to leave, when once the industrial start was accomplished.

Personally I believe that underdeveloped countries do not have, and cannot easily acquire, knowledge of the supply market all over the world where such partners would be available. I have therefore sometimes urged officials of developed countries, concerned about development of underdeveloped countries, to take an interest in the problem, to prepare standard contracts, and to bring the matter to the attention of the many individual firms that have seldom or never thought of the possibility of selling their management and technological know-how without having to tie themselves to long-term investments.

Among the conditions that underdeveloped countries normally want to set up is this: *foreign investment should be limited to certain sectors of their economy.*

No developed country would want to have its public utilities owned by foreign investors. In all developed countries, except the United States, the decision was long ago taken that normally they should even be publicly owned and managed. Even the United States put them under federal regulations and would hardly like to have them owned by foreigners.

It is difficult to believe that underdeveloped countries in the long run would not feel the same desire of excluding foreign interests from public utilities. A similar comparison supports the opinion that they will feel that foreign interests should be excluded from ownership of mines and of land in the form of big estates.

They will also feel that foreign interests should be prevented from becoming too dominant in various manufacturing industries, particularly if the enterprises are branches of very large firms from very large countries, which practically means from the United States.

On these points underdeveloped countries in Latin America, but not only there, have inherited a situation that might have to be changed by *nationalizations of a type that create serious conflicts of interest.* Such nationalizations have been carried out, and it is not difficult to foresee that there will be more of them.

The conflict is often rooted in an unfortunate historical legacy. The land and the concessions were once acquired at exceedingly low remunerations, sometimes by not too clean methods. The government will therefore be unwilling to pay compensations that correspond to present market values. It will anyhow be under pressure at home not to do it. The foreign concerns, on their side, find these demands unjustified, as sometimes the property and regularly their own shares have changed owners since then, often many times.

If the foreign interests are concerns in the United States, they will more or less forcefully demand to be backed by the United States government. One incidental effect will be, in any case, the discouragement of new foreign investments.

It is not difficult to foresee an increasing number of such conflicts in regard to old American investments in Latin America, where governments will continue to change in the future as in the past. But it is a burning issue in other parts of the underdeveloped world also.

The World Bank has focused its interest upon the problem of applying mediation and arbitration to such conflicts, in order to keep them from poisoning the political climate of international cooperation between developed and underdeveloped countries in regard to foreign investment as well as in all other fields.

Peaceful solutions of such conflicts would be more possible if the Bank, under certain conditions, would be prepared to make loans available to facilitate well-motivated nationalizations—in the same way as I suggested in Chapter 8 for land reform.

In both the developed and the underdeveloped countries, the discussion about private direct investments in the latter countries is carried out in terms of the *national interests of development* of those countries.

At this point, however, we should recall that most underdeveloped countries have a very inegalitarian social structure. They are often ruled by one or another constellation of persons in an upper-class oligarchy.

This situation opens the way for policies that are not necessarily in line with what can be considered long-term national interests. Private interests of members of that oligarchy are involved, sometimes in ways that could not stand the light of day.

From one point of view, this situation may make the operation of the foreign concern investing in an underdeveloped country easier. In any case, it becomes almost necessary to cooperate with those who are in power.

As is often observed, foreign investments are bound, at least in the short run, to strengthen what is commonly referred to as the "private sector" in an underdeveloped country. As has been touched upon in Chapters 3 and 8, they will thereby also increase the economic, social, and political power of the oligarchic upper stratum in such a country—even in the absence of illegitimate transactions.[21]

Ordinarily, however, this upper stratum is split into competing factions. The political regime is usually not very stable, as witnessed by the frequency of *coups* in underdeveloped countries.

Most of them imply only a reshuffling of political power positions within the oligarchy. But in some of the underdeveloped countries, not least in Latin America, there is more than the beginning of a more broadly based opposition movement, sometimes extending down not only to the "middle class" but even touching elements among the masses.

The foreign concern, which has had to cooperate with those who were in power, and which often has profited from doing it, can easily find itself in a compromising situation. Both the concern and—if it is an American firm —the United States government, easily become involved in the internal power game in an underdeveloped country.

This is a situation that is not "comfortable" for either the United States or its concerns investing abroad—to use Meyer's term.

The conclusion is that increasing American foreign direct investment all over the globe is not necessarily in the American or in the international interest, as is commonly assumed in the propaganda for increasing these investments.

Another conclusion is that the United States and, indeed, all the developed countries share with the underdeveloped nations their interest in *stamping out corruption in high places, and in ending the type of oligarchic power monopoly, which is the germinating bed of corruption*—and thereby also of lessening uncomfortable involvements in their internal power game.

Chapter 11

AID

I   The European Recovery Program

Much that has been happening in the field of public aid to underdeveloped countries since the Second World War has a prehistory that should be sketched in order that we may better understand the confusion of thought among people in the developed countries in regard to their relations to underdeveloped countries.[1]

When the Second World War ended, the United States found itself in a historically unique situation. Unlike its allies it was not only undamaged by military action but much better off economically than at the beginning of the war. It had entered the war in a state of depression and severe protracted unemployment, but the war had accomplished what the New Deal failed to accomplish, rapidly raising employment and levels of income and living.

In this situation the United States undertook almost singlehandedly the responsibility for rendering the financial assistance that was felt to be needed for reconstruction and recovery. *By far the larger part of this assistance went to the countries of Western Europe,* which in any international comparison—apart from the South European countries—must be included with North America and Australasia as part of the small minority of countries that

are industrially advanced and economically well off, even
though they were temporarily crippled because of the war.

The rescue action under the Marshall Plan and the
European Recovery Program implied that one rich country helped other potentially rich countries very substantially. A "sharing of wealth" seemed natural to Americans
and to most Europeans. But it was a sharing only among
the rich.

The same European-focused bias could at that time be
observed in many other fields. The internationally organized efforts to help refugees were concentrated on the displaced and drifting persons in Europe, while, for instance,
India and Pakistan had to take care of their own refugees
as best they could.

The generosity of the United States to the West Euro-
peans at that early time was almost boundless. The American government showed the utmost restraint in the use
of its power. It advised the European governments to
make up their own minds, promising to support, financially and otherwise, any constructive policy they might
agree upon among themselves.

In the field of trade the United States permitted the
West European countries to discriminate bluntly against
its export. It actually assisted in planning the discriminatory policies against itself, sometimes overcoming strong
pressures from business interests at home. It intervened,
at least once, against the American oil monopolies, prohibiting them from applying a price policy that would
have hurt Western Europe. This was a policy line that
could not be more different from the stand the United
States—as well as most other developed countries—took
when the underdeveloped countries later asked for special
considerations in foreign trade (see Chap. 9, above).

The main dish served to Western Europe was, however,
financial assistance. Excluding military aid, it amounted
in the end to the enormous sum of around $30 billion—
reckoned in dollars that then had a very much higher real

value than after the ensuing inflation of prices. *More than two thirds of it was outright grants.*

I felt at that time that all this assistance should have been given in loans to be repaid when Western Europe had regained its viability. *I never believed—and I do not believe today—that the giving of aid as a gift from one government to another is a necessary, natural, or even wise policy—except when the beneficiary is an under-developed country, with deep-seated, structural disabilities to overcome.*

And I find a confirmation of my opinion at that time in reflecting upon what happened later. The whole international exchange situation would have been more wholesome now and in the past decade if the United States could have called for repayments of loans from the West European governments—gradually and with due considerations. Its record during the Marshall era should guarantee that such considerations toward Western Europe would have been informed with a spirit of rational generosity.

Instead, the grants—and the long maturing period for loans—permitted the continental West European countries, when they had once recovered, to assemble overgrown reserves of gold and currency. This development implied a threat even against the United States' exchange position. We all know that under de Gaulle, France—one of the bigger recipients of grants—could, for a time, exert pressure which nearly amounted to blackmailing the United States.

But *the United States at that early time wanted to give gifts.* I myself can testify how American officials kindly but unsuccessfully prodded their Swedish colleagues also to take grants—which Sweden did not need and did not want—in the interest of "equality" and "cooperation."

In particular, the United States insisted on lumping together as "aid" open grants, loans not necessarily to be repaid on agreed terms, and straight credits. When that pattern was first established in the Marshall era it was due to what I then looked upon as American overgenerosity. It was made more possible because of the United States' unstable background in international finance and its sad experiences with its large credits to Germany and Latin America in the period between the two world wars.

I found at that time, however, few if any European economists or politicians who shared my critical views or even wanted to discuss the problem. They were all happy about the large grants and were ready also to accept that credits were labeled as aid, which created a vague uncertainty as to whether and how they should be repaid. A pattern of confused thinking was thus established that is still with us.

But *a terminological muddle that was then mainly an outflow of what I considered American overgenerosity toward potentially rich and developed countries is now turned into a means for stinginess toward poor and underdeveloped countries.* Any type of capital inflow, private or public, now becomes "assistance" or "aid." History is often so paradoxical.

I want first, however, to probe a little deeper into the thinking and feeling in the United States during the Marshall era.

The American government chose *from the beginning, in the summer of 1947, to motivate the Marshall program in terms of anti-Communism.* As I was often told by American officials at that early time, this line was taken partly on tactical grounds: in order to assure its easier and wider acceptance in Congress and to gain fuller support from the American people.

As the cold war later flared up, actively promoted by a strange "cooperation" with Stalin,[2] and especially after the Communist victory in China in 1949 and the ascendancy of McCarthyism in America, this particular reason for aiding the West European countries gained in importance.

But at that time the program had already been launched and had only to be continued.

The role the anti-Communist appeal played was, on the whole, kept outside the main European Recovery Program. Anti-Communism was used, however, to motivate tying (by Congressional riders) the European governments as well as all other non-Communist governments to the American discriminatory export licensing policy toward the Communist countries.[3]

It is my considered opinion, however, that in the beginning the main motivation of the American people—the farmers and the workers, the teachers and the preachers, the lawyers and the merchants—and of their representatives in Congress to line up behind the Marshall Plan was *much more the positive one of sympathy and solidarity* with nations which were badly off and to which they felt related by cultural and blood ties. This was more important than the negative motivation of saving the Europeans from Communism and of having them as allies in the cold war—even though the anti-Communist appeal undoubtedly gave an extra emotional spur to the emotions, and increasingly so as the cold war intensified.

A peculiarity of the American motivation in the Marshall Plan was, however, that from the beginning all who talked and wrote tried to convince themselves and others that *they were acting "in the best interest of the United States."* To me this was only a further demonstration of the strange and basically inopportune suspicion on the part of the Americans of their own generous motives, which I once analyzed as a slightly perverted element of their Puritan tradition.

Important for what would happen in the future relations of the United States with underdeveloped countries was the European reaction to the American discussion on the home ground. The confession that Americans were acting selfishly was too often eagerly seized upon in Europe as a reason why no repayment, even in gratitude, was really called for.

This was the reaction particularly in the large aid-receiving European countries. At that time the only countries in Europe without a trace of anti-Americanism were Switzerland and Sweden, which were not beneficiaries of grants-in-aid.

I recall a member of the British Labor government explaining at a social party of Europeans that the United States badly needed, and for the foreseeable future would continue to need, to give away a large part of its exports in order to prevent depression at home. The Americans could be happy that Western Europe provided a convenient dumping ground for their surpluses.

All the West European governments reluctantly went along with United States blockade policy against the Communist countries, though with a lot of open and concealed acts of what from an American point of view must have looked like sabotage. This angered members of the United States Congress, although the Administration had to grin and bear it.

When the flow of Marshall money came to an end toward the middle 1950's, the West European governments rapidly joined together and torpedoed the whole American-inspired embargo policy, which they had never believed in, anyway.[4] Thereafter the United States alone abstained from normal trade relations with the Communist countries. This was not against European business interests, as has sometimes been pointed out in the United States.

II Aid to Underdeveloped Countries

There is no doubt in my mind that the American experience with the Europeans during the Marshall era had in several respects deep and lasting effects upon United States policy toward the underdeveloped countries.

To begin with, the huge Marshall Plan, lasting into the middle 1950's, tended to crowd out other demands on

American resources—similar to the way that, in recent years, preoccupation with the Vietnam war, or with landing men on the moon, and attendant costs have crowded out the anti-poverty program at home.

Let me spell out an experiment of thought to clarify what I mean. Imagine that there had been no reconstruction task to be carried out in Europe, but that otherwise nothing was different.

I feel rather certain that as the colonies were then becoming liberated—which on a deeper ideological level touched sympathetic cords in America—and as knowledge about the great difficulties encountered by newly emerging and other underdeveloped countries was disseminated, efforts to aid them would have been forthcoming earlier and more strongly from a United States coming out of the war with feelings for its responsibility in the world—feelings that had then not yet hardened in the way they later would, partly under the influence of the experiences with the West Europeans during the Marshall era.

I can, indeed, very well conceive of the United States launching something like a Marshall Plan for the underdeveloped world. And even if nothing on that enormous scale had been set afloat, aid on a substantial scale *could have been more successfully propagated.*

I will not in this context attempt to give the history of public aid to the underdeveloped countries.[5] It had a very slow start and remained, for years, of a diminutive size—with the partial exception of the aid given by the United States to its former colony, the Philippines.

And at that early time little of what was given to underdeveloped countries was, like the aid to Europe, aimed at economic reconstruction and development. It was mainly intended to meet political and military emergencies and to provide relief to severely depressed civilian consumption.

When, around 1950, the United States' foreign-aid

budget rather suddenly began to grow more rapidly, *the main motivation was less a desire to meet the development needs of underdeveloped countries than it was the intensified cold war.* This was particularly the case in that large part of the underdeveloped world which I have studied most intensively, South Asia. The alignment, and in some cases already a not unfriendly neutrality, of an underdeveloped country became of political interest to the United States, which dominated the scene, providing 80 percent or more of all grants and credits to the region.

The political purpose of the aid was plainly reflected in its distribution among countries. Pakistan, besides military aid, received in economic aid twice as much per inhabitant as India, in remuneration for its political and military alliance to the United States—which in more recent years, however, has not turned out to be very dependable.

And during 1954–58 Laos and South Vietnam received from the United States grants and loans almost equal in sum to those received by India and Pakistan. For the same period, South Korea received more aid (designated economic) than all of India, Pakistan, the Philippines, Burma, and Ceylon. India alone has a population ten times bigger than the three small but strategically important countries taken together.

I argued above that when the Marshall Plan was launched as an anti-Communist policy and explained to be "in the best interest of the United States," this was, at least in the beginning, largely a sort of pious and inopportune self-deception. That motivation had no serious effects on the program itself (except for the peripheral export-licensing policy added later).

But at that later time, under the influence of the intensified cold war and after Korea, *the aid program for underdeveloped countries was actually shaped so as really to be in the political interest of the United States* and, indeed, in its strategic and military interests, as those interests were then conceived by the American government and largely by the American people. At the same time, it was more vaguely conceived of as a development program for underdeveloped countries.

What had been inopportune self-deception now became instead highly opportune, introducing *a duplicity in thinking that still accounts for part of the insincerity and hypocrisy in public discussion* referred to at the end of the preceding chapter.

It is impossible to say how much of the "aid" at that time was misplaced from a development point of view, but that much of it was wasted or even actually inhibited essential reforms by supporting reactionary regimes cannot be denied. This is not an afterthought of mine but was foreseen when this line of strategic aid policy was first introduced, and not only by the present author but by many others.[6]

Among those I quoted in 1954 to support my critical views of this new political "realism" was a wise European historian of diplomacy, A. J. P. Taylor, who explained that "when one state is completely dependent on another, it is the former which can call the tune; it can threaten to collapse unless supported and its protector has no answering threat in return." [7] The American government has since then repeatedly experienced the truth of this in its relations with successive puppet governments in South Vietnam—at heavy financial and moral cost.[8]

Eugene Staley—in a book on United States policy toward the underdeveloped countries written from the explicitly stated viewpoint of how to save these countries from Communism and draw them into political alliance with the United States in the cold war—formulated the practical dilemmas that confront such a strategic aid policy:

> If we do not give vigorous support to governments that are trying to move in progressive, democratic directions when

they need it and want it, we are likely to be forced into the position later of having to back a government that is bad by our standards for the sole reason that it is the only available alternative to a Communist regime.... When in order to prevent a Communist seizure we have to back a corrupt or unpopular or foreign-dominated government, we do immense political harm to our world position.... In that case, also, the appropriations are likely to go mainly for military measures, with bad political repercussions, much more than might have been required to get better results by forehanded economic aid.... How long will it take us to learn that when a progressive reform government happens to be in power in an underdeveloped country we should go all out in aiding it to grapple with its economic and political problems? [9]

And Adlai E. Stevenson warned:

A policy based just on anti-Communism and military potency is not in the spirit of this great movement of the twentieth century and will win few hearts. The challenge to us is to identify ourselves with this social and human revolution, to encourage, aid and inspire the aspirations of half of mankind for a better life, to guide these inspirations into paths that lead to freedom. To default would be disaster.[10]

There were from the beginning elements in the United States foreign aid policy of that broader, more humanitarian, and in my opinion, more rational conception as argued by liberal Americans throughout this period. And it may perhaps be said that as the 1950's drew to a close and the 1960's began, those elements were gradually winning in relative importance—though the narrowly political, military, and strategic motives were continually given primary attention.

But thereafter the United States' ever deeper involvement in the Vietnam war, proceeding not in a planned way but as a blind destiny,[11] gradually changed the whole situation. *During the further course of that war venture, the foreign-aid program, like many other promising developments in the United States, was to become a casualty of the American people's deep frustrations*—though the cause of the deterioration of the foreign-aid program as the 1960's came to a close is a more complicated process.

The drive from the beginning of the 1950's to fashion and adopt an aid program for underdeveloped countries so as to fit the United States' political and strategic interests in the cold war had *several important general consequences* which should be briefly examined.

For one thing it implied that the United States was reluctant and unwilling to support attempts to implement the type of multilateral and cooperative action for aiding the underdeveloped countries that the United Nations Charter—worked out under the close guidance of Franklin D. Roosevelt—looked toward.

For its political and strategic aid the United States had to adopt a national foreign policy whose instrumentality was unilateral economic and military aid. Other developed countries, particularly the larger ones, as they gradually entered the field of aid on a greater scale, were encouraged by this example set by the United States also to follow a narrow national policy line, even though it was less and less of the military and strategic variety.

A second consequence was undoubtedly the beginning of a gradual hardening of hearts in the United States. When the aid policy had once been firmly established on this political, military, and strategic line, there was no longer, as in launching the European Recovery Program, an American enthusiasm for giving grants-in-aid. Otherwise grants would have been better motivated, indeed, in relation to poor underdeveloped countries than to the potentially rich and developed countries in Western Europe.

In any case, while the aid to underdeveloped countries in the first years after the war was on a very small scale— and even at the beginning of the 1950's when it was starting to rise—it was given almost 100 percent in the form of grants. At the beginning of the 1960's that portion had sunk to around 50 percent. And both aid and credits were increasingly becoming tied to export from the United States.

Also in this respect, the United States set a pattern that was for the most part followed by the other developed countries as they gradually entered the field of aid on a larger scale.

I pointed to the intellectual duplicity implied in identifying a political and strategic aid policy in the national interest of the United States with a program for aiding the underdeveloped countries to develop. One unfortunate effect of this identification was that when that type of aid policy backfired, as it often did, it resulted in a general disillusion about aiding underdeveloped countries.

The history of the American aid policy in the era of the cold war was punctuated by the revelations of scandals implying gross corruption and other improprieties. They were splashed across the newspapers and often investigated in Congressional committees. The impression conveyed to the American people and Congress too often motivated the feeling that the aid was diverted into "ratholes," to use an American expression. This impression was then, however, often carelessly related to aid to underdeveloped countries in general.

On a deeper psychological and ideological level it was actually foreseen that this type of unilateral aid would not meet the moral aspirations of the people, least of all in the United States.

> ... in the United States itself, this hard-boiled policy, which is so definitely out of line with the cherished humanitarian traditions of the nation, will not be an inspiring one. I personally doubt very much whether a comprehensive and lasting policy of international aid on a strategic basis will ever have the chance of becoming accepted in the United States. To the minor—and, from the point of view of real economic needs and real effects in promoting economic development, rather haphazard—extent that this

policy has been tested out, the results abroad are not very encouraging. The effects at home of unilateral, strategic aid policy will in the longer run almost certainly be disappointment and frustration, compunction and bitterness over the aid-receivers' ingratitude; *in the end the result is likely to be a reduction in the amount of aid forthcoming from the United States.*[12]

... in present political conditions unilateral aid on any large scale is bound to have the most serious effects both in the United States and in the receiving underdeveloped countries: at home it can hardly be motivated except as a political device in the cold war; this lowers moral and economic standards in the distribution, direction, and utilization of aid, creates resentments and political splits in the receiving countries, and *will in the end only provide valid reasons in the United States for radically cutting down the appropriations.*[13]

The fifteen years that have elapsed since I made this prediction have unfortunately not proved me wrong.

The solemn designation in 1961, by a resolution of the U.N. General Assembly on a proposal of President John F. Kennedy's, of the 1960's as the Development Decade, with the implicit and explicit promises of more substantial financial aid to the underdeveloped countries from the developed countries, *almost exactly coincided with a stagnation and, soon, a downward trend of the United States aid budgets.*

To judge the real impact of the downward trend of foreign aid, a number of points will have to be borne in mind that all *imply a lower real value of the dollars allocated for aid to underdeveloped countries.* For one thing, prices have been rising, not least in the United States.

It is a fact worth noting that while in other respects, for instance in regard to the gross national product and to wages, it is always felt to be necessary to translate nominal values into real values, no such need is usually revealed in measuring aid to underdeveloped countries—a bias quite in line with the generally opportunistic tendencies of which this book gives so many examples.

The tendency toward giving aid in the form of *loans instead of grants*, which was apparent by the latter part of the 1950's, has now proceeded still further. The efforts made to keep down rates of interest and to prolong the amortization period have in recent years been reversed. Even more important is that nearly all aid, whether in terms of grants or loans, is now *tied to exports from the United States.*

This protective practice—which extends also to shipping and to private investments, particularly when public agencies such as the Export-Import Bank are involved—is in blunt contradiction to what was the self-evident principle at the time when the old private capital market was still functioning and responsible for furnishing funds, mostly in the form of portfolio credits. It is one of the reasons for the present author's feeling of nostalgia for the time when international finance was handled by private credit institutions.[14]

Tying aid to exports implies a curtailment of the aid-receiving underdeveloped country's freedom to buy the most suitable commodity and at the most favorable price. In the latter respect it has variously been estimated to increase costs by 20 to 40 percent.

In polite form this practice has been pointed to, on the side of the underdeveloped countries, as implying a subsidy rendered to the American economy. Thus Galo Plaza of the Organization of American States (OAS) explains:

> A semantic cloud hangs over United States aid programmes and makes it difficult to see them as they really are. Most U.S. aid under the Alliance for Progress is not a gift [but] is in form of loans that are being repaid. . . . it is not at all unreasonable to turn the picture around, and think about the benefits accruing to the United States as a result of what we call aid. . . . Nearly all of this [the loans] is being spent in the United States on United States goods. In this way, they help create jobs for U.S. workers. They generate

earnings for U.S. manufacturing enterprises and their stockholders, and taxable income for the U.S. Government. They give the U.S. a surplus in its balance of payments with Latin America.[15]

To the receivers of loans this practice of tying them to exports from the "donor country" seems the more unjustified as the loans have to be serviced in dollars that, on the contrary, can be fully used without any restriction.

Within the context of the struggle by Latin American countries to get the United States to give them more favorable export outlets, which in 1969 flared up considerably,[16] the criticism of the United States' practice of tying all loans and grants to American exports increasingly takes a much harsher tone and is being labeled exploitation. As I write this, the newspapers report that the United States now feels constrained to relax somewhat the requirement that the funds made available to Latin American countries should be tied to import of commodities originating in the United States.

When American services or commodities are directly awarded to underdeveloped countries in the form of grants or grantlike contributions, the high prices attached to these gifts often imply, or seem to imply, an unjustified padding of the amount of aid.

When I was in Karachi, Pakistan, a few weeks before Ayub Khan's putsch in 1958, a government report was confidentially circulated showing that the American experts placed at the disposal of the Pakistan government were reckoned to cost, on the average, around $40,000— including all the amenities, fringe benefits, and working facilities of various sorts added to the high salaries. The Pakistanis implied that they could buy such services very much cheaper elsewhere, if they instead were given the dollars for free use. The new government repaid the friendly reception their putsch was given by the United States by suppressing that report, among other things.

Likewise, the food provided under PL 480 was counted at the prices on the protected home market in the United States, rather high above the prices at which it could be bought on the international market. Shipping it to the aid-receiving country was also largely reserved for American protected high-cost shipping and charged to the aid-receiving country.

At that time, moreover, the disposal of the bulging food surpluses was very much an American interest. The question could therefore be raised, and often was, whether in a realistic analysis the cost of these food deliveries, or a large part of it, should not have been charged as national agricultural aid instead of as foreign aid.

A most important reason for discounting the development value of the aid was, of course, the fact that the motivation for it, and largely its direction, was political, military, and strategic. *When politics goes into aid whether at home or abroad, it is unavoidable that standards both of morality and of effectiveness are apt to be radically lowered.* I have already touched upon this frequent happening.

As the 1960's progressed toward its close, there was a tendency for *this political character of aid to become ever more pronounced.* The main operative factor was, of course, the United States' Vietnam policy. South Vietnam —or rather, that part of it controlled by the military forces of the Saigon government and of the United States—became the "country" that was given by far the biggest slice of the aid program—one quarter, or more than that if we include certain parts of the aid to the governments of a few satellite countries in Southeast and East Asia that were helping the United States in its war efforts.

Nobody outside the United States, the Asian governments that are its co-belligerents, and, of course, the secretariat of the Development Assistance Committee (DAC) —indeed, I believe, very few in the United States itself if they really thought the matter through—would reckon this as aid, in the same sense as, for instance, aid to India, even though in this era also that latter aid carries strong political overtones.

But if we subtract that very big item in the aid appropriations and disbursements, which is directly part of the United States political and military involvement in Vietnam, the low level of development aid and its tendency to fall still lower in the course of the 1960's become even more accentuated.

If, in addition, we make proper discounts for all the other reasons given above, *probably considerably less than half of the American appropriations and disbursements, reckoned as "public financial flow" in the DAC statistics, would remain as genuine aid to underdeveloped countries.* This would imply an almost ridiculously inadequate fulfillment of many emphatic declarations.

I mentioned in Chapter 3 that some influential Congressmen have come to regard foreign aid as a danger for bringing the United States into new military involvements of the same type as that in Vietnam. This, and similar feelings outside Congress, mean that aid to underdeveloped countries now lacks the wholehearted support of even all the liberal forces in the country.

People also sense, and dislike, the duplicity of aims for aid which has been introduced by using it as a means for national military and strategic policy—which, moreover, ended in failure and is in danger of doing so in other regions, in Latin America for instance. That this duplicity goes against the grain of American moral traditions has already been pointed out.

During the next few years I am afraid that we will see only a continuation of the present downward trend of foreign aid, without any great changes in direction of, and conditions for, aid. I cannot be a defeatist, however. There must come a time, and, one hopes, rather soon, when the forces for a thorough reconsideration of the whole issue can unite.

What we need is a new philosophy of aid to underdeveloped countries. We need to reconsider its motivation, its direction, and the conditions under which it is given. And we must see it as the international issue it is—not in terms of "the best interests of the United States," which is a much too narrow view.

The most recent report by a high-level committee, the so-called Perkins Committee, appointed by President Lyndon B. Johnson to reconsider the whole foreign aid issue but presented as a program for the new Administration, starts out by complaining that "in America today a mood of malaise and withdrawal is enfeebling U.S. development assistance efforts." [17] Before he retired as the Johnson government's Administrator of the Agency for International Development, William S. Gaud said bluntly: "The bitter truth is that we in the United States are doing badly. Our program is shrinking. We are falling short. . . ." [18]

Summarizing my explanation for this "tide of withdrawal that is now so strong," I want to stress that *the American people and the American Congress have been furnished with, and have been giving themselves, reasons why they should render aid to underdeveloped countries, which are obviously insufficient.*

And those doing the arguing and politicizing have convinced themselves and others that these insufficient reasons were the true reasons why they were acting the way they did.

Moreover, *they have allowed the aid program to take shape from those reasons*—until, at one end, they have no longer been able to feel that they are really good reasons for giving aid to underdeveloped countries.

One reason was long ago proved by experience to be illusive: "Aid cannot even guarantee gratitude from those it helps." [19] If, then, aid is used as a bribe or a political pressure, this is not a reason that can ensure popular support in a nation like the United States.

As I have stressed, aid has in the United States traditionally and commonly been propounded, and is propounded today, for the general catch-all reason that "it is in the basic interest of the United States" to give aid.[20] To the ordinary citizen and Congressman this reason must remain a very vague conception.

It does not become much clearer or more prompting to him when it is explained that the development of underdeveloped countries, which can be made possible by aid, contributes to a more stable and secure world.[21] The more sophisticated can even point to examples where a little development aid does not make people more peaceful—particularly when, at the same time, they are furnished with the training of the officer corps and with armaments as "military aid" or permitted to buy them with what funds they can dispose of, funds that are increased by the aid.

To anybody the relation between aid and the political development in the underdeveloped world must seem highly speculative and uncertain. The "basic interest of the United States," however, becomes concrete when translated into precise military and strategic interests of the United States. But that is a reason which has gone sour in the frustration after the failure in the Vietnam war and other pending failures of the policy inherited from the Dulles era.

To many in Congress and among the people, the "basic interest of the United States" now often is a reason for not giving aid, in order not to involve the United States in political and military commitments that may be implied in the aid-giving.

Then there is the reason that the aid in reality does not cost the United States very much—except in taxes for the federal budget. This reason is often amplified by the assertion that "aid is good for business." As we have seen, the aid program has also increasingly been adjusted to serve this alleged national interest, particularly by being tied to expenditures in the United States. As Gaud explains:

> The biggest single misconception about the foreign aid program is that we send money abroad. We don't. Foreign aid consists of American equipment, raw materials, expert services, and food—all provided for specific development projects which we ourselves review and approve.... Ninety-three percent of AID funds are spent directly in the United States to pay for these things. Just last year some 4,000 American firms in 50 states received $1.3 billion in AID funds for products supplied as part of the foreign aid program.[22]

But the American taxpayer and his representative in Congress have for a long time been suspiciously watchful of that type of handout to private business—if not big and widespread enough, as in recent years the armament expenditures have often been, so that a majority of the people and of Congress feel they get their share or more.

Then there is, of course, the simple moral reason. After having stated "the national stake" in terms of the reasons reviewed above, the Perkins Committee added as the "*second*" national interest in giving aid "the humanitarian reason": "We ought to try to help poor countries and poor people improve their lot...."[23] President John F. Kennedy had said that the United States should give aid because it is "right."

And in presenting his first message to Congress on foreign aid President Richard M. Nixon—after having accounted for all the other reasons enumerated above—added: "These are all sound, practical reasons for our foreign aid programs. But they do not do justice to our fundamental character and purpose. There is a moral quality in this nation that will not permit us to close our eyes to the want in this world...."[24]

I fully agree with the last assertion in this quotation.

But with all the strained selfish reasons given such a prominent place in public discussion and public opinion, and with the whole aid program being so definitely shaped by these reasons, *the light and the power have been taken out of the moral imperative.*

I have focused my attention on the United States as provider of aid to underdeveloped countries. The other developed nations have, particularly from the middle 1950's, become more important contributors of aid, partly under American prodding that they should take on their share of the aid burden.

For reasons similar to those enumerated in regard to the United States, the DAC statistics on the "official flows" from all the other developed countries cannot be accepted at their face value as measuring what is really aid to underdeveloped countries. The figures would have to be discounted, on the whole.

The deflation necessary to take care of the rising prices would tend to change the trend from apparent stagnation in the programs to actual lessening of aid.

As in recent years there has not been in most other developed countries anything corresponding to the radical shrinking of United States foreign-aid appropriations, their share in the aid activity should, in the next few years, be a rising one. It will then be less possible to conclude from the DAC statistics that the United States stands for half, or more than half, of all aid to underdeveloped countries, as is commonly asserted now.

By making these observations, we are still moving on a superficial level, however. Among other reasons than rising prices for discounting the figures for the "official flows" when estimating what is aid, the practice of tying aid by various devices, thereby decreasing its value to the recipient countries, is common in almost all countries and is, if not increasing, in any case not becoming less important.

A closer study would probably reveal that reasons of national policy are a prominent motivation for all the larger countries in the rest of the Western world. But such aid has decreasingly taken the crude forms of military and strategic designs that are such a strong reason for discounting American figures for aid, as exemplified by the "aid" to Vietnam.

The political interests are more directed toward winning influence and trade advantages. For France and Britain, continued close relations with their former colonies have played a dominating role, as is visible in the direction given to countries receiving their aid.

The considerations backing this direction of aid have largely been, of course, the need to protect their own remaining business connections and investments, but undoubtedly also a feeling of responsibility for the future of the newly independent states.

France, and less conspicuously Britain, have been more interested in preserving in their former colonies a political and cultural tie to the old motherland. In its relatively large foreign-aid budget France has included various items of doubtful character. Part of the expenditure for aid has also been lost in corruption or, more often, in what could be called the "collective corruption" of providing inordinately high salaries and all sorts of excessive amenities to a ruling oligarchy, kept allegiant to French policy.

Britain under the Wilson government has been struggling with extraordinary financial difficulties, and it should be pointed out as rather remarkable that it has not decreased its aid budget more. It is perhaps not unnatural that the British government, in defending its policy of keeping up its aid, has pointed to trade advantages flowing from its aid activity. Earl Grinstead, until recently the Minister of Overseas Development, explained:

> About two-thirds of our aid is spent on goods and services from Britain. . . . trade follows aid. We equip a factory overseas and later on we get orders for spare parts and re-

placements. . . . We shall [spend on aid] . . . because it is
right and because it is in our long term interest.[25]

A Parliamentary Committee studying Britain's aid program stated more bluntly:

> Aid plays an important part in stimulating trade. Subject
> to the basic moral purpose of the aid programme, aid
> should be increasingly concentrated in those countries
> which offer the greatest potential markets for goods origi-
> nating from Britain.[26]

This type of motivation is probably rather representative
of the feelings behind the aid activity of most of the developed countries, also of France and, in particular, of
Japan and Germany.

Although, without much deeper studies than have as
yet been carried out, it is impossible to give quantitative
expression to definite conclusions, the general impression
from what is commonly known is that the aid figures for
almost all these other countries have to be discounted—
particularly because so much aid is tied—but not nearly as
much as the American figures must be discounted.

If so discounted, the United States is probably already
now giving considerably less than half and probably not
much more than a third of what can be counted as genuine aid to underdeveloped countries. And its share of total
aid will be falling as the effects of the shrinking appropriations in recent years determine future disbursements.

The true level of aid from the other developed countries
to underdeveloped countries is, of course, also totally
inadequate. The trend is generally not upward but downward, though not as definitely and rapidly as that of the
United States.

The former President of the International Bank for
Reconstruction and Development, George D. Woods, in
an important address from which I have already quoted
expressed his dismay at the trend of aid in the following
words:

The high-income countries do not seem to be thinking about tomorrow. Their aid policies have tended as much to mirror their own narrowest concerns as to focus effectively on the situation of the developing countries and its long-term meaning for the world as a whole. It is possible to overstate the case, but nevertheless it is true that up to now, bilateral programs of assistance have had as one of their primary objectives helping the high-income countries themselves; they have looked toward financing export sales, toward tactical support of diplomacy, toward holding military positions thought to be strategic.[27]

The only encouraging signs are certain recent developments in some of the smaller developed countries. As a prelude to the policy conclusions I will draw in Section III of this chapter, I shall permit myself to review briefly the recent development of the aid program in one of these smaller countries that I know well, Sweden.

A comparison with the United States is particularly relevant for reasons of the similarities between Swedes and Americans. There is, in fact, no other nation more resembling the Americans in general cultural traits and basic moral inclinations than the Swedes. If anything, the Americans have a legacy of more charitable intentions in regard to the whole surrounding world than Swedes normally have.

The idea that aid to underdeveloped countries would be in "the best interest of Sweden" does not occur naturally to the Swedes. The explanation for this lacuna may in part be that, fortunately, Sweden is not oversized like the United States. Also, with somewhat less of a puritanical heritage, that particular turn of thought implied in wanting to state every impulse to do a right thing in this selfish way has never become a tradition, as in the United States. After a century and a half without war, the Swedes in any case do not feel tempted to turn aid into serving the military and strategic interests of Sweden.

With the principle of sound and competitive commerce firmly established, and conservatively upheld through more than a generation of Social Democratic rule, the Swedes are not inclined to find an excuse for aid in the opportunity to use it for spreading haphazardly a subsidy to private individuals and business firms at home.

The Swedes thus find that, for them, *there cannot be any other reason for giving aid than the simple humanitarian impulse to feel solidarity with those who are poor, hungry, diseased, and illiterate, and who meet difficulties in their efforts to rise out of poverty.*

The Swede never acquired much of a colonial empire outside Europe—less because of a desire to abstain from the competition for overseas dependencies than because of bad luck when they tried. The King sold the last small piece of colonial territory well over a hundred years ago.

With no colonial dependencies, their universities seldom, and then almost by accident, devoted much interest to what is now called the Third World. There were no colonial officials returning. The few businessmen and missionaries who had personal experience from these regions did not stimulate research or wider national interest. With that weak background, the Swedes, even in recent years, have made practically no original contributions to increasing the knowledge about the underdeveloped countries and their problems.

But an academic and intellectual basis is not really necessary for informing ordinary people about the misery in these countries, the sufferings of their peoples, and their need for aid. It took, however, some considerable time, beginning about the middle 1950's, before the aid problem received much publicity in Sweden. And the aid budget was, and still is, quite small.

But the interesting thing is the very recent trend. In 1968 the Parliament decided that the aid carried in the national budget from then on should be increased *every year* by 25 percent until, in the fiscal year 1974–75, it reaches 1 percent of the gross national product (which is about 25 percent higher than the national income, still the common measuring rod elsewhere). *Nobody has assumed that this rapid rise should not continue thereafter.*

This percentage was calculated on public aid, pure and simple. *"Private flows" are thus not included in the Swedish calculation of aid.* When aid is given in the form of a public loan it will normally be given for twenty-five years or more, with a grace period of ten years, and an interest rate of 2 percent or less. When working in cooperation with the International Development Association (IDA) of the World Bank, loans can be given for fifty years without interest, except for a small administrative fee.

Moreover, *aid is normally not tied to expenditures in Sweden* (except when a national surplus is given away, for instance in some years paper). There has been some pressure from business also to tie Swedish aid. A rather telling reason could be put forward for this suggestion. When Sweden is the only country not to tie its aid, while all other countries do it, Swedish business is being discriminated against by what amounts to unfair competition. But as the government's position was known to be firm, the pressures never amounted to much.

The question which interests us in the present context is: *How did all this, and particularly the decision to increase aid so substantially and fast, happen?* It goes contrary to the usual trend abroad, and particularly in the United States where people are so similar to Swedes.

So far as the static factors are concerned—preserving a clear distinction between aid and business, and not tying aid—the credit is due to the government and Parliament. They have conservatively stuck to old-fashioned "principles of sound finance and commerce."

But when it was decided to begin raising aid so substantially and rapidly, this move was hardly initiated by the political establishment. I believe it is fair to state that the government and the political parties have reacted as instruments of the will of the people—as, incidentally, they have had to do in developing their policy toward the American military involvement in Vietnam or the Russian invasion of Czechoslovakia. And in the vanguard among the people were the popular organizations—the political, religious, youth, and women's movements, and the mighty cooperative and trade union movements.

The political establishment simply had to follow popular demands. The two political parties immediately to the right of the government party even found it advisable in their search for popular support to overbid the government bill by demanding, as an opposition, a still more rapid rise of the aid budget, reaching the first goal of 1 percent of the gross national product by the fiscal year 1972–73.

The almost clean laboratory case of Sweden, whose people could not really feel any other motivation for aid to underdeveloped countries than the simple humanitarian one, *demonstrates the conquering strength of that moral imperative*—when it is not confused in opportunistic duplicities and then buried in failure and frustration, as in the United States.

Besides this main inference, there are two other interesting observations to make. When aid-giving in this way is purified from motives of national and, particularly, military and strategic interests, and when no aid is tied to expenditures in the donor country, the reluctance to channel aid through the intergovernmental organizations in the United Nations family diminishes. About half of the Swedish aid budget goes to these organizations for multilateral aid-giving. For the rest of the developed countries, this portion is still only around 10 percent.

The second observation is that the absence of motives other than the moral one liberates the policy interests among the Swedes from inhibitions preventing them from trying to influence underdeveloped countries. In the popular debate, which is always ahead of the political and administrative establishment, more and more pressure is now exerted to steer the aid to progressive underdeveloped countries carrying on radical reforms of the type discussed in Chapters 3 through 7 in this book. Under this pressure the establishment is gradually beginning to move in that direction.

I have hesitated to tell this story, feeling that it would sound nationalistic. But I have overcome that hesitation, as I want to be scrupulously honest and as I need to cite this actual experience in a laboratory case for the policy conclusions I want to draw in the next section. There is nothing unusual about the Swedes except that they are placed in a situation where *the only reason they could have for aid to underdeveloped countries is the moral one of solidarity with people in distress*—the same principle upon which they have built their successful welfare state at home.

Sweden is not alone in showing that type of improved climate for increasing genuine aid to underdeveloped countries. Several among the smaller, highly developed countries are in a similar situation where national interests are of minor and fading importance, so that aid *has to be* motivated solely on moral grounds. When those other national interests drop out, these countries are then found to be *not decreasing but increasing their aid,* or to be preparing to do so.

Among these countries I would definitely reckon Canada and the Netherlands, and perhaps also soon Switzerland, Denmark, Austria, Finland, and Norway. There is still a difference though it might not be lasting, namely, that all of these other countries named have as yet not given up tying their aid to exports, and have not so bluntly placed private investments in another and different category from public aid, demanding sacrifices through taxation.

III Policy Conclusions

I am now ready to draw my policy conclusions.
From all we know about the levels and direction of pro-

duction and consumption in underdeveloped countries and the difficulties that meet their development efforts, it stands out as imperative that *the developed countries should be prepared to increase aid appropriations very considerably.* This would agree with the type of general declarations so generously made but not with the practices actually followed thus far.

In a realistic view, it should also be evident that the need for aid in the larger part of the underdeveloped world cannot be thought of as a short-term exigency but *will be long-lasting.* How long it will take before a particular underdeveloped country has accomplished what is popularly—and in a logically unclear way [28]—described as its "take-off" into a "self-generating" or "self-sustaining" growth, will, besides the size of foreign aid and the reform of the commercial policies of developed countries, depend upon that country's willingness and ability to tackle the radical reforms at home discussed in Part Two of this book.

When the government in a developed country, in order to secure easier passage for an aid bill, gives an overoptimistic idea about the future development in underdeveloped countries, this is bound to increase the difficulty of winning support for aid later, when its prognosis has been proved wrong.

The need for aid in underdeveloped countries and the concern expressed in general statements made on behalf of developed countries should motivate those responsible to see that *aid appropriations in the budget gradually approach the size of what developed countries spend for other important national purposes,* as, for instance, social security or education, not to mention defense. They should at least be a substantial portion of the expected annual increase of their national incomes.

In countries like Sweden, Canada, and the Netherlands, such a development may be well on its way toward the end of the 1970's. In the United States we shall probably see these appropriations continuing to plunge downward for a time. But for reasons I will dwell upon below I am not excluding the possibility but, rather, expecting that we shall see a change in that trend within a few years. This is, anyhow, what we have to strive for.

I assume then that developed countries can afford to raise aid appropriations substantially. This problem *depends solely on the importance that people in the developed countries attach to aid for the underdeveloped countries.*

That foreign-exchange difficulties can only be a false pretense for lowering aid appropriations as well as for not changing commercial policies in the interests of underdeveloped countries, I have pointed out in Chapter 9.

In the future, we should try to move toward a common recognition of aid to underdeveloped countries as a collective responsibility for the developed countries, the burden of which should be shared in an agreed fair way, amounting to *an approach to a system of international taxation.*

In order to promote such a development it is necessary that *we purge our conceptions and our practices of a number of opportunistically biased and false ideas and misrepresented devices,* the prevalence of which has been pointed out throughout this chapter, and, indeed, throughout the book. For the carrying out of this cleansing operation a special responsibility falls on the independent students. Experts and officials of governments and intergovernmental organizations are apparently unable to liberate themselves from the powerful opportunistic biases of their employers, one or several governments.

This purge would be in the interest of intellectual clarity and honesty. It has, therefore, a general and independent value in our type of civilization. Specifically—and as they obviously serve the function of protecting a guilty conscience—purging them would make it easier to win popular support for increasing aid.

We should thus draw *a distinct line between benefi-*

cence, ordinarily requiring sacrifices, and business, assumed instead to be profitable.

If aid is given in the form of a loan—which in many cases is practical not only for securing an easier passage through a national legislature—it is the grace period and the submarket interest rate during a prolonged amortization period that constitutes aid. It can be calculated by discounting payments to the present time and subtracting the sum of them from the loan.

Private capital inflow, particularly direct investment, as well as trade can—with several important reservations which we have spelled out in Chapters 9 and 10—be most important for development in an underdeveloped country. Aid can often improve the economic basis in an underdeveloped country, and that in its turn can cause an increase in private investment. This belongs then to the *ameliorating effects of aid.* Aid can even be applied in order to *subsidize and increase private investment;* the subsidy, but not the investment itself, may then, under certain conditions, be counted as aid.

But the possible, though not always present, advantageous effects of normal business transactions should not be taken as a pretext for calling them aid or assistance. Such transactions occur, of course, much more frequently, and are of a much greater scope, between developed countries. They are then never assumed to be aid or assistance, however beneficial they often may be for all parties concerned.

Private investments in underdeveloped countries are really worthy of a better fate than being used to confuse the statistics on aid and pamper peoples' beliefs in developed countries about how much they are sacrificing to help underdeveloped countries.

When a developed country—and it is now almost only a question of the United States as practically no other Western country would be contemplating doing it—is giving "aid" for what it considers its own military interests, whether it consists of armaments, military training facilities, or anything else, this type of aid, including "supporting aid," should be *removed from the aid budget and carried as national defense expenditures.*

A most important cleansing operation is, moreover, to abolish the *tying of aid to deliveries from the donor country.* The main victims of these practices are the underdeveloped countries, which should be aided. It is they whose freedom to choose in the world market becomes restricted, and this increases costs, among other unfavorable effects.

For the developed countries these practices are of doubtful advantage. They imply a lack of confidence in the competitive ability of a country's own business enterprises.

With almost all countries now tying most of their aid— and also private investments insofar as they can get a hold over them—these practices work toward a segregative economic system. For one country to break out of it may imply losing business.

It should nevertheless imply an advantage, as generally a freer trade even in a protectionist surrounding tends to harden and strengthen business. As the trade statistics reveal, Sweden's experience with its free-trade policies in this as in other respects rather confirms this old-fashioned belief of the economists over many generations.

But certainly it would be easier to abolish these malpractices by an international agreement, binding all developed countries. The underdeveloped countries are pressing for such an agreement in UNCTAD and elsewhere. But most developed countries are shortsightedly resisting this pressure, and the malpractices have tended to increase in the 1960's.

One form of tying aid is present when a developed country directly provides commodities and services as unilateral aid. It would be healthy even in such cases if the supplies were acquired in the international market or, at least, counted at international market prices.

The World Bank has in its lending activity stood as a tower of strength, insisting, against the spreading practices of tying aid, that the funds it provides should be used freely for buying where it is most advantageously done. It is fortunate that it stubbornly adheres to this principle and does not succumb to the temptation to compromise in order to increase the funds at its disposal.

The other intergovernmental organizations operating in the aid field, and in particular the executive agencies of the United Nations Development Program, have also tried to stand firm against tying aid. One tendency that has to be watched, however, is the pressure of government delegates for subcontracting to consulting firms. Too often they are put in a position to steer the placing of orders, thus bypassing the rule of making the aid-receiving country able to deal with a competitive international supply market.

My next point is not entirely uncorrelated with this purging of the concept of aid and the practices when giving aid. It is my firm conviction, founded upon study and reflection, that *only by appealing to peoples' moral feelings will it be possible to create the popular basis for increasing aid to underdeveloped countries as substantially as is needed.*

To put it clearly and convincingly, the moral reason for aid has to be separated and cleansed from all the spurious reasons of national interest that I have criticized in relation to United States aid policy. And the aid concept must be expressed in terms of real sacrifices to be borne by the people in the form of taxes. These sacrifices should not be falsely distended by the various opportune devices I criticized above, which mainly imply a lower level of genuine aid than pretended.

I am not saying this as a moralist. It is certainly true that it agrees with my personal valuations as well as with my quest for honesty and clarity as a student of economic issues. But quite apart from that, I want the statement to be considered as an assertion by a social scientist about facts and factual relations as they are revealed by study of economic policies in our contemporary world. And I have illustrated my thesis by comparing the different and counter-directed recent trends in two very like nations, the United States and Sweden.

Ordinary people in our Western civilizational milieu— and they are the ones who in the final instance determine the trend of policies in our countries over the years—*can* be brought to act on the basis of feelings of compassion and solidarity. But they soon become cold toward alleged national interests, particularly when, as regularly happens, those turn out to have been spurious and misdirected.

This is, as I see it, one important lesson that we can learn from our experiences after the war. When politicians and experts become so timid about giving due importance to moral motivations in this and many other fields, true realism is absent.

At the bottom, such timidity is an unwarranted condescension on the part of the articulate toward the common people. They have become so entangled in special considerations to all sorts of short-term advantages and to vested interests that they cannot see the forest for the trees.

Frankly, *I believe it is unrealistic and self-defeating to distrust the moral forces in a nation.* And what in the United States has been happening to the Congressional appropriations for aid to underdeveloped countries in the 1950's and 1960's bears me out. As Robert E. Asher reflects: "The American public appears massively indifferent [to the aid program], perhaps because its humanitarian and fundamental decency have not been properly appealed to." [29]

One thing that can sap the strength from the feelings of moral responsibility in the developed nations for the welfare of underdeveloped nations is the knowledge that *these countries often have a very inegalitarian social and economic stratification* and that the trend is working toward increasing internal inequalities.[30]

Most often they are ruled by various and rapidly shifting constellations of persons in upper-class oligarchies. Members of these oligarchies are rich, sometimes fabulously rich. They escape direct taxation by various means, while indirect taxes are heavy on the masses of people. The states are soft and corruption is widespread and usually spreading further.

Even those policies that are motivated as being in the interests of the poor are perverted to favor, instead, the not-so-poor. And foreign aid, either as a natural result of the market forces as they operate in such a society or because of collusions and illegal practices, often goes to line the pockets of the already very rich.

It is unrealistic not to be aware of the fact that ordinary people in the developed countries will easily have their feelings of moral obligation to the impoverished underdeveloped countries blunted by the knowledge of these facts of life in underdeveloped countries. "Why don't they tax their own rich people before they come with their begging bowl to our door?" is a natural reaction.

There are two ways of trying to overcome this obstacle to popular response to aid appeals. One is to play down these facts. This is also opportune for the articulate upper strata in underdeveloped countries and is, of course, done on a large scale.

It represents, indeed, a major cause of biases in the discussion of these problems, as illustrated throughout the first two parts of this book. These systematic biases, generally leading to the avoidance of awkward and embarrassing problems, have for this and other reasons also become determinative for the scientific work, as stated in Chapter 1.

In line with these biases the whole discussion of development in underdeveloped countries has become focused on "economic growth." It is simply defined as an increase in aggregate national product or income, without considering income distribution and changes in the other social conditions that are determining development, particularly in the somewhat longer run. This "growth" is then measured by means of "growth rates," whose extreme unreliability was commented upon at the end of Chapter 8.

From a policy point of view one weakness of this is that such abstract notions as "growth" cannot appeal to people's moral conscience in the developed countries. This is particularly so when experts associated with the national and international aid authorities succeed, by an uncritical use of this insufficient concept of development and these faulty statistics, in convincing themselves and others that underdeveloped countries are well on the road to rapid development. Unfortunately, this delusion—and self-delusion—is common.

When this biased approach is then complemented by information about the poverty, and often plain misery, of the masses of people, the implication of the conventional approach is regularly that a rise in that aggregate income will raise the level of income of those poor masses. This invites a sort of satisfied complacency in developed countries, but not a greater willingness to carry burdens and make sacrifices.

But it can usually not altogether conceal what I called the facts of life in most underdeveloped countries and particularly the harsh inequalities and their tendency to increase. As this cannot be reconciled with the superficial and biased definition of development as "growth" calculated in the grossly imperfect way I referred to, the result is intellectual confusion. This is not favorable for the integrity of the moral judgment.

It is a mistake to believe that knowledge of these awkward facts can be excluded from popular knowledge in developed countries. They will be known, in spite of the biased approach in economic analyses, and in spite of the political discussion becoming opportunistically directed toward withholding that knowledge from public debate.

I am firmly convinced that even from the point of view of letting the moral feelings resound full-toned in popular and political debate, it is of great importance to uproot these opportunistic biases. People will then demand that aid not be used to pamper the oligarchies. They will demand that aid be given to countries making serious efforts toward social reform and even that it be given on condition that such reforms are undertaken; indeed, the aid may be given to make such reforms more possible. Often this will mean that aid should not be given to strengthen reactionary regimes that are bent upon resisting reform.

Aid policies cannot be morally neutral (see Chap. 8, above). And popular support as a response to a moral commitment will not be found for a neutral aid policy. Moral feelings are never neutral to social conditions.

That has been felt by some governments. When the Swedish government early in 1962 for the first time outlined the broad aims for aid to the underdeveloped countries, it stated:

> The concept of human dignity and the claims to social equality, that have marked development in the majority of Western countries during the past century, no longer halt at the frontiers of nationality or race. . . . The growing feeling of international solidarity and responsibility reflects a deeper insight into the facts that peace, freedom and welfare are not an exclusively national concern, but something increasingly universal and indivisible. The idealistic motives behind assistance are thus at the same time highly realistic. . . . No other kind of motive is needed for the extension of assistance by Sweden to underdeveloped countries.
>
> . . . *we can reasonably try so to direct our assistance programs that they do, to the best of our judgment, tend to promote political democracy and social equality. It is not*

*consistent with the motives or aims of Swedish assistance
that it should help to preserve anti-progressive social structures.*[31]

It is fair to say that what there has been of actual aid
policy pursued by Sweden has not corresponded very
closely to this declared ideal. Gradually it will begin to do
so, however. I have already pointed out that this will be
the result of popular pressure upon the political and bureaucratic establishment. This was confirmed at the Conference of the Social Democratic Party in September,
1969.

In the United States the feelings of moral responsibility
among liberal Congressmen that American aid should be
used in the interest of the broad masses of people in the
underdeveloped countries found its eloquent expression
in the adoption of Title IX in the Foreign Assistance Act,
L, 1966. This declaration of intention, however, has not
had much influence on the practical decisions by Congress
and the activity of the Agency for International Development on how to direct and use the aid appropriations.

In Chapter 4, Section III, I exemplified this by pointing
out that such a paramountly important development problem as land reform was kept under the rug even when the
discussion was on the level of the principles of Title IX.
The main practical efforts to promote land reforms were
focused on South Vietnam—and long before the murder
of Ngo Dinh Diem.

These efforts were, however, motivated as a tactical
move in the competition with the National Liberation
Front for the souls of the Vietnamese people. The United
States government even declared its aim to be a "social
revolution" in South Vietnam. This tactical policy, however, was largely made ineffective by the resistance of the
consecutive Saigon governments. However they shifted,
the landlord interests were dominating their actions.[32]

More generally, it is a fact that in practice American
aid policy has often deviated utterly from that moral point

of view expressed in Title IX. The United States almost regularly found itself propping up reactionary and corrupt regimes in underdeveloped countries. Without doubt, this has to be given its due weight when explaining why popular support for aid has been faltering in the United States, not least among liberals.

One major element that will be needed in the new philosophy, if aid is to be increased as substantially as is called for, is undoubtedly *to direct it toward spurring reforms in the interests of the masses of people in underdeveloped countries, and to get away from motives that appear cynical from a moral point of view.*

Among the underdeveloped countries are several that are particularly poor or that for various reasons meet greater difficulties in their attempts to engender development. When transforming aid according to the new philosophy, where the moral motivation becomes the decisive one, a corollary is that *these "most underdeveloped" countries must be given special considerations.*

This goes contrary to what has become the established principle, particularly in the United States. Under cover of the popular slogan that aid to underdeveloped countries should be "help to self-help," which undoubtedly is a sound principle, the inference has too often been drawn that priority should be given to those underdeveloped countries showing the best prospects for rapid development. This is a more doubtful proposition.

If it means that aid should first be directed to countries with governments intent upon internal reforms, which is such an essential precondition for development, this meets no objections. It is in line with the political non-neutrality principle toward the type of governments and government policies declared above. But if it means that the poorest countries struggling with the greatest difficulties should be excluded from aid, this cannot be accepted as a policy rule for the way in which the developed countries should discharge their worldwide responsibilities.

Under collective pressure from the underdeveloped countries, this has commonly been accepted as an abstract proposition. A special resolution of the Second Session of UNCTAD invited the United Nations organizations "to devote particular attention to the needs of the least developed countries in the drawing up of their programs of assistance, and in identifying viable projects and promoting their financing." [33] In the same spirit the new President of the World Bank, Robert S. McNamara, in his first address to the Board of Governors in 1968, declared on behalf of the Bank:

> In particular, we will exert special efforts to right one up-side-down aspect of Bank Group operations: the fact that many of our poorest members, despite their greater need, have had the least technical and financial asssistance from the Bank Group. About ten of these have had no loans or credits at all. This is largely because of their inability to prepare projects for consideration. In these cases we will provide special assistance to improve economic performance and to identify and prepare projects acceptable for Bank Group financing. [34]

Neither in the UNCTAD resolution nor in any other connection has anything been said, however, about the much bigger assistance presently flowing through unilateral channels.

The UNCTAD secretariat has made attempts to identify these most underdeveloped countries. [35] It has also tried to outline by what means they could be helped. [36] Its list of policy measures which is also echoed in the UNCTAD resolution—including special considerations in commodity agreement, in regional cooperation, etc.—does not convince one that something substantial will come out of their proposals.

The main thing must simply be aid, given partly on the principle of the social policy that has been instituted in the developed countries' national welfare state. It is then taken for granted that no region and no group of people shall have its living standard held down under a national minimum level, and that all individuals should be given a fair chance of improving their lot. Social services should be provided at standardized levels, and paid for by contributions from the public purse.

Likewise the international community should make their contribution for raising living levels in the poorest countries. If such aid is directed to raising levels of nutrition, and to educational and health facilities, this would in the somewhat longer run also be the most effective help to development.

Like all underdeveloped countries, these most underdeveloped countries show great differences. Tanzania may be almost as poor and underdeveloped as Ethiopia. But the government of Tanzania is bent upon internal reform, while Ethiopia is a politically stagnant, feudal country. That the Tanzanian government should have a greater right to be aided than Ethiopia's government by a morally motivated aid policy is clear from what has already been said.

If agreement could be reached among the developed countries to abstain from tying aid to exports from the donor country, which would be rational from every point of view, this would also decrease the vested national interest in keeping aid unilateral and make it possible increasingly to *transfer aid to be handled by multilateral, intergovernmental organizations.*

Among the favorable factors for such a reform should be counted the fact that the intergovernmental organizations in the aid field have been relatively successful. The outstanding example of this is, of course, the International Bank for Reconstruction and Development.

From the beginning, under exceptional personalities as presidents, the Bank has, in fact, shown an unusual independence of judgment, even toward the United States, and can be expected to proceed further in that direction. The Bank needs to increase its activity in relation to very poor underdeveloped countries and also countries with leftist regimes—which often means countries which are really attacking their internal reform needs in a serious and radical manner.

But also the United Nations Development Program and its executing agencies and resident representatives have, on the whole, been successful and increasingly so, even if reforms are needed. There are rumors—and sensational prepublication indiscretions in newspapers—that the forthcoming *Jackson Report* is going to highlight and exaggerate critical views. It then appeals to the inbuilt adverse attitudes toward multilateral aid among the bureaucracies of the national agencies for unilateral aid in the developed countries and of many in the legislative assemblies and among government officials concerned with these problems.

The effect might be to provide those people in developed countries with new arguments to hold down or even decrease the contribution to this type of multilateral aid. This outcome is the more probable as there are many in the legislative assemblies and among the general public who are suspicious of all aid to underdeveloped countries and who will have got grist for their mill. Because in most developed countries, particularly the United States, the prospects for increasing substantially even unilateral aid are bleak, the result might be an added spur to a contiuued decrease of total aid in real terms, at least for a time.

The fact is, however, that with all weaknesses, the multilateral programs in the board field of technical assistance and capital aid have, on the whole, been more successful and increasingly so than the national unilateral programs. I have reached this conclusion both from my experience as a United Nations official for ten years, and also by observations I have made since then in various parts of the Third World. In the present context my judgment has to be left as an *obiter dictum,* though I hope to come back to the problem at a later time.

The most general reason for a multilateralization of aid generally is, of course, that it would restrict the role of narrow national interests in decisions on aid. And besides this major reason, it would improve the whole atmosphere surrounding aid. As Asher puts it:

> Even the most scrupulously-designed bilateral program, mounted by a rich and powerful nation, will be suspect in the eyes of poor and weak recipients as compared with enlarged multilateral efforts. In consequence, the enduring interests of the United States in the development of low-income countries and in progressing toward a better world order will in all probability be better served by a vastly increased emphasis on the multilateral administration of development assistance.[37]

An earlier President of the World Bank, Eugene Black, sees the argument for multilateral aid in terms of efficiency:

> Are we likely to get the best results if these funds are supplied on a bilateral basis—direct from one government to another—or should they be channeled through, and administered by a multilateral agency? ... I do believe that the emphasis should and can be changed, away from bilateral and toward multilateral aid. Bilateral aid is usually—and unfortunately, increasingly—tied to purchases of the giver's products. However well intentioned a lending government, it is vulnerable to pressure from its own commercial interests to help finance the sale of particular goods for projects abroad, whether the projects themselves are well justified or not. And, however sensible the government of the recipient country, it may have difficulty in resisting offers of finance, even for low-priority projects and on terms that often are not suited either to the circumstances of the country or the requirements of the project.
>
> My most serious criticism of bilateral aid programs, however, is their susceptibility to political influences, whether overt or otherwise. At its worst, aid is offered or exacted as a price in political bargaining that takes no account of the actual economic requirements of the recipients. But even at best, there is always the risk that political influences may misdirect development aid, since they may bring in considerations that are irrelevant to the real needs. I have

known cases where, as a result, a splendid new sports sta-
dium has been built, while the highway system remains
primitive; or where the national airport has acquired a
strikingly modern terminal building, while parched but
fertile land is left without irrigation. Economic priorities
are inevitably confused when economic objectivity is lost—
and economic objectivity is not easy when aid is influenced by political ends. Moreover, the problem goes deeper
than the simple waste of a given amount of money. Aid
directed to a government that is unwilling to meet the real
needs of a country has a pernicious consequence. The most
obvious result of some of the bilateral lending of the past
decade has been to make it possible for countries to put off
undertaking needed reforms; because well-meant but ill-
judged offers of aid have been forthcoming, governments
have been able to postpone such essential but disagreeable
tasks as the overhaul of systems of taxation or essential
currency reforms.[38]

The resistance against gradually transferring aid from
unilateral to multilateral administration comes, of course,
from governments in the developed world who want to
be free to use the aid for pursuing national interests of
various sorts. To some extent, though much less, it comes
from governments in such underdeveloped countries who
feel that their chances of exploiting their relations with a
specific country, mainly the United States, are particularly
great.

Most underdeveloped countries are, however, eager to
place the political element in a wider, international context. They want to have more of a say themselves, to share
in the laying down of principles and guidelines.

Paradoxically enough, the United States, which most
bluntly has pursued national interests in its aid policy, is
probably the one among the larger developed countries
which is now becoming prepared to multilateralize aid.
The explanation is, of course, that its experiences in giving aid "in the best interests of the United States," have
ended in foreign policy failures and in bitter frustrations.

Senator J. William Fulbright has led this ideological
movement. He wants aid transferred "from a national

charity, and an investment of cold-war competition, to an international responsibility" and to end "the peculiar and corrosive tyranny which donor and recipient seem to exercise over each other in bilateral relationships." [39] Fulbright's idea has been getting increasing support among American Congressmen and from the more informed among the American people.

And Henry H. Fowler, former Secretary of the Treasury, stated in the 1968 annual meetings of the board of the World Bank:

> It is no longer open to question that a strong multilateral approach holds the greatest promise for marshalling major amounts of funds for development on an equitably shared basis. . . . Because of the confidence they now enjoy, the multilateral institutions are in a unique position to exercise constructive leadership in the critical process of mobilizing development resources that will be adequate in relation to the demands of the developing world. . . . This kind of objective leadership cannot and should not be undertaken by any single nation, either donor or recipient. Only by making full use of the leadership potential of the international financial institutions can we mount the most effective attack on the problems of development finance. [40]

In Sweden—used in this book as a second reference country—the government started out by giving definite and explicit preference for multilateral aid. One of the reasons given was that it would strengthen the intergovernmental organizations in the United Nations group. Sweden still channels about 50 percent of its aid through the agencies in the United Nations family.

At the same time, however, the Swedish government created an agency for a residual unilateral aid activity. One reason for bilateral aid was that until very recently Sweden and the other Scandinavian countries were the only ones that felt free to give aid to underdeveloped countries for spreading birth control among the masses (see Chap. 5, above).

Once a bureaucratic agency had been established, however, it developed its own momentum to grow. And it also grew rapidly as the combined effect of what is popularly referred to as empire-building and Parkinson's law. Watchful over its public relations, it also succeeded in creating a sort of national pride in its various undertakings in underdeveloped countries, even when they were not very distinguished. It has even succeeded in forestalling much of a public discussion of the crucial question of the problem whether aid should be unilateral or multilateral.

This agency is presently intent upon enlarging the unilateral aid program to become more than 50 percent of total aid, in spite of the decided rapid increase of aid. As the true national interest in this shift to unilateral aid is not overwhelming, I feel, however, that the tide could be turned if there were a general movement among developed countries toward multilateralization of aid or even only a definite move by the United States. Sweden would support such a move.

The countries which can be expected to put up the strongest resistance to the multilateralization of aid are middle-sized countries like Japan, Germany, France, and England. They are now successfully using aid in their national interests. But among these interests nowadays are not many military and strategic ones, the kind that have caused such feelings of failure and frustration in the United States.

Quite aside from whether the prospects of success are easy or not, the rational reasons for playing down unilateral aid and pressing for enlarging the scope of multilateral aid are so strong that we should strive for the latter. And again we should not be taken in by what I called false internationalism. The fact that some countries might try to adhere to unilateral aid should not hinder other countries, least of all the United States, from transferring more of their aid to the intergovernmental organizations.

A further decrease in United States foreign aid is to be foreseen in the years just ahead. I have already said that I am not a defeatist, however. *I foresee a change in this trend to be possible and worth striving for.*

The decrease of American aid, having taken the direction I have described, might in the end come to appear to have been a precondition for building up an aid program in all the developed countries that is both much bigger and more in line with what I consider to be also the American ideals.

We have to see the present situation in its historical perspective. Immediately after the Second World War, the United States stood out as the one over-rich country that had not been hurt by the war but, instead, had become very much better off. It was natural for peoples and politicians, both in the United States and in Europe, to accept as a normal and right thing that the United States should take upon itself practically the whole financial burden of providing aid to any part of the world where it was needed.

This situation has changed. Other developed countries are also rich. And an international redistribution system, like a national one, must be based on a fair and equitable sharing of the burden.

It is natural if the ordinary American has not followed too closely what has happened. He probably believes that his country still provides most of the aid. And the public discussion, in the United States, often even that of the experts, is proceeding in a queer way on the assumption that American aid is the one important thing. This is another example of the extreme provincialism that is a particular danger in a large country.

The American's idea about the overwhelming importance of his country in the aid field is not correct, however. If we make all the discounts necessary to arrive at the true aid picture, the United States is hardly paying more than its share, if that. And still less will it be doing so after the further scaling down of the aid budget that is probably coming.

In the early 1950's, I felt reason to wish a short-term

decrease in American willingness to give international aid. I saw this as a condition for putting international aid on a more stable foundation and for increasing it substantially, as we needed.[41] That condition has now been effected. And the United States has burned its fingers in using aid for all sorts of national interests instead of following the moral imperative.

Nevertheless, under any fair scheme of international distribution of the burden of aid to underdeveloped countries, *the share of it to be borne by the United States must be large.*[42] This is due to the fact that the United States is so big. The United States is also relatively very rich, although not so rich by far as Americans generally believe.

In an international comparison its wealth and national income have to be decreased very substantially by what I call its "debt to the poor," which must be paid if the nation is not going to disintegrate or become a police state. This debt, together with the current expenditures caused by a less integrated and well-organized society than the other most advanced developed countries, is much bigger than is commonly accounted by Americans.

Some of the most advanced Western nations probably are now as rich as the United States, primarily because they have never put themselves in such a debt, or, if they did, paid it long ago, but also because they do not squander so relatively much of their national incomes on wars and preparation for war and on expensive adventures in space and other types of conspicuous public consumption.

But even taking all these things into account, the United States' contribution to aid has to be very large in a multilateralized scheme, and all the more so when the level of total aid from developed countries is raised as substantially as is called for.

The feeling in the United States after the war that aid to underdeveloped countries was mainly an American responsibility was part of the general delusion of American omnipotence in the world. This lasted a long time, and may not be entirely expunged yet.

Asher quotes President John F. Kennedy who maintained that:

> We in this country... are—by destiny rather than by choice—the watchmen on the walls of world freedom.

and adds dryly:

> The interventionist policy in the Truman Doctrine in 1947 is finding its final fateful expression in Vietnam. At the very time the United States has come to question most seriously the rationale for its involvement in the less developed countries, it has been most deeply involved.[43]

The grim failure of the Vietnam involvement and several other imperialist adventures, particularly in Latin America, where the United States has been going it alone, is bound to end an era in American and world history. There will be those who will choose some sort of withdrawal into a Fortress America.

But there will also be those who will see that what caused the disasters was the United States' insolent claim to the right to police the world *on its own terms*—by virtue of its might. This was what the Greeks called *hubris,* and they held that when it was not stopped it always led to self-destruction.

During the Second World War I wrote a book, *An American Dilemma,* about America's internal problems of justice, liberty, and equality. I was led to consider in the last chapter of that book the role in the world that I foresaw for the United States when it became "America's turn in the endless sequence of main actors on the world stage." I wrote then, and I want to repeat it: "America has now joined the world and is tremendously dependent upon support and good-will of other countries. Its rise to leadership brings this to a climax. None is watched so suspiciously as the one who is rising." [44]

I refuted the idea that even then I found common in

America, namely, that financial and military power could be a substitute for the moral power of earning the good will of all decent people in the world. Without followers, the leader is no longer a leader, but only an isolated aberrant. And if he then is strong, like America, he becomes a dangerous aberrant, dangerous for himself and the world.

The leadership the world now needs from the United States must spring from clear thoughts, rational analysis, and devotion to peaceful living and to development. It should be possible to move more courageously toward putting a stop to the armaments race and toward giving the poor, non-white nations of the world trade outlets and financial aid.

And the United States must put an end to its effort to convince itself that what it is prepared to do to aid the poor countries is being done for a national political purpose—"in the best interest of the United States" or even "for the security of the United States." That type of motivation for foreign aid is not effective in calling forth a national sacrifice at home or in other rich countries, nor is it soliciting good will in the poor countries or anywhere else in the world.

The international leadership from the United States must be in the form of vigorous attempts to strengthen international compassion and solidarity, necessary to build up intergovernmental cooperation within the United Nations for disarmament, global peace-keeping, and joint responsibility for the development and welfare of the poor countries. Such leadership is needed. National selfishness is as dangerous for building up a peaceful, progressive international community as rugged individualism has proved to be for consolidating the nation-state at home.

Part Four

THE POLITICS OF DEVELOPMENT

Chapter 12

A LOADED
MISCONCEPTION

When the amount of aid to underdeveloped countries began to increase in the 1950's—at first mostly from the United States—this was mainly a move in the intensifying cold war (see Chap. 11, Sec. II, above). *Governments that could be relied upon to stand firm against Communism were given not only military aid and "supporting aid" but also aid for development.*

Insofar as such aid strengthened that type of government in their own countries, this made sense in terms of military strategy. The economists at that time added a more humane note by explaining that development aid, in particular, would make the masses of people less inclined to become infected by Communist thought. This would hold true not only of countries whose governments had been brought to come out as allies in the cold war, but also of countries like India, whose government did not take a stand in the cold war but remained neutral.

Communism was depicted as the "counsel of despair." It could win easier access, it was held, to the minds of people who were very poor and saw little prospect of improving their lot. Those who were somewhat better off and feeling more assured about their future would be immune to Communism.[1]

This assumption was supported by the theory of a "revolution of rising expectations." Without any attempt at empirical research, this type of mental reaction was assumed to affect the masses of people in underdeveloped countries.

The theory had, on the one hand, an optimistic slant. When the impoverished masses were touched by the rising expectations, it was believed that the new hopes would bring them to change their world outlook, inspire them to modernize their life and work, and bring about development. This effect would be stronger if aid from developed countries came to their support.

The theory implied also a threat. The rising expectations had to be satisfied. If their hopes were frustrated, those masses would be apt to rise in revolt and become susceptible to Communist propaganda.

In the United States, this line of thought became in the aid field an auxiliary to the "containment policy," developed in the late 1940's and early 1950's and given doctrinal structure and theological nerve by Secretary of State John Foster Dulles. Development aid so motivated became part of the Western armor in the steadily intensified cold war.

The slightly ironical note to be added is that this idea—that poverty-stricken masses, feeling hopeless about their future, would be prone to revolt—stems from Marx's simplistic theory about class struggle and the proletarian revolution. The modern idea of the revolution of rising expectations was indeed only an amplification of Marx's theory, in that it would make an uprising of the masses likely even without a process of actual impoverishment.

In regard to Marx's basic theory, as in regard to many of his other doctrines which Western writers have unwittingly taken over in their crudest form, Marx himself made many qualifications and reservations. These would have been worthy of careful study by Western writers— had they been more aware of the history of their thinking.

This motivation for aid to underdeveloped countries has for some years been given somewhat less emphasis, at least in writings with scholarly pretensions. Behind this shift in thought are a number of developments.

For one thing the cold war has been abating—or the intellectuals in the Western countries have been hoping that it has. The "purpose" of the theory of containing Communism by aid to underdeveloped countries has stood out as relatively less important.

It should be added that it was very much a theory manufactured for use in the United States. Other developed nations, and particularly those in Western Europe who had more experience of colonial rule over backward regions, were from the beginning skeptical about the need for giving aid for that purpose.

As a matter of historical record, really impoverished peoples have seldom revolted. When there was crop failure in some district of India, the poor who had no food usually just went hungry. Some contracted disease and some died. Some took to the road, with a hope of finding food somewhere else. They did not revolt.

It is an old experience all over the world that it is the somewhat-better-offs who are apt to become rebellious, and not least so when their lot is slightly improving. These rather obvious facts became more difficult to escape as time went on and people came to reflect on what they were saying.

Particularly persons with scholarly pretensions must have felt it increasingly embarrassing to rely upon the theory of the revolution of rising expectations as applied to the masses of people, without ever attempting to use observations to confirm or refute it. It is my conclusion from studying conditions in South Asia that that type of expectancy regularly does not touch these masses much—though, of course, it often does touch the articulate among the upper class, including the "middle class."

When it has been asserted—and occasionally is asserted even today, by indigenous intellectuals as well as by observers from the developed countries—that the masses are actually being moved by rising expectations, this has in my opinion been a false rationalization. It reflects how they feel they themselves would react if they had to live in the dire and often hopeless poverty of the masses. It undoubtedly also reflects their bad conscience when confronted by extreme inequality, which most often is increasing.[2]

It is true that there are plenty of "revolutions" in the underdeveloped world. With few exceptions, however, they are in the nature of coups or putsches, through which one group of persons in the upper class overthrows another group that has been in power. They usually follow a trend of altering the system of government to become more authoritarian.

As I pointed out in Chapter 3, seldom, and never in that large part of the underdeveloped world which I have studied more intensively, South Asia, have these "revolutions" risen in response to organized rebellion among the masses. They have all occurred at levels high above the masses.[3]

In *Asian Drama* I expressed skepticism about the possibility of foreseeing how "revolutions" of this type would evolve in South Asia. Having taken a wider view of the whole underdeveloped world, I now feel that it is not feasible to forecast with any certainty, even for five years ahead, what kind of government any one of the several underdeveloped countries will have eventually.

Even more substantial revolutions aimed at improving the conditions of life and work for the masses of poor people and in some measure supported by those masses, at least *post factum,* that have occurred and can come to occur, including the rise and spread of some sort of nation-alistic Communism, are equally difficult to foresee. If such revolutions should occur on a large scale, which is not to be excluded, it will depend upon any one of a great num-ber of factors, among which increasing impoverishment of the masses hardly figures, except in some specific cir-cumstances as a broad underlying condition.[4] I shall come back to this important question in the third section of this chapter.

As an economist I am humiliated to recall how many of our profession in that era yielded to the temptation of urg-ing aid to underdeveloped countries by stressing that it could help save them from Communism. It was simply as-sumed that this was so—without bothering to undertake any serious research or even to apply critical thought to the socio-political processes implied, in regard to which the conventional economists had developed blinkers.

It was undoubtedly done for the best of purposes: to make development aid more palatable to the politicians and the general public in the United States and other developed Western countries. But in the end, a good pur-pose cannot be served by paltry thinking. Nothing but critical awareness of our ignorance and hard-boiled re-search seeking to establish truth can serve a good purpose. This is the inherited faith of every honest student.

The cold warrior's argument for development aid has in more recent years been changed into a much looser and more general proposition, namely, that economic progress rendered possible by aid contributes to making under-developed countries more democratic, more stable inter-nally, and more peaceful in their international relations. I have in Chapter 11 pointed out that this thesis in its general form is equally unfounded by experience and re-search and therefore equally frivolous.

By what I have said, of course, I do not mean to warn the economists against going into the broader questions of the socio-political processes in underdeveloped countries, with which the following chapters will deal. Quite the contrary: they should do so if they want to make their studies realistic and conducive to rationality in policy formation.

But they should then feel under the same restraints of the necessity for critical analysis and empirical study of the facts as they are prepared to accept, at least in principle though not always in practice, when working on narrowly restricted "economic" problems in line with their own research experiences in developed countries, where it is more possible to isolate those problems.

Chapter 13

A FATEFUL DEVELOPMENT

One of the potentially most fateful developments in the underdeveloped world today concerns the conditions that determine *social and economic stratification and the distribution of opportunities among different classes* in the national communities. Before attempting to draw conclusions in regard to political dynamics from the analysis in the preceding chapters, I shall, as a preparation, focus attention in this chapter on the effects of two forces of economic and social change now at work: the population development (Chap. 5, above) and the technological advance in agriculture (Chap. 4, above).

In regard to *population,* a main effect of the spread of birth control, if an effective program were begun, would be to raise levels of living through a changed age distribution, with many direct and indirect further effects to raise labor efficiency. These favorable effects would be of major importance in every underdeveloped country, independent of the man/land ratio.

Not all governments in underdeveloped countries have reached a decision to go all out for a policy of spreading birth control among the masses. Still fewer governments have shown the willingness or the ability to take firm action to implement such a decision.

The task of giving effect to a policy of spreading birth control among the masses, if once seriously faced, is a most difficult one, particularly in the poorest countries and generally among the poorer classes of people. Even with the availability of the new birth-control technology, the administrative problem of reaching down to the individual families in the villages meets almost overwhelming obstacles and inhibitions.

Because of the youthfulness of the populations, which itself is an effect of the high fertility up till now, it will be a long time before lower fertility will effect a substantial decrease in population growth. In particular, the future labor force—like the cohorts of future parents— are already born, or will soon be born while birth control is gradually being spread. The labor force will therefore continue to grow by something between 2 and 3 percent until the end of the century.

Industry will not be in the position to increase net labor demand very much very soon. Because of "backwash effects," the total number of workers employed in manufacturing, including crafts and traditional industry, may for a considerable time even decrease as a result of industrialization.

The other urban occupations, and particularly retailing and services, are already packed with grossly underutilized labor. Even where the refugees from agriculture in the city slums are rapidly increasing, as is the case almost everywhere in the underdeveloped countries, the agricultural labor force will not decrease but will usually increase, in some countries very rapidly.

The growth of the labor force in agriculture has an inherent tendency to increase fragmentation of land holdings. More generally it will tend to force people down the economic and social ladder, making owners tenants and tenants landless workers, while the size of the small farms will decline. Population increase is thus in itself one of the forces that work for increasing social and economic inequality in agriculture.

As a general proposition it holds true that agriculture in underdeveloped countries tends to be *extensive and not, as usually assumed, labor intensive.* Too many in the labor force do not work at all and those who work put in short hours during the day and are often without work for periods during the year. Their labor intensity is low. The labor force is thus at present grossly underutilized. A rational agricultural policy must aim at raising labor input and efficiency, and thereby labor productivity and yields.

That this should be possible is demonstrated by the fact that average yields are not only very low but that they vary a great deal among units of cultivation, even when conditioning factors are held constant: size, soil, climate, and the available and generally known technology.

Technological improvement cannot regularly be applied without raising the demand for increased labor input and efficiency. Its application should thus advance the prospects for an agricultural policy aimed at decreasing the underutilization of the labor force.

There are many difficulties that have to be overcome in order to accomplish the fuller application of a more advanced technology, whether already known or newly made available. They have almost all a root cause in *a system of landownership and tenancy* that, though differing in different underdeveloped countries, generally holds down labor utilization and, more specifically, prevents the wide utilization of improved technology.

The quest for land reform is motivated not only by the craving for economic and social justice but primarily by the urgent need for higher productivity of land and labor. Only in combination with land reform can all other attempts to raise yields by improvement of agricultural technology have their full effects.

Land reform should take different forms, depending upon the conditions in the several underdeveloped countries. From a productivity point of view, what every land reform should accomplish is to create such *a relationship between man and land*[1] that can make possible and create the incentive for the tiller to work more, work harder and more effectively, to invest whatever funds he can lay his hands on for raising yields and improving his land, and in the first place to invest his own labor for these purposes.

In most underdeveloped countries, though not all, land reform has been a sham, reflecting the inegalitarian distribution of power. In recent years even the discussion of land reform has mostly died down in both underdeveloped and developed countries.

Contrary to the motivation generally pretended, all other attempts at institutional reform, subsidized aid of various types handled through local self-government and various schemes of cooperation, have in the absence of land reform implied a bypassing of the equality issue. These other reforms have actually tended to favor the higher strata in the villages, thus increasing instead of decreasing inequality in agriculture.

I have permitted myself to repeat in a summary fashion, and to stress, some of the main conclusions reached in Chapters 4 and 5. The problems of inequality and low productivity in agriculture have in recent years been brought to a head by *the availability of new high-yield varieties of cereals and the vision of the "green revolution"* (see Chap. 4, Sec. III).

In many countries, as for instance two of the very poorest and also most populous underdeveloped countries, Pakistan and India, the availability of improved seed grains has for some substantial and progressive farmers in some districts meant a remarkable rise in yield, often to several times what it had been. There is fair reason to hope that this development can spread to other districts in these countries and also to other parts of the under-developed world.

This development has given rise to what I have called a technocratic euphoria. One important effect has been that almost all further thoughts about land reform are on the way to being finally buried.

The expectation is expressed that food-deficient countries, among them the two mentioned above, shall soon become "self-sufficient in food," meaning independent of food imports. The pending hunger crisis in the Third World should thus be on the way to being prevented, or at least delayed.

This expectation as usually pronounced apparently *does not envisage any improvement in the undernourishment and malnourishment* that is prevalent among the masses in underdeveloped countries and to which I referred in Chapter 4, Section I. Such an improvement would pre-suppose that the lower strata would come to earn so much more that they could raise an effective demand for more calories and for more protein and protective food that, in turn, would often raise the need for still larger starchy crops. The "self-sufficiency in food" taking these needs into account would require a much higher level of production.

The type of substantial and progressive farmer who can embark upon the type of farming where the new seed grains can be used is undoubtedly responsive to prices. When fears are now expressed of an oversupply of food that might exert pressure downward on prices and make even that type of farming less profitable or even unprofitable, this is again a confirmation that an increase in effective food demand by those who are now underfed is not expected on any large scale.

But so far I have only scratched the surface of the economic and social problems raised by the vision of a "green revolution." The important thing is that the new opportunities are open only to farmers with irrigated land and with capital resources to buy fertilizers and other necessities and implements for intensive farming. They will be more able to do so, as they will regularly escape taxation, however profitable their enterprises become. For the larger part of the subsistence cultivators, whether working as sharecroppers or on mini-farms of their own, *the new opportunities are out of reach.*

I stressed in Chapter 4, Section II, that improved technology will generally raise the demand for labor. This is, indeed, true for mechanization also, when it is not directly labor saving. Through import controls and controls over the direction of enterprise and investment in industry, the government in an underdeveloped country regularly has it in its power to stop labor-saving mechanization in this new type of capitalist farming.

But the big question is whether it really will do so. These agricultural entrepreneurs will have their place, or take their place, in the power elite of a country. The government and the administration on all levels are "soft" toward demand and pressure from that class and are easily drawn into collusion. It is more probable than not that there will gradually be substantial investments also in labor-saving machines, thereby decreasing the demand for labor.

As pointed out in Chapter 4, Section II, a tendency to introduce labor-saving technology is clearly visible in some Latin American countries. In a country like India, it is a disquieting fact that there are no indications of either policy or research being directed toward the combined objective of labor-intensive and at the same time high-productivity agriculture.

The introduction of labor-saving technology will then add its effects to all the other developments that tend to increase social and economic inequality in underdeveloped countries and to press down the lower strata in agriculture. The main one is the rapid increase of the labor force that is imprisoned in agriculture—to the extent that it is not fleeing to the slums in the cities.

I have focused my observations on agriculture, which is by far the most important part of the economy in all underdeveloped countries.

There is, in the presently prevailing trends in most underdeveloped countries, no sign that the social and economic inequality in agriculture will not continue to widen, indeed at an accelerating rate. The quest for land reform is almost everywhere weakening, partly under the influence of the vision of the "green revolution," which is hailed as the solution to the agricultural problem.

In the absence of effective land reform there is little basis for a hope that all the other institutional reforms—such as community development, agricultural extension, and credit cooperation—will not continue to become perverted to serve the interests of the better-offs. The availability of the new agricultural technology will tend to make the governments inclined to aid those who are best able to put it into use, which means those with resources.

If then, as I fear, these entrepreneurs also begin to introduce labor-saving machines, decreasing the demand for labor, while the labor force is already underutilized and rapidly rising, the end effect of the "green revolution" will be an increase of the underutilization of labor to an unprecedentedly high level.

What is popularly but inadequately called "unemployment" and "underemployment" in agriculture could then in the 1970's—supposed to be the Second Development Decade—rise to truly damaging proportions. The other side of such a development would be increasing poverty among the rural masses.

The exodus to the city slums will under these conditions almost certainly continue and probably swell in numbers. The growth of modern industry will, as I said, not open up many new employment opportunities that are really a net increase of labor demand. Other urban occupations in underdeveloped countries are overfilled by largely under-utilized labor.

These refugees from agriculture in the miserable slums of the cities are not really integrated into the urban community. They are in reality only a dislocation of some of those in the rural underclass who have become superfluous in agriculture as the result of the increase of the labor force in a rigidly stratified society, where technological advance is also restricted and increasingly misdirected from the point of view of making use of that labor force.

This underclass in the cities may easily become the great majority in most cities in the underdeveloped countries. Even in the cities the overwhelming problems will be that *labor becomes increasingly superfluous and goes to waste, with mass poverty as a result.*

Meanwhile there are other trends supporting the preservation or even increase of inequality in underdeveloped countries. Thus *education* is in most underdeveloped countries, particularly the poorest ones, not effectively used as an agency for inducing social and economic change (see Chap. 6, above).

In many countries education is not now directed at counteracting economic and social inequality, or even upon preparing the masses to use what chances they may have for participation in development. Instead, it is often used as a means for upholding the upper-class monopoly of education and their inherited claim of not having to soil their hands. It becomes then, in effect, anti-developmental. The strivings to make the masses of people acquire functional literacy are frustrated in various ways.

Political power in almost all underdeveloped countries is held by upper-class groups who have generally prevented effective reforms aimed at protecting and advancing the interests of the masses. With the aid of Western and indigenous economists they have even equipped themselves with a theory that inequality, and a growing inequality, are natural in a "developing country" and, indeed, a precondition for economic progress. This theory is false (see Chap. 3, above).

Corruption is everywhere rampant and is usually increasing. This issue is ordinarily wrapped in silence in the development literature. Occasionally it is even falsely said to be favorable for development in a "developing country" (see Chap. 7, above).

The *influence exerted by the developed countries*— through direct private investments and public aid—has seldom been directed toward creating greater equality. It has more often than not tended to foster social and political reaction (see Chaps. 9–11, above).

Meanwhile, *the pending "hunger crisis"* in the restricted sense in which it is mostly used—implying that production is not increasing fast enough to meet effective demand at the low nutritional level of the poor classes in the underdeveloped world—may be prevented or delayed.

Meanwhile also, modern industrial plants will be set up by the state and by indigenous capitalists and foreign concerns, often working through joint enterprises. *The whole modern sector of the economy will be growing.*

Including industry, transport, power, the financial agencies, and the facilities for higher technical education, the growth of this sector could have important constructive possibilities for the transformation and growth of the entire economy. This would assume, however, that it had been directed by planned policy to have this effect and, in particular, coordinated with efforts to increase labor utilization and productivity in the subsistence sectors in agriculture and in the urban slums.

This has regularly not been the case. The modern sector remains mostly in isolation. There has been and will be legislation on working conditions and social security for employees working in that sector, inspired by the International Labour Organization (ILO), and earnings will be considerably higher than in the surrounding urban slums or in agriculture. They will often approach a "middle-class" status.

If, at the same time, underutilization of the labor force and consequently poverty will be rising in subsistence farming and among landless laborers and also among people in the urban slums, the small modern sector will have even more of an enclave nature than in colonial times. The "spread effects" are weak now [2] and may become weaker as the gap widens between the upper class and the underclass groups.

None of the policy measures for protection of the workers is applicable to conditions of these underclass groups. If legislated, they will not be implemented. They cannot be implemented.

Meanwhile, finally, the conventional economists and the secretariats of the intergovernmental organizations, uncritically using the flimsy aggregate figures for "growth" of the national income or the national product and taking no consideration of what is growing, whether it is real growth from a national point of view or merely costs caused by negative developments, of how the product is distributed, and, generally, of the "non-economic factors," may convince themselves and the general public that *the "developing countries" are really developing* (see Chap. 8, above).

Before turning to the political dynamics in the underdeveloped countries, I need to add one more clarifying note. The economic and social situation and development in these countries are often characterized as *exploitation*. For the most part this conception is kept loose and equivocal, when it is not related to the classical theory of value in the specific form into which it was molded by Marx.

I leave aside in this context the fact that the classical theory of "real value"—defined by Marx as well as Ricardo as the cost in terms of labor required for the production of a commodity—is metaphysical and an outgrowth of the natural-law philosophy,[3] and thus not useful in scientific analysis. The definition of exploitation given by Marx is the "surplus value" of which the employer robs the worker.

The underutilized labor force in agriculture and the urban slums is much worse off, however, than could ever be grasped by that or any other definition of exploitation in terms of a part of the produce stolen from the workers. The real affliction of the underutilized labor force and the main cause of their impoverishment is that they are producing very little or nothing at all.

That in this situation landowners, moneylenders, and, indeed, the upper strata in general can "exploit" labor by paying workers very little and, as landowners, can retain an extraordinary share of what little the tenants produce, and that generally a lot of cheating of the poor and powerless goes on, are merely symptoms of this much more fundamental trend of underutilization of the labor force. Attempts to fight poverty by attacking these symptoms but not the deeper causes are in vain, as is fully proved by much legislation, for instance in India, that attempts to establish minimum wages in agriculture and provide for protection of tenants.

Looking closer at what actually has been happening and is now happening in underdeveloped countries, the increasing underutilization of the labor force and the consequent mass poverty are caused by the combined effects of its rapid increase and the economic and technological changes, as they evolve in a very inegalitarian economic, social and political system. *A large and increasing part of the labor force is simply superfluous or becoming superfluous.*

Likewise, the widening income gap between developed and underdeveloped countries, and the poverty of the latter countries, are caused by developments in these countries dealt with in Part Two of this book and by their economic relations with the former countries as analyzed in Part Three and, particularly, Chapter 9, above. It is not the result simply of exploitation in any meaningful and clear sense of the term.

Indeed, if the whole Indian subcontinent with what will soon be a population of one billion people should sink into the ocean tomorrow, this would cause only minor disturbances to the curves of international trade, production and consumption, wages and other incomes, values of financial stocks, etc., in the developed countries.

It would hardly be noticeable in their national economies. The developed countries need so little of what is produced in Pakistan and India, while these countries need so much from them.

Like many other problems in underdeveloped countries, this one also has a close parallel in the poverty problem in the United States. There is certainly a lot of petty cheating of the slum dwellers—by charging exorbitant rents and other prices and underpaying labor in sweatshop trades, etc. And there is plain discrimination, particularly against Negroes.

But the basic difficulty for America's large underclass in its rural and urban slums is that they have not been given the education and the skills and other personality traits they need in order to become effectively in demand in the modern economy. The parallel is even closer: there is a trend working to decrease the effective demand for the work of that underclass, making them, in fact, more and more superfluous.[4]

If in the United States the unemployed and underemployed slum inhabitants could vanish, yes, even if all inhabitants of the slums were to vanish, there would be transitional adjustments to make but no major affliction to the national economy. After these adjustments, majority America would be as well off as before—indeed, better off, as it would have gotten rid of the large running costs for living with its slums and slum dwellers. This is the horrible truth, even if the ordinary American is not prepared to face it.

For America the remedy is to invest heavily and for a prolonged period in the education and the general well-being of its underclass, in order to bring them into the mainstream of the nation's life and work by increasing their ability to become effectively in demand. This is what I have called America's "debt to its poor." [5] It must be paid, if the nation is not going to blow up and disintegrate.

I have no doubt that these huge investments will be profitable—in the very long run. And America can well afford it. But in the short run it will be a burden on its annual income.

When ordinary Americans, liberals as well as reactionaries, brag about the richness of their country—and feel so free to indulge in all sorts of public expenditure of little or no value for satisfying the needs of its population—this demonstrates that they have not, as yet, taken due account of their debt to the poor.

The inequality issue both within the underdeveloped countries themselves and between them and the developed countries—as within the United States—can certainly be viewed from *the moral point of view of justice and the need for redistributional reforms*. And this we have done throughout this book.

In the internal issue of greater equality within the underdeveloped countries, the whole economic system should be altered, particularly in regard to landownership and tenancy. In regard to the international equality issue, the developed countries should give more aid, and they should inaugurate commercial policies favoring underdeveloped countries instead of, as now, discriminating against them.

In the first place, this should be done out of human solidarity and compassion. Particularly in regard to the internal equality issue, reforms are needed also in order to *improve productivity of labor and land*.

Reforms should be urged straight on these lines of justice, equality, and productivity. The issues are merely confused, and at the same time made to appear much too easy to solve, by clothing them in the old metaphysical theory of surplus value and exploitation.

Foreign investors in underdeveloped countries, for example, can often refer to their paying much higher wages than the corresponding market rates, without that fact settling the issue of whether it is really advantageous for the underdeveloped countries to have them there and doing what they do.

These themes have been developed at some length in the earlier chapters of this book. My main thesis is that development should be defined as *a movement upward of a whole system of interdependent conditions,* of which "economic growth," assuming that it could be properly defined and measured, is only one of several categories of causally interrelated conditions.[6] A halt to improvement of other conditions, usually called "social conditions," and still more an actual deterioration of them, will cause a trend toward disintegration of these newly founded national communities. Sooner or later, if present trends are permitted to continue, it will bring the whole development process to a grinding lame walk and, finally, general retrogression.

This is what the use of the biased postwar approach to the development problem in underdeveloped countries has tended to conceal (Chap. 1, above). The argument has recently been spelled out in a United Nations report of an Expert Group meeting in Stockholm,[7] from which I will permit myself to quote the first paragraph.

> It has been common in the past to draw a distinct line between "economic" phenomena on the one hand and "social" ones on the other, opposing social to economic development, economic objectives to social objectives and economic factors to social factors etc. This is partly due to the rather narrow approach to the development process

characteristic of past thinking in economics which relied heavily on simplistic econometric models with highly aggregated variables. This school of thinking has influenced planning methods and techniques on the national level (in the developing countries) and also economic projections of a wider scope as well as the work of the United Nations in this area. This approach using relatively simple models with easily quantifiable variables, such as GNP, capital investment, exports and imports leads to a neglect of certain very important factors and aspects of the development process. Thus neglected are all matters relating to differences in incomes and levels of living—between classes, regions, sectors, age groups, town and country, matters relating to human development—health, education, children, matters relating to consumption—nutrition, housing, social services. To these neglected factors should be added the crucial problem of social stratification and many other aspects outside the sphere of the narrow economic models, particularly the vast underutilization of labour. Considering the great importance of those aspects for the development process, the Group believed that *the time has now come when the economic approach to development analysis and planning has to be integrated with a social approach which is different in nature and would be more relevant to the problems of developing countries in the coming Decade.* [Italics added.]

Chapter 14

POLITICAL
DYNAMICS IN
SOUTH ASIA

The conspectus in Chapter 13 of the economic and social changes under way in underdeveloped countries is painted with a broad brush. There are great differences between countries. Nevertheless, I believe the developments I have sketched are more or less typical of what the great majority of people in underdeveloped countries are now experiencing—and will continue to experience if trends are not altered by radically changed policies.

Even when economic and social conditions and trends are fairly similar, political events cannot be expected to be so. In *Asian Drama,* in my survey of the political developments in the several countries of South Asia, I noted that *in regard to political developments the differences were greater than in other respects.*[1] The model I sketched for studying the political development in India[2] was thus of only slight relevance for the analysis of that same type of development in the other countries of the region.

More generally speaking, I have *little use for the highly simplified, general models for political development in underdeveloped countries* which have recently been worked out by a new school of political scientists, emulating the economists.

These models have no predictive value. I have already stated my considered opinion that it is not possible to predict the type of government any single underdeveloped country will have five years from now.

Reflections on the future political development in these countries will have to deal instead with a spectrum of *alternative possibilities,* and with the consequences of one or the other of these possibilities being realized. It is true that there are also some general trends—for instance, the increasing importance of the military establishments. This trend, however like those in the social and economic fields, can have different effects as to the policies actually followed in different countries.

Inherent in all social research is the tendency to analyze a development in terms of broad sets of forces. When considering political developments, however, we should remind ourselves that *history is not destiny but is manmade,* and that its course will depend on decisions and actions yet to be taken. Individuals or groups of individuals often happen to be placed in a strategic position where their choice of action can have profound and long-lasting effects, even far outside the political field.

In India Jawaharlal Nehru had a towering and in the beginning an almost uncontested position in politics, especially after Sardar V. J. Patel's death. He constantly stressed the need for a social and economic revolution to follow the political liberation from the British Raj. He had spelled out in his own writings the direction of the radical reforms needed and had succeeded, together with the radical wing in the National Congress, in getting many of them endorsed in resolutions of the Congress.

If Nehru then, even at the risk of splitting the Congress Party, had not been satisfied with continually spelling out the radical ideals in his speeches while postponing the social and economic revolution, but instead had inaugurated vigorous political action for their speedy realization, India's history would have been different.[3]

What would have happened if Mohandas Gandhi had not been assassinated right at the start of India's independence era, and if he had retained his earlier vitality, is also open to speculation. So is the question of what position he would have taken, for instance, on the shelving of land and tenancy reform through a nationwide pattern of collusion and corruption.

If in Pakistan Ayub Khan, after a successful and promising start in 1958,[4] had had a more open mind to the need for social and redistributional reforms in his very poor and inegalitarian country, and if he had purged corruption and to begin with kept himself and his family from corrupt practices, he might still be in power there. And Pakistan's history during the last decade and in the decades to come might have been very different.[5]

The point I want to drive home is that although there are broad social and economic conditions and trends—such as those toward underutilization of labor stressed in the preceding chapter—these mainly raise problems for those active in the political arena, or set restraints on what they can accomplish.

I have felt it necessary to spell out all these caveats. A main point to stress is *the utterly fragile nature of all generalizations about underdeveloped countries in the field of political dynamics.*

One conclusion of the analysis in this book is *the need for radical reforms in most or all underdeveloped coun-*

tries. And if the dangerous trends toward increasing un-derutilization of labor among the masses of poor people in the rural and urban slums is to be averted, it is *urgent* to initiate and rapidly carry out these reforms.

The needed reforms are spelled out in Part Two of this book. They center on breaking up inegalitarian and rigid economic and social stratifications. In agriculture, land reform stands out as the crucial issue. Birth control must be spread among the masses of people. A fundamental redirection of education and a vigorous adult education campaign are needed. Corruption must be stamped out and stricter social discipline enforced.

Reforms in this direction would be the rational policy choices. Bringing about their rapid realization would amount to *an economic and social revolution.*

Before I proceed to comment upon actual policy choices, a theoretical problem of facts and factual rela-tionships should be touched upon: How does a tradition-alist society react to changes, once they are imposed upon it? The answer should be of crucial importance in all rational planning for development.

More specifically, *does a large and rapid thrust against prevailing attitudes and institutions raise such forceful and continual resistance that the only choice is to proceed with small and gradual reforms?* [6]

Unfortunately, very little empirical research has so far been devoted to this important problem. A few modern anthropologists are becoming prepared to tackle it, react-ing against an old school that tended to use a static approach and in the main saw change as disturbance of an established equilibrium.

Benjamin Higgins quotes Margaret Mead, summing up her conclusions from a revisit to Manus of the Admiralty Islands after it had been exposed to a massive occupation by American troops during the Second World War. She says that provided the thrust of modernization is strong enough, a traditional society can be rapidly changed to its great advantage without meeting strong popular forces of resistance and reaction.[7]

Higgins' own view is:

> There is nothing we know *for certain* that would suggest to us that a "big push," including massive efforts at education and re-education, will fail, or that it will be particularly painful to a society. On the other hand, there is a good deal of evidence that gradualism will fail, and that it will be very painful indeed in a great many developing countries. . . . development economists should fight tooth and nail any line of argument that might result in a reversion to gradualism as a basis for development policy.[8]

In my study of conditions and trends in South Asia I have grown more and more convinced of the realism of the hypothesis that most often it is not more difficult, but easier, to carry out a big rapid change than a series of small gradual changes—"just as a plunge into cold water is less painful than slow submersion."

What policies are then felt to be available for carrying out reforms? Bigger and more rapid changes ordinarily must be attained by resolutely *altering institutions* within which people live and work, instead of trying, by direct or indirect means, to induce changes in attitudes while leaving institutions to adjust themselves to the changed attitudes.

But institutions—for instance the distribution of land ownership—can usually be changed only by resorting to what in South Asia is called compulsion—legislating obligations on some people and giving rights to others, and supporting these changes by state force.

Whatever resistance is called forth by any one gradual step forward will usually be more effectively mustered against the next step, whereas there is less chance for continued resistance when the change is rapid and big. This is particularly true if the small changes are attempted halfheartedly and if reliance instead is placed either on the indirect effects induced by economic changes or on persuasion, exhortations, or threats. The forces of resistance may then be fed and intensified.

Worse still is the practice, common in all underdeveloped countries that pretend they are taking radical reform measures, of pronouncing or even legislating large-scale institutional reforms but not implementing them. This breeds cynicism, creates uncertainty about what actually is the established law, and builds up further resistance to implementing the reforms and continuing them.

I shall leave this question of big rapid changes versus small gradual changes after these brief remarks. It needs to be further explored, taking into consideration the nature of the changes, the advance preparation—social, political, and administrative—that is possible, the character of the leadership that pursues reforms, etc.

In theory, the radical reforms required to meet the dangerous trends could be carried out *peacefully*.

The need to carry out radical reforms is commonly recognized—as an abstract proposition. Indeed, political and ideological leaders in practically every underdeveloped country—in Brazil as well as in India—freely indulge in exuberant pronouncements of the necessity for a social and economic revolution. They often attempt to dress in these terms the policies they actually inaugurate.

The extravagantly radical vocabulary used for this purpose was commented upon in Chapter 3, above. All governments profess to be for greater equality, while the actual development goes in the opposite direction.

Generally speaking, none of the reforms I pointed to as necessary for reversing the sinister trends is tackled in the underdeveloped countries with the resoluteness that is called for—with the partial exception, in a few of these countries, of promoting birth control among the masses. While the general pronouncements have been radical and often revolutionary, the policies resorted to have been piecemeal and gradualist in the extreme, even at the planning stage. In actual practice they have most often been perverted and have increased inequality by favoring the better-offs.

These developments must be explained by the *power situation in underdeveloped countries.* The partial exception of population policy can be understood when we note that, though very difficult to carry into effect, it is cheap and does not call for any sacrifice on the part of the upper-class groups.

In this respect there is little difference between the countries that have succeeded in establishing and retaining a system of parliamentary democracy and those that by "revolution" have brought to power an authoritarian government of one type or another. Power almost always belongs to varying factions of the upper class, taken in its wider meaning as including the so-called middle class.

While reasoning in terms of class and power, *I do not assume class solidarity,* least of all on the level of conscious intent. The upper-upper class of high officials, substantial businessmen, and big, usually absent landlords ordinarily do not act in any overt institutional cooperation to defend their common interests.

The "middle class," on the one hand, includes the "rural elite" of landowners living in the villages, moneylenders, merchants and other middlemen, and local officials. As a group they are often the most reactionary elements in the national community.

In the cities the "middle class" is a very disparate category, containing not only a striving bourgeoisie of small merchants, industrialists, and better-placed employees of the larger industrial and commercial firms, as well as officials in the middle range, but also a lower stratum of white-collar workers in private and public service. To this "middle class" belong also teachers, at least in the secondary and tertiary schools, students, and other "intellectuals," except those who have advanced into the upper-upper class.

There is, indeed, very little all these variegated groups have in common except *their distance from the poverty-stricken masses,* who ordinarily lack functional literacy. The interests of these inarticulate masses are not felt as their concern. Indeed, the masses are usually not within their vision, except as part of the landscape.

This is possible because of the *passivity of the masses.* The attitude I am trying to describe is less a commonly shared and consciously felt interest among the upper class in preserving a *status quo,* since they are privileged in various degrees compared with the masses and have in most underdeveloped countries actually become better off in recent decades, particularly in urban areas. It is more *a common disregard for the interests of these masses* which are not effectively brought to their attention.

But, as pointed out in Chapter 3, the higher strata in this upper class have been *the vehicles for the moderniza-tion ideals,* including the quest for equality. Gradually, these ideals have spread to most of the lower strata in the upper class, though least to the "rural elite." They have to varying degrees become common to all the "educated"— schooling being the main dividing class line in these countries.

Those in the upper class who try to intellectualize their policy attitudes are found to harbor two sharply opposing views simultaneously. On the one hand, they see the need for radical reforms that must reach deep and be brought about fast. This explains the common clamor for a social and economic revolution. On the other hand, they fall back on the belief that change must proceed with utmost caution, so as not to upset the inherited pattern of social relations.[9]

To explain the latter view, which dominates their ac-

tual policy choices, they invoke the traditionalist conservatism, supported by religious taboos, of the masses of
people. On that point, they adhere to an ideology cultivated by the colonial powers in support of their laissez-
faire policy in regard to the social and economic conditions that had become customary. This is, in fact, a sort of
"neo-colonialism," though one pronounced and practiced
by the articulate in the indigenous upper-class groups
that succeeded in holding power after liberation.

The contradiction between the acceptance of the necessity for radical reforms in principle and the reluctance to
undertake them in practice is bridged by *an overoptimistic assumption about the magnitude and rapidity of the
spread effects from developments in modern industry.*[10]
Confidence in that assumption, which is rooted in Marx's
thinking, has become widely shared by Western and indigenous economists, usually without their recognizing its
origin.

This assumption is slipped in without evidence that it is
realistic. It is, in fact, most often left implicit. It does not
agree with historical experience and with what we know
about what is actually happening.[11] The trend toward
underutilization of the labor force, sketched above, implies that such spread effects of industrialization are
minor and easily overpowered by other forces.

In support of the gradualist approach, *analogies to the
historical development in Western countries* are also ad-
duced. The fundamental differences in initial situation
(see Chap. 2, above) then fade from thought. This happens the more easily because of the common use of a
biased Western approach in research and planning that
broadly implies abstraction from those types of social and
economic facts that represent differences in initial situation.

Even *the ideal of democracy* is introduced to defend
abstention from radical reforms, particularly in South
Asia. It is then assumed that the upper strata would resist

them. That resistance would have to be broken and this would necessitate compulsion, which is associated with Communism and a totalitarian system of government.

It is now often said that under a totalitarian government radical reforms could be carried out that are not feasible within a democracy. This view of democracy is in fact opposed to the tradition and commitments of the liberation movement, at least in India. It was assumed there that basing the government on the will of the people would have an immediate effect on the whole social and economic structure of the national community (see below).

This has not happened, and anti-Communism has, in fact, been used as an argument against all reforms that do not leave the interests of the upper-class groups undisturbed. It is used in countries that rely upon elections as the basis of their governments as well as in countries under authoritarian regimes.

The anti-Communist argument has had a sweet smell in the United States and, though less so, in most other Western countries. The absence of efforts even to enforce what laws and rules have been promulgated has been quietly accepted, without much criticism.

The Western world, for instance, puts on blinkers to keep corruption out of its sight. As we have seen, this opportunistic considerateness even afflicts the writings of economists and other social scientists.

More generally, it is a fact that with all the cruelty, arbitrariness, and abuse of individual power, there is in underdeveloped countries an astonishing reluctance to use social controls that have been resorted to freely and successfully in Western democracies. The "soft state" can from one point of view be defined as a relative absence of effectively enforced rules, leaving people largely free to do what they please and what they have the power to do.[12]

In this sketch of how the absence of urgently needed

radical reforms is rationalized and reflected ideologically, I have had in mind primarily South Asia, where by far the greater part of the people in underdeveloped countries live and whose conditions I have studied more intensively. The somewhat different conditions in Latin America are dealt with in the Appendix.

I pointed to the *two contradictory views* on social change simultaneously harbored in the minds of more thoughtful members of the upper class: the urgent need for radical reforms and the necessity to proceed very cautiously. With some the two views—the revolutionary and the gradualist—even take on an almost schizophrenic character.

It is, for instance, not unusual to hear a successful businessman, particularly if he is young and well educated, declare bluntly that nothing but a Communist revolution could save his country from the ills of underdevelopment. This does not affect his political behavior, however, nor indeed prevent his simultaneously expressing the philosophy of gradual change and of free and undisturbed private enterprise.

In India, which has by far the most sophisticated public debate in South Asia and, indeed, in the whole underdeveloped world, it is customary to appoint special commissions to spell out in concrete terms, and urge, radical reforms. The policy proposals in their reports are thereafter left unimplemented and are rapidly forgotten.

There have been several such commissions on land reform, for instance, and on education and on eradication of corruption. The persistent pattern of having such commissions appointed and giving them directives to propound radical reforms seems to indicate that they are aimed at serving a function in the national life: to keep the ideals alive even when they are not followed in practice.

Jawaharlal Nehru occasionally hinted at such a function for ideals being propounded even if not practiced.[13] And his perseverance in using every opportunity in his speeches, often several a day, to hammer in the modernization ideals points in the same direction.[14] Undoubtedly Nehru was sincere and honest in doing this. It was to him an attempt to prepare the ground for change, not a cautious evasion.

Nehru was not alone in this. Similar impulses motivate many other Indian politicians and intellectual leaders. Indian newspapers give so much space to their speeches that they, too, appear to be mainly concerned with enlightening their readers along the lines of the modernization ideals.

In the tradition established immediately after independence, legislation is frequently used for the same purpose, even when it must be clear that the intentions and spirit of the laws are being nullified in practice. The Five Year Plans have formulated general reform goals remote from their practical proposals and still more from the implementation of the Plans.

The annual conferences of the Congress Party, and sometimes the Parliament, have been persuaded to adopt resolutions far in advance of the actual policies pursued. The trend in this general ideological activity was, in Nehru's time as well as today, toward more explicit, radical commitments, whereas practical policies moved in a pragmatic and generally conservative direction.

The situation in India is of particular interest not only because of its huge population but also because of the freedom of public discussion that has been zealously preserved together with its parliamentary system of government founded on universal adult suffrage.

Not unexpectedly,[15] the Congress Party in India is now —at least for the time being—split into two wings. A lively debate, engaging the articulate section of the population, is taking place and is well reported in the Indian press, which is of high quality when it comes to mirroring what is happening in the country. What does the debate center around?

Prime Minister Indira Gandhi's wing of the Congress Party is claiming a more radical attitude. This was symbolized by the nationalization of the banks. That change, however, had been prepared by resolutions of the Congress Party before the split.

In practice it may not imply much difference one way or another. It can hardly be counted as one of the major radical reforms India urgently needs in order to counteract the trends toward underutilization of the labor force and impoverishment of the masses.

The opposite wing, led by what is commonly called "the syndicate," was not in principle against putting the banks under more effective control but urged caution against rash action. Otherwise it is now competing with the other wing in generally radical pronouncements in the tradition of Jawaharlal Nehru.

Neither of the two competing groups has much to say about land reform. Least of all do they show any desire to discuss that problem in concrete, practical terms. Nobody talks about the need for higher taxes, particularly on land, or for preventing tax avoidance and tax evasion.

The proposals in the truly outstanding report of the Educational Commission in 1966 have been quietly buried without either group coming out for their realization. The important public health reforms are similarly left almost in oblivion. Even family planning is not much of a burning issue in the public debate in spite of the serious non-attainment of announced goals.

Revealed individual cases of corruption among politicians and officials are eagerly seized upon by both sides as weapons to destroy political adversaries. But the urge to do something on a large scale and systematically to stamp out corruption, which had a brief span of public interest after the excellent report of the Committee on Prevention of Corruption in 1964, has died down.

The breakdown since 1966 in India's established tradition of planning does not seem to be of much concern to either group. The opposition group has begun to ask for a redrafting of last year's Draft Fourth Five Year Plan— which was produced after a lapse of three years without a Plan—in order to give more emphasis to employment. But they have very little to propose of a more concrete character. Generally, there is a lack of interest in the broad issues of how to direct the national economy.

What we witness is that resort is taken to non-commital general declarations—in favor of a "socialist pattern of society" or the like—to which everybody can agree. Concrete issues of a national character that could cause a rift are avoided.

If any specific proposal is taken up, usually within a rather narrow "middle-class" perspective, both groups seem to be maneuvering to be for it, though perhaps wanting to postpone its realization for a shorter or longer time. One recent example is the issue of abolishing the privy purses of the former princes.

Like the nationalization of the banks, this is surely not unimportant. Neither is another issue that has been broached by leaders of the more radical wing, that of nationalizing a large part of foreign trade, particularly imports.

More than ten years ago a firm decision was taken to nationalize the wholesale trade in grains. Only partial, halfhearted, and largely vain efforts have been made to implement this decision. The issue has now been revived by the more radical wing but without their showing conviction that they are willing and able to accomplish much against the vested interest of landowners, moneylenders, and middlemen.

Under these conditions the political struggle becomes

unduly centered on unreal doctrinal differences, and on personalities and the sometimes unstable alliances between them, issues that have a strong gossip appeal. The other political parties in India do not act very differently.

The Communist Party is split into three groups with differing affiliations to the Soviet Union and China. They mostly carry on internecine struggles on doctrinal issues and between individual leaders. Meanwhile they stress general issues like the need to decrease unemployment and to nationalize industries and foreign trade.

Under these conditions *intensified party dissent does not contribute to bringing crucially important national problems to public attention.* It provides instead a sort of exciting stage play which distracts from the really important problems now facing India. It helps make it more possible to forget about pending developments and the necessity to meet them with daring and rationally planned political action.

In this connection it is important to recall how exceedingly small the articulate sector of the Indian nation is, mainly confined to the upper class, including the so-called middle class. A very rich and highly integrated country like Sweden, with only a little more than one percent of India's population, has probably as many politically articulate people as all of India. And they are immensely more effectively organized for purposeful political participation.

What is lacking in India is organized pressure from below on the part of the masses of people, effectively directed toward defending and promoting their interests. This has made possible a political stability that is tantamount to stagnation in regard to the urgently needed economic and social reforms.[16] The recent development referred to above may risk this political stability without inaugurating an era of radical reform.

A political "revolution" of the type that has brought a

more authoritarian government to power in other countries in South Asia is not excluded in India, but is less
likely for several reasons: the prestige of the parliamentary democracy and its success in "functioning" fairly
undisturbed until now; the special character of the military establishment, particularly its having been less involved in politics than, for instance, it had been in Pakistan for a long time; the more highly developed national
trade-union system in the organized sector of the economy; and, indeed, the size and diversity of the country, as
long as it does not break up into separate regional parts.

If the parliamentary system were to break down and be
succeeded by a more authoritarian government in India,
too, this would not be due to organized, concerted political activity by the huge underclass in agriculture and in
the city slums. And it would hardly increase the prospect
for far-reaching economic and social reforms—though it
would not decrease it either. As elsewhere, it would
merely imply a regrouping of the holders of power in the
upper class, restricting the freedom of a large number of
that class to play the role they play today, and sacrificing
free public discussion and the largely uninfringed civil
liberties.

The fatalism and apathy of the masses is a fact of
immense importance in a country like India, as in most
other underdeveloped countries. It narrows the group
within which political dynamics evolve to the upper class,
or rather to those of them who care. The politically active
can deal with the masses as an object for policy, re-
strained only by their power passively to resist policies.

The interesting question is whether this mass passivity can be changed—and *whether the masses can then
be expected to demand rational reforms in their own interest.* Mere activization of the masses may be useless or
actually bolster reaction if the masses move against birth
control, against cow slaughter, against efforts toward

greater social discipline, indeed, against rational reforms. They must be educated to see their own true interests.

I have likened the Indian village to *a complex molecule among whose clusters of atoms extreme tensions have been built up.*[17] But the tensions crisscross in a manner that maintains equilibrium so that the social system remains at rest. The molecule can be brought to explode, however, which implies a rearrangement of its atoms so as to engender joint action by some or all members of the village community. The question is, How and with what consequences?

Such an explosion can be ignited from within. But it can also be caused by a thrust from outside that works on accumulated inflammable tensions inside the local community. A rather common pattern of reversal of the peaceful passivity of the masses is *riots animated by religious fanaticism or ethnic jealousies, combined with an opportunity to steal from one's neighbor.*

The partition of British India into the Indian Union and Pakistan caused a horrifying wave of mass murder and looting in both countries. In India since then, occasional outbreaks of this type of mass activity, setting Hindus against Moslems, have in recent years followed rather an upward trend. It recently culminated in the religious riots in Gujarat, costing several hundreds of lives.

The Malayan riots of Malays against Chinese are of the same type. Because of the precariously balanced size of the Malay and other ethnic groups, the so-called Alliance, an association of the wealthy leaders of the three main ethnic groups which up till then had permitted a system of government based on elections, has now broken up. The country is under a *de facto* authoritarian government with the power held by Malays.[18]

In independent Africa all signs point to continued uprisings and wars on ethnic grounds that in many parts of the continent will dominate the political development for a long time to come.

In the present context, the main point is that this type of political activity on the part of the masses not only lacks rational policy goals but actually *distracts the masses from organizing to press for their real and common interests.*

There are, however, a number of trends that should *promote mass solidarity in purposively and effectively pressing for their interests.* One is *the spread of education.*

In countries like Ceylon and Malaya, now approaching a situation where almost all children get at least elementary schooling,[19] resulting in nearly universal literacy among the younger generation, this trend could gradually succeed in awakening the masses, particularly if stress were also laid on adult education. But India and still more Pakistan are far away from such a situation. As pointed out in Chapter 6, the educational system in these two countries rather tends to preserve, if not actually increase, the class chasm.

The functioning of a parliamentary system founded on universal adult suffrage, as in India and Ceylon, should itself serve as an educational process and one directly focused upon politics. Proudhon said that giving the people the vote was political dynamite. Mohandas Gandhi, as well as Nehru and the whole radical wing of Congress, firmly believed that radical social and economic reforms were inevitable once independence was won and power vested in the Indian people.[20]

The winning of independence, however, did not touch off the anticipated social and economic revolution. But is it not possible to believe that with some delay, elections and the whole political process evolving in a system founded on elections will gradually make the masses alert?

It is true that much electioneering becomes directed upon less rational issues—such as caste or ethnic group, language or regional allegiance, and personalities—or is carried out under one form of bribery or another. In spite of this—and however much status, authority, and power determine how the masses of people vote—the idea should gradually dawn upon the lowly and the poor that the secret vote gives them potential power.

This could build upon the sullen dissatisfaction that anyone can observe among the disadvantaged masses. The transistor radio and other contacts with the outside world should undergird the propensity to use the vote for pressing their interests to improve their condition.

In India, particularly the political behavior of the lower classes in local elections of panchayats has been studied rather intensively. Many of the studies are published in the remarkably problem-conscious *Economic Weekly*, now the *Economic and Political Weekly*. The main question has been to what extent these voters continue to adhere to the traditional line of political behavior, simply following commands of leaders in the upper brackets, or whether they begin to use the new opportunities to elect members from their own class.

Conclusive results that can be applied to the whole country have not been reached, but a tendency toward independent action on the part of the disadvantaged has occasionally been recorded.[21] Yet even in such cases, there has generally been little purposeful striving to organize for demanding concrete reforms.

The positive factors—education and participation in elections of various types—can thus only be expected to have important results *in the rather long run*.

In India, as well as in the rest of South Asia, the land-reform issue is, for instance, just as dead in elections—local, state, and national—as at present in the public discussion among the political and intellectual leaders and among the economists.[22]

Should there really be a popular upsurge of political radicalism in questions of primary importance for the masses, it could create a situation where a more authoritarian government could take over, precluding elections when they became dangerous for the upper strata.

But such an upsurge is not in sight. It would be an exception to the rule in the region.

One more question should be raised: whether the amassing underclass in the urban slums would be more prone to demand egalitarian reforms.

It does not seem so. This rapidly growing underclass, characterized above as really not integrated in the cities where they live, remain displaced poor people from the rural areas.

Just as, after some riotous outbreaks immediately following the war, there has not been much of a popular movement for land reform in the rural areas,[23] so the city slums have remained remarkably quiet. A study of the slum dwellers in Old Delhi, for instance, even found that the overwhelming majority, with an average monthly income of about $4 per head, considered their present situation "secure."[24]

Still, there are many elements of uncertainty for the future that should be stressed. It is conceivable that a national leader or several of them will rise above the little-minded pattern of Indian politics and frame the practical but radical reform program that is needed to save India from increasing underutilization of the labor force and mass poverty.

To have any chance of success, such leaders would need high national prestige. In the present state of political demoralization, that is not easy to acquire.

The upper-class groups would not by themselves support them or even tolerate them, at least not until they had succeeded in arousing considerable pressure from below. To reach down among the masses while still retaining a following among upper-class groups would be immensely more difficult for a national leader today than for Gandhi in the liberation struggle when the issue was so simple and the enemy so visible.

A Nehru could perhaps have done it, in the first years after liberation when the time was so much more propitious. But he chose to postpone the social and economic revolution.

Under the strong influence of the postwar approach, he relied too much upon the spread effects of "economic" development, meaning the growth of modern large-scale industry and the use of modern technology. The population explosion came as a surprise to him, as to everyone else, and he never saw the full effects of it. He underestimated the difficulties raised by the rural economic and social structure. There were also many "immediate" problems to solve, and he was deluded by the success India had in solving them.[25]

Could he have done more today? Nehru was not concerned about the problem of what would come after him. He believed, as all his friends knew, that when difficulties towered aloft, the men and women to master them would come forth. And deeper still was his faith in the long-term development of democratic institutions in a very underdeveloped country where, as he hoped, even the poor would increasingly make their voices heard and would become educated to press for their own interests.

The actual political development in Nehru's later years and after his departure has made it ever more evident how essential is increased participation among the masses. Who could now be the vehicles for such a change?

Preoccupied with doctrinal issues and personal maneuvering, the Communist parties have shown an astonishing reluctance or inability to organize the rural and even the urban poorer strata. When in some parts of the country they have reached out in the villages, they have seldom tried to establish a class front by raising the issue of land reform, but have often played the game of caste and even worked on the grievances of the more articulate "middle-class" groups. This might be changing, however.

Moreover, there is the possibility that local leaders may emerge to bring the complex and motionless molecule to explode while directing the movement upon constructive issues. Eventually there might be cooperation among insurgents over a wider area, involving rebel leaders from the upper class. There have always been localized spurts of this sort in India, and they may be on the increase.

The universities may conceivably come to furnish intellectuals who overcome their individualistic quietism or cynicism, their disgust for the villagers and their torpid life, and go out into the rural areas to organize the masses for political action. Up till now—except in periods of civil war, as recently in Indonesia—students in South Asian countries have seldom expressed their rebellion in political activity or even in clearly defined goals.[26]

Riots by students in South Asia have mostly had only spurious and trivial reasons and causes: wanting easier examinations or lower bus fares, or following out ethnic and caste animosities. Their riots are, in a way, parallel to the mass riots commented upon above. But this might not be so forever.

But there is quite clearly a possibility or even perhaps a probability that *in India or indeed in the larger part of South Asia there will be neither much evolution nor revolution.*

What the political repercussions will be if nothing very effective is done in the reform field while the trend toward increasing underutilization of the labor force is permitted to work for ever greater impoverishment of the masses—somewhat in the perspective of the demographers' dictum, when they see a reactivation of the Malthusian checks if population increase is not stopped—eludes my power of analysis.

Is there a limit to the misery human beings can bear without revolting? Or is there no such limit? The utterly miserable living conditions quietly endured by many in the rural and urban slums today would suggest that there is no such limit.

But would such a development stir up factions in the upper class, in the first place students and intellectuals in general? Would they be *moved to raise more determined demands for radical reform?* Would they back these demands by going out among the poor masses to try to educate and organize them? What success would they have? I do not know.

Again I need to stress the volitional, unforeseen, and unforeseeable elements of individuals and groups of individuals acting contrary to established patterns. I see a spectrum of alternatively possible political developments, but I am not prepared to forecast what actually will happen in Indian politics—not in five years' time and still less in the more distant future.

I feel much the same about the other countries in South Asia—however, with a similar possibility of utter and increasing impoverishment much less likely, or at least placed further ahead on the time axis, in countries like Malaya and Ceylon than in India, Pakistan, and even Burma.

Vietnam shows a radically different political development from that in other South Asian countries. The crucially important difference is that the masses there are no longer passive politically, certainly not in the wholesale manner that is typical of the rest of the region. And they are intent upon reforms that are in their own interests.

As I pointed out in Chapter 3, Section II, the explanation lies first in the different character of French colonial rule and then, after the Second World War, in the French colonial war. The latter war was supported by the United States—against the clear intentions of Franklin D. Roosevelt before he died—and after 1954 was taken over entirely by that country, with token participation of some dependent governments in the region. It has now lasted for more than a quarter of a century.

To an increasing number of the Vietnamese people, it became a war of liberation, and more precisely *a fight against military intrusion by a foreign, white, and rich nation*—first the French and later, on an increasing scale, the Americans.[27]

A *resentful nationalism* developed. As pointed out in Chapter 3, such feelings, more than any one of the modernization ideals, have easy access even to the masses.

From there the masses moved to economic and social *consciousness of their interest in radical reforms,* primarily land reform. The fact that the white intruders in the French and later in the American phase of the war sought, and had to seek, their support among the privileged upper class, in the general setting of the cold war *led the masses toward a sort of nationalist Communism.*

The war is already lost for the United States. Their mistake was not to see this awakening of the masses and how their military intervention spurred it. The United States under successive administrations has put its trust in puppet governments in South Vietnam which, however they shifted, had their support mainly among privileged upper-class groups.

When the United States government, emulating its adversaries, began to press for land reform and to speak in terms of economic and social revolution, as had already happened in Eisenhower's and Diem's time, the Saigon government and its officials and supporters regularly obstructed it—as, indeed, the similar holders of power have done in other South Asian countries. But in Vietnam, under the impact of aroused resentful nationalism, the masses were no longer passive.

Western interference, particularly when it takes the form of military action, can become a force which oper-

ates to bring the masses in an underdeveloped country to a higher degree of political awareness and activity. Nationalism takes the character of being anti-Western and, indeed, anti-white. In the setting of the cold war, where aid can come only from the Communist countries, it then also becomes easily identified with Communism.

A somewhat similar process was under way in Indonesia, which the Dutch had not left peacefully. It was crushed by the carnage in the fall of 1965, calmly reported in the Western press as a victory against Communism.

There are many reasons to feel doubtful about the future political development in Indonesia.[28] Among many other things, if it is difficult to awaken the masses, it is also difficult to calm them down when once awakened. They cannot all be killed or imprisoned forever.

In the southern region of Africa—South Africa, South-West Africa, Rhodesia, and the Portuguese colonies—a situation is developing where the majority populations of non-whites are suppressed by white minorities, supported by the United States and almost the entire Western world. For this development I refer the reader to Chapter 3, Section II.

This development of anti-white and anti-Western emotions in some underdeveloped nations, experiencing an onslaught of white military and police forces and seeing this backed by Western solidarity, tends to spread to other underdeveloped countries that are largely non-white. From the point of view of the value premises adhered to in this book, *it is a frightening prospect to have to fear that the relations between developed and underdeveloped countries will become infested by the color complex.*

From a Western point of view the tendency toward alignment with Communism of underdeveloped nations is equally unfortunate, giving a new dimension and an additional *raison d'être* to the continuation of the cold war that is costing the world so much in armament expenditures and is threatening peace.

Even more fundamentally, to me, as a student in the great liberal tradition of the Enlightenment, it is a hateful experience to be driven to the conclusion that the awakening of the masses and their becoming conscious of their interests and prepared to fight for the radical reforms needed for development shall happen in a world political constellation where *they find themselves projected into a movement of national Communism.*

A primary cause of this development is *gross misjudgment of facts and betrayal of ideals* on the part of Western nations and, in the first instance, by the United States. This development would not have been necessary—in Southern Africa or in Vietnam—with more foresight and accurate knowledge and with more faithfulness to our ideals. Studies and some political experience have driven me to see ever more clearly the role of stupidity and ignorance in world history. These are not innocent shortcomings but, like selective knowledge, opportunistically stressed by interests, often petty and short-term. They become undergirded by the biases in "realistic" and polite research. This is what gives such a paramount importance to the attempt to cleanse our thinking of biases.

It is a bitter thought that in the wider perspective of world history the repressive and hostile positions taken toward these underdeveloped nations by the United States and other Western governments have served to awaken the masses to their interests, a primary condition for reform and, in the longer run, development. Could not the rich, developed countries have found other more effective and less destructive means to help these peoples reach that goal?

The question is unhistorical, as the social scientist's queries must often be. *The goal of the developed countries and, in particular, the United States has not been that the masses should be awakened in order to make possible genuine democracy and the radical reforms needed.* All their sympathies were with the privileged classes in the underdeveloped countries and not with the impoverished masses. They were readily prepared to condone the absence of reforms in underdeveloped countries, or the perversion of reforms, preferring stability—in fact, a sort of continuation of colonial practices.

Finally, I feel the need to stress one more point. As explained in *Asian Drama,* and touched upon already in Chapter 3 above, my study led me to the conclusion that in regard to preparedness for radical reforms, there is not much difference between what happens in a country like India, with a parliamentary system of government based on universal suffrage and a wide range of civil liberties, and a country with a more authoritarian regime. In both cases the power belongs to groups and factions in the upper class while the masses tend to remain passive.

This is a statement about facts. So is the possibility — though not the necessity—that an authoritarian regime will come under leadership that is prepared to carry out reforms that would not have been enacted under a "democratic" regime. From the point of view of the value premises, it would then be preferable.

These conclusions of my research *go against my grain, though I have to accept them.* I certainly feel no neutrality in regard to democracy.[29] And I am eager to stress certain possible advantages of general elections and free discussion even in the South Asian setting.

Democracy and, in particular, elections may in time contribute to making the masses more alert and better educated. Freedom of speech and action in a democratic system of government can even encourage individuals and groups in the upper classes to take a stand for radical reforms and to attempt to stir up and educate the masses. They will, at least, not be prevented from doing so.

Also, the suppression of public discussion in authoritarian countries can make the government less well informed. For instance, I believe that one important reason for the Burmese military regime's spectacular lack of success in social and economic policies has been its protection from criticism.[30]

Chapter 15

THE RESPONSIBILITY
OF ECONOMIC
SCIENCE

The problem of policy choices has two dimensions. One is that policy choices follow as inferences from value premises and from the knowledge of facts acquired by the use of these premises. These *rational policy choices* have been spelled out in Chapters 3 through 11 above. The other dimension concerns the political development that, in turn, determines *what policy choices will actually be made.*

The two dimensions of the problem are interrelated. The social scientists represent the main link between rational and actual policy choices. Among them we economists, as planners and advisers to peoples and their governments, dominate that interrelation.

On the one hand, we have been influenced by the political forces in all our countries to take a biased approach to the development problems in underdeveloped countries.

In Chapter 1 of this book, I have given a general characterization of this biased approach. In the following chapters I have persisted in demonstrating how these biases have manifested themselves in the several specific problems.

At the same time, we economists undoubtedly also exert influence upon actual politics and the policy choices that are being made. John Maynard Keynes's observation that people are moved by defunct theories is wrong only to the extent that actually they are also moved by quite fresh and current theories, at least in part and after a time lag that need not be too long.

Indeed, Keynes's own mostly *posthumous* success in the fields of monetary and related policies all over the world is proof of that. In Sweden before this, a similar adjustment of actual policies in these fields had given the same confirmation of the practical importance of the theories of Knut Wicksell and his Swedish followers, who had anticipated those of Keynes.

Before I go further, I have one most earnest reminder that I want to stress. When I accuse my fellow economists in the conventional line of gross biases in their approach to the development problems of underdeveloped countries, *I do not imply personal dishonesty.*

Since my early youth I have lived as a member of the worldwide academic community. In many lands I have acquired intimate knowledge of, and friendship with, hundreds of my confreres in the pursuit of economic science. Extremely few have been cynical in regard to their work. Even fewer have I seen intentionally adjusting their writings to selfish interests.

In this respect I believe our whole profession, and particularly those who have made the outstanding contributions, have adhered to the great tradition of the classical economists, whom Alfred Marshall once characterized in the following words:

> The fact is that nearly all the founders of modern economics were men of gentle and sympathetic temper, touched with the enthusiasm of humanity. They cared little for wealth for themselves; they cared much for its wide diffusion among the masses of the people. . . . They were without exception devoted to the doctrine that the wellbeing of the whole people should be the ultimate goal of all private effort and all public policy. . . . The rights of property, as such, have not been venerated by those master minds who have built up economic science.[1]

He noted, however, their reluctance to give their backing to distributional reforms and the fact that they "appeared cold" to the needs of the poor. This he explained as follows: "the range of vision even of the greatest seers of that age was in some respects narrower than is that of most educated men in the present time."

What Marshall alludes to here is that classical economics was biased by the influence of the dominant political forces in England one and a half centuries ago. There is to my mind no question that if these economists had retained a broader "vision," to use Marshall's euphemism, and had not been biased in the way they were, this would have had considerable influence on practical politics.

Karl Marx liberated himself from the biased failure of Ricardo to draw the radical conclusions implicit in his own value theory.[2] And certainly Marx came to have great influence on the political development in the world, not least by his theory of surplus value and exploitation.

But as the classical value theory, in Marx's as well as in Ricardo's version, under the influence of the natural-law philosophy is intrinsically metaphysics of the teleological variety, as are many other of Marx's theories, we can have little use for his approaches. This does not mean that there are not observations and pieces of analysis of continuing importance in his as well as Ricardo's writings.

And we still need to know their writings in order to have a historically critical view of our own thinking. I have often observed in the foregoing chapters how economists today show the lack of such knowledge when they follow Marx's lead in an uncritical and often only implicit way.

The conventional economists today are not, any more than were their forebears in earlier times, subjectively dishonest when they apply biased approaches. But *they are naïve in regard to the logic of their research.*

In a sense and to an extent, they are apt to be more naïve than their precursors generations ago. When men like F. Y. Edgeworth and Henry Sidgwick developed their welfare theories, they still believed in objective values and could base their theories on these as value premises. They did not have to shrink from such a foundation, as do the modern welfare theorists.[3] This undoubtedly made their reasoning less crammed and illogical.[4]

The prevailing, and for the last two generations increasing, naïveté among conventional economists and generally among social scientists makes the plea for *a sociology of social science and scientists* important and urgent.[5] There is danger in economists carrying on their research while remaining ignorant of how they are conditioned by the surrounding society—and also, of course, by tradition and their personal inclinations.

This sociological research can be centered directly on our work. It should be easier to carry out than most other social research. The *corpus delicti* can be placed on the table right before the researcher. It consists of our published articles and books.

A lead can be gained by logical criticism, showing up non sequiturs and arbitrary assumptions. This criticism will have to be immanent, as the assumptions are most often left implicit. When these logical defects are seen to be tending in a systematic direction, this should be a signal that sociological research is needed to explain in terms of cause and effect the social conditioning that has had that result.

A guide for this sociological research should be the principal question asked in every detective work: *Cui bono?* What interests are served? Those interests are seldom or never the interests of the individual researcher but of the powers dominating the society that surrounds him.

Research, when not purged from bias, becomes *opportunistic* in the service of the interests of the power collectivity as commonly understood by those making up that collectivity and determining its policy choices. Causation along this line escapes the conscious knowledge of the researcher. Biases, as I said before, are not intentional.

A closer analysis shows that even the interests of the power collectivity are mostly not rationally conceived. In particular, these interests are ordinarily not long-term but short-term interests, and often misconceived even in the short run.

The demand for a sociology of science and scientists is motivated by the need to make the researcher less innocent about his own work and more aware of how easily it becomes irrationally conditioned. The type of logical criticism carried out in this book should be helpful in the same direction.

It would be maximally effective if it would induce the researcher to define explicitly the value premises that determine his approach, that is, the viewpoint he applies, the questions he raises, and the concepts he uses in his analysis.

These reflections on the causes of bias in economic research and on the need for fresh and extended analysis in terms of both the sociology of science and scientists and the logic of science are placed here, after the chapter on political dynamics, with a purpose. There is no doubt that *economic research as an influence on the development of politics and on the policy choices being made in underdeveloped as well as developed countries.* There-fore, a model for political development that neglected the influence of what we economists are writing would be inadequate to reality.

Generally speaking, a purge of bias from economic re-search will lead to policy conclusions demanding radical reforms in underdeveloped countries and radical changes in the aid and trade policies of developed countries, as broadly specified in the earlier chapters of this book. A reorientation in that direction of the research carried on by the many thousands of economists in developed and underdeveloped countries cannot fail to have an effect on politics. That people do want to be rational in their policy choices is also a part of social reality.

It may seem *utopian and politically "unrealistic"* to study the development problems of underdeveloped coun-tries from the viewpoint of value premises, even though they correspond to the ideals everywhere expressed. These ideals obviously have little correspondence in an actual willingness by those in power, in underdeveloped as well as developed countries, to make sacrifices for attaining them.

The important point to stress in this connection, how-ever, is that *even a move in the direction of the realization of these ideals is desirable.* Likewise, a move in the oppo-site direction is undesirable. To work for a turning of the trend and for the speeding up of such a movement toward better realization of the ideals should not be deemed offhand as politically "unrealistic." Indeed, striving for such a change must be the obvious purpose of a policy study carried out in scientifically rational terms.

Moreover, to take for granted that things will remain as they are at present, including people's attitudes toward social change, is certainly not realistic. People's attitudes can alter, as well as the support their attitudes are ren-dered in institutions and power structures. And *they can be induced to alter.* Under certain circumstances induced changes that are big and sudden may even meet less popular resistance than small, gradual changes (see Chap. 14, above).

But quite aside from all policy considerations, it should be stressed that studying the problems of underdeveloped countries from the viewpoint of explicitly stated value premises that are relevant, significant, and feasible is primarily *a logical device for preventing the study of economic, social, and political reality from becoming biased, and thus faulty, in regard to the establishment of the facts.*

The views expressed in *Asian Drama* and recapitulated in this book are often said to be "pessimistic." I disavow this criticism. I claim instead that the methodological principle adhered to in these and other studies of mine is the only means, provided by logic, to attain *realism.*

The greater "optimism" in most of the economic literature—and in many studies by the economic secretariats not only of government agencies but often of intergovernmental organizations, and in special reports of experts working under the auspices of these agencies and organizations—is the result of their falling prey to gross biases in their very approach to research.

This fact is amply exemplified in the previous chapters of this book. The conventional economist is unaware of his biases. He believes he is "objective" and simply "factual." He is, therefore, utterly unwilling even to discuss the problem of bias. For this reason, I have made it my duty in this book to pursue the common biases and to nail them down.

I cannot feel hopeless about such a reorientation of economic science taking place. In part it will occur even before a full awareness on the part of the researchers of the now prevalent biases, and before they have become prepared to bring the valuations into the open by explicitly stating their value premises.

Up to a point, *all honest research has a self-healing capacity.*[6] As Knut Wicksell once stated, the scientist is superior to his own chosen approaches. He cannot help finding truths which he has not looked for.

It should be noted at this point that my criticism in the foregoing chapters has regularly been in terms of logic and of the demand for stringent scientific observation and analysis and for circumspection. I have pointed out defects in scientific approaches which, if my criticism is correct, cannot be defended by any economist, whether or not he shares my general conclusion that they are caused by biases.

This judgment of lack of stringency and circumspection applies to our tendency to restrict the analysis to what we call, without ever defining the limitation implied, "economic" factors, and to disregard other factors—in spite of general declarations of their importance. It applies to the misuse of concepts which, though useful in the analysis of our Western economies, are largely inadequate to the economic realities in underdeveloped countries—for example, "unemployment" and "underemployment." It applies to the use of aggregates and market terms with reference to national economies where for the large part markets either do not exist or are highly imperfect.

To this corresponds an inadmissible carelessness in the use of statistics, for instance those relating to the national product or income, without scrutinizing either how the terms are defined in underdeveloped countries or the observational basis for their calculation. Without clarifying what they are doing, the conventional economists then commonly identify the rate of change of the product or income with "development."

This is usually done without even mentioning the distributional aspect and, still less, the significance of other than "economic" factors in the process of development of underdeveloped countries. This negligence serves the purpose of the tendency to bias, as otherwise it would not be possible to use the figures in the way they are commonly used.

Much more generally, the statistical observations and compilations are made with the use of categories which are inappropriate to the conditions in underdeveloped countries. As a result the statistical figures become grossly misleading and often meaningless. Besides the figures for national product or income, this is true of aggregate figures for "savings" and, quite particularly, for "unemployment" and "underemployment."

The faults in statistics generally follow an opportunistically biased line. Some important facts, for instance those about landownership and tenancy, are not only faulty but are often even prevented from being collected, or suppressed when collected, by the influence of powerful vested interests.

As I have pointed out throughout this book, but particularly in Chapter 6, other statistics, for instance those on literacy and enrollment in schools, have been produced and used in an uncritical way. As these figures commonly exaggerate educational accomplishments, they also serve the purposes of the "optimistic" biases.

The UNESCO secretariat has not made any serious attempts to check or improve upon these figures, though this would not be too difficult. It could make a beginning by merely carrying out an intensive observational study in a few districts of the real literacy situation and the number of children that actually go to school, and comparing the findings with the figures in the censuses and in the school statistics which they so uncritically use. No secretariat in the other intergovernmental organizations and none of the individual students quoting these figures has ever suggested that they do so. It has served their common and biased purposes to accept those figures without questioning their validity or accurateness.

We have permitted a veritable jumbling of the statistics

on public aid and capital streams from developed to underdeveloped countries, in spite of the fact that statistics
in the former countries are so much more accurate and
complete than those in underdeveloped countries that it
should be possible to give an honest and correct account
of the facts. It serves the opportunistic interests in developed countries to feel that they have undergone greater
sacrifices than they actually have in order to aid underdeveloped countries in their development efforts.

We have often allowed our scientific terminology to be
invaded by expressions from popular, politically oriented
discussion, such as "developing country" when we simply
mean an underdeveloped country, or "the free world"
when we mean the non-Communist world. To me this is
not an unimportant semantic inadvertence but an indication of deeper bias. And it should be disturbing even on
logical grounds.

I simply cannot believe that the massive research now
being devoted to the problems of underdeveloped countries and their relations with developed countries will not
on point after point come up with criticism against, and
correct, these and many other gross defects of economic
science. Any deeper empirical study of the educational
problem in an underdeveloped country, for instance, will
show up the superficiality and incorrectness of the financial approach to that problem in terms of "investment in
man."

And any thorough study of the agricultural problem—
the underutilization of its labor force and the threat that
this will increase still more as a result of the population
development and recent trends in agricultural technology
—will, of course, uncover again the problem of land reform which has recently been swept under the rug in both
developed and underdeveloped countries.

When one economist after another becomes aware that
the errors he and others detect and correct are systematic
and follow a common interest line, he will be forced to

ask: *Why and how?* He will then be on the verge of seeing and inquiring about the biases that are the driving force.

The valuations will then be brought into the open. And he will be driven by the logic of his situation as researcher to ask what his own value premises are. *This is the true and overwhelmingly important "value" problem in economics and the social sciences generally.*

When this has happened, he will have seen a light that will lead him on still further in the detection of defects in economic science and in correcting them. The reform of our science will come more surely, though with some time lag, in this pragmatic and heuristic way than as a result of improving our basic philosophy of science. That is the reason why I have not restricted myself to giving the general philosophical criticism in Chapter 1, but have pursued that criticism into the several problems, taking up one after another.

In particular, I want to stress *the urgent need to improve statistics* in underdeveloped countries. For this, we economists—as the main users of statistics in our analysis and the definers of the concepts and, therefore, of the questions asked—must carry a primary responsibility. My accusation against the conventional economists is that they have filled their books with flimsy figures and built their conclusions upon that material without applying the critical scrutiny that should be incumbent upon us as scientists.

When it comes to quantification, our knowledge is extremely weak. No serious researcher who comes to scrutinize the procedures leading up to published statistics should escape an awareness of their extreme unreliability. This is true even of a country like India where, within the tiny group of the intellectual elite, the discussion has been so free and on such an unusually high level of sophistication.

One cause of statistical insufficiency is that observations and compilations are made according to categories which are inadequate to reality in underdeveloped countries. The resulting figures are grossly misleading or even meaningless. A second cause is the great carelessness shown in defining the questions asked and in carrying out the actual basic observations.

The need in underdeveloped countries is not primarily for a large number of high-flown statistical theoreticians, which might seem beyond what can be rapidly provided. What is needed is well-trained persons who have substantive knowledge about conditions in underdeveloped countries and the critical ability to formulate questions about the material that are adequate to social reality in these countries. They should know how to direct and organize their observations effectively, and in addition have an elementary knowledge of sampling techniques and a few other simple statistical methods.

To help train cadres of such professionals in the underdeveloped countries would seem a type of technical assistance from the developed countries that should be given a very high priority. It would be natural *to give the several statistical services in the intergovernmental organizations in the United Nations group a major role in carrying out this worldwide technical assistance.* They should be instructed to provide—at the request of the governments—missions of expert personnel to organize, teach, and train. And they should be given the necessary funds to carry out these tasks.

But before attempting to meet these new demands, they first need to clean up their own shops. They must be made to realize that at present *their own output of statistics from underdeveloped countries is often stale and defective.*

Above all, these agencies cannot possibly pretend to meet professional standards so long as they uncritically accept figures from the governments and merely reproduce them. The first condition for their coming to exert leadership in the attempt to improve statistics in underdeveloped countries is that they begin to criticize the figures handed to them. And they must also break away from the camaraderie among themselves which makes them reproduce each other's obviously faulty statistics—and, even more often, permit the substantive departments of their own agencies to use those sorts of statistics in their analyses (see Chap. 10, above).

I have no doubt that a growing realization in the statistical services of these organizations that *"science is criticism"* and, in particular, an increasing attempt actually to improve statistics will make it more possible for them to recruit highly qualified statistical personnel. This, in turn, will give momentum to the general movement to improve the statistics in underdeveloped countries for which I am pleading.

I have said that we economists represent the main connecting link between rational policy choices and actual ones. And certainly a main responsibility rests on us as analysts and policy advisers.

But we are not working in an intellectual vacuum. We are only part of the articulate people in developed and underdeveloped countries. These people form the intellectual milieu in which we live and work. They reason, as we do, in terms of cause and effect, and goals and means. Science is never anything else than highly rationalized common sense.

These people who are apt to emulate our ways of thinking make up the ruling oligarchies in all the underdeveloped countries and their entourages, and they include all reflecting persons whatever their present influence is. In developed countries they vote, legislate, and administer, and they shape and express public opinion, which itself is composed of the feeling and thinking of articulate people.

The economist who wants to influence actual policy

choices must in the final resort convince ordinary people, not only his confreres among the economic scientists. This is why I have written this book in as simple terms as possible, without, I hope, sacrificing logical stringency.

I also am aware that the fight against bias in economic science would have greater prospects of rapid success if examination and criticism of our ways of thinking could be nurtured among intelligent laymen. The social forces that condition economic research and drive it into bias would then be considerably weakened.

Appendix

THE LATIN AMERICAN POWDER KEG

Asian Drama was not a book on the development problems of underdeveloped countries in the whole world. As I felt it my duty to repeat insistently, it referred to South Asia, the only part of the underdeveloped world I had studied intensively.

When for the purpose of the present book I had to give attention to conditions in other regions, I was surprised to find that with all the obvious differences, not least in historical background, *economic and social conditions were relatively similar and had resulted in policy problems of much the same character.*

Most underdeveloped countries show the same pattern of gross social and economic *inequalities,* and the inequalities seem to be increasing almost everywhere. Most of these countries, whatever their form of government, are ruled by *small though shifting oligarchies.* They are almost without exception *soft states,* and *corruption* is prevalent and is generally on the increase.

Land reform, even when stated as a major policy goal, has almost regularly been frustrated. All underdeveloped countries face the same type of *population problem.* They can all be seen moving toward a policy of fertility control, though they are at different distances from making it a definite government program.

Even in the *educational field,* the problems turn out to be astonishingly similar. Adult education has been irrationally neglected everywhere in the non-Communist world. Too much stress has been laid on the quantity of education, that is, the number of children and youths enrolled in schools, at the expense of quality. Almost everywhere, dropouts and repetitions are seriously damaging the effectiveness of elementary education. Contrary to the programs commonly advertised, secondary and particularly tertiary education have been given precedence over elementary education, even though they are much more expensive. Schools on all levels are too "academic" and "general" and are not related to practical, vocational, or professional needs.

Within this setting of fundamental similarities there are differences between individual countries and more broadly between regions, especially in regard to political development.

The political development in Latin America deserves special attention. Divided into over twenty separate countries, some very small, others quite large, the whole Latin American region has only about half as many inhabitants as India. But its importance in the present context is great.

For one thing, the political development in Latin America has reached a stage of *violent clashes of ideas as well as violent action.* It cannot be expected to exhibit much political stability of the type poverty-stricken India has been able to show, at least up till now.

The Latin American countries, moreover, are geographically nearer the United States. For much more than a century the United States has pronounced, and succeeded in establishing, very *special relations* with these countries. Much of the present political dynamics in Latin America has been determined by these relations.

Between these countries there are *great differences in economic conditions as well as in ethnic composition.* Even the poorest among them usually have a higher level of income than any Indian state, except perhaps Punjab. But the poverty in the rural and urban slums in most of Latin America is appalling.

Generally speaking, *the inequalities are even greater than in India.* Parts of many cities are striking examples of wealth and modernity, providing a luxurious life for an entrenched upper-upper class and a fairly comfortable one for a striving "middle class"—for both groups, a life very different from that of the increasing numbers of slum dwellers so closely surrounding them. It can be doubted whether in most Latin American countries the poorer third, or in some countries half, of the population during recent decades has gained much or indeed anything of rising levels of living—the "quality of life," to quote the title of the Rockefeller Report.[1]

Many, though not all, of the Latin American countries, and particularly some of the bigger ones, have *more modern manufacturing industry than India.* But that industry and the whole modern sector of their economies are even more isolated.

The commodities and services are mainly produced and sold within that sector itself, meeting demands for its growth and the needs of those who live within it, while not having much development impact outside it. There has been even less of rational planning to steer industrialization in such a way as to have beneficial effects on the rest of the economy. It is no wonder that American economists specializing in Latin America have arrived at the development theory of "unbalanced growth." [2]

The threatening social and economic trends toward underutilization of the labor force and impoverishment of the underclass in the rural and urban slums, sketched in Chapter 13 above, *are moving faster in Latin America.*

Population increase is proceeding more rapidly, and except for some vain and mostly private attempts, no serious efforts have been directed toward spreading birth control among the masses. At the same time *the replacement of labor by machines* in large-scale agriculture has gone further. Land reform is not being promoted effectively (see above, Chap. 4, Sec. II).

Urbanization has proceeded further and is at present proceeding faster. Many Latin American countries now have much less than half of their population in agriculture. But the rural population is nevertheless still increasing, though usually much more slowly than in India.

Much of the economic life in Latin America is *dominated by foreign business, mostly American.* Directly or indirectly, through joint enterprises and other arrangements, United States corporations now control or decisively influence between 70 and 90 percent of the raw-material resources of Latin America, and probably much more than half of its modern manufacturing industry, banking, commerce, and foreign trade, as well as much of its public utilities. These are rough estimates but are probably not far from the truth.

It is of particular importance that whatever dynamism there is—or could be without radical changes in economic and social structures—in Latin American economies, mainly emanating from industrialization and the extraction of mineral resources, becomes controlled directly or indirectly from abroad, mostly from the United States. But even much old-fashioned plantation agriculture, pro ducing for export, is run for foreign profit. The United Fruit Company alone controls over 50 percent of the foreign earnings and therefore the entire economic life of six Latin American countries.

Primary products—from agriculture and from mineral extraction—make up about 90 percent of Latin American exports. These products can, of course, have only a very small market in Latin American countries that do not have complementary economies.

Moreover, as modern manufacturing industry has grown up behind high walls of protection, it is mainly limited to producing for the national home market. The total intra-regional trade is still quite inconsiderable.

Modern manufacturing industry, and that sector alone, has therefore a strong interest in forming free-trade associations or common markets, facilitating sales in a larger protected market. As that sector is dominated by foreign interests, the enthusiasm for economic integration has not been very strong among the Latin Americans themselves, except for those who are involved with foreign interests. This is part of the explanation why the integration movement has not made much progress in the present nationalist era.

None of the Latin American countries has anything resembling a diversified economy. In most of them one single product makes up more than 40 percent of total export sales, in some of them much more.

Most Latin American countries are vainly struggling against price inflation that sometimes reaches figures of a yearly increase of 20 or 30 percent and occasionally even more fantastic heights. This makes all economic calculations extremely difficult, encourages an unsound speculative mood in business, and generally tends to discriminate against the low-income strata.

Many of the earlier large-scale American enterprises in Latin America for export production of agricultural products and minerals, including oil, have left *memories of grossly unfair practices* at the time when the land and the concessions were originally acquired.

This has continuous importance, as this legacy has left property rights and concessions acquired in this way in foreign and primarily American hands. They have been challenged, are now being challenged, and in all probability will be challenged even more in the future.

As an American businessman active in Latin America explained to an interviewer from *U.S. News and World Report:*

> Part of the problem . . . is that foreign companies are being called to account for what Latin Americans sometimes term "the rapacious history" of the U.S. business dealings.[3]

That history undoubtedly created a tradition that still influences the business policies of some American ventures in Latin America toward making deals with those in power which cannot bear the light of day.

The explanation for this damaging legacy is partly that the Latin American countries became independent long ago, after having been ruled by the Spanish and Portuguese at a time when those two Catholic nations were becoming backward and out of line with the general development in Europe toward liberalism and the strong and incorrupt state. They did not, as India did, profit from the progressive elements of British rule.

There is no need to ignore the darker side of colonialism in order to see *its positive contribution, as in its British incarnation in India,* which is the part of the underdeveloped world with which I will compare Latin America in this chapter.

After liberation India succeeded in establishing a parliamentary government with universal suffrage and extensive civil rights and, in spite of all difficulties, was able to keep to these political institutions much more firmly than almost all Latin American countries. This was due to what the Indians had learned from their British rulers and, in part, to what the British had begun to put into effect before they left. This much every thoughtful Indian intellectual, however critical he is of the British, will readily admit.

Moreover, almost from the beginning and ever more strongly as the nineteenth and twentieth centuries proceeded, the British colonial government and the Indian civil service, while certainly not unresponsive to British business interests, felt the urge to prevent the most outrageous and offensive practices by their own and other countries' businessmen.

The Latin American countries did not experience that type of wholesome influence from colonial rule. Influences from the ever more dominant American business corporations and the United States government could the less counteract this weakness in Latin American institutions as the United States itself was, and still is, less free from corruption and shady deals between business and public authority than Britain and Northwestern Europe generally (see Chap. 7, above).

The increase of the "middle class" in Latin America is alternatively seen as a force for "stability," in the American sense of the word (see below), including if possible a cautious and gradual internal reform activity, or as a force for nationalist revolt. The truth is probably that it is neither—or that various portions of it can under different conditions turn out to be one or the other.

The "middle class" is extremely heterogeneous and divided in Latin America as in most other underdeveloped regions. It nowhere approaches being a cohesive, self-conscious grouping of like-minded people feeling a community of interests.

The people in "middle-class" positions are astonishingly *individualistic,* on the whole even more so than in the

United States. Concerted, organized action in defense of common interests is not their natural inclination.

The larger part of the "middle class," particularly in the older generation, individually are undoubtedly bent upon preserving what they have and upon climbing socially and economically. They envy the established upper-upper class of landowners and indigenous industrial or commercial barons, though they have to serve them in order not to lose their opportunities and often do so with feelings of loyalty.

They must often find American or American-dominated firms more willing and able to meet their aspirations and to give them chances to advance economically and socially. This does not necessarily mean that they do not share in the spreading resentful nationalism. People's minds are seldom very congruent.

When they are younger, before they are fully involved in the struggle for a living and for individual advancement, many in the "middle class" can embrace rebellious ideas, as is evidenced by the spreading unrest in the universities. Even these movements show the effects of their individualism.

Generally, people of the "middle class" have nowhere in Latin America shown much willingness or ability to go out into the urban and rural slums to teach and to stir up and organize the masses for political activity in their own interest. Those of them who join urban and rural guerrilla bands are a very few.

The small number of workers in modern manufacturing industry, which is not labor intensive, form as in other underdeveloped countries an annex to the "middle class" with considerably higher incomes than the poor masses in the urban slums. In many Latin American countries they have responded to whatever practical possibilities for unionization were left open to them. They can be brought to fight for their own interests, but they practically never

feel a solidarity of interest with the real underclass in the
rural and urban slums.

Something similar can be said about the workers in the
huge mineral-extracting industry, except that they, like
the workers on agricultural plantations, often remain
much more of a real proletariat, far below the "middle-
class" level.

If a large number of people in the "middle class" in
Latin America were brought to revolt or even to nurse
revolutionary sentiments, this would be due to the spread
and intensification of *resentful nationalism,* which in the
Latin American setting simply means anti-Americanism.

Nor is the upper-upper class immune to that type of
nationalism. A few have reason to regard American competition as a threat to their own interests, although more
commonly they seek and win advantages by collaborating
with American corporations. Ordinarily they must also
share the American interest in political "stability," to
which they give the same interpretation as the Americans.
Nevertheless, anti-American feelings are prevalent also in
large sections of that upper-upper class.

Before we take up this theme of growing anti-Americanism, it should be pointed out that the frequent "revolutions" in Latin American countries, which in recent decades have regularly been putsches and coups, and the
now increasing spread of actions of violence, *should not
deceive us into believing that the masses more generally
have become, or are now becoming, activated.* Many of
the romantic enthusiasts for violent revolution among leftist intellectuals in Western Europe and the United States
are suffering from that deception.

To begin with, even when there is some degree of
political democracy and elections are held, it can be observed that the participation rate is most often astonishingly low. It is safe to assume that the non-voters are
mostly the underclass.

Literacy is often a requisite for registration. Also, people in the city slums live without an address. The registration procedures are complicated. But most of the poor apparently *do not care to vote. When they do vote, they vote for parties that are boss ridden and corrupt, and that do not have their interests at heart.*

In the rural areas they often vote as they have been ordered by the landowners, upon whom they depend. These often use more brutal methods of intimidation and engender more complete compliance than in India. But there is seldom a protest movement raised against these practices.

There are exceptions, but in general the behavior of the lower classes in elections, when such elections are held in Latin America, does not testify against the thesis that the masses have not been awakened to political interest and activity.

Also, the failure of the several guerrilla movements to take root among the masses—at the present time most notably in Colombia, Bolivia, Guatemala, and Venezuela and spasmodically in Argentina, Brazil, Peru, and Ecuador—cannot be explained only by the effectiveness of the American-supported and often American-led armies and police forces, as a comparison with the experience in Vietnam should demonstrate.

It is true that there are sporadic attempts among workers and mini-farmers in agriculture to organize unions to fight for better conditions. Though a basic difficulty that such attempts meet is the underutilization and the oversupply of labor, it happens to some extent even in such a very poor district as Northeastern Brazil.

Leadership is occasionally provided by the Church. A small but growing number of Catholic priests are becoming socially and economically radical and sometimes revolutionary. This trend might in time become important in Latin America as well as in the rest of the world, as new signals in the same direction are coming from Rome.

But the main impression is undoubtedly one of great passivity on the part of the underclass in urban and rural slums. As most of them do not have functional literacy, as they are undernourished and weak, and as they have grown up and are now often living under the most brutal suppression, this should not be so surprising.

In Latin America even less than in India do these experiences necessarily mean that the masses could under no circumstances be brought to revolt. It would hardly be possible to initiate and steer a revolt through a democratic process, however, as such a process would be stopped by force.

The Dominican Republic was for several decades under dictatorial rule of the most hideous type by Rafael Trujillo. The United States government supported that regime warmly until toward the very end, when it came to appear as a threat to its interests. A special tariff was then imposed on Dominican sugar, and in 1960 the United States government broke diplomatic relations with the Trujillo regime. It had by then already established contact with the underground opposition. The following year Trujillo was murdered.

From that time on, the United States government was continually involved by all available means. Under President John F. Kennedy it offered support to Juan Bosch, who came to power in 1962, heading a reform party, but was driven from office after seven months.

When opposition against the military junta in power was becoming organized in the spring of 1965, it was crushed by direct American military intervention ordered by President Lyndon B. Johnson. Juan Bosch, writing a book in his Paris refuge, concludes from his experiences that under Latin American conditions general elections and formal democracy cannot be the road to reform. What he recommends instead is a dictatorship, supported by the people.[4]

The crux even of that proposal is that the masses of people are mostly too passive to rise or even to support a political movement that tries to help them, at least in the beginning.

The revolution in Cuba cannot be invoked as an example of a revolt by the masses. What it can prove, however, is that *after a successful revolution,* if it is not crushed at the start, a reform government can engender mass support—if an effective appeal is then made to the masses and policies declared and enacted to serve their interests.

This assumes, of course, that the new government is not overthrown right at the beginning by adversary forces in the country and/or by American intervention. Such a *post factum* support by the masses is more likely to emerge when they are less impoverished.

Cuba was one of the richest countries in Latin America, though the growth of its economy had slowed down in recent decades. In spite of very great inequalities, there was some spread downward of educational and health facilities. There was a stronger and better organized trade-union movement in Cuba than almost anywhere else in Latin America.

When Fidel Castro started out, he certainly did not have substantial support from the "middle class." It was anyhow deeply split, as is usually the case in Latin America. Neither did he in the beginning have support from organized labor, which did not heed his appeal for a general strike. The Communist Party, stronger and better organized than in any other Latin American country, only came forth in his support when he was already winning.

Nor did he initially have any consolidated support from the unorganized lower strata of farmers and rural labor or from the people in the urban slums, even if his guerrillas were fed and occasionally given protective concealment by the poor in rural districts where they appeared. Castro's revolution was not the result of an uprising of the masses. His guerrillas never numbered more than a couple of hundred men, mostly students and intellectuals and only a very few workers, all of whom had joined him individually and not because of mass appeal. Their ideology, and his, was nebulous but generally of the radical liberal variety.

Castro's conversion to the "Socialist camp" developed much later, when the revolution had already succeeded. It was a result of the cumulative effects of the interaction between his and the United States' policy actions toward each other and of the support from the Soviet Union, which came at a time when, because of the United States blockade, it was very badly needed. In fact, the liquidation of the Batista regime had initially met with much sympathy in the United States.

This delay prevented the United States from nipping the Cuban revolution in the bud. At an early stage, this would not have been impossible, particularly as the United States had a military force in the Bay of Guantánamo. Later the badly prepared CIA-directed Bay of Pigs invasion failed because at that time Castro had already stabilized his regime.

The Cuban revolution must forever stand out as one of the strangest occurrences in modern history. I doubt that anyone foresaw it in the United States or anywhere else, or that it could have been foreseen. A basic precondition, however, was undoubtedly the unifying force of the widespread nationalist resentment caused by the United States' economic and political domination that weakened resistance in the upper class, demoralized the regime, and then emasculated the support it could have had from the United States. These were very special circumstances, and I doubt that such a revolution could easily be emulated today in other Latin American countries. The extraordinary personal qualities of Fidel Castro and some of the men around him certainly also played an important role.

The foregoing remarks are not intended as an evaluation of the Cuban revolution, the difficulties it met, or its accomplishments in terms of planned economic changes and radical social reforms. My only interest in this context has been the causal mechanism through which the revolution succeeded to begin with.

The United States government drew several conclusions from what had happened in Cuba. They were partly contradictory.

On the one hand, under the leadership of President John F. Kennedy and his liberal policy advisers, it was felt that the United States should attempt to influence the Latin American governments to prepare for *reforms in order to change the grossly inegalitarian social and economic stratification.* As mentioned in Chapter 4, stress was laid on land reform and more equal and effective taxation, but educational and health reforms also stood high on the list of policy priorities. American aid policies were to be oriented toward making such social and economic reforms more possible. The result was the Alliance for Progress, agreed upon with the Latin American governments in the Charter of Punta del Este in 1961.

The adherence of most Latin American governments to the principles adopted in the Alliance for Progress was halfhearted, to put it mildly. It even happened that individual members of the ruling oligarchies branded Kennedy as "Communist inspired." How on the whole land reform was effectively sabotaged was touched upon in Chapter 4, Section III. There was not much progress in other fields either.

The American corporations working in Latin America were not much interested in these new liberal intentions either, particularly as the demand for reforms mostly did not agree with the inclinations of the oligarchies with whom they had to cooperate. Partly under the influence of this development, the United States Congress did not live up to the aid promises implied in the Alliance.

During the Johnson Administration fewer and fewer references were made to the social and economic reform aims stressed in the Charter. The Alliance for Progress was increasingly looked upon as a failure. The vague proposals in the Rockefeller Report in line with those aims in the Charter do not explicitly refer to the Alliance. Also, these proposals are not among those which the Nixon government is likely to pursue very actively.

The other set of conclusions from the traumatic shock of the Cuban development certainly did not fit in with the liberal thinking that originally motivated the American government's interest in the Alliance for Progress. On the contrary, they share in the responsibility for the failure of the Alliance.

The events in Cuba were taken to confirm the inclination in America to believe that *all insurrections against a conservative or even plainly reactionary government lead to Communism*—and, indeed, that such insurrections are Communist inspired from the beginning.

The United States also became prepared to interfere against any government that could be feared to lean toward Communism, in that extraordinarily inclusive sense of the term. For all its often declared interest in reforms, "stability" had first priority, stability too often meaning plain reaction.

These were not new ideas in the United States, although they became fortified by the Cuban experience. In Guatemala in 1954 the United States government, applying clandestine methods and using neighboring states as bases of operation, had organized the toppling of a constitutionally elected reform government that established freedom of speech and the press, legalized trade unions, and proclaimed land reforms. The United Fruit Company was quite unashamedly behind these actions, though the land reform was to touch only some of their uncultivated areas. As already mentioned, in 1965 the United States government, for the most flimsy reasons, intervened with military force in the Dominican Republic.

These blunt proofs of United States interference in the internal affairs of Latin American countries served to feed and intensify anti-American nationalist resentment in all of Latin America. They only punctuated and accentuated a great number of less dramatic interferences and pressures continually being exerted in all Latin American countries by the United States government and American business corporations, often working in consonance.

In the world at large and in Western Europe in particular, the United States had enjoyed great prestige and much genuine popular sympathy as the great and kindly democratic country that had saved the world from the Fascist onslaught and helped West European reconstruction through the Marshall Plan. This moral capital of good will now began rapidly to dissipate, and the United States policy in Latin America was an important cause of this. The view began to spread that the United States was *imperialist* and grossly indiscriminate in regard to the means by which it promoted its business interests in weaker countries abroad.

Indeed, Guatemala and later Vietnam fed an increasing popular animosity against the United States throughout the world. As most governments were financially and militarily dependent on the United States, the American people were kept from knowing much about this development of public opinion. The excellent American journalists, who to a particular degree monopolize the conveying of news from abroad to the American people and government, have shown a glaring inefficiency in regard to the development of popular opinion in this and other fields of interest.

This is not due to their being intentionally prohibited. It is more a demonstration of their astonishing lack of interest, shared by other Americans, in how people abroad, other than officials, feel. It is also understandable because of their lack of critical judgment of the biased sample of people they can talk with, restricted as they usually are to those who speak English. I have seen particularly outlandish reporting from Asia, for instance, on what the Indian "public opinion" is or how "the Thai nation" feels on various issues, but also about popular reaction to American policies in various West European countries, where the people as a whole are politically articulate.

In Western Europe, the generation who have no personal memories of the fears of a Fascist victory during the Second World War and the United States' role in averting it are most susceptible to anti-American feelings. Among them they easily turn into a doctrinal anti-capitalism and, in particular, into anti-American-capitalism. They see the interests of big business as steering the United States government's foreign policy—for which Guatemala was something of a telling example. Vietnam should certainly have been less so.

The race riots in northern American cities from the middle of the 1960's gave further nourishment to anti-American feelings, spreading to ever wider strata.[5] The blame was again quite commonly laid to American capitalism, which in regard to this particular problem is a doubtful theory.

The United States will never again be permitted to deal with its problems in and with Latin America as "hemispheric" problems. They have, and are increasingly bound to have, worldwide repercussions.

Most Americans are naïvely unaware of this, liberals as well as conservatives. The Rockefeller Report is typical, or overtypical, of this trust in the possibility of confining the problem to "the Americas."

In an old American tradition of high-flown rhetoric, which has become even more reckless in recent decades because of the use of ghost writers, the Report opens with the pathetic declaration: "We went to visit neighbors and found brothers. We went to listen to the spokesmen of our sister republics and heard the voices of a hemisphere." Considering the type of reception the governor and his entourage had been given, this way of speaking is bound to sound insincere and even ridiculous not only in Latin America but even more in the rest of the world.

The understandable reluctance of dependent governments in the whole "free world" to disturb their relations with the United States government, and their preoccupation with pressing problems nearer home, will continue to help prevent the American people and their government from considering realistically how its policies toward Latin American countries influence feeling and thinking about the United States among the peoples.

This concerns the United States' "image" abroad. That a country that must exert, and wants to exert, world leadership is to a particular degree dependent on trust and good will abroad was stressed at the end of Chapter 11.

The rise of resentful nationalism in Latin American countries represents a certain parallel to what has happened in Vietnam and is now happening in Southern Africa, though in Latin America there is practically *no anti-Western and certainly no anti-white feeling.* It is more simply and exclusively anti-American.

Neither is there much of the same *direct relation to the cold war,* allying the resentful nationalism to Communism of one type or another. The Soviet Union has its hands full supporting Cuba, which has turned out to be an expensive affair. It has apparently little confidence in the possible success of any leftist revolt, at least in the near future. It may also fear that such a revolt would upset the United States too much and would risk another world war.

The Soviet government seems more interested in opening political and trade relations with even the most reactionary governments in Latin America than in supporting a revolution against any one of them. The extremely weak Communist parties in Latin America are now commonly careful not to get involved in or even to show sympathy for the guerrilla movements in some countries.

A third and most important difference is that *the anti-American sentiments are mainly an upper-class phenomenon.* For the time being they do not effectively reach deep down among the rural and urban masses, who are generally passive. But we know from other parts of the world that resentful nationalism is one of the attitudes that can most easily spread to the masses.

Anti-American feelings everywhere in Latin America and in all classes—except in large sections of the silent underclass—have now reached such a pitch that apparently no single Latin American government can afford not to pay homage to these feelings. Again to quote the *U.S. News and World Report,* which cannot be suspected of harboring "un-American" sentiments:

> U.S. businessmen in Latin America are a beleaguered lot these days—beset by the political left, the right, the military and even the clergy. . . . U.S. executives are frankly concerned over the outlook. . . . An American executive in Bogotá, the capital [of Colombia], says flatly that private enterprise has a bad name in the country and, "We're worried about it." . . . A persistent fear among U.S. executives in Brazil and throughout Latin America is that they will suffer reprisals for the actions of the U.S. Government—or of a local government considered too friendly with the U.S.[6]

Governor Nelson A. Rockefeller and his experts and advisers, returning from a violence-marred mission to Latin America for the Nixon Administration, found that:

> The United States has allowed the special relationship it has historically maintained with the other nations of the Western Hemisphere to deteriorate badly. . . . The curve of nationalist sentiment is generally rising. . . . If the current anti-U.S. trend continues, one can foresee a time

when the United States would be politically and morally isolated from part or much of the Western Hemisphere. . . . A great many and probably a majority of the citizens of hemisphere nations regard United States private investment as a form of exploitation or economic colonialism. . . . Fear of domination by the United States companies is expressed frequently.[7]

Assuming that these views on the part of Latin Americans are "mistaken"—and presumably also that they will be corrected when United States investment in Latin America has reached still greater magnitude—the Report recommends that *the United States should provide maximum encouragement for private investment throughout the hemisphere.*[8]

From a *political* point of view, this would seem a strange judgment. In Chapter 10, Section III, I argued not only that further nationalization of foreign investments in land, natural resources, and public utilities must be expected, but also that it would be in the interest of the United States to slow down its new investment in Latin America in manufacturing industry, while welcoming investment from other countries that do not fill the Latin Americans with so much fear of domination.

Probably in no other respect, however, does the Report more definitely express the opinion of the United States government, as well as its business opinion. We see here a great nation bent on continuing along the road that has already brought it to an almost disastrous impasse.

With all its obvious differences, speeding up United States investment in Latin America is not unlike that government's decision in early 1965 to escalate the war in Vietnam when it was going badly. It did not see, or underestimated, to what extent the protest against the Saigon government was due to the palpable fact that it was totally dependent on American military support.

The overwhelming influence of American corporations in the economic life of Latin American countries and their support from the United States government are not the only leverage of American power in these countries. Since the beginning and intensification of the cold war from the end of the 1940's, *military aid* has been an important part of the United States' worldwide foreign policy.

Precise figures are difficult to calculate, but the Agency for International Development has recently confirmed that "military assistance, defense support, and related expenditures for keeping internal order" represent the larger part of the total assistance budget to all countries for the years 1950–67.[9] Loans from the Export-Import Bank used to finance military purchases should be added to this estimate and, of course, the expenditure for the CIA, amounting to perhaps some $3 billion a year.

Military aid to the Latin American countries began during the Second World War. In recent years it has been given on a decreasing scale. The furnishing of Latin American governments with more sophisticated modern weapons systems has met with criticism from progressive Congressmen in Washington, and Congress has even stipulated as a condition for aid of other types that the aid-receiving countries abstain from squandering their resources in buying weapons from West European countries.

Since the agreement on the Alliance for Progress in 1961, there have been sixteen military coups leading to military governments that now rule over the majority of people in Latin America. That the military aid from the United States, even when restricted to equipping the armed forces with weapons dating mostly from the Second World War or shortly thereafter, has eased the way for military juntas to take over the government is obvious and indisputable.

Nevertheless, the Nixon Administration is trying to argue against this,[10] asserting also that this military aid is consistent with the United States' "overall concern: social

and economic reform leading to a better and more rewarding life for our Latin American neighbors." [11]

The alleged connection is that military aid counteracts
"instability" by "strengthening the Latin American national capabilities to counter Communist sponsored or
supported insurgency movements." [12] In an almost naïve
way, not the slightest suspicion is uttered that this type of
"stability" as it is actually interpreted can counteract the
United States' expressed concern for social and economic
reform.

American military aid takes many forms. Furnishing
weapons or facilitating their purchase in the United
States is actually the smallest item in terms of cost. *Training* Latin American officers, either in the United States or
at the United States Southern Command School in Fort
Gulick in the Panama Canal Zone, is another item of
military aid. This training has more and more been directed toward increasing the *counter-insurgency capabilities* of the Latin American army and police forces, in
recent years drawing upon the American experiences in
Vietnam.

Particularly in the larger countries of Latin America,
the United States has also maintained regular *military
service missions* to support its own forces and to train
them. In all Latin American countries—as in other countries all over the world—more *secretly operating units* are
active, working under the direction of the CIA, sometimes
almost independently of the State Department and its
embassies and even the Pentagon. In Latin America they
have been particularly active and have become engaged
in supporting or, as the case may be, counteracting the
national government. More generally, they are important
in counter-guerrilla warfare.

In American academic life there has been an increasing
tendency for the military agencies, the State Department,
or the CIA to finance *research on Latin American prob-*

lems by special units, either within or outside the universities. Whether carried out in Latin American countries or in the United States, that research is directed toward the "defense of American interests" and, in particular, "national security" in that region. It has often been closely connected with the CIA's activity in these countries.

In January 1969 an *ad hoc* committee of Latin American specialists in the United States made a declaration that was signed by 273 professors, researchers, and graduate students in Latin American studies, protesting against this prostitution of independent scientific and scholarly work. They ascertained that this research activity was contrary to the ideals of American academic scholarship, that it had not contributed to international understanding, and, more particularly, that "the distrust of American intellectuals in Latin America and elsewhere in the world will not be overcome until such a time as it is made clear that the American Scholars and their professional organizations have totally disassociated themselves from the interventionist activities of the U.S. government agencies. . . ." [13]

These military, police, and research activities of an open or clandestine nature may have been welcomed by the governments in Latin American countries, particularly the military ones, in regard to which the United States government's interest was usually but not always in counterinsurgency and not in insurgency. Among the articulate strata at large, however, it has undoubtedly given *a further spur to anti-American sentiments*.

Finally, there is the American *development aid*. In the Alliance for Progress it was assumed to be aimed at and coordinated with large-scale internal reforms, particularly taxation and land reform.

How the Alliance was rapidly emasculated by interaction between the holders of power in Latin America, including the American corporations working there, and the United States government and Congress is commented upon above.

The Rockefeller Report, which I quote as the latest available authoritative American attempt at an overall assessment of the Latin American situation, takes a rather sinister outlook on what is now happening in Latin America:

> Forces of anarchy, terror and subversion are loose in the Americas. . . . The inflation, urban terrorism, racial strife, overcrowding, poverty, violence and rural insurgency are all among the weapons available to the enemies of the systems of the free nations of the Western Hemisphere. These forces are quick to exploit for their own ends the freedoms afforded by democratic governments. . . .[14]

The Report is correct about the regrettable facts, although its analysis in terms of "forces," "the nations," and "freedoms afforded by democratic governments" is topsy-turvy. It warns:

> At the moment, there is only one Castro among the 26 nations of the hemisphere; there can well be more in the future. And a Castro on the mainland, supported militarily and economically by the Communist world, would present the gravest kind of threat to the security of the Western Hemisphere and pose an extremely difficult problem for the United States.[15]

Under these circumstances the Report takes comfort in finding it possible to "predict," though with some reservations for the difficulty of making any forecasts, the *"continuation of the trend of the military to take power."* [16] The welcoming of this trend toward military dictatorships can be asserted by no American without serious qualms of conscience, for as the Report stresses, quite correctly and I believe honestly:

> Commitment to representative responsive democratic government is deeply imbedded in the collective political consciousness of the American people. We would like to

see strong representative government develop in the other nations of the hemisphere for both idealistic and practical reasons.[17]

As the Report also foresees *a rising trend of anti-Americanism,*[18] it has certainly posed a most difficult problem for American policy-makers.

Apart from increased private United States investment, about which I have expressed grave doubts, the Report proposes measures to make it possible for *Latin American exports to win easier access to the American market.*[19] This is sound advice. Particularly if action could be taken on a world scale, favoring other underdeveloped countries' exports as well, it would be a move in the right direction (see Chap. 9). Unfortunately in this regard the United States government, if it chose to follow the advice, would meet the resistance of strong vested interests at home. It is not possible to believe in any very great change in United States commercial policies toward underdeveloped countries in the near future.

A third proposal of the Report is to turn the trend and *increase development aid to the Latin American countries,* to use multilateral agencies for that purpose to a greater extent, to abolish a number of encumbering conditions for and restrictions on aid, to lower interest rates for loans, and to agree to a rescheduling of debt service requirements, etc.[20] These are all excellent proposals, but it must be doubted to what extent they will be carried out by the Administration and Congress.

In regard to *military aid*[21] the Report recommends a reversal of the recent trend by increasing assistance for training of security forces and a more definite direction of this training toward defense against the growing subversion. At the same time, it recommends a withdrawal of the permanent military mission in some countries as "too visible."

Although the Report, as is usually the case in the United States, looks upon the military establishment in Latin American countries as primarily a means against internal subversion, it proposes that the United States take a more permissive attitude toward the Latin American military establishments' ambition to acquire modern, sophisticated weaponry such as jet planes and the like. This proposal, as well as perhaps the Report's demand for the increase of other military aid, though in line with the intentions of the Nixon government,[22] will probably meet resistance in the Congress as it is presently composed.

One proposal that in itself is sound is that the United States government relinquish the pretension it has maintained, contrary to its practices, of wanting *diplomatic relations only with democratic governments.* "It should recognize that diplomatic relations are merely practical conveniences and not measures of moral judgment." [23]

If the United States, for its worldwide diplomatic activity, were prepared to go back to this old principle established by the Vienna Conference after the Napoleonic wars and still adhered to by more conservative countries like Britain and Sweden, this would simplify international relations very much. As to its relations with Latin American countries it would not seem to introduce any change from present policies—except making the support of military juntas even more uninhibited.

When looking over the policy recommendations of the Rockefeller Report, and considering also the extent to which they have a chance of becoming realized, *it is difficult to believe that they will change the gloomy trends* as fairly realistically assessed in the Report.

In particular, the Report's forecast of *a continual trend toward military governments may well be realized.*

Generally speaking, the potential power of the military establishment in every country is in modern times tremendous and is steadily increasing because of the development of weapons and military technology.

In Latin America there is almost nowhere any firm tradition of genuine democracy or of civilian control of the military. The political power of the military establishment can therefore be used with fewer inhibitions and hindrances.

Moreover, governments and political parties are commonly inept and often corrupt. It is easier to plead the necessity for the military to take over the rule in order to create effective, incorrupt government and enforce social discipline. That this will often not be the result is another matter.

Particularly as the masses remain passive, it would seem likely that, at least in the near future, the sporadic guerrilla movements will remain inconsequential. However, their very existence, even on a small scale, will create a feeling of unrest and uncertainty. This, in turn, will support the trend toward military governments.

As generally observed, there has been in some Latin American countries a tendency toward *increasing guerrilla activity in urban districts.* The size and density of the population in a city and the complexity of its life provide "jungles," under cover of which serious damage and disturbance can be inflicted.

This development has come to a head in Brazil, but is on the increase in other Latin American countries as well. Small bands with apparently little cooperation among themselves are acquiring funds for their activity by robbing banks. Public facilities are being destroyed, resulting in temporary disorder. It has even happened that officials, indigenous or American, have been captured and held at ransom, or killed.

One almost certain effect of this is that the police and security forces find reasons to take less consideration. In Brazil, at least, groups of them have formed teams who take it upon themselves to pursue rebel bands or mere suspects ruthlessly, using methods not generally condoned or actively ordered by their superiors or the government.

It is possible to foresee a sort of warfare between the police and security forces and these rebel bands that would gradually take on serious proportions and generally come to motivate abnormal restrictions on civilian life. If unrest should grow, it cannot be considered unthinkable that *some sort of Latin American Fascism* would be the outcome. Some countries have proceeded far on that road already.

This Fascism would have its own Latin American stamp but would be more of the Italian, Spanish, or Portuguese type. It would be different from German Nazism, as it would not imply racial persecution. I then make an exception of the continual killing of Indians in remote rural districts in Brazil and a few other Latin American countries, which has gone on all the time and has aroused extraordinarily little interest at home and in the rest of the world.

Much more generally there is, in Latin America, if not persecution on racial grounds, nevertheless much hereditary oppression of Negroes and Indians. The racial harmony in Latin America is largely a myth. The racial woofs in the class stratification are one of the features that are apt to facilitate the development of Latin American Fascism.

When the Rockefeller Report—which on this particular issue is representative of official American policy—attempts to look forward to a happier development in spite of accepting without question the continuation of the trend toward military governments, this is because it senses a *fundamental change in the character of military officers in Latin America*. It finds that

> a new type of military man is coming to the fore. . . . the new military man is prepared to adapt his authoritarian tradition to the goals of social and economic progress.[24]

As explanation, the Report develops a theory:

> . . . the military was traditionally a conservative force resistant to change. Most officers came from the landowner class. In recent years . . . the military service has been less attractive to their sons. As a result, opportunities have opened up for young men of ambition and ability from poor families who have neither land nor professional and business connections. *These ambitious sons of the working classes have entered the military. . . . This pattern has become almost universal throughout the American republics to the south. . . . their emotional ties are often with the people. Increasingly, their concern and dedication is to the eradication of poverty and the improvement of the lot of the oppressed, both in rural and urban areas.*[25]

According to what we know, both the assertion of a very big change in the class origin of military officers and the other assertion that this is happening everywhere in Latin America are obvious exaggerations. The facile assumption of a strong and simple relationship between such a change and the social and political orientation of the officer corps does not, of course, stand up to scientific scrutiny.

But these are minor observations. Even without such a change in class origin or any important effects of such a change on political orientation, it is indeed possible that *a military establishment under progressive leadership might undergo a change of heart* and become interested in radical reforms and in activating the masses in support of it.

With the strong tendency toward political contagion within the region, if that happened in one or a few Latin American countries it could have spread effects to other countries—though I believe that the traditional tendency of military governments to defend vested interests in most of these countries would be stronger, at least in the near future.

In fact, a different turn in a radical direction might now be happening in Peru. Whether the military government under General Juan Velasco Alvarado as President will prevail in its announced radical policy line is uncertain but, of course, possible.

If it does prevail, *it will meet strong resistance from most of the upper class*, whose privileges will have to be curtailed. To overcome this resistance the military will have to keep together without split or stint. They will also have to mobilize mass support. We shall then see *radical reforms carried out by a military government that has gradually to involve and activate the masses*.

With the rising anti-Americanism in the region, a military reform government would be tempted to direct its onslaught, particularly in the beginning, against the American companies. This is what happened in Peru.

The difficulties that a military reform government would meet would be immense. Many of these difficulties would come from almost automatic reactions on the part of American business. No general declarations in favor of reforms would prevent the United States companies in the country from working along with the indigenous oligarchy to stop the reforms or else bring the government to collapse.

And no general declarations of continuing and speeding up private investment in Latin America would hinder the virtual holdup of new investments in such a country. It is, moreover, difficult to believe that American aid to such a country would be continued, even if the Hickenlooper amendment should be abolished or put out of use.

These difficulties might cause the military government *to slow down and compromise its reform activity*. This would seem to be a likely course. If instead it should continue its reform policies, it would have to take ever more radical measures and ask for greater and greater sacrifices on the part of its people.

It would then put an increasing distance between itself and the United States policies. It would have to play on, and itself magnify, the anti-American resentments which anyhow are on the rise and would be apt to increase still more—now partly because of the withholding of American capital investment and aid.

The vision, extremely unclear in its contours, of radical reform activity in the Latin American countries under military governments—supported, as the Rockefeller Report indicates, by the youth and the Church, prevented from becoming too revolutionary, and, by "young management" in business, brought to feel "a social concern for workers and the public" [26]—and, in particular, the idea that such a development would lead, against the rising trend of anti-Americanism, to the welcoming acceptance of an increased flow of private investment by United States corporations, while generally inaugurating an era of friendly understanding with the United States, seems *illusory in the extreme.* To Americans of good will it has sentimental and almost romantic overtones. But it does not belong to this world.

It is as illusory as the contrary vision of young rebels against the Establishment, in the United States as well as in Europe—equally unclear, romantic, and sentimental—that Latin America now is inevitably driving toward a violent clash between the impoverished masses and the ruling oligarchies. The masses are too passive and the weapons in the hands of the military too efficient and plentiful.

There will probably, as the Report foresees, be still more military governments. As I said, I do not exclude the possibility that one or several of them could be moved to try to carry out the social and economic revolution needed for development, though the difficulties, particularly the economic ones, would be formidable.

If these difficulties did not rapidly stop such a military reform government short of going very far, which is probable, there would be attempts to overthrow it. Such attempts might involve the American government in clandestine activity through the CIA and in other ways. This would be in line with established traditions and existing machinery, the dismantling of which neither the Rockefeller Report nor the Nixon Administration proposes. Even open military intervention by the United States cannot be excluded—though after the experience of Vietnam, resistance against such ventures is growing in the United States.

The regular way of overthrowing a military government bent upon reform would be to sow dissent in the military establishment itself. This would simply mean another military coup, though this time not directed against a civilian government.

It could be carried out without disturbing the masses or indeed the civilian population generally. The result would be a retreat on the reform front—if that retreat had not already been made under the pressure of mounting difficulties.

Returning to the other type of illusory vision, common in the United States and in Western Europe among the critics of American foreign policy, to foresee a revolt by the masses in Latin America directed against the governments and the oligarchies seems as unrealistic as the official policy of the United States. It has become associated with *a strange glorification of violence.*

No sane person can be in favor of violence for its own sake. On the other hand, if the ruling oligarchies in Latin American countries could be overthrown by revolt, the needed violence could be defended as necessary for the purpose. The Mexican Revolution some decades ago cost between one and two million lives. Neither was the American Revolution two hundred years ago carried out without violence.

In the Latin American situation gross violence is, moreover, exerted all the time, mostly against poor people to keep them suppressed. The whole economic and social order perpetuating underutilization of the labor force and causing impoverishment of the masses must rightly be seen as "institutionalized violence."

Barrington Moore, Jr., in an important book published a few years ago, *Social Origins of Dictatorship and Democracy: Lord and Peasant in the Making of the Modern World,* to which I could not refer in *Asian Drama,* makes the point

> that the way nearly all history has been written imposes an overwhelming bias against revolutionary violence. . . . the use of force by the oppressed against their former masters has been the object of nearly universal condemnation. Meanwhile the day-to-day repression of "normal" society hovers dimly in the background of most history books.[27]

And he goes on to illustrate the immense cost in human life and happiness of "going without a revolution." The same argument has been made by Robert L. Heilbroner and other authors.

But then everything hangs on the two questions: *whether there will be a mass revolt, and whether it has a chance of succeeding.* The glorification of violence, now becoming so popular in leftist writing on the Latin American situation, assumes that the answer to both these questions is affirmative. This is most bluntly revealed in the careless and enthusiastic exaggeration of the importance of the guerrilla movements operating at present in many Latin American countries.

On these two points I diverge. The masses are initially too passive. Even more important is the fact that every attempt to activate them will at the start meet overwhelming military and police power, supported by the indigenous oligarchy—and by the United States, which believes that it has learned a lesson from the Cuban experience.

I see little chance for any large-scale, successful revolt against the present economic, social, and political power structure in Latin American countries. The exceptions would be the perhaps not very likely possibility of a military government cutting its ties to both the indigenous oligarchy and the American corporations—and soon the American government—and arousing the masses in its support. *But such a revolt, led by a military government itself, would not need to use much violence.*

The careless and ignorant indulgence in, and apparent enjoyment of, fantasies of violent revolt must be judged as *morally* the more reprehensible as it is done by persons living comfortably in secure circumstances without a thought of going down themselves to fight and die in a struggle for the suppressed and subdued underclass in Latin America.

Intellectually, it is rationalized in a vulgarized so-called "Marxism" which would cause Karl Marx to turn in his grave.[28]

Another possible development that should not be excluded altogether for all Latin American countries would be *relatively peaceful change,* even without a new type of military dictatorship. To be successful, it would have to be rather speedy on account of the pending social and economic trends. And it would need the appearance of honest and enlightened leadership bent upon fundamental changes in the prevalent economic and social power structure and the gradual realization of more genuine democracy.

For a relatively rich country, like Argentina, or one with firmer traditions of general elections, like Chile, or with a background of a true revolution that has now lost its momentum, like Mexico, such a development might perhaps be in the range of possibility. Within such a development even popular uprisings might have a role, at some stage. In any case the development would need to engender *more pressure from below,* which in these countries and some others should be possible to realize.

The third and perhaps most likely possibility would be *the continuation of the present trends.* As in South Asia this would imply that there would be *neither evolution nor revolution.* As already said, in some and perhaps many countries, or even in all of them, this could amount to a development toward some sort of Latin American Fascism, firmly guarded by an overpowering police and military force.

It would also be supported by the United States government—unless American policy changed in fundamental respects. Fascist governments in Latin America would appear to Americans as *the only alternative to Communism.*

In regard to Europe, this was the appeal to the world of Hitler, Mussolini, Franco, and Salazar. As we all remember, their regimes won some favorable response and considerable credulity, particularly in the United States—as does the Greek military junta today. We also remember how Fascist regimes were credited with efficiency of administration and even with being bent on progressive reforms in the interest of the people, somewhat along the line of the Rockefeller Report's exuberant hopes about Latin American military regimes.

When Franklin D. Roosevelt and other liberals succeeded in winning over the American people from this simplistic view of Fascism in Europe, it was before the McCarthy-Dulles era had exerted its still lasting impact on America. And they were helped by an increasing awareness that Fascism would lead, and finally did lead, to world war.

Latin American Fascism, however dehumanizing its effects in Latin America, would have little prospect of leading to wars outside the subcontinent itself, particularly as the Soviet Union shows no inclination to become involved in opposing it. Liberals in the United States would under these circumstances have an uphill fight to withdraw

American support from Fascist regimes in Latin America.

I definitely do not want to exclude, however, the possibility of *a redefinition of the United States policies toward Latin American countries in terms of the American nation's cherished liberal traditions.* This is what we have to fight for.

Such a redefinition of policies would be almost the opposite of the new "pragmatism" that is the beacon of the Nixon Administration. It would imply cooperation with any progressive forces there are in the several Latin American countries and the cold-shouldering of reactionary regimes. It would mean returning to the principles of the Alliance for Progress, though including the preparedness to make greater sacrifices to ensure its success.

It would imply taking a stern and critical look at the United States furnishing Latin American countries with weapons and training for their officers. Surreptitious activities through the CIA and uncalled-for meddlesomeness by the embassies are in the longer run sure means of aggravating the anti-American complex among all except those few who have a direct interest in being supported in this way. Steering research in the interest of the "security of the United States" as exemplified above has equally an almost sure boomerang effect.

This redefinition of policies would also imply taking a fresh look at the problem of American investments in Latin America. The United States should be prepared to tolerate large-scale nationalization of American enterprises, particularly in land, natural resources, public utilities, and even some manufacturing industries.

Indeed, in cooperation with the Bank for International Reconstruction and Development, the United States should take an active hand in financially facilitating such nationalizations. This would make more possible agreements on terms of compensation that did not sow lasting discord.

From a liberal point of view, *there is no necessity that the political development in Latin America should continue to develop under the strong influence of a rising trend of anti-Americanism.* Indeed, it is possible to outline a policy for the United States that without implying unbearable sacrifices could lead to a close and friendly cooperation for common goals.

This has been an attempt at an overview of the political dynamics in Latin America. At the end of my discourse I need to stress again *the great uncertainty of what there is in the future.*

My tentative conclusions are probably more reliable when they are in the negative, setting out what is not likely to happen. Positively, there remains a spectrum of alternative possibilities, of which only some are seen to be entirely unlikely. The outcome may well be very different in the several countries of Latin America.

The main value premise which has steered my inquiry is, as in Chapter 14 on South Asia, the urgent need for radical reforms. If they are not carried out, I must predict not only stagnation of development in general but, in particular, still greater inequality and impoverishment of the masses.

What the effects of this would be politically *in the somewhat longer run* is beyond my power to judge—for the same reasons as were indicated toward the end of Chapter 14 on South Asia.

The political development in the several Latin American countries should be studied by political scientists with a minimum of opportunistic bias—that is, without blinkers adapted to popular and official beliefs of what is in the interest of the United States or of the ruling oligarchies in these countries.

Meanwhile, we economists have to try to familiarize ourselves with the broad facts of the political dynamics in these countries. Otherwise any attempt to study their development problems is bound to be grossly superficial and misleading. That is the excuse for this appendix as well as for the chapter on South Asia.

It should perhaps be mentioned that the Catholic Philippines, with the legacy of several centuries of Spanish colonial rule and half a century of dominance by the United States, is in many ways *more a Latin American country than a South Asian one.* Its development, however, is still at an earlier stage than several of the present Latin American trends.[29]

During the American era the pattern of regular elections and of allowing their outcome to determine what government shall be in power became more firmly established in the Philippines than it has almost anywhere in Latin America. Even though up till now these elections have been kept from concerning the issues really important for the masses of the people, this does not necessarily imply that they could not be changing in that direction. Reforms, and radical reforms, could then be emerging in a peaceful way. This is not certain, however.

Anti-Americanism is rising along the Latin American pattern and has broadly the same basis, though as yet it is much weaker. But to quote once more an American weekly that cannot be suspected of views critical of business or the present administration, *U.S. News and World Report:*

> Signs are growing that Asia's most durable East-West partnership—the close alliance between the Philippines and the U.S.—is starting to fall apart. . . . Now you find Philippine leaders from President Ferdinand Marcos on down saying Americans must be prepared to give up air and naval bases here that have been vital to U.S. military operations in Asia since 1945. . . . some officials are calling for "critical scrutiny" of all treaties with the U.S., including those protecting large private American investments in these islands.[30]

But the American bases and the personnel stationed there generate about 5 percent of the calculated national income of the Philippines, which is equivalent to about 18 percent of its export earnings.

It therefore seems likely that for the near future at least, the Philippine government is going to use the spreading anti-American sentiments only to put pressure on the United States government to be generous in giving advantages to the Philippines.

NOTES

Preface

[1] For the definition of South Asia and other regions referred to in this book, see *Asian Drama: An Inquiry into the Poverty of Nations* (New York: Twentieth Century Fund and Pantheon Books, 1968), Chap. 1, Sec. 1, p. 41.

Part One. THE APPROACH

Chapter 1. Cleansing the Approach from Biases

[1] For definitions of underdevelopment and development, see *Asian Drama*, Appendix 1 (pp. 1839ff.) and Appendix 2, Secs. 5–7 (pp. 1859ff.), 12 (pp. 1878ff.). The problems of development planning are discussed in Chap. 15 and Appendix 2, Parts III and IV.

[2] For a fuller development of the thoughts in this first chapter see *Asian Drama*, Prologue; Chap. 2; *et passim*.

[3] Myrdal, *Objectivity in Social Research* (New York: Pantheon Books, 1969), and other sources referred to in that book.

[4] *Asian Drama*, Chap. 21, Secs. 6–7 (pp. 977ff.).

[5] *Ibid.*, Prologue, Sec. 2 (pp. 8ff.).

[6] *Ibid.*, Chap. 21, Sec. 8 (pp. 984ff., particularly p. 989).

[7] *Ibid.*, Prologue, Secs. 3–4 (pp. 10ff.); *et passim*.

[8] *Ibid.*, Appendix 1 (p. 1839), "Diplomacy by Terminology." This is not the only example of diplomatic terminology. Sometimes heavily loaded propaganda terms, like "the free world," creep into the scientific literature; see *Asian Drama*, Prologue, Sec. 4 (pp. 12ff.).

[9] *Asian Drama*, Prologue, Sec. 5 (pp. 16ff.).

[10] *Ibid.*, Prologue, Sec. 7 (pp. 24ff.).

[11] In *Asian Drama* I used the term the "modern approach" (Chap. 21, Sec. 1 [pp. 961ff.]) to denote the same thing.

[12] *Ibid.*, Chap. 21 and Appendix 6.

[13] *Asian Drama*, Prologue, Secs. 5 (pp. 16ff.), 8 (pp. 26ff.); Appendix 2, Secs. 8–11 (pp. 1870ff.), 19–20 (pp. 1901ff.); Appendix 3, Sec. 3 (pp. 1946ff.); *et passim*.

[14] *Ibid.*, Appendix 2, Sec. 21 (pp. 1912ff.); *et passim.*

[15] *Ibid.*, Prologue, Sec. 6 (pp. 20ff.).

[16] *Ibid.*, Appendix 2, Secs. 20–21 (pp. 1903ff.); *et passim.*

[17] *Ibid.*, Appendix 2, Secs. 12–15 (pp. 1878ff.); Appendix 3, particularly Sec. 8 (pp. 1961ff.).

[18] *Ibid.*, Chap. 21; Appendix 6; Appendix 2, Sec. 19 (pp. 1901ff.).

[19] *Ibid.*, Chap. 21, Secs. 10–13 (pp. 995ff.).

[20] *Ibid.*, Chap. 21, Part III.

[21] *Ibid.*, Prologue, Sec. 8 (pp. 26ff.).

[22] *Ibid.*, Appendix 2, Sec. 20 (pp. 1903ff.).

[23] *Ibid.*, Chap. 24, Secs. 7–9 (pp. 1184ff.); Chap. 25, Sec. 5 (pp. 1225ff.); *et passim.*

[24] *Ibid.*, Chap. 21, Secs. 7, 9 (pp. 981ff., 989ff.).

[25] *Ibid.*, Chap. 14, Sec. 2 (pp. 677ff.); Appendix 10.

[26] *Ibid.*, Appendix 2, Secs. 19–20 (pp. 1901ff.); *et passim.*

[27] Myrdal, *Economic Theory and Under-Developed Regions* (London: Duckworth, 1957), published in the United States under the title *Rich Lands and Poor* (New York: Harper & Row, 1958), pp. 129ff. (This and all subsequent page references are to the English edition.)

[28] *Asian Drama*, Preface; Prologue, Sec. 8 (pp. 26ff.).

[29] In *Asian Drama* two lines of emphasis that may make the book less accessible for easy reading but to the author have been essential have been the clarification of concepts and the criticism of the statistical material available; they are interrelated for the reasons already given in the text. See, for instance, *ibid.*, Chap. 11, Secs. 1–4 (pp. 474ff.); Chap. 12, Secs. 1–2 (pp. 529ff.); Chap. 13, Sec. 1 (pp. 581ff.); Chap. 14, Sec. 1 (pp. 674ff.); Chap. 17, Secs. 1–3 (pp. 799ff.); Chap. 18, Sec. 1 (pp. 849ff.); Chap. 19, Sec. 1 (pp. 902ff.); Chap. 21; Chap. 27, Sec. 1 (pp. 1387ff.); Chap. 29, Sec. 1 (pp. 1533ff.); Chap. 30, Sec. 1 (pp. 1553ff.); and Appendices 1–8 *passim.*

[30] *Objectivity in Social Research*, Sec. 8.

[31] *Asian Drama*, Prologue, Sec. 8 (pp. 26ff.).

[32] *Ibid.*, Chap. 29, Secs. 4–7 (pp. 1540ff.).

[33] *Ibid.*, Appendix 4; cf. Appendix 2, Sec. 22 (pp. 1919ff.), *et passim.*

[34] *Ibid.*, Appendix 2, Part II.

[35] *Ibid.*, Appendix 2, particularly Secs. 5–11, 19–21 (pp. 1859ff., 1901ff.).

[36] *Ibid.*, Prologue, Sec. 8 (pp. 31f.).

[37] See also *ibid.*, Appendices 2 and 3.

[38] *Ibid.*, Appendix 2, Secs. 19 and 20 (pp. 1901ff.); Appendix 3, particularly Sec. 3 (pp. 1946ff.).

[39] *Ibid.*, Prologue, Sec. 9 (pp. 31ff.); Chap. 2, Secs. 1–2 (pp. 50ff.). I have made an attempt to present in simplified terms, and with references to earlier contributions, the main line of thought in *Objectivity in Social Research,* particularly Secs. 11–14.

[40] *Asian Drama,* Chap. 2, Secs. 3–4 (pp. 54ff.); cf. Part IV.

[41] Somewhat disturbing to the author, in view of his personal valuations, is his conclusion that political democracy is not a necessary element among the modernization ideals. Unlike the other value premises, this ideal is not essential to a system comprising all the other modernization ideals. This does not imply, however, that the substitution of an authoritarian regime for a more democratic one gives any greater assurance that policies will be directed toward the realization of these modernization ideals, or that, if so directed, they will be more effective. See *Asian Drama,* pp. 67f.; *et passim.*

[42] *Asian Drama,* Chap. 2, Sec. 3 (pp. 54ff.).

[43] *Ibid.*, Postscript, Sec. 2 (pp. 1834ff.).

[44] I do not use the common term "values" for reasons explained in *Asian Drama,* p. 32, fn. 2.

[45] *Asian Drama,* Chap. 3, Sec. 1 (pp. 71ff.).

[46] *Ibid.*, Chap. 3, particularly Sec. 2 (pp. 74ff.).

[47] *Ibid.*, Chap. 3, Sec. 3 (pp. 81ff.); Chap. 33, Secs. 3, 4, 6 (pp. 1728ff., 1743ff., 1768ff.).

Chapter 2. Differences in Conditions

[1] Concerning the definitions of the technical terms "inhibitions" and "obstacles" and the role of these two concepts in a development model, see *Asian Drama,* Chap. 3, Sec. 1 (pp. 71ff.); Appendix 2, Sec. 12 (pp. 1878ff.).

[2] *Asian Drama,* Chap. 14, Sec. 5 (pp. 688ff.).

[3] *Ibid.*, Chap. 14, Sec. 9 (pp. 700ff.).

[4] *Ibid.*, Chap. 14, Sec. 2 (pp. 676ff.); Chap. 11, Sec. 7 (pp. 510ff.).

[5] *Ibid.*, Chap. 14, Sec. 2 (pp. 677ff.); Appendix 10.

[6] *Ibid.*, Chap. 14, Sec. 3 (pp. 681ff.).

[7] *Ibid.*, Chap. 27, Sec. 2 (pp. 1389ff.); Appendix 11; *et passim.*

[8] *Ibid.*, Chap. 28, Secs. 1–3 (pp. 1464ff.).

[9] See for this section, *Asian Drama,* Chap. 14, Sec. 4 (pp. 682ff.); Chap. 13, particularly Secs. 1, 5, 6 (pp. 581ff., 595ff., 603ff.).

[10] *Asian Drama,* Chap. 10, Secs. 7–8 (pp. 442ff.).

[11] *Ibid.*, Chap. 13, Secs. 12–15 (pp. 640ff.).

[12] *Ibid.*, Chap. 13, Sec. 14 (pp. 649ff.); *et passim.*

[13] *Ibid.*, Chap. 13, Sec. 16 (pp. 661ff.).

[14] *Ibid.*, Chap. 13, Sec. 17 (pp. 669ff.); Chap. 19, Sec. 7 (pp. 926ff.), *et passim;* Chap. 24, Sec. 2 (particularly 1158f.); Appendix 8, Part I.

[15] *Ibid.*, Chap. 14, Secs. 6–7 (pp. 691ff.).

[16] *Ibid.*, Chap. 14, Secs. 8–9 (pp. 697ff.).

[17] *Ibid.*, Chap. 14, Sec. 9 (pp. 700ff.).

[18] *Ibid.*, Appendix 2, Secs. 19–20 (pp. 1901ff.).

[19] *Ibid.*, Chap. 14, Sec. 1 (pp. 674ff.).

[20] *Ibid.*, Appendix 2, Sec. 3 (pp. 1847ff.).

[21] *Ibid.*, Prologue, Sec. 6 (p. 22; *et passim*).

Part Two. THE NEED FOR RADICAL REFORMS IN UNDERDEVELOPED COUNTRIES

Chapter 3. The Equality Issue

[1] *Asian Drama*, Chap. 16, Sec. 10 (pp. 769f.); *et passim.*

[2] For conditions and trends in South Asia, see *Asian Drama*, Chap. 12, particularly Secs. 7–8 (pp. 563ff.); Appendix 14; Chap. 15, Sec. 8 (pp. 737f.); Chap. 16, Secs. 6–10 (pp. 756ff.); Chap. 18, particularly Sec. 12 (pp. 883ff.); Chap. 19, Sec. 7 (pp. 926ff.); Chap. 22, Sec. 5 (pp. 1052ff.); Chap. 26, Secs. 12–20 (pp. 1301ff.); Chap. 33, Sec. 7 (pp. 1790ff.); *et passim.*

[3] I have developed this theme in *The Political Element in the Development of Economic Theory* (London: Routledge and Kegan Paul, 1953; published in the United States by Harvard University Press in 1965), and in Part II of *Economic Theory and Under-Developed Regions* (London: Duckworth, 1957; published in the United States as *Rich Lands and Poor* by Harper & Row in 1969). See also *Objectivity in Social Research*, Secs. 17–23.

[4] Myrdal, *Beyond the Welfare State* (New Haven: Yale University Press, 1960), Part I.

[4a] Gustav R. Papanek, *Pakistan's Development: Social Goals and Private Incentives* (Cambridge: Harvard University Press, 1967), pp. 178, 242.

[5] *Asian Drama*, Chap. 16, Sec. 3 (pp. 745ff.).

[6] *Ibid.*, Chap. 16, Sec. 1 (pp. 741ff.).

[7] *Ibid.*, Chap. 15, Sec. 2 (pp. 712ff.).

[8] *Ibid.*, Chap. 16, Sec. 2 (pp. 743ff.); *et passim.*

[9] Jawaharlal Nehru, *The Discovery of India* (4th ed.; London: Meridian Books Ltd., 1956), p. 513.

[10] "Strategy of the Third Plan," *Problems in the Third Plan—A Critical Miscellany* (New Delhi, 1961), p. 50.

[11] *Loc. cit.*

[12] *Asian Drama,* Appendix 4, Secs. 1–2 (pp. 2005ff.).

[13] *Ibid.,* Chap. 16, Sec. 3 (pp. 745ff.).

[14] *Ibid.,* Appendix 2, Sec. 21 (pp. 1912ff.).

[15] "Recent Social Trends and Developments in Asia," *Economic Bulletin for Asia and the Far East,* Vol. XIX, No. 1 (June, 1968), p. 58.

[16] *Asian Drama,* Chap. 22, Secs. 5, 10 (pp. 1052ff., 1083ff.). For an illustration from another part of India, see Kusum Nair, *Blossoms in the Dust* (London: G. Duckworth & Co., 1961), pp. 27ff.

[17] *Asian Drama,* Chap. 12, Sec. 7 (pp. 567f.).

[18] *Ibid.,* p. 1806, fn. 1; *et passim.*

[19] *Ibid.,* Chap. 3, Secs. 5–7 (pp. 93ff.).

[20] *Ibid.,* Chap. 16, Secs. 1–2 (pp. 741ff.).

[21] "Recent Social Trends and Developments in Asia," *op. cit.,* p. 57.

[22] *Asian Drama,* Chap. 16, Sec. 9 (pp. 765ff.).

[23] For the development in South Asia, see *Asian Drama,* Chap. 12, Secs. 7–8 (pp. 563ff.); Chap. 16, Sec. 6 (pp. 756ff.); *et passim.* Cf. footnote 2 above.

[24] *Ibid.,* Chap. 16, Sec. 8 (pp. 763ff.).

[25] See, for example, *Asian Drama,* Chap. 16, Sec. 6 (pp. 756ff.); Chap. 22, Sec. 5 (pp. 1052ff.); *et passim.*

[26] See, for instance, *Asian Drama,* Chap. 26, Secs. 18–20 (pp. 1334ff.); cf. "Recent Social Trends and Developments in Asia," *op. cit.,* particularly pp. 49f.

[27] *Asian Drama,* Chap. 16, Sec. 9 (pp. 765ff.); *et passim.*

[28] *Ibid.,* Chap. 16, Secs. 7, 9 (pp. 761ff., 765ff.); *et passim.*

[29] *Ibid.,* Chap. 6.

[30] *Ibid.,* Chap. 26, Sec. 12 (pp. 1301ff.).

[31] *Ibid.,* Chap. 7, Secs. 4–5 (pp. 281ff.); Chap. 16, Secs. 9, 12, 13, 14 (pp. 765ff., 775ff.).

[32] *Ibid.,* Chap. 16, Sec. 13 (pp. 779ff.).

[33] *Ibid.,* Chap. 8, Secs. 3–6 (pp. 315ff.).

[34] *Ibid.,* Chap. 8, Sec. 9 (pp. 338ff.).

[35] See Gustav F. Papanek, *Pakistan's Development: Social Goals, and Private Incentives.*

[36] Joseph Lelyveld, "Difficulties in Pakistan Cause Reassessment of Her 'Success,'" *New York Times,* March 9, 1969.

[37] *Asian Drama,* Chap. 8, Sec. 9 (pp. 338ff.).

[38] *Ibid.,* Chap. 8, Sec. 3 (pp. 315ff.).

³⁹ *Ibid.,* Chap. 8, Sec. 9 (pp. 338ff.).

⁴⁰ *Ibid.,* Chap. 4, Sec. 12 (pp. 169ff.); Chap. 5, Sec. 13 (pp. 221ff.); Chap. 9, Sec. 16 (pp. 398ff.).

⁴¹ *Ibid.,* Chap. 4, Secs. 4, 5, 7, 13 (pp. 138ff., 149ff., 173ff.).

⁴² *Ibid.,* Chap. 7, Secs. 3–7 (pp. 273ff.); cf. Chap. 4, Sec. 7 (pp. 149ff.); *et passim.*

⁴³ *Ibid.,* Chap. 4, Sec. 11 (pp. 162ff.); Chap. 5, Secs. 11–12 (pp. 213ff.); Chap. 9, Secs. 9–10 (pp. 373ff.).

⁴⁴ *Ibid.,* Chap. 9, Sec. 10 (pp. 376ff.).

⁴⁵ Bronfenbrenner, "The Appeal of Confiscation in Economic Development," *Economic Development and Social Change,* April, 1955.

⁴⁶ *Asian Drama,* Appendix 9, pp. 2112ff.; *et passim.*

⁴⁷ *Newsweek,* December 30, 1968.

⁴⁸ *Asian Drama,* Chap. 17, Sec. 9, particularly p. 823, fn. 4.

⁴⁹ *Ibid.,* Chap. 16, Secs. 1, 2, 4, 5 (pp. 741ff., 749ff.).

⁵⁰ *Ibid.,* Chap. 16, Sec. 6 (pp. 756ff.).

⁵¹ Myrdal, *Economic Theory and Under-Developed Regions* (U.S. title: *Rich Lands and Poor*), Part II.

⁵² *Objectivity in Social Research,* Secs. 3–5.

⁵³ For a condensed exemplification from South Asia, see *Asian Drama,* Chap. 16, Sec. 7 (pp. 761ff.); *et passim.* Cf. "Recent Social Trends and Developments in Asia," *op. cit.,* pp. 49f.

⁵⁴ *Asian Drama,* Chap. 16, Sec. 9 (pp. 765ff.).

Chapter 4. Agriculture

¹ The background for this chapter, so far as South Asia is concerned, can be found in *Asian Drama,* Chaps. 22, 26.

² *Ibid.,* Chap. 10, Sec. 2 (pp. 417ff.).

³ Food and Agriculture Organization, *The State of Food and Agriculture* (Rome, 1968), Fig. III–3, p. 78; *et passim.* See also FAO reports, published under the same title, for other years.

⁴ *Asian Drama,* Chap. 11, Secs. 5–6 (pp. 546ff.); Chap. 10, Secs. 7–8 (pp. 442ff.); Chap. 17, Sec. 3 (pp. 808ff.); *et passim.*

⁵ *Ibid.,* Chap. 26, Sec. 8 (pp. 1278ff.).

⁶ *Ibid.,* Chap. 26, Sec. 2 (pp. 1244ff.).

⁷ *Ibid.,* p. 1245, fn. 5.

⁸ FAO, *The State of Food and Agriculture* (1968), pp. 9ff.; *et passim.*

⁹ *Ibid.,* pp. 75ff.

¹⁰ *Ibid., et passim.*

[11] In regard to South Asia, see *Asian Drama*, Chap. 12, Secs. 3–4 (pp. 538ff.); Chap. 30, Sec. 11 (pp. 1602ff.); *et passim*. For the rest of the underdeveloped world, see a great number of publications by FAO, besides *The State of Food and Agriculture*, various years, particularly *Third World Food Survey* (Rome, 1963), and the excellent American study prepared by the President's Science Advisory Committee, *The World Food Problem* (Washington, D.C., 1967). The last-mentioned source was not available when I finished *Asian Drama*.

[12] *Asian Drama*, Chap. 30, Secs. 11–13 (pp. 1602ff.).

[13] *Ibid.*, Chap. 3, Sec. 5 (pp. 93ff.), and Chap. 30, Secs. 11, 13 (pp. 1602ff., 1616ff.).

[14] Quoted in Myrdal, *1965 McDougall Memorial Lecture*, November 24, 1965, Rome, Food and Agriculture Organization Conference, Thirteenth Session.

[15] *The State of Food and Agriculture* (1968), pp. 78ff.; *et passim*.

[16] *Asian Drama*, Chap. 26, Secs. 1, 3 (pp. 1241ff., 1251ff.); Chap. 10, Secs. 3–5 (pp. 417ff.).

[17] For the definition of underutilization of labor and these other concepts mentioned, see *Asian Drama*, Chap. 21, particularly Sec. 15 (pp. 1012ff.). See also *ibid.*, Appendix 6.

[18] *Asian Drama*, Chap. 21 and Appendix 6.

[19] *Ibid.*, Chap. 22.

[20] *Ibid.*, Appendix 2, Parts I and II.

[21] *Ibid.*, Chap. 26, Sec. 3 (pp. 1251ff.).

[22] *Ibid.*, Chap. 21, Sec. 14 (pp. 1007ff.); Appendix 6, Secs. 6–7 (pp. 2050ff.); Chap. 26, Secs. 3, 11 (pp. 1251ff., 1294ff.); *et passim*.

[23] *Ibid.*, Chap. 26, Sec. 21 (pp. 1356ff.).

[24] *Ibid.*, Chap. 26, Sec. 11 and Secs. 6–10 (pp. 1294ff., 1261ff.); *et passim*.

[25] Economic Commission for Latin America, *Economic Survey of Latin America 1966* (United Nations, New York, 1968), Part III, particularly pp. 351–352.

[26] *Asian Drama*, Chap. 26, Secs. 11, 25 (pp. 1294ff., 1377ff.).

[27] *Ibid.*, Chap. 26, Secs. 6–11 (pp. 1261ff.).

[28] *Ibid.*, Chap. 24, Sec. 1 (pp. 1150ff.).

[29] *Ibid.*, Appendix 1.

[30] *Ibid.*, Chap. 24, Secs. 2, 11 (pp. 1155ff., 1202ff.); *et passim*.

[31] *Ibid.*, Chap. 17, Secs. 6–10, 14, 15 (pp. 815ff., 840ff.).

[32] *Ibid.*, Chap. 24, Sec. 1 (pp. 1153f.); *et passim;* Appendix 6, particularly Sec. 10 (p. 2061).

[33] *Ibid.*, Chap. 24, Secs. 1, 5 (1153f., 1172ff.); *et passim*.

[34] *Ibid.*, Chap. 24, Secs. 5, 10, 11; *et passim.*

[35] *Ibid.*, Chap. 24, Sec. 6; Chap. 21, Sec. 1.

[36] *Ibid.*, Chap. 10, Sec. 11.

[37] *Ibid.*, Chap. 11, Sec. 4; Chap. 23, Secs. 4, 9; Chap. 26, Sec. 1.

[38] *Ibid.*, Chap. 23, Secs. 4–5 (pp. 1112ff.).

[39] *Economic Survey of Latin America 1966*, Table 283, p. 326; *et passim.*

[40] *Asian Drama*, Chap. 26, Sec. 2 (pp. 1244ff.); Appendix 4, Sec. 2 (pp. 2008ff.).

[41] *Ibid.*, Appendix 2, Secs. 18–20 (pp. 1897ff.); *et passim.*

[42] *Ibid.*, Chap. 24, Sec. 4 (pp. 1168ff.); Chap. 14, Sec. 6 (pp. 691ff.).

[43] *Ibid.*, Chap. 25, particularly Secs. 3, 5–9 (1217ff., 1225ff.).

[44] *Ibid.*, Chap. 26, Sec. 1 (pp. 1241ff.).

[45] *Ibid.*, Chap. 14, Sec. 7 (pp. 696f.); Chap. 26, Sec. 3 (pp. 1251ff.); *et passim.*

[46] *Ibid.*, Chap. 26, Sec. 3 (pp. 1253f.); Chap. 14, Secs. 7–8 (pp. 696ff.); *et passim.*

[47] *Ibid.*, Chap. 21 *passim;* Chap. 22, Secs. 7–9 (pp. 1070ff.); *et passim.*

[48] *Ibid.*, Chap. 26, Sec. 10 (pp. 1288ff.).

[49] *Ibid.*, Chap. 22, Sec. 4 (pp. 1047ff.); *et passim.*

[50] *Ibid.*, Chap. 22, particularly Secs. 5–11 (pp. 1052ff.).

[51] "Recent Social Trends and Developments in Asia," *Economic Bulletin for Asia and the Far East*, Vol. XIX, No. 1 (June, 1968), p. 51.

[52] *Economic Survey of Latin America 1966*, Part III (United Nations, New York, 1968).

[53] *Ibid.*, p. 312.

[54] *Asian Drama*, Chap. 26, Secs. 12–17 (pp. 1301ff.).

[55] *Economic Survey of Latin America 1966*, pp. 334ff.

[56] *Ibid.*, p. 338.

[57] *Ibid.*, pp. 353f.

[58] *Asian Drama*, Chap. 26, Secs. 18–20 (pp. 1334ff.); see also Chap. 18, particularly Secs. 12–13 (pp. 883ff.). Cf. "Recent Social Trends and Developments in Asia," p. 52.

[59] "Recent Social Trends and Developments in Asia," p. 52.

[60] *Asian Drama*, Chap. 18, particularly Sec. 12 (pp. 883ff.); Chap. 26, Secs. 18–19 (pp. 1334ff.).

[61] *Asian Drama*, Chap. 26, Sec. 19 (pp. 1339ff.).

[62] For some estimates for India, see *Asian Drama*, p. 1344, fn. 4.

[63] *Asian Drama,* Chap. 26, Sec. 25 (pp. 1377ff.).

[64] *Ibid.,* Chap. 22.

[65] *Ibid.,* Chap. 19.

[66] *Ibid.,* pp. 1352, 1382f.

[67] *Ibid.,* Chap. 26, Secs. 22–24 (pp. 1366ff.).

[68] *Ibid.,* Chap. 26, Sec. 20 (pp. 1346ff.).

[69] *Ibid.,* Chap. 26, Sec. 4 (pp. 1255ff.); *et passim.*

[70] *Ibid.,* Chap. 21 and Appendix 6.

[71] *Ibid.,* Chap. 21, Secs. 12–14 (pp. 1001ff.); Appendix 6, Secs. 8–9 (pp. 2055ff.).

[72] *Ibid.,* Chap. 21, Secs. 12, 14 (pp. 1001ff., 1007ff.); Appendix 6, Sec. 10 (p. 2061).

[73] *Ibid.,* Chap. 25, Sec. 1 (pp. 1210ff.); Chap. 26, Sec. 21 (pp. 1356ff.); *et passim.*

[74] *Ibid.,* Chap. 26, Secs. 22–24 (pp. 1356ff.).

[75] *Ibid.,* Chap. 26, Sec. 12 (p. 1304, fn. 2).

[76] *Ibid.,* Chap. 26, Sec. 4 (pp. 1255ff.).

[77] *Ibid.,* Chap. 26, Sec. 5 (pp. 1259f.).

[78] *Ibid.,* Chap. 26, Sec. 4 (pp. 1257ff.) and Chap. 22, Sec. 6 (pp. 1064ff.).

[79] *The State of Food and Agriculture* (1968), pp. 81ff.

[80] *Loc. cit.*

[81] "Heretofore, reliance upon seed selected by individual farmers meant that neighboring farms growing the same crop usually planted two or more different varieties or strains. This heterogeneity provided a built-in protection against widespread plant diseases, since not all varieties are equally susceptible. But where a single variety is introduced, covering large contiguous areas, the dangers of pathologic susceptibility are multiplied. . . . The outbreak of any major disease which wipes out the harvest of thousands of farmers is far more likely to be blamed on the producers and spreaders of the miracle seed than on Fate. Agricultural development could be set back several decades." (Clifton R. Wharton, Jr., "The Green Revolution: Cornucopia or Pandora's Box?" *Foreign Affairs,* April 1969, pp. 468f.)

[81a] *The State of Food and Agriculture* (1968), pp. 81ff.

[82] Hiroshi Kitamura, "The Economic Situation in Asia," *Economic Bulletin for Asia and the Far East,* Vol. XIX, No. 1 (June, 1968), p. 41.

[83] Lester R. Brown, "New Directions in World Agriculture," *Studies in Family Planning,* No. 32 (June, 1968); Lyle Schertz, *Challenge of the "70's": Improve Agriculture in the Less Developed Countries,* United States Department of Agriculture, 435–69 (February 11, 1969), mimeographed.

[84] "The Agricultural Revolution in Asia," *Foreign Affairs*, Vol. 46, No. 4, July, 1968.

[85] Cf. *Asian Drama*, Chap. 26, Sec. 19 (pp. 1342ff.).

[86] *Ibid.*, Chap. 26, Sec. 19 (pp. 1345ff.), *et passim*.

[87] The papers are published under the title *Development and Change in Traditional Agriculture: Focus on South Asia*, mimeographed (East Lansing, Michigan; November, 1968).

[88] *Ibid.*, p. 59.

[89] Agency for International Development, *Primer on Title IX of the United States Foreign Assistance Act* (Washington, D.C., 1968).

[90] *The Role of Popular Participation in Development*, published in mimeographed form by the Center for International Studies, Massachusetts Institute of Technology (Cambridge, Massachusetts; November, 1968).

[91] *Ibid.*, p. 1.

[92] Gunnar Myrdal, *Challenge to Affluence* (New York: Pantheon Books, 1963; Vintage Books edition, 1965), Chap. 10, particularly p. 144. (This and all subsequent page references are to the Vintage edition.)

[93] See *Report of the World Land Reform Conference, 1966*, United Nations, 1968, particularly Part III, "An Analysis of the Main Issues of the Conference," by Erich H. Jacoby and John Higgs.

[94] Food and Agriculture Organization of the United Nations, *Provisional Indicative World Plan for Agricultural Development, A Synthesis and Analysis of Factors Relevant to World, Regional and National Agricultural Development*, Rome, August, 1969, 3 vols. The main report is supported by four almost equally voluminous regional studies on West Asia, Latin America, Africa south of the Sahara, and South and East Asia.

[95] *1965 Report on the World Social Situation* (United Nations, New York, 1966).

[96] *Ibid.*, pp. 79f.

[97] United Nations, 1963; mimeographed, A/7248, E/CN.5/417.

Chapter 5. Population

[1] See *Asian Drama*, Chaps. 27 and 28 on population prospects and population policy.

[2] *Asian Drama*, Chap. 11, particularly Sec. 1 (pp. 474ff.).

[3] *Ibid.*, Chap. 12, Secs. 1–2 (pp. 529ff.).

[4] *Ibid.*, Chap. 21 and Appendix 6.

[5] *Ibid.*, Chap. 27, Sec. 1 (pp. 1387ff.).

[6] *Ibid.*, Chap. 27, Sec. 2 (pp. 1389ff.).

[7] *Ibid.*, Chap. 27, Sec. 13 (pp. 1448ff.).

[8] *Ibid.*, Chap. 27, Secs. 4–6 (pp. 1402ff.); Chap. 30, Secs. 5–6 (pp. 1567ff.).

[9] *Ibid.*, Chap. 27, Sec. 4 (pp. 1402ff.).

[10] *Ibid.*, Chap. 27, Sec. 5 (pp. 1408ff.).

[11] *Ibid.*, Chap. 27, Secs. 7–11 (pp. 1422ff.).

[12] *Ibid.*, Chap. 27, Sec. 12 (pp. 1443ff.).

[13] *Ibid.*, Chap. 27, Sec. 2 (pp. 1391ff.).

[14] *Ibid.*, Chap. 28, Sec. 3 (p. 1470).

[15] *Ibid.*, Chap. 30, Sec. 1 (pp. 1554f.).

[16] *Ibid.*, Chap. 28, Sec. 9 (pp. 1496ff.).

[17] For an example, see Jan Tinbergen, *The Design of Development* (Baltimore: Johns Hopkins Press, 1958), p. 14.

[18] *Asian Drama*, Appendix 7, Sec. 1 (pp. 2063ff.).

[19] *Population Growth and Economic Development in Low-Income Countries* (Princeton: Princeton University Press, 1958).

[20] *Asian Drama*, Chap. 28, Sec. 1 (pp. 1464f.).

[21] *Ibid.*, Chap. 28, Sec. 2 (pp. 1465ff.).

[22] See also *ibid.*, p. 1469, fn. 1.

[23] *1968 Annual Meetings of the Boards of Governors, Summary Proceedings* (Washington, D.C., 1969).

[24] *Asian Drama*, Chap. 28, Sec. 3 (pp. 1467ff.).

[25] *Ibid.*, Appendix 11.

[26] *Ibid.*, Chap. 28, Sec. 4 (pp. 1471ff.).

[27] *Ibid.*, Appendix 7, Sec. 3 (pp. 2066ff.).

[28] *Ibid.*, Chap. 28, Sec. 14 (pp. 1513ff.).

[29] *Ibid.*, Chap. 28, Sec. 5 (pp. 1473ff.).

[30] *Ibid.*, Chap. 28, Sec. 14 (p. 1523).

[31] *Ibid.*, Chap. 28, Sec. 5 (pp. 1473ff.).

[32] *Ibid.*, Chap. 28, Sec. 12 (pp. 1505ff.).

[33] *Ibid.*, Chap. 28, Sec. 5 (pp. 1474f.).

[34] *Ibid.*, Chap. 28, Sec. 13 (pp. 1507ff.).

[35] *Ibid.*, Chap. 28, Sec. 14 (pp. 1515ff.); Appendix 12.

[36] *Ibid.*, Chap. 28, Sec. 13 (pp. 1512f.).

[37] *Ibid.*, Chap. 28, Sec. 14 (pp. 1518ff.).

[38] International Planned Parenthood Federation, *Family Planning in Five Continents* (London: August, 1969).

[39] *Asian Drama,* Chap. 28, Sec. 15 (pp. 1526ff.); Appendix 12, Sec. 4 (pp. 2161).

[40] *Ibid.,* Chap. 28, Sec. 15 (pp. 1526ff.); Postscript, Sec. 1 (pp. 1831ff.).

[41] *Ibid.,* Chap. 30, Sec. 8 (pp. 1582ff., particularly pp. 1593ff.).

[42] *Ibid.,* Postscript, Sec. 1 (pp. 1831ff.). See also Sajal Basu and Sankar Ray, "Impact of Intra-Uterine Contraceptive Devices," *Economic and Political Weekly* (June 8, 1968).

[43] *Asian Drama,* Chap. 28, Sec. 5 (pp. 1473ff.). For the colonial era, see Secs. 6–8 (pp. 1480ff.).

[44] *Ibid.,* Chap. 28, Sec. 5 (pp. 1475ff.).

[45] *Ibid.,* Chap. 28, Sec. 8 (pp. 1489–1495, particularly pp. 1494f.).

[46] *Ibid.,* Chap. 28, Sec. 13 (pp. 1507–1513, particularly p. 1509).

[47] Carl E. Taylor, "Health and Population," *Foreign Affairs* (April, 1965), and "Five Stages in a Practical Population Policy," *International Development Review* (December, 1968).

Chapter 6. Education

[1] *Asian Drama,* Chap. 32, Sec. 4 (pp. 1670ff.).

[2] *Ibid.,* Chap. 32, Sec. 4 (Fig. 32–2 on p. 1677 and p. 1671, fn. 2).

[3] *Ibid.,* Chap. 32, Sec. 4 (p. 1671, fn. 3).

[4] *Ibid.,* Chap. 33, Sec. 2 (pp. 1714ff.), *et passim.*

[5] *Ibid.,* Chap. 33, Sec. 2 (p. 1715, fns. 4, 6).

[6] *Ibid.,* Chap. 11, Secs. 1–2 (particularly Table 11–1, p. 477); Appendix 13 (pp. 2165ff.).

[7] *Ibid.,* Chap. 29, Sec. 4 (particularly p. 1544), *et passim.*

[8] *Ibid.,* Chap. 29, Secs. 4–7 (pp. 1540ff.).

[9] *Ibid.,* Appendix 3, Sec. 7 (pp. 1956ff.).

[10] *Ibid.,* Chap. 29, Sec. 5 (pp. 1567ff.).

[11] In the more than 250 pages of these chapters I attempted a fresh analysis of the educational problems in South Asia. These chapters constitute one of the parts of my study where I thought that I pierced deeper than merely to present a "theory" and motivate a different approach. I would be disappointed if they did not catch the attention of the specialists in education, simply because they are contained as the last part of a book with a much more general scope and title, written by an economist.

[12] *Asian Drama,* Chap. 31, Secs. 3–4 (pp. 1632–1650).

[13] *Ibid.,* Chap. 31, Sec. 3 (pp. 1632ff.).

[14] *Ibid.,* Chap. 31, Secs. 3 (p. 1641, *et passim*) and 4 (*passim*).

[15] *Ibid.,* Chap. 33, Sec. 5 (pp. 1757ff.).

[16] *Ibid.*, Chap. 10, Sec. 9 (pp. 454ff.), *et passim.*

[17] *Ibid.*, Chap. 31, Sec. 3 (pp. 1640f.); Chap. 33, Sec. 7 (pp. 1806ff.).

[18] *Ibid.*, Chap. 32, Sec. 2 (pp. 1653ff.).

[19] *Ibid.*, Chap. 32, Sec. 3 (p. 1659, *et passim*); Chap. 33, Sec. 8 (pp. 1810f.).

[20] *Ibid.*, Chap. 33, Sec. 1 (pp. 1703ff.; particularly Table 33–2).

[21] *Ibid.*, Chap. 33, Sec. 1 (pp. 1708ff., particularly Table 33–3).

[22] *Ibid.*, Chap. 32, Sec. 4 (pp. 1670ff., particularly Table 32–3 on p. 1672).

[23] *Ibid.*, Chap. 11, Secs. 1–2 (pp. 474–492).

[24] In this book I continually refer to Malaya as the relatively more homogeneous part of the bigger unit which has more recently been created, Malaysia.

[25] *Asian Drama*, Chap. 32, Sec. 2 (pp. 1655ff.).

[26] *Ibid.*, Chap. 32, Sec. 3 (pp. 1657ff.).

[27] *Ibid.*, Chap. 32, Sec. 4 (pp. 1666ff.).

[28] *Ibid.*, Chap. 32, Sec. 5 (pp. 1687).

[29] *Ibid.*, Chap. 32, Sec. 3 (pp. 1657ff.).

[30] *Ibid.*, Chap. 32, Sec. 5 (pp. 1685ff.).

[31] *Ibid.*, Chap. 33, Sec. 2 (pp. 1724ff.) and Sec. 7 (pp. 1801f.), *et passim.*

[32] W. S. Woytinsky, *India: The Awakening Giant* (New York: Harper & Row, 1957), p. 137.

[33] *Asian Drama*, Chap. 23, Sec. 6 (pp. 1124–1131).

[34] *Ibid.*, Chap. 32, Sec. 5 (particularly pp. 1690ff.).

[35] *Ibid.*, Chap. 32, Sec. 3 (pp. 1657ff.).

[36] *Ibid.*, Chap. 32, Sec. 3 (particularly Table 32–1, p. 1660); see also Chap. 33, Secs. 4, 6 (pp. 1743ff., 1768ff., particularly table on p. 1778), and 7 (pp. 1803f.).

[37] *Ibid.*, Chap. 32, Sec. 3 (p. 1666).

[38] *Ibid.*, Chap. 32, Sec. 3 (pp. 1665f.).

[39] *Ibid.*, Chap. 33, Sec. 2 (pp. 1712ff., particularly Table 33–4 on p. 1718); cf. Secs. 4, 6 (pp. 1743ff., 1768ff.).

[40] *Ibid.*, Chap. 32, Sec. 3 (particularly p. 1659).

[41] *Ibid.*, Chap. 33, Secs. 2 (*passim*) and 7 (pp. 1791ff.).

[42] For India see Agricultural Economics Research Centre, University of New Delhi, *Primary Education in Rural India: Participation and Wastage*, New Delhi, May 1968 (mimeographed).

[43] *Asian Drama*, Chap. 33, Sec. 2 (particularly pp. 1724f.).

44 *Ibid.*, Chap. 33, Secs. 1 (pp. 1702f.) and 2 (pp. 1725f.).

45 *Ibid.*, Chap. 33, Sec. 3 (pp. 1728ff.).

46 *Ibid.*, Chap. 33, Secs. 3 (pp. 1730ff.) and 5 (pp. 1766ff.). Cf. Chap. 31, Sec. 4 (pp. 1644f.).

47 *Ibid.*, Chap. 33, Sec. 3 (pp. 1741ff.); cf. Chap. 3, Sec. 3 (pp. 81ff.).

48 *Ibid.*, Chap. 3, Sec. 3 (pp. 81ff.).

49 *Ibid.*, Chap. 32, Sec. 2 (pp. 1655f.) and Chap. 33, Sec. 3 (pp. 1737ff.).

50 *Ibid.*, Chap. 33, Sec. 4 (pp. 1743ff.).

51 *Ibid.*, Chap. 33, Sec. 5 (pp. 1756ff.).

52 *Ibid.*, Chap. 31, Sec. 3 (pp. 1642f.).

53 About the social problem of "educated unemployed," see *Asian Drama*, Chap. 23, Sec. 6 (pp. 1124ff.).

54 *Asian Drama*, Chap. 33, Sec. 6 (pp. 1768ff.).

55 *Ibid.*, Chap. 33, Sec. 6 (pp. 1781ff.).

56 *Ibid.*, Chap. 33, Sec. 6 (pp. 1784ff.).

57 *Ibid.*, Chap. 33, Sec. 6 (pp. 1774ff.).

58 *Ibid.*, Chap. 33, Sec. 6 (pp. 1776ff.).

59 *Ibid.*, Chap. 33, Sec. 6 (particularly Fig. 33–5, p. 1778).

60 *Ibid.*, Chap. 33, Sec. 5 (p. 1760, *et passim*), Sec. 6 (pp. 1776ff.), Sec. 7 (pp. 1792ff.).

61 *Ibid.*, Chap. 9, Secs. 5–9 (pp. 360ff.).

62 *Ibid.*, Chap. 30, Sec. 4 (pp. 1565f.); Chap. 31, Sec. 3 (pp. 1633f.); Chap. 32, Sec. 5 (pp. 1691f.); and Chap. 33, Sec. 3 (p. 1739).

63 *Ibid.*, Chap. 33, Sec. 7 (pp. 1798ff.).

64 *Ibid.*, Chap. 33, Sec. 6 (pp. 1774ff.).

65 *Ibid.*, Chap. 33, Sec. 7 (pp. 1801ff.), *et passim* in earlier sections of that chapter.

66 *Ibid.*, Chap. 3, Sec. 8 (pp. 113ff.); Chap. 15, Sec. 6 (p. 730); Chap. 16, Sec. 13 (pp. 781f.) and Sec. 19 (p. 796).

67 *Ibid.*, Chap. 33, Sec. 8 (pp. 1827f.).

68 *Ibid.*, Chap. 33, Sec. 8 (pp. 1810f.).

69 *Ibid.*, Chap. 33, Sec. 8 (pp. 1811ff.).

70 *Ibid.*, Chap. 33, Sec. 8 (pp. 1813f.).

71 *Ibid.*, Chap. 32, Sec. 3 (pp. 1658ff.) and Chap. 33 (*passim*), particularly Sec. 8 (pp. 1814ff.).

72 *Ibid.*, Chap. 33, Sec. 8 (pp. 1816ff.).

73 *Ibid.*, Chap. 33, Sec. 8 (pp. 1814ff. and p. 1826).

74 *Ibid.,* Chap. 32, Sec. 5 (pp. 1685ff.) and Chap. 33, Sec. 8 (p. 1809).

75 *Ibid.,* Chap. 33, Sec. 8 (pp. 1822ff.).

76 *Ibid.,* Chap. 33, Sec. 8 (pp. 1820f.).

77 *Ibid.,* Chap. 33, Sec. 8 (pp. 1824ff.).

78 *Ibid.,* Chap. 32, Sec. 3 (p. 1659 with footnotes).

79 *Ibid.,* Chap. 31, Sec. 1 (pp. 1622f.).

Chapter 7. The "Soft State"

1 *Asian Drama,* Chap. 2, Sec. 4 (pp. 66f.); Chap. 3, Sec. 8 (particularly pp. 117f.); Chap. 16, Sec. 13 (pp. 779ff.); Chap. 18, Sec. 13 and, particularly, Sec. 14 (pp. 895ff.); Appendix 2, Sec. 20 (particularly pp. 1908ff.).

2 *Ibid.,* Appendix 2, Part II (pp. 1859ff.).

3 *Ibid.,* Chap. 8, Secs. 4–9 (pp. 319ff.).

4 *Ibid.,* Chap. 9, Secs. 7–8 (pp. 365ff.).

5 *Ibid.,* Chap. 16, Secs. 12–13 (pp. 775ff., particularly p. 780).

6 *Ibid.,* Appendix 2, Sec. 6 (particularly p. 1866); *et passim.*

7 *Ibid.,* Chap. 18, Sec. 5 (pp. 859ff.), Sec. 14 (pp. 895ff.); cf. in Chaps. 22 and 23 (*passim*).

8 *Ibid.,* Chap. 18, Sec. 14 (pp. 897f.).

9 *Ibid.,* Chap. 18 (*passim*); cf. Chap. 2, Sec. 2 (pp. 51ff.).

10 *Ibid.,* Chap. 19, Sec. 3 (pp. 910ff., particularly pp. 912ff.).

11 *Ibid.,* Chap. 16, Sec. 7 (pp. 761ff.); Chap. 26, Secs. 18–20 (pp. 1334ff.); *et passim.*

12 *Ibid.,* Chap. 18, Sec. 12 (pp. 883ff.).

13 *Ibid.,* Chap. 18, Sec. 13 (pp. 891ff., particularly pp. 894f.).

14 *Ibid.,* Appendix 2, Sec. 20 (pp. 1903ff., particularly pp. 1909ff.).

15 *Ibid.,* Chap. 16, Sec. 8 (pp. 763ff.); Chap. 7, Sec. 5 (pp. 292ff.).

16 *Ibid.,* Chap. 26, Sec. 12 (pp. 1303ff.); cf. Chap. 22, Sec. 5 (pp. 1052ff.).

17 *Ibid.,* Chap. 26, Secs. 12–17 (pp. 1301ff.).

18 *Ibid.,* Appendix 8, Secs. 8 and 9 (pp. 2096ff., particularly pp. 2098ff.).

19 *Ibid.,* Chap. 15, Sec. 8 (pp. 737f.); Chap. 16, Secs. 7–8 (pp. 761ff.); cf. Chap. 26, Secs. 12–20 (pp. 1301ff.) and Chap. 18, Sec. 12 (pp. 883ff.).

20 *Ibid.,* Chap. 16, Sec. 13 (pp. 780ff.).

21 *Ibid.,* Chap. 19, Sec. 4 (pp. 916ff.); cf. Chap. 23, Sec. 3 (pp. 1103ff.).

22 *Ibid.,* Chap. 10, Sec. 7 (p. 445); Chap. 11, Sec. 5 (pp. 506ff.).

23 *Ibid.,* Chap. 11, Sec. 9 (pp. 521ff.).

²⁴ I distinguish between *positive* controls—or inducements—and *negative* controls—or restraints and curtailments. Controls can be *discretionary* when their application involves an individual decision by administrative authorities or *non-discretionary* when application follows automatically from the laying down of a definite rule or from induced changes in prices, the imposition of tariff duties or excise duties, or the giving of subsidies to a particular branch of industry without the possibility of discrimination in favor of particular firms. This last distinction is, on the whole, identical with that between "direct," or "physical," controls and "indirect" controls, as described in the literature. See *Asian Drama*, Chap. 19, Sec. 1 (pp. 903ff.).

²⁵ *Asian Drama*, Chap. 19, Sec. 2 (pp. 905ff.).

²⁶ *Ibid.*, Appendix 5 (p. 2031).

²⁷ *Ibid.*, Chap. 19, Secs. 5–6 (pp. 919ff., *passim*); Appendix 8 (pp. 2077ff.); cf. Appendix 5 (pp. 2031ff.).

²⁸ *Ibid.*, Chap. 19, Sec. 4 (pp. 918ff.).

²⁹ *Ibid.*, Appendix 2, Sec. 23 (pp. 1923ff.).

³⁰ *Ibid.*, Chap. 19, Sec. 1 (pp. 901ff.) and Sec. 2 (pp. 905ff.).

³¹ *Ibid.*, Chap. 19, Sec. 7 (pp. 926ff.); Appendix 8 (p. 2077, *et passim*).

³² See also *ibid.*, Chap. 13, Sec. 17 (pp. 669ff.) and Chap. 24, Sec. 2 (pp. 1158f.).

³³ See particularly *ibid.*, Chap. 19, Sec. 7 (p. 930, footnote 6).

³⁴ *Ibid.*, Chap. 20 (pp. 937ff.).

³⁵ *Ibid.*, Chap. 20, Sec. 1 (p. 939).

³⁶ *Ibid.*, Chap. 20, Sec. 5 (pp. 951ff.).

³⁷ *Second Public Services International Asian Regional Conference*, November 14, 1968, mimeographed.

³⁸ *Asian Drama*, Chap. 20, Sec. 2 (pp. 940ff.).

³⁹ *Ibid.*, Chap. 20, Sec. 3 (pp. 942ff.).

⁴⁰ *Ibid.*, Chap. 20, Sec. 4 (pp. 947ff.).

⁴¹ *Ibid.*, Chap. 18, Sec. 5 (pp. 859ff., particularly p. 861); Chap. 20, Sec. 3 (p. 949, footnote 3).

⁴² *Ibid.*, Chap. 20, Sec. 2 (p. 941).

⁴³ *Ibid.*, Chap. 20, Sec. 5 (pp. 951ff.).

⁴⁴ *Ibid.*, Chap. 20, Sec. 5 (pp. 953ff.).

⁴⁵ *Ibid.*, Chap. 20 (pp. 937ff.).

⁴⁶ *Ibid.*, Prologue, Sec. 9 (pp. 31ff.).

⁴⁷ Myrdal, *An American Dilemma, The Negro Problem and Modern Democracy* (New York: Harper & Row, 1944), Chap. 1, Secs. 6–12 (pp. 12ff.). I reverted to the problem in several later chapters on specific problems.

[48] Myrdal, *An International Economy: Problems and Prospects* (New York: Harper & Row, 1956), pp. 204ff.; *Beyond the Welfare State* (New Haven: Yale University Press, 1960), pp. 99ff.

[49] Myrdal, *Challenge to Affluence* (New York: Vintage Books, 1965), pp. 96ff.; cf. *American Dilemma*, Chap. 33 (pp. 709ff.).

[50] *Asian Drama*, Chap. 11, Sec. 4 (pp. 502ff.); Chap. 23, Sec. 9 (pp. 1145f.); *et passim*.

[51] *Ibid.*, Chap. 20, Sec. 5 (pp. 953ff.).

[52] *Ibid.*, Chap. 20, Sec. 6 (pp. 955ff.).

[53] *Ibid.*, Chap. 20 (pp. 937f.).

[54] *Ibid.*, Chap. 15, Sec. 4 (p. 724); Chap. 17, Sec. 1 (pp. 801ff.); *et passim*.

Chapter 8. Not an Alibi but a Challenge

[1] *Asian Drama*, Chap. 30 (pp. 1553ff.).

[2] *Ibid.*, Chaps. 24–25 (pp. 1149ff.).

[3] *Ibid.*, Appendix 2, Part II, particularly Sec. 5 (pp. 1859ff.) and Sec. 7 (pp. 1866ff.).

[4] *Ibid.*, Appendix 2, Sec. 7 (pp. 1868ff.).

[5] *Ibid.*, Chap. 11, Sec. 1 (pp. 474ff.).

[6] *Ibid.*, Chap. 11, Secs. 3–4 (pp. 492ff.).

[7] *Ibid.*, Chap. 12, Sec. 2 (pp. 530ff.).

[8] *Ibid.*, Chap. 11, Sec. 1 (pp. 482); Appendix 13 (pp. 2165ff.).

[9] *Ibid.*, Prologue, Sec. 8 (pp. 30f.).

[10] *Ibid.*, Chap. 27, Sec. 1 (pp. 1387ff.).

[11] Morgenstern, *On the Accuracy of Economic Observations* (2nd ed.; Princeton: Princeton University Press, 1963).

[12] *Ibid.*, p. 282.

[13] *Ibid.*, p. 300. Italics in the source.

[14] "Comparative Social Research in the United Nations," *Comparing Nations: The Use of Quantitative Data in Cross-National Research*, ed. Merritt and Rokkan (New Haven: Yale University Press, 1966), pp. 528, 535.

Part Three. THE RESPONSIBILITY OF THE DEVELOPED COUNTRIES

Chapter 9. Trade and Capital Movements

[1] The highly simplified argument in the text has been more fully developed in my *Economic Theory and Under-Developed Regions* (London: Duckworth, 1957), published in the United States as *Rich Lands and*

Poor (New York: Harper & Row, 1958), particularly Chaps. 1 (pp. 3ff.) and 11 (pp. 147ff.). The page numbers here and in later footnotes refer to the English edition.

[2] *Economic Theory,* Chap. 10 (pp. 135ff.).

[3] *Ibid.,* Chaps. 1 and 11.

[4] *Ibid.,* Chap. 3 (pp. 23ff.).

[5] *Ibid.,* Chap. 2 (pp. 11ff.) and particularly Chap. 5 (pp. 50ff.).

[6] *Asian Drama,* Chap. 5, Sec. 4 (pp. 188ff.).

[7] *Asian Drama* contains, of course, more specific observations on this problem so far as South Asia is concerned; see in particular Chap. 10, Secs. 7–9 (pp. 442ff.).

[8] The foreign trade of underdeveloped countries has been analyzed in considerable detail in the *World Economic Surveys* of the United Nations, the *Economic Surveys* of the regional Economic Commissions, GATT, and more recently, by a great number of studies by the secretariat of UNCTAD.

Exports and imports are concepts more clearcut than other economic concepts, such as national income or production, savings, etc. The statistical observations are also more accurate and comprehensive. See *Asian Drama,* Chap. 13, Sec. 1 (p. 583).

In regard to the development and prospects of trade of the South Asian countries, see *Asian Drama,* Chap. 13 (pp. 581ff.), particularly Sec. 5 (pp. 595ff.) and Secs. 12–15 (pp. 640ff.).

[9] *Asian Drama,* Chap. 13, Sec. 5 (pp. 595ff.); Sec. 12 (pp. 640ff.).

[10] For South Asia, see *Asian Drama,* Chap. 13, Secs. 13, 14, 15 (pp. 643ff.).

[11] *Asian Drama,* Chap. 13, Sec. 17 (pp. 669ff.); Chap. 24, Sec. 3 (pp. 1160ff.); Appendix 8, Sec. 3 (pp. 2085ff.).

[12] *Ibid.,* Chap. 13, Sec. 9 (pp. 621ff.) and Sec. 16 (pp. 661ff.).

[13] See, for instance, United Nations, *Problems of Policies of Financing,* UNCTAD, Second Session, New Delhi, Vol. IV (New York, 1968), pp. 28ff.

[14] *Ibid.,* p. 33. See also *Asian Drama,* Chap. 13, Sec. 16 (pp. 664ff.).

[15] Myrdal, *An International Economy: Problems and Prospects* (New York: Harper & Row, 1956), now republished as a Harper Torchbook (1969), Chap. 13, particularly pp. 288ff.

[16] Myrdal, *Beyond the Welfare State* (New Haven: Yale University Press, 1960), Chap. 5 (pp. 77ff.), *et passim:* see also *Economic Theory and Under-Developed Regions* (U.S. title: *Rich Lands and Poor*), Chap. 4, particularly pp. 47ff.

[17] Myrdal, *Beyond the Welfare State,* Chap. 10 (pp. 77ff.), *et passim.*

[18] Myrdal, *Challenge to Affluence* (New York: Vintage Books, 1965), Chap. 7 (pp. 95ff.); Myrdal, *An American Dilemma* (New York: Harper & Row, 1944), Chap. 33.

[19] United Nations, *The Significance of the Second Session of the United Nations Conference on Trade and Development,* Report by the Secretary-General of UNCTAD (New York, 1968), p. 1.

[20] *Ibid.,* p. 20.

[21] For brief accounts of the result, see *ibid.* and Branislav Gosovic, *UNCTAD: North-South Encounter,* International Conciliation, Series published by the Carnegie Endowment for International Peace (May, 1968), No. 568, pp. 51ff.

[22] *Asian Drama,* Chap. 13, Sec. 15 (pp. 656ff.).

[23] United Nations, *United Nations Conference on Trade and Development,* Second Session, New Delhi, Vol. 1, *Report and Annexes* (New York, 1968), Resolution 23 (II), p. 51.

[24] *Ibid.,* Resolution 27 (II), p. 38.

[25] *Ibid.,* Resolution 29 (II), pp. 40ff.

[26] *Ibid.,* Resolutions 30 (II) and 31 (II), p. 42ff.

[27] *Ibid.,* Resolution 32 (II).

[28] Alvin Hansen, *The Dollar and the International Monetary System* (New York: McGraw-Hill Book Company, 1965); see particularly the Preface by Gunnar Myrdal, pp. ixff.; see also Myrdal, *1965 McDougall Memorial Lecture* (Rome: FAO, 1965), pp. 10ff.

[29] United Nations, *United Nations Conference on Trade and Development,* Second Session, op. cit., Resolutions 16 (II), 17 (II), 18 (II), 19 (II), 20 (II), pp. 34ff.

[30] *Ibid.,* Resolutions 2 (II)–14 (II), pp. 45ff.

[31] *Ibid.,* Resolution 9 (II), p. 30.

[32] *The Significance of the Second Session of the United Nations Conference on Trade and Development,* Report by the Secretary-General of UNCTAD, *op. cit.,* p. 3.

[33] United Nations, *United Nations Conference on Trade and Development,* Second Session, *op. cit.,* Resolution 21 (II), p. 38.

[34] Stated by the Prime Minister and all the leaders of the other parties when questioned by a youth group at the time they faced a general election to Parliament, *Dagens Nyheter,* September 6, 1968.

Chapter 10. The Opportunistic Juggling of Aid Statistics: The "Financial Flows"

[1] Stockholm International Peace Research Institute (SIPRI), *SIPRI Yearbook of World Armaments and Disarmament 1966/69* (Stockholm: Almqvist & Wiksells, 1969).

[2] Organisation for Economic Co-operation and Development, *Development Assistance Committee, Statistical Tables for the 1969 Annual Aid Review,* Paris, July 17, 1969.

[3] Press release from the Swedish Ministry of Finance, February 14, 1969.

[4] *Ibid.*

[5] DAC (69) 32, Paris, June 4, 1969.

[6] Sweden—and also Switzerland—abstained for a long time from participating in DAC. It held in principle to the view that problems of development aid should, rather, be dealt with in regional or worldwide organizations where the underdeveloped countries also have a voice. It has remained critical of DAC's activity and so, in particular, of the statistics its secretariat compiles. Sweden is, as far as I know, the only country where the DAC statistics are criticized—and even in popular journals and the daily newspapers. Sweden is thus, as in some other respects, an exception that, by being an exception among the developed countries, confirms the rule as stated in the test.
Concerning the underdeveloped countries' reaction to DAC's statistics, see below.

[7] Myrdal, "The Intergovernmental Organizations and the Role of Their Secretariats," *Canadian Public Administration*, 1969.

[8] The last one, with the subtitle *International Flow of Long-Term Capital and Official Donations, 1962–1966* (New York, 1968), includes a chapter, "The Problem of Reverse Flows," pp. 50ff.

[9] Remarks of Senator Charles McC. Mathias, Jr., prepared for delivery at the University of Maryland Summer School, July 22, 1969; mimeographed.

[10] UNCTAD, Trade and Development Board, *Report of the Committee on Invisibles and Financing Related to Trade,* Supplement No. 2 (United Nations, New York, 1969), Annex D, 2, p. 20.

[11] George D. Woods, *Address before the United Nations Conference on Trade and Development,* February 9, 1968, p. 12; cf. *Asian Drama,* Chap. 13, Sec. 9 (pp. 623f.).

[12] United Nations, *United Nations Conference on Trade and Development,* Second Session, New Delhi, Vol. I, *Report and Annexes* (New York, 1968), Resolution 33 (II), pp. 44f.

[13] United Nations, *Panel on Foreign Investment in Developing Countries,* Amsterdam, February 16–20, 1969 (New York, 1969).

[14] Charles A. Meyer, "Latin America, What Are Your Priorities?" *The Department of State Bulletin,* Vol. LX, No. 1561 (May 26, 1969), p. 442.

[15] *Panel on Foreign Investment in Developing Countries,* p. 5.

[16] *Asian Drama,* Chap. 13, Sec. 9 (pp. 621ff.).

[17] Meyer, "Latin America, What Are Your Priorities?" *op. cit.,* p. 440 (italics added).

[18] *Quality of Life in the Americas,* Report of a U.S. Presidential Mission for the Western Hemisphere, Nelson A. Rockefeller, 1969 (mimeographed), p. 80.

[19] Myrdal, *An International Economy: Problems and Prospects* (New York: Harper & Row, 1956), p. 117.

[20] It has recently again been taken up by Paul Streeton in an article "Improving the Climate," *Ceres* FAO Review, Vol. 2, No. 2 (March–April, 1969).

[21] See, for example, a statement by the chief of the Indian Planning Commission, Professor D. R. Gadgil, *Asian Drama*, Chap. 17, Sec. 9 (pp. 823f., fn. 4).

Chapter 11. Aid

[1] The problems dealt with in this chapter and the positions taken by the author have been more fully dealt with in *An International Economy: Problems and Prospects* (New York: Harper & Row, 1956), based on a text written in 1954 (republished as a Harper Torchbook in 1969). See pp. 111ff., 119ff. See also "Trade and Aid," *The American Scholar*, Vol. 26, No. 2 (Spring 1957), pp. 137ff.; and *Challenge to Affluence* (New York: Vintage Books, 1965), pp. 193ff.

[2] Gunnar Adler-Karlsson, *Western Economic Warfare 1947–1967. A Case Study in Foreign Economic Policy* (Stockholm: Almqvist & Wiksells, 1968), Preface, p. xi, *et passim*.

[3] *Ibid.*

[4] *Ibid.*

[5] Concerning South Asia, see *Asian Drama*, Chap. 13, Secs. 10–11 (pp. 625ff.), *et passim*. See also *An International Economy*, Chap. 9 (pp. 119ff.).

[6] Myrdal, *An International Economy*, Chap. 9 (pp. 124ff.); cf. *Asian Drama*, Chap. 13, Sec. 11 (pp. 636f.).

[7] Taylor, *The Struggle for Mastery in Europe 1848–1918* (Oxford: Clarendon Press, 1954).

[8] *Asian Drama*, Chap. 9, Sec. 6 (pp. 398ff.); cf. Chap. 4, Sec. 12 (pp. 169ff.) and Chap. 5, Sec. 13 (pp. 221ff.).

[9] Eugene Staley, *The Future of Under-Developed Countries* (New York: Harper & Row, 1954), pp. 362ff.

[10] Adlai E. Stevenson, *Call to Greatness* (New York: Harper & Row, 1954), p. 92.

[11] *Asian Drama*, Chap. 9, Sec. 16 (pp. 398ff.).

[12] Myrdal, *An International Economy*, Chap. 9, pp. 127f. Italics added.

[13] *Ibid.*, p. 329. Italics added.

[14] See Myrdal, *An International Economy*, Chap. 8 (pp. 112ff.).

[15] *Ceres*, FAO Review, Vol. 2, No. 2 (March–April, 1969).

[16] There was recently a ministerial meeting in Viña del Mar, Chile, where Latin American ministers agreed on a common protest, directed at the United States' commercial and financial policies. See *The Latin American Consensus of Viña del Mar*, May 7, 1969, mimeographed.

[17] *Development Assistance in the New Administration. Report of the President's General Advisory Committee on Foreign Assistance Programs,*

October 25, 1968, reprinted by the Agency for International Development (Washington, 1969), p. 1. The committee was headed by James A. Perkins.

18 "Development—A Balance Sheet," *The Department of State Bulletin,* Vol. LIX, No. 1540 (December 30, 1968), p. 705.

19 William S. Gaud, "Foreign Aid: What It Is; How It Works; Why We Provide It," *The Department of State Bulletin,* Vol. LIX, No. 1537 (December 9, 1968), p. 605.

20 *Development Assistance in the New Administration,* p. 1.

21 *Ibid.,* p. 6.

22 William S. Gaud, "Foreign Aid: What It Is; How It Works; Why We Provide It," *op. cit.,* p. 603.

23 *Development Assistance in the New Administration,* p. 6.

24 *News Bulletin,* United States Information Service, Stockholm office, June 2, 1969.

25 Reported in *Overseas Development* (November, 1968), p. 9.

26 *Survey of International Development,* Vol. VI, No. 1 (January 15, 1969).

27 Address by George D. Woods, President, World Bank Group, before the United Nations Conference on Trade and Development, New Delhi, February 9, 1968.

28 *Asian Drama,* Appendix 2, Sec. 18 (pp. 1897ff.); cf. Sec. 3 (pp. 1847ff.).

29 *Toward a Predominantly Multilateral Aid Program,* Foreign Policy Studies Program (Washington, D.C.: The Brookings Institution, March, 1969), mimeographed.

30 Myrdal, *An International Economy,* pp. 133ff.

31 Swedish Government Bill No. 100 (Kungl. Maj:ts Proposition Nr. 100), Stockholm, 1962. Italics added.

32 *Asian Drama,* Chap. 9, Sec. 16 (pp. 398ff.).

33 United Nations, *United Nations Conference on Trade and Development,* Second Session, New Delhi, Vol. I, *Report and Annexes* (New York: United Nations, 1968), Resolution 24(II), pp. 54f.

34 International Bank for Reconstruction and Development, *1968 Annual Meetings of the Boards of Governors. Summary Proceedings* (Washington, 1968), p. 11.

35 "The Problem of Identifying the Least Developed among the Developing Countries: Report by the Secretariat of UNCTAD" (TD/17/ Supp. 1), *United Nations Conference on Trade and Development,* Second Session, New Delhi, Vol. V, *Special Problems in World Trade and Development* (New York: United Nations, 1968).

36 "Special Measures To Be Taken in Favour of the Least Developed among the Developing Countries: Report by the Secretariat of

UNCTAD" (TD/17), *United Nations Conference on Trade and Development*, Second Session, New Delhi, Vol. V, *Special Problems in World Trade and Development* (New York: United Nations, 1968).

[37] *Towards a Predominantly Multilateral Aid Program*, p. 2.

[38] International Bank for Reconstruction and Development, *Address* of Eugene R. Black, President, to the Boards of Governors of the World Bank, the International Finance Corporation and the International Development Association, in Washington, D.C., September 18, 1962, p. 8.

[39] J. William Fulbright, *The Arrogance of Power* (New York: Vintage Books, 1966), pp. 238ff.

[40] International Bank for Reconstruction and Development *1968 Annual Meetings of the Boards of Governors, Summary Proceedings*, Washington, D.C. (1968), pp. 91f.

[41] Myrdal, *Challenge to Affluence*, pp. 131ff.,

[42] Myrdal, *An International Economy*, pp. 130ff.

[43] *Toward a Predominantly Multilateral Aid Program*, p. 1.

[44] Myrdal, *An American Dilemma: The Negro Problem and Modern Democracy* (New York: Harper & Row, 1944), p. 1020.

Part Four. THE POLITICS OF DEVELOPMENT

Chapter 12. A Loaded Misconception
[1] *Asian Drama*, Chap. 16, Sec. 19 (pp. 795ff.).

[2] *Ibid.*, Chap. 3, Sec. 8 (pp. 114f.); Chap. 16, Sec. 19 (pp. 795ff.); *et passim.*

[3] *Ibid.*, Chap. 16, Sec. 13 (pp. 780ff.).

[4] *Ibid.*, Chap. 16, Sec. 19 (pp. 796ff.).

Chapter 13. A Fateful Development
[1] Erich H. Jacoby is now undertaking a study at the Stockholm University Institute for International Economic Studies from this point of view. It will be published by André Deutsch in London with the title *Man and Land. The Key Issue in Development*. He intends to give special attention to Latin American conditions.

[2] *Ibid.*, Chap. 24, Sec. 9 (pp. 1196ff.), *et passim.*

[3] Myrdal, *The Political Element in the Development of Economic Theory* (Cambridge, Mass.: Harvard University Press, 1965), Chap. 3 (pp. 61ff.).

[4] Myrdal, *Challenge to Affluence* (New York: Vintage Books, 1965), Chap. 3 (pp. 40ff.), *et passim;* and *An American Dilemma Revisited: The Racial Crisis in Perspective* (New York: Pantheon Books, 1970).

[5] *An American Dilemma Revisited.*

[6] *Ibid.*, Appendix 2, Part II (pp. 185ff.).

[7] United Nations, *Report of the Expert Group Meeting on Social Policy and Planning*, Commission for Social Development, Twenty-first Session, Geneva, March 4–10, 1970 (E/CN.5/445, October 21, 1969), mimeographed.

Chapter 14. Political Dynamics in South Asia

[1] *Asian Drama*, Chaps. 7–9 (pp. 257ff.).

[2] *Ibid.*, Chap. 7, Sec. 3 (p. 280).

[3] *Ibid.*, Chap. 7, Sec. 3 (pp. 273ff.); Sec. 6 (pp. 296ff.).

[4] *Ibid.*, Chap. 8, Sec. 7 (pp. 325ff.).

[5] *Ibid.*, Chap. 8, Sec. 9 (pp. 338ff.).

[6] *Ibid.*, Chap. 3, Sec. 8 (pp. 115f.); Appendix 2, Secs. 18–20 (pp. 1897ff., particularly p. 1910, fn. 1).

[7] Benjamin Higgins, *Economic Development: Principles, Problems, and Policies*, rev. ed. (New York: W. W. Norton & Co., 1968), p. 262.

[8] *Ibid.*, pp. 265f. Italics in the source.

[9] *Asian Drama*, Chap. 3, Sec. 8 (pp. 116ff.).

[10] *Ibid.*, Chap. 24, Sec. 7 (pp. 1184ff.); *et passim.*

[11] *Ibid.*, Chap. 24, Secs. 7–9 (pp. 1184ff.); *et passim.*

[12] *Ibid.*, Chap. 18, Sec. 14 (pp. 895ff.).

[13] *Ibid.*, Chap. 18, Sec. 12 (p. 885, fns. 3 and 4).

[14] *Ibid.*, Chap. 7, Sec. 6 (pp. 296ff.).

[15] *Ibid.*, Chap. 7, Sec. 7 (pp. 301ff.); Postscript, Sec. 1 (pp. 1831ff.).

[16] *Ibid.*, Chap. 7, Secs. 3–7 (pp. 273ff., particularly pp. 295f.).

[17] *Ibid.*, Chap. 22, Sec. 5 (pp. 1061ff.).

[18] *Ibid.*, Chap. 9, Sec. 11 (pp. 381ff.).

[19] *Ibid.*, Chap. 33, Sec. 7 (pp. 1791ff.); cf. Sec. 2 (pp. 1716ff.).

[20] *Ibid.*, Chap. 16, Sec. 16 (pp. 786ff.); cf. Sec. 5 (pp. 753ff.).

[21] *Ibid.*, Chap. 7, Sec. 6 (pp. 299f.).

[22] *Ibid.*, Chap. 26, Sec. 12 (pp. 1301ff.).

[23] *Ibid.*, Chap. 26, Sec. 12 (pp. 1301ff.); cf. Sec. 14 (pp. 1311ff.).

[24] *Ibid.*, Chap. 23, Sec. 5 (pp. 1121ff.).

[25] *Ibid.*, Chap. 7, Sec. 3 (pp. 273ff.); *et passim.*

[26] *Ibid.*, Chap. 33, Sec. 6 (pp. 1787ff.).

[27] *Ibid.*, Chap. 4, Sec. 12 (pp. 169ff.); Chap. 5, Sec. 13 (pp. 221ff.); Chap. 9, Sec. 16 (pp. 398ff.).

[28] *Ibid.*, Chap. 4, Sec. 11 (pp. 162ff.); Chap. 5, Sec. 12 (pp. 217f.); Chap. 9, Secs. 9–10 (pp. 374ff., particularly pp. 379ff.).

[29] *Ibid.*, Chap. 2, Sec. 4 (p. 65, fn. 2).

[30] *Ibid.*, Chap. 9, Sec. 8 (pp. 369ff., particularly pp. 374f.).

Chapter 15. The Responsibility of Economic Science

[1] Myrdal, *Economic Theory and Under-Developed Regions* (London: Duckworth, 1957), p. 120; published in the United States as *Rich Lands and Poor* (New York: Harper & Row, 1958).

[2] Myrdal, *The Political Element in the Development of Economic Theory* (London: Routledge & Kegan Paul Ltd., 1953; Cambridge, Mass.: Harvard University Press, 1954), Chap. 3 (pp. 56ff., particularly pp. 78f.); cf. *Economic Theory and Underdeveloped Regions*, Part II (pp. 107ff., particularly pp. 114ff.).

[3] Myrdal, *The Political Element in Economic Theory*, Chap. 4 (pp. 80ff.).

[4] *Asian Drama*, Appendix 3, Sec. 2 (p. 1944, fn. 3); Appendix 7, Sec. 1 (p. 2063, fn. 1); cf. Appendix 2, Sec. 14 (pp. 1884ff.).

[5] *Ibid.*, Prologue, Sec. 1 (pp. 5ff.).

[6] Myrdal, *Objectivity in Social Research* (New York: Pantheon Books, 1969), Sec. 8 (pp. 39ff.).

Appendix. The Latin American Powder Keg

[1] Nelson A. Rockefeller, *Quality of Life in the Americas*, Report of a U.S. Presidential Mission for the Western Hemisphere (Washington, D.C., 1969), mimeographed.

[2] *Asian Drama*, Appendix 2, Sec. 24 (pp. 1932ff.).

[3] *U.S. News and World Report*, July 14, 1969, p. 68.

[4] Juan Bosch, *Pentagonism: A Substitute for Imperialism*, trans. Helen R. Lane (New York: Grove Press, 1969).

[5] Myrdal, *An American Dilemma Revisited: The Racial Crisis in Perspective* (New York: Pantheon Books, 1970).

[6] *U.S. News and World Report*, July 14, 1969, pp. 68–69.

[7] *Quality of Life in the Americas*, pp. 5, 14, 25, 80.

[8] *Ibid.*, p. 80.

[9] Richard J. Barnet, *Intervention and Revolution: The United States in the Third World* (New York: The World Publishing Company, 1968), p. 19, fn. 8.

[10] See, for instance, a testimony by Charles A. Meyer, Assistant Secretary for Inter-American Affairs, before the Subcommittee on Western Hemisphere Affairs of the Senate Committee on Foreign Relations on

July 8, 1969, published as "U.S. Military Assistance Policy Toward Latin America" in *The Department of State Bulletin,* Vol. LXI, No. 1571, August 4, 1969.

[11] *Ibid.,* p. 100.

[12] *Ibid.,* p. 101.

[13] *Declaration of Latin American Specialists on Professional Responsibility,* January 1969, mimeographed. It should be mentioned that this type of direct engagement of social scientists in American foreign policy and subversive activity abroad is not restricted to Latin America. The Indian official journal, *Indian and Foreign Review,* Vol. 6, No. 10, March 1, 1969, contains an unsigned and presumably editorial article, "Academic Colonialism," specifying in very critical terms complaints of the same type in regard to India.

[14] *Quality of Life in the Americas,* p. 49.

[15] *Ibid.,* p. 25.

[16] *Ibid.,* p. 21. Italics added.

[17] *Ibid.,* p. 45.

[18] See above and *ibid.,* pp. 14 and 22.

[19] *Ibid.,* pp. 61ff.

[20] *Ibid.,* pp. 72ff.

[21] *Ibid.,* pp. 42ff.

[22] Charles A. Meyer, "U.S. Military Assistance Policy Toward Latin America," *op. cit.,* p. 102.

[23] *Quality of Life in the Americas,* p. 46.

[24] *Ibid.,* p. 18.

[25] *Ibid.,* pp. 17f. Italics added.

[26] *Ibid.,* pp. 15ff.

[27] Barrington Moore, Jr., *Social Origins of Dictatorship and Democracy: Lord and Peasant in the Making of the Modern World* (Boston: Beacon Press, 1966), p. 505.

[28] I have not found it possible to use "Marxism" as a technical term in scientific analysis (*Asian Drama,* Chap. 15, Sec. 5 (p. 726, fn. 1), *et passim.*). It is commonly used to characterize several types of theories and ideologies, many of which are left unclear and indistinct.

(1) One clear meaning of "Marxism" would, of course, be Marx's own conceptions. If this were the only meaning attached to the term, I would be prepared to delete the quotation marks. Marx's own ideas are in some respects difficult to construe, and to an extent they have changed over time. But "Marxism" in the sense of what Marx wrote can, in principle, be clarified by analytical study. In contemporary writings this meaning is seldom or never given to "Marxism," except by some who call themselves Marxists; see (5), below.

(2) As I have often pointed out in this book and other writings, Western economists have to a very large extent adopted Marx's theories

without accounting for their origin or even being aware of it. As this has been done unwittingly and often without much knowledge of Marx's writings, the theories have not been refined and qualified as Marx understood them. They are often left as implicit assumptions. When revealed by immanent criticism, they tend, therefore, to be vulgarizations of Marx. For the same reason, they are not recognized as Marxism either by the Western writers themselves or by anyone else. To trace this hidden "Marxism" and bring this doctrinal heritage out into the open would be a good topic for several doctoral theses.

(3) Then, of course, we have the doctrines and theories expounded in writings by authors in the Communist countries and by those who are lined up with them in various Communist parties in the Western world. These authors explicitly and emphatically announce their works as "Marxian," and they display much diligent exegesis to prove it. In reality, their "Marxism" is in many respects further away from Marx's own thinking than even the hidden "Marxism" of Western economists.

(4) Particularly in the United States, "Marxism" is used by "non-Marxists" as a loose and very inclusive term to characterize all sorts of leftist thinking, not least that in underdeveloped countries. Much literature on "Marxism" in Asian countries is, for instance, of this nature, particularly the American literature. It is a most unclear concept.

(5) Finally we have the thinking of many leftist writers who characterize themselves as Marxists without necessarily toeing the Communist Party line. Few of them are clear and consistent. When they are, their thinking is in many respects quite different from Marx's own. This is recognized by some of them, who look upon their constructs as developments of Marx's thought.

These reflections were called forth more specifically by the fact that those critics of the imperialist policies of the United States toward Latin America who indulge in visions of an imminent clash between the masses and the ruling oligarchies supported by the United States often call themselves Marxists.

I do not share their hopes for an early revolt of the masses in Latin America. But I also feel inclined to stress that Marx, behind all his interest in constructing abstract models of "the laws of movement" of capitalist society, was fundamentally an *empiricist*. He was therefore against using anyone as an *authority* for conclusions about the shape of reality. At least twice in his writings he expressed scorn for "Marxists" of his time. It seems likely that a hundred years later he would have been even sterner in his condemnation of the exegetes.

If Marx were living today he would know and take into account all that we now know but that he could not have known a century or more ago. He would also, of course, stand freer from dependence on Hegel and other German philosophers who were more or less his contemporaries.

Even more important, he would, I believe, have been freed from the impact of the mighty tradition of teleological natural-law philosophy, under which both he and his adversaries, the classic liberal thinkers, labored, although he as well as they repudiated it on principle. This last-mentioned, and main, philosophical influence is seldom observed in the writings on Marx, because so many "anti-Marxians" as well as "Marxians" are still under its spell.

He would most certainly not be a "Marxist" of any of the present varieties. From a study of how he worked, I rather believe that in regard to Latin America he would have reached conclusions not very far from those presented in this appendix, though of that I cannot, of course, be certain.

These brief remarks on Marx and "Marxism" are made parenthetically. To make them specific and to prove them would require much elaboration.

[29] *Asian Drama,* Chap. 4, Sec. 6 (pp. 147ff.); Chap. 9, Sec. 12 (pp. 386ff.).

[30] *U.S. News and World Report,* January 27, 1969, p. 63.